A CONCISE ENCYCLOPEDIA *of* HINDUISM

D0062439

Other books in the same series:

A Concise Encyclopedia of Christianity, Geoffrey Parrinder, ISBN 1–85168–174–4
A Concise Encyclopedia of Judaism, Dan Cohn-Sherbok, ISBN 1–85168–176–0

Other books on Hinduism published by Oneworld:

The Bhagavad Gita: A Verse Translation, Geoffrey Parrinder, ISBN 1–85168–117–5
Hindu and Muslim Mysticism, R. C. Zaehner, ISBN 1–85168–046–2
A Short Introduction to Hinduism, Klaus K. Klostermaier, ISBN 1–85168–163–9

A CONCISE ENCYCLOPEDIA *of* HINDUISM

KLAUS K. KLOSTERMAIER

ONEWORLD
OXFORD

A CONCISE ENCYCLOPEDIA OF HINDUISM

Oneworld Publications
(Sales and Editorial)
185 Banbury Road
Oxford OX2 7AR
England

Oneworld Publications
(US Marketing Office)
160 N. Washington Street
4th floor, Boston
MA 02114

© Klaus K. Klostermaier 1998

All rights reserved
Copyright under Berne Convention
A CIP record for this title is available
from the British Library

ISBN 1-85168-175-2

Cover design by Design Deluxe
Typesetting by Transet, Coventry
Printed in England by Clays Ltd, St Ives plc

Contents

Acknowledgements

The author and publishers wish to thank the following for permission to reproduce material in this volume:

Circa Photo Library (p. 60); The High Commission of India (p. 8); International Society for Krishna Consciousness (p. 86); Laura Marrison and Ben Steiner (p. 87); Moojan Momen (p. 153 and cover); Peerless (pp. 25, 36, 54, 71, 100, 115, 121, 125, 136, 148, 167, 197).

Every effort has been made to trace and acknowledge ownership of copyright. If any credits have been omitted or any rights overlooked, it is completely unintentional.

Preface

To write a concise encyclopedia of Hinduism is a daunting task considering the enormous diversity of what is called 'Hinduism' and its history of over five thousand years. There is not a single statement that would be accepted by all Hindus as expressive of their religion, not a single symbol that all would agree upon as typifying what they worship.

The many different religions and philosophies embraced by the over 800 million Hindus in India and the 45 million Hindus all over the world today supply the background to what is offered in this *Concise Encyclopedia of Hinduism*. The followers of particular paths within Hinduism will probably find the information offered on their specific traditions insufficient – there simply is no way to do justice to any of them within the context of this enterprise. Nor is it possible to do justice to all the great persons, women and men, who over the millennia have contributed through their lives and thoughts to one or more aspects of the Hindu traditions.

The purpose of this encyclopedia is to provide basic information on many expressions of Hinduism and to explain important terms that one might encounter reading more technical literature in the field. Many of the entries interlock and the reader is requested to consult terms and expressions that are capitalized in the text itself. Unless otherwise noted, the technical terms used are Sanskrit. English translations have been supplied in one place only. Given the uncertainties of Indian chronology in many cases dates attached to authors or works are tentative; other sources may have different dates.

Care was taken to establish a balance between people and places, scriptures and philosophical systems, art and architecture, mythology and history. However, given the vastness of the country, the huge population, the long history, the rich mythology, choices had to be made. One of the choices made was *not* to include entries on living scholars of Hinduism. The names of some of them will be found as authors in the bibliography.

A great many entries are concerned with mythology. While mythology has its own truth, it goes without saying that no historical truth claims are associated with the stories told, often in a variety of versions, that cannot be harmonized. Even the stories connected with historical personalities before the modern period are often inextricably interwoven with mythical elements, and are hagiographic rather than critically biographical. Hindus have always placed greater emphasis on meaning than on factual correctness. It would be pointless to qualify every entry by adding disclaimers like 'Hindus believe' or 'Hindu tradition reports' etc.

Likewise, given the enormous diversity of traditions within Hinduism, it goes without saying that no Hindu believes or accepts everything that is here presented as 'Hinduism'. It would again be rather tedious to underscore that fact by specifying in each and every instance where Hindus are mentioned, that 'some Hindus' or 'many Hindus' believe or think this and that. Using inclusive terms like 'Hindu' and 'Hinduism' implies always and by necessity a certain blurring of real and important distinctions and generalizations that have to be taken with a grain of salt.

Given the constraints of space and the very nature of such a work the *Concise Encyclopedia of Hinduism* is no substitute for comprehensive monographs on either Hinduism as a whole or any of the topics mentioned. The bibliography is meant to direct the user of this work to more detailed descriptions of issues that by necessity could only find brief mention herein.

Since is was decided that Sanskrit words would be transliterated with diacritics, as they are used in scholarly works, a few hints as regards pronunciation will be in place. Most Sanskrit vowels (a, e, i, u) are pronounced like Italian vowels – a macron (ā, ī, ū) indicates doubling the length of the vowel. Diphthongs (ai, au) are pronounced like double vowels. There are three semi-vowels: ṛ (pronounced ri), y (pronounced like y in yes), v (pronounced like w in Swami). The pronunciation of most of the consonants is similar to that of their English equivalents. A major difference are the aspirates: kh, gh, th, dh; the h sound is clearly perceived like the h in hot-h̲ouse. Sanskrit has many different t and d and n sounds, expressed in transliteration through dots under the letter (ṭ, ḍ, ṭh, ḍh). While the difference (and the marking) is important to recognize the meaning of the word, English does not have equivalent sounds. Ś and ṣ are pronounced like sh.

Sanskrit is fond of compounding words, which makes it difficult for most non-Sanskritists to pronounce them. To facilitate reading, the

Concise Encyclopedia of Hinduism separates the various elements of compounds through short dividing dashes. Sanskrit words do not have accents. The basic rule is to stress the first syllable, unless there are long vowels in later syllables. All long vowels in a word receive a stress, even if there are more than one.

Proper names of individuals and organizations have usually been reproduced as used by these, without attempting to transliterate them according to the system mentioned above. Indian words that have become part of the English vocabulary have also been left without diacritics. Plural formations have been made by adding an -s to the singular, disregarding the Sanskrit inflections. Likewise no distinction has been made between masculine and neutral noun formations; the final -m indicating (in many cases) that the neutral form has been dropped.

Information has been drawn from many sources. Instead of attaching references to individual entries, a bibliography has been added at the end, which should allow the reader to pursue the issues raised here in greater depth. Cross-references within the entries are intended to provide fuller information by directing the reader to similar or related matters. They are indicated by text in small capitals, e.g. AVATĀRA. For readers wishing to explore Hinduism from a thematic viewpoint, the Thematic Index on pp. 236–43 will refer them to the appropriate entries. The Chronology on pp. 216–21 gives a full picture of the major events through the life of the faith.

Many people associated with Oneworld Publications have been involved in the production of this encyclopedia. I would like to single out Mary Starkey, the copy editor, for thanks and praise. Through patient and intelligent questioning and by skilfully rephrasing awkward expressions she has made this a much better book than it would otherwise have been. I am truly grateful to her.

Klaus K. Klostermaier
Winnipeg, 31 July 1998

Introduction[1]

Hinduism has no known founder, no known historic beginnings, no central authority, no common creed. It has many founders of diverse schools and sects, many spiritual leaders, many scriptures, many expressions. Hinduism is an overwhelming reality in today's India: it is visible in thousands of temple cities, audible in exuberant festivals, alive in hundreds of millions of people.

The word 'Hindū' was not created by the Hindus themselves. It probably was a designation coined by the ancient Persians for the people who lived beyond the Indus river, the eastern border of the outermost province of Persia. The term 'Hinduism' is an invention of eighteenth-century European scholars who were fond of '-isms' and had no exposure to the reality of Indian religions. By now, however, the designation 'Hindū' has been taken over by the Hindus themselves, and while it may be impossible to define Hinduism as one 'religion', it makes sense to use the term to describe a family of religions that developed over the past several thousand years in South Asia which have much in common and share many historic roots.

Hindus are fond of saying that Hinduism is more than a religion: it is a way of life. As such it suffuses all aspects of public and private life, it is part of India's social fabric as well as of its entire culture. On the one hand, that makes Hinduism so fascinating and so 'real', while on the other it makes it difficult to describe to outsiders. Instead of merely interpreting a scripture or unfolding a set of doctrines we have to look at the geography and the history of India that brought forth such a unique phenomenon as Hinduism.

The Geography of Hinduism

India, the homeland of the Hindus, is a vast subcontinent with a great variety of geographic regions inhabited by a multitude of different populations. Side by side with the Hindus there always lived adherents of other traditions, autochthonous tribes and immigrants from other parts of the world. Hinduism, however, developed a quite unique bond with the land of India, whose very physical features are filled with religious meaning for Hindus.

The earliest self-designation of Hinduism was *vaidika dharma*, the way of life laid out in the Veda. The codes that determined that way of life clearly specified the Āryāvarta, 'the 'country of the noblemen', as the geographic area within which the followers of the *vaidik dharma* were to live.

The original Āryāvarta was identical with the Saptasindhava, the area around the seven great rivers of north-western India, that later became the Panjāb, the Five-River-Country, after the Saraswatī had dried out and the Yamunā had changed its course. With the expansion of the Vedic way of life, the rest of much of South Asia became Holy Land to Hindus. If in the beginning it was predominantly the (now dried-out) mighty Saraswatī river that inspired the seers and represented divine power and blessing to them, in the course of time all the great rivers first of Northern, and then of Southern India – the Gaṅgā, the Yamunā, the Indus, the Brahmaputra, the Nārbadā, the Kṛṣṇā, the Kauverī and many others – were worshipped as divinities and the thousands of *tīrthas* on their banks became the destination for millions of pilgrims.

Similarly the mountain ranges of India became associated with Hindu gods: the entire Himālaya, and specific peaks within its ranges, the Vindhyās and the Western ghāṭs, the Nilgiris and the Eastern ghats. Sanctuaries were built high up in the mountains, hermits sought out caves and built their huts on the hills, thus transforming them from mere natural phenomena into religiously meaningful realities.

Millions of temples dot India's landscapes: from small cubicles which contain a rudimentary figure to large temple cities with huge edifices that emulate the mountains, housing artistically exquisite huge *mūrtis*. By virtue of its ceremony of installation these images become for Hindus the Presence of God and the temples the places where humans can come and see God, have *darśana* and receive *prasāda*. Existing Hindu law recognizes the temple as house of God: all property attached to it is registered in God's name.

For the Hindu India is defined by its holy places and all of India is holy land. When Indians fought for liberation from colonial rule they did it in the spirit of liberating the Goddess Mother India from the fetters by which she was tied down by foreigners. The attachment of Hindus to holy mounts, holy rivers and sacred places is much more than aesthetic or sentimental: it is deeply religious. That is evident in the

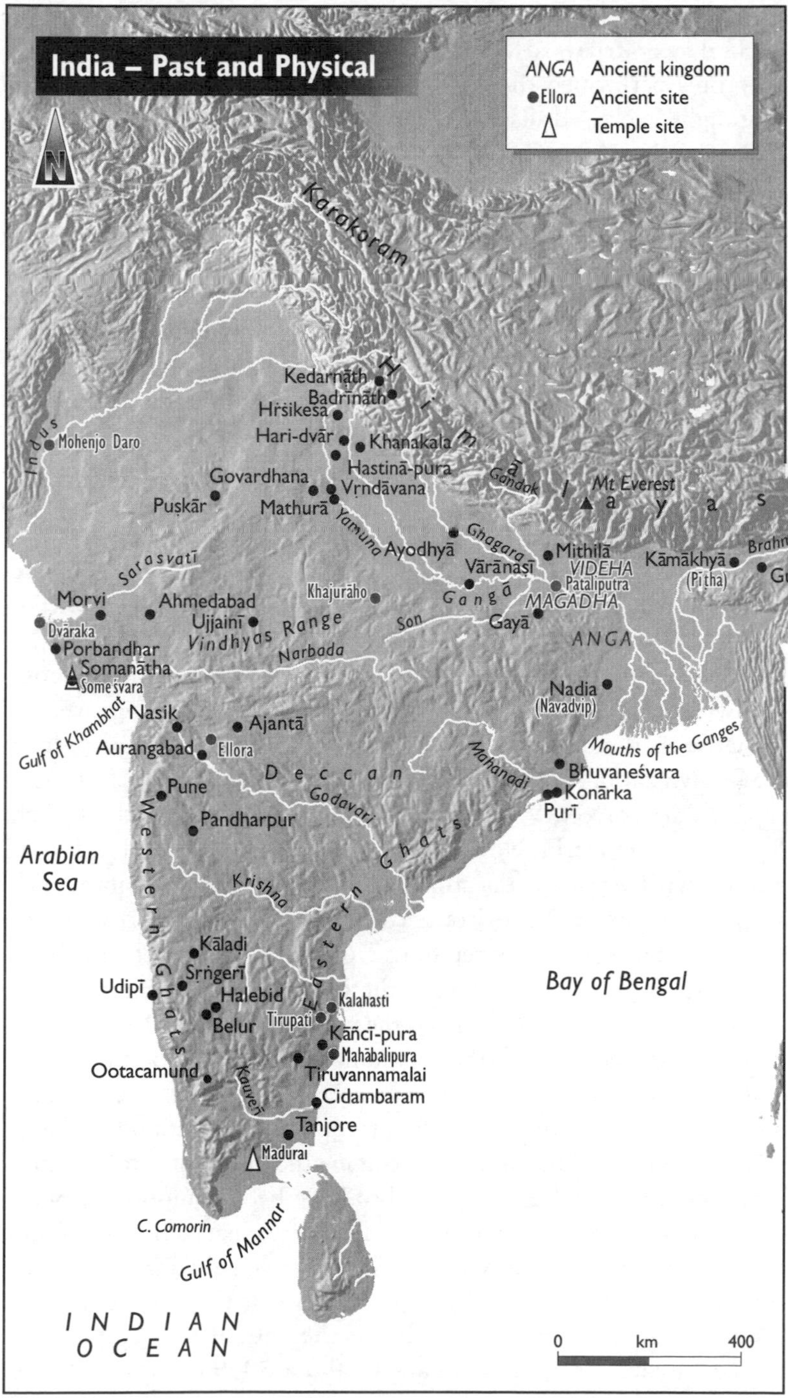
India – Past and Physical
ANGA Ancient kingdom
Ellora Ancient site
Temple site
N
Karakoram
Himālayas
Mt Everest
Indus
Mohenjo Daro
Kedarnāth
Badrīnāth
Hṛṣikesa
Hari-dvār
Khanakala
Hastinā-pura
Govardhana
Vṛndāvana
Puṣkār
Mathurā
Yamuna
Gandak
Ghagara
Ayodhyā
Mithilā
Vārāṇasī
VIDEHA
Pataliputra
MAGADHA
Kāmākhyā
(Pīṭha)
Guvāhati
Brahmaputra
Naga Hills
Sarasvatī
Morvi
Ahmedabad
Khajurāho
Gangā
Gayā
Dvāraka
Ujjainī
Vindhyas Range
Son
ANGA
Porbandhar
Narbada
Somanātha
Someśvara
Nadia
(Navadvip)
Gulf of Khambhat
Nasik
Ajantā
Aurangabad
Ellora
Mouths of the Ganges
Mahanadi
Deccan
Bhuvaneśvara
Pune
Godavari
Konārka
Purī
Pandharpur
Western Ghats
Eastern Ghats
Arabian Sea
Krishna
Kālaḍi
Sṛṅgerī
Udipī
Halebid
Kalahasti
Belur
Tirupati
Kāñcī-pura
Mahābalipura
Ootacamund
Kaveri
Tiruvannamalai
Cidambaram
Tanjore
Madurai
Bay of Bengal
C. Comorin
Gulf of Mannar
INDIAN OCEAN
0 km 400

millions of people who visit these places, not as tourists but as pilgrims. Many Hindu expatriates attempt to get back to India to die and to have the holy rites performed there. If that is not possible they have their ashes brought back and dispersed into the sea or a river in India. An age-old conviction animates Hindus to consider India as unique among all countries as the only one where religious rites bring fruit and where liberation from *saṁsāra* can be gained.

The History of Hinduism[2]

India is the birthplace of many religions besides Hinduism, and has become in the course of its long history the home of many others from abroad. Buddhism, Jainism and Sikhism, to mention only the best known, arose in India. Jews, Christians, Zoroastrians, Muslims and many others have found homes in India during the last two thousand years as well.

Assuming, with recent Indian researchers, that Vedic civilization was not imported into India through nomadic invaders from outside from places such as Ukraina or Central Asia, but developed within north-western India in the country identified in the *Ṛgveda* as Saptasindhava around 4000 BCE, the so-called Indus civilization, whose best-known sites are Mohenjo Daro and Harappa (extending over an area of more than a million square kilometres) must be seen as part of late Vedic civilization flourishing between 2700 and 1750 BCE. If these assumptions are correct, Vedic civilization was one of the earliest High Civilizations of the world, with large urban centres, advanced technical skills and extensive trade connections with the rest of the ancient world.

When in the course of a drought lasting more than two hundred years a large belt of land stretching from Asia Minor to northern India became largely uninhabitable, the big cities in the Indus valley were abandoned and the majority of the population moved eastwards, into the dense forests of the Yamunā–Gaṅgā doab. The river Sarasvatī, worshipped in the *Ṛgveda* as the mightiest stream, had dried out by 1900 BCE and the focus of both civilization and worship moved to the Gaṅgā, with Vārāṇasī becoming the most important centre.

For a long time the Veda, believed to have been composed around 1500 BCE, was the only evidence used in the reconstruction of Vedic civilization and religion. Now, increasingly, archaeological and other scientific evidence is being utilized to complement the picture derived from literary sources alone. Not only has the date of the composition of the Vedic hymns been pushed back to about 3000 or 4000 BCE, the understanding of these hymns and their position in the Indian tradition has undergone a dramatic change as well. Whereas in India the mantras of the *Ṛgveda* were preserved as an integral part of the ritual routine, nineteen-century Western scholarship read them as lyrics, somewhat clumsy expressions of nature worship. It did not seem to matter that many passages either could not be translated or did not make sense; scholars such as Max Müller confidently passed judgement on them and developed systematics of Vedic religion from them.

Indian traditional scholars always considered Itihāsa-Purāṇa the source for ancient Indian 'history', literature that had not seemed worthy of study by serious scholars in the West, because of its often sectarian and occasionally wildly imaginative character. Based on the latter, Indian scholars reconstructed a chronology that differed widely from the one established in Western textbooks.

For traditional Indian historians the great watershed in ancient Indian history is the Mahābhārata War which most date at 3002 BCE, based on astronomical cues. They also identify with this date the beginning of the Kali Yuga, the 'Age of Strife'.

For most of its known history India was divided into a large number of kingdoms that feuded with each other. Some of these succeeded in establishing themselves as major powers and becoming centres for religion and culture.

Thus the Mauryas, who established an empire in north-western and central India from 323 BCE to 183 BCE became supporters of Buddhism. The most famous Maurya descendant, Emperor Aśoka (269–32 BCE), sent Buddhist missionaries to many countries in the East and the West and proclaimed the Buddha's message in dozens of inscriptions throughout his empire.

The Kuśāṇas, invaders from the north-west, who founded a large empire in the early first century CE, continued this tradition and supported Buddhist establishments in their realm.

Under the imperial Guptas (320–540 CE) Hinduism experienced a major renaissance. With their protection, brahmins launched a major campaign to re-hinduize the country. The Guptas built temples, encouraged the growth of the Purāṇas and the cultivation of Sanskrit literature that elaborated themes from the epics. The time of the rule of the imperial Guptas is often called the 'Golden Age' of Hindu culture.

In South India the Cālukyas, based in the Godāvarī area, and the Pallavas, ruling over the country along the Kāverī, established themselves as major powers and patrons of Hindu religion and art. Under the Pallavas, Indian religion reached out to Java (Indonesia), Champā (Thailand) and Cambodia. They were eventually overthrown by the Colas, who became famous not only through the major irrigation works in the Kāverī delta region but also through the exquisite sculptures of Hindu gods and goddesses that were created under their patronage.

Smaller but locally important kingdoms, patronizing various branches of Hinduism, were emerging in the middle ages in the Deccan (Rāṣṭrakūṭas, Hoyśaḷas, Yādavas, Kākatīyas and others); eventually all of them were conquered by the invading Muslims and amalgamated into the Muslim empire that grew from the eighth century CE onwards until it was abolished by the British in 1808. Even during Muslim rule a powerful new Hindu empire succeeded in establishing itself on the Deccan: the Vijayanagara empire, lasting from 1336 to 1565 CE, when it was reduced to a part of the Mogul empire. Its rulers were strong supporters of Hindu religion and culture. In the eighteenth century the Mahrattas carved out a kingdom in central and north-western India, which was pronouncedly Hindu.

The Muslim rulers, who dominated India for half a millennium, did not all follow the policy of the first conquerors, who wanted to stamp out 'idolatry'. Under the enlightened rule of Akbar 'the Great' (1556–1605) Hindus enjoyed great freedom and respect, while Aurangzeb (1658–1680) repressed Hindus and razed many temples that his predecessors had allowed to be built. Important new developments like the Caitanya movement and the great Bhakti revival in North India invigorated Hindu life and culture during Muslim rule, not least under the challenge of Islamic monotheism.

With the takeover of India by the British – first the East India Company, then the Crown – and their declared policy of non-interference with indigenous religion, a slow but steady recovery of Hinduism took place. The government paid the salaries of priests in major temples, the edition and translation of important Hindu texts by Indian as well as Western scholars was encouraged and Hindus themselves began diverse reform movements, such as the Brahmo Samāj, to adapt their religion to the new times and circumstances. Other new religious movements, such as the Ārya Samāj, attempted to purge traditional Hinduism of its medieval accretions and revive Vedic religion and culture.

Since the establishment of the Republic of India (Bhārat) in 1947 Hinduism experienced a major renaissance. While the first prime minister of India, Pandit Jawaharlal Nehru (1947–64), Western educated and a

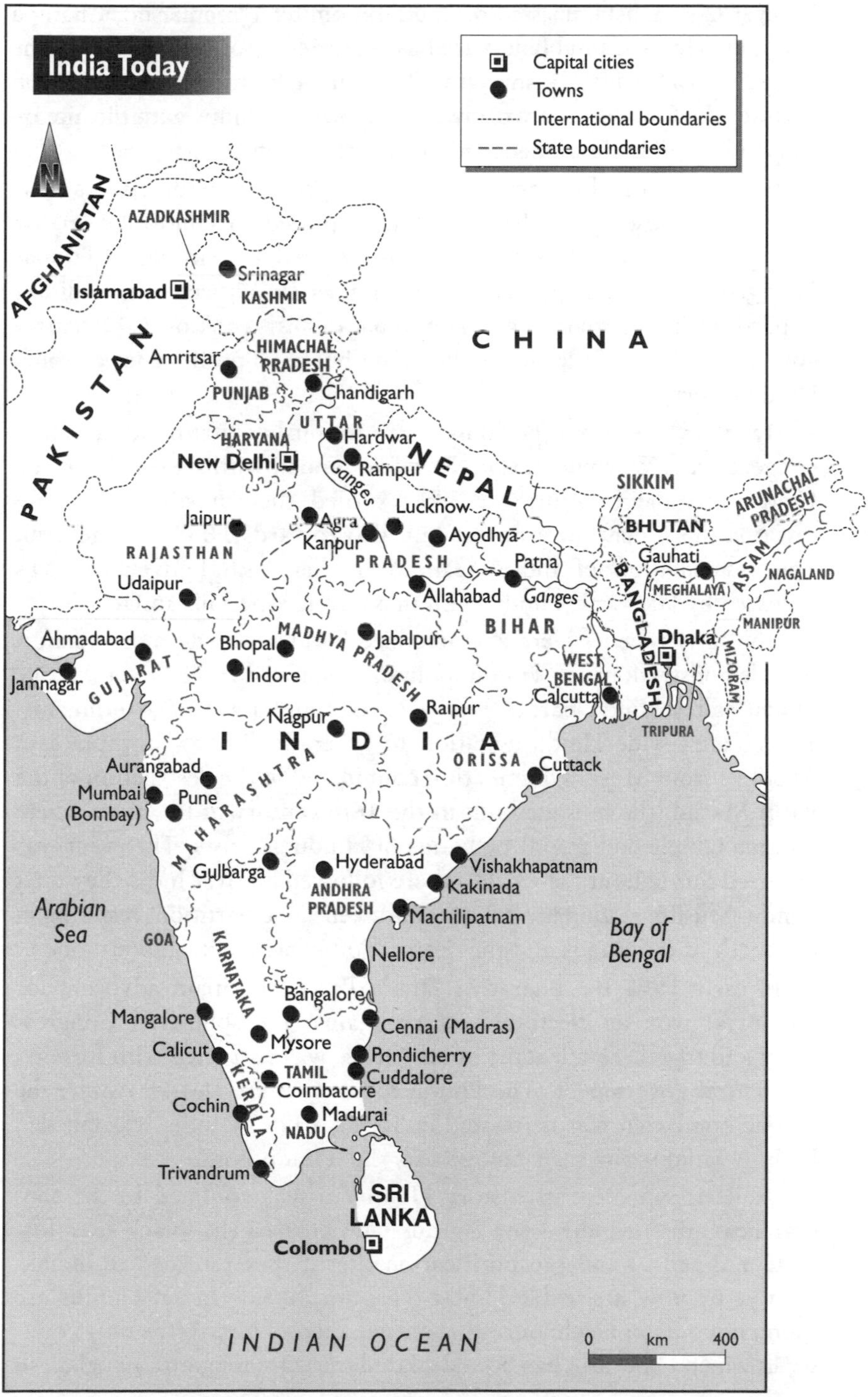
India Today
Capital cities
Towns
International boundaries
State boundaries
AFGHANISTAN
AZADKASHMIR
Srinagar
Islamabad
KASHMIR
CHINA
PAKISTAN
Amritsar
HIMACHAL PRADESH
Chandigarh
PUNJAB
UTTAR
HARYANA
Hardwar
New Delhi
Rampur
Ganges
NEPAL
SIKKIM
ARUNACHAL PRADESH
BHUTAN
Lucknow
Jaipur
Agra
Kanpur
Ayodhya
RAJASTHAN
PRADESH
Patna
Gauhati
ASSAM
NAGALAND
BANGLADESH
Udaipur
Allahabad
Ganges
MEGHALAYA
BIHAR
MANIPUR
Ahmadabad
MADHYA PRADESH
Jabalpur
Dhaka
Bhopal
WEST BENGAL
Jamnagar
GUJARAT
Indore
MIZORAM
Calcutta
Raipur
Nagpur
INDIA
TRIPURA
ORISSA
Aurangabad
MAHARASHTRA
Cuttack
Mumbai (Bombay)
Pune
Gulbarga
Hyderabad
Vishakhapatnam
Kakinada
ANDHRA PRADESH
Arabian Sea
Machilipatnam
GOA
KARNATAKA
Bay of Bengal
Nellore
Bangalore
Mangalore
Cennai (Madras)
Mysore
Calicut
Pondicherry
TAMIL NADU
Cuddalore
KERALA
Coimbatore
Cochin
Madurai
Trivandrum
SRI LANKA
Colombo
INDIAN OCEAN
0 km 400

believer in socialism, insisted on India becoming a 'secular democracy', under his successor, Bal Bahadur Shastri (1964–6), organized Hinduism gained considerably in strength. Thus in 1964 the Vishva Hindū Pariṣad was founded as a worldwide alliance of Hindus with the aim of consolidating Hindu influence in all spheres of life.

Increasing disillusionment with Congress governments added strength to those political parties that appealed to Hindu nationalist sentiments. When Indira Gandhi was ordered to end the 'National Emergency', with its largescale repression of civil liberties, a coalition of parties with a strong core of Hindu nationalists took over the central government in 1977. It did not last long but gave prominence to some Hindu leaders.

By the early eighties the Sikhs began seriously agitating for an independent state. When operation 'Blue Star' ended with shoot-outs at the Golden Temple in Amritsar, Sikhs turned their hostility not only towards the Indian government but also towards Hindus in general. The assassination of Indira Gandhi by her Sikh bodyguards was followed by largescale Hindu–Sikh massacres, especially in Delhi.

The early nineties were characterized by increasingly more vociferous demonstrations of Hindu political aspirations. In several large Indian states Hindu parties won elections and formed governments. The country-wide Hindu agitation to 'liberate' Rāma's birthplace in Ayodhyā from Muslim domination culminated in the destruction of the Babri Masjid (the mosque built in the 16th century at the place where a Rāma temple had stood) by bands of Hindu activists. The event was televized throughout the world. There followed all over India the worst Hindu–Muslim rioting the country had seen since partition, resulting in the death of thousands and the destruction of whole neighbourhoods.

In early 1998 the Bhāratīya Jānata Party, the main advocate for Hindūtva, won an electoral victory against the splintered Congress Party and together with some other parties was entrusted with forming the central government. The Hindu thrust is quite clearly visible; the atomic bomb that was detonated in Spring 1998 by India was labelled both by Hindus and their antagonists the 'Hindu bomb'.

While for most of its history Hinduism was confined to the geographical area of India – the Hindus who crossed the 'black seas' lost caste and had to undergo purification rites if they returned to India – there is by now a sizeable Hindu diaspora outside India. Hindus are found not only in neighbouring countries such as Nepal (the only country in which Hinduism has been declared the state religion), Bangladesh (the former East Bengal) and Śrī Laṅkā, but also in Europe, in North America, in Africa, Australia and Oceania. Hindu temples have been built in all these places and Hindu ceremonies are performed there by Hindu priests. The Hindū Viśva Pariṣad is very active among the Hindus in the diaspora, promoting both a sense of Indian national pride and a non-sectarian kind of Hinduism.

In India itself a great number of Hindu temples has been built in recent times, large masses of people participate in Hindu religious festivals, and Hindu religious authorities exercise much influence, as anyone can observe who visits India. A visitor will also be struck by the juxtaposition of archaic and ultra-modern, the continuity of ancient ways of life and worship, and the emergence of new expressions of Hinduism.

The Sacred Books of Hinduism

Hinduism comprises the entire life of Hindus: their religion, culture, society, laws and literature. While it would be incorrect to say that all of Indian culture is 'Hindu' or that all of Indian art is 'religious', it is indeed often difficult to separate the 'religious' from the 'secular' in India. Thus the 'sacred books of the Hindus' contain much that is 'non-religious' from a Western perspective, that takes its definition of 'religion' from the model of biblical religions.

Ancient, 'classical' sacred Hindu literature has come down through the ages mainly in two major streams: Vedas and Itihāsa Purāṇa. The first is the literature of the religious professionals. These books contain the information required for the performance of Vedic rituals, deemed indispensable by all. It was the prerogative of the brahmins alone to perform these. The second genre is the literature of the common people: it contains creation narratives, the histories of kings and patriarchs, the myths of gods and goddesses, edifying stories, wisdom of life, eschatological lore.

Both kinds of literature contain, besides religious, essentially 'secular' elements, which, however, are integral to their 'religious' purpose. The Vedas, for example, also deal with astronomy and grammar, Itihāsa Purāṇa contains instructions in statecraft cosmography, genealogies and many other matters.

In addition to these more or less universally accepted sacred books there is a huge mass of literature that could be termed 'sectarian', as long as one understands that 'sect' in Hinduism does not mean a breakaway from a 'mainstream' tradition, but a denomination or a school of thought that developed within Hindu mainstream tradition and is an expression of it.

Since Hinduism as such has no central authority, no common creed, no magisterium, but consists essentially of a large number of parallel developments, the term 'sect', which is the usual translation of the Sanskrit word *saṁpradāya*, does not have the pejorative meaning that it has in the context of biblical religions with their insistence on conformity. Thus the large communities of worshippers of Viṣṇu (Vaiṣṇavas), Śiva (Śaivas) and Devī (Śāktas) have their own extensive 'special' revelations laid down in a great many books, sacred only to the members of specific *saṁpradāyas*: the numerous Saṁhitās, Āgamas and Tantras.

The interpretation of the Veda, undertaken since the early Indian middle ages from various standpoints, led to the further development of schools of thought that established traditions of their own. Thus Śaṅkara became the founder of the school of Advaita Vedānta, which since the eighth century has had its own institutions and its literary traditions, adhered to by a galaxy of brilliant exponents of a monistic understanding of the Upaniṣads.

In the course of time ten different such schools of Vedanta developed, each with its own large and growing literature in defence of a particular reading of the same texts. The creation of new branches of Hinduism, and with it the creation of sacred books, continues right now. Followers of major contemporary religious leaders often note down their words and get them published as inspired literature – continuing the revelations of old and creating new sacred books of Hinduism.

The Languages of Hinduism

The language of the most ancient literary documents of Hinduism, the Vedas, 'Vedic', is an archaic form of Sanskrit, the 'refined language' which became standardized around 600 BCE by the famous grammarian Pāṇinī. Sanskrit was considered to be the 'language of the gods', a sacred language, to be used only by persons of higher rank. It became the language of Hindu scholarship as well as Hindu religious literature: the epics, the Purāṇas, the Āgamas, the Tantras are all composed in Sanskrit, albeit not always in conformity with Pāṇinī's grammar. Not by coincidence did the 'heretical' Buddhists and Jains use Prākrits, 'natural' languages, whose vocabularies have strong affinities to Sanskrit, but which were not considered 'sacred' by the brahmins. (In classical Indian drama, only the most eminent persons, brahmins and kings speak Sanskrit, while all other characters have to use Prākrits.) When the popular *bhakti* movements became the predominant form of

Hinduism, the vernaculars became the preferred linguistic medium. Most of the *bhakti* poets came from backgrounds that precluded the knowledge of Sanskrit, and the addressees of their songs and hymns were the ordinary folk of their own neighbourhoods. Thus languages like Tamil, Mahratti, Telugu, Avadhi, Brajbhāṣa, Bengali and others acquired a large religious literature that was also used in certain forms of worship. Śrīvaiṣṇavas in particular felt so strongly about the Tamil compositions of the Āḷvārs that they considered them equal to the Sanskrit texts and used them side by side with Sanskrit in temple worship. While Sanskrit continued to be the preferred medium of Hindu scholarship (even now there are conferences where Hindu pandits read to each other papers in Sanskrit and where debates are conducted in Sanskrit), Tamil (in South India) as well as Hindī (in North India) and Bengali (in Eastern India) were used to write scholarly and theological treatises as well. With the development of virtually all the major vernaculars into literary languages Hinduism adopted all of them as vehicles for religious instruction: Sanskrit religious texts have been translated into all the major Indian languages and original compositions in these are becoming the main source for ordinary people to appropriate Hinduism.

The Beliefs of the Hindus

Considering the breadth of the spectrum of sacred books of the Hindus it will not astonish anyone to learn that it is not possible to find a creed to which all Hindus subscribe or even a single doctrine which all Hindus understand and accept the same way. Recent compilations, often by Western converts to a particular Hindu *saṁpradāya*, claiming to offer a 'Hindu catechism', i.e. a concise and systematic presentation of the articles of faith of Hinduism, are artificial and idiosyncratic attempts to give universal validity to the teachings of a particular sect. The closest to a common foundation of Hindu beliefs is the nominal acceptance of the Veda as revealed 'scripture', and a general agreement on the factual reality of *karma* and rebirth. Looking at the many different ways in which the Veda is understood by various Hindu schools and the controversies among Hindus about strategies to cope with *karma* and rebirth, even those minimal foundations seem somewhat shaky.

Rather than attempting to list beliefs shared by all Hindus and establish a kind of common creed of Hinduism, it is more meaningful to study the literatures of specific *saṁpradāyas* and learn what their followers believe and think. Thus the authoritative books of particular schools within Vaiṣṇavism, Śaivism or Śāktism would narrate in great detail the specific teachings on God and creation, human life and salvation, heavens and hells, commandments and prohibitions.

Each *saṁpradāya* exercises fairly strict control over doctrines taught and practices permitted and reprimands of 'heretics' or even excommunications of non-conformers are not unheard of. Since popular Hinduism is concerned with the worship of images in temples, much of the teaching of most Hindu schools is focused on the proper (sectarian) way of ritual.

Philosophies of Hinduism

India has never known the division between philosophy and theology that has characterized much of modern Western intellectual history. This has had two consequences that distinguish Hinduism from current biblical religions. First, it makes it appear natural for Hindus of an enquiring bent to analyse and investigate philosophically the teachings of their traditions. Second, it allows professional philosophers to deal with ultimate issues in a meaningful way.

Among the philosophies of Hinduism several take the Veda as a basis, considering their task not the creation of new truths but the interpretation of revealed texts. Thus (Pūrva) Mīmāṁsā investigates the injunctions of the Veda relating to ritual; it does not question them but attempts to get at their precise structure and meaning.

Vedānta (also called Uttara Mīmāṁsā) is essentially a reflection on the Upaniṣads, presupposing that what the Upaniṣads say is true and that they contain a truth that could not be obtained through unaided human reason. The task the Vedāntins set themselves is not to question or dissect the truth of Upaniṣadic utterances but to make sure that they are properly understood.

When Hindu scholars debate matters of religion the point is not to argue for or against the content of a scriptural statement but to ascertain whether an assertion is scriptural. Once that is done, there is no further discussion possible.

Hindu philosophical systems, although called *darśanas* ('theories'), are not mere abstract verbal constructs concerning God, world and humankind but intellectual and ethical endeavours to realize the meaning of life. Among the qualifications required for beginning philosophical study is the earnest desire to find liberation from the sufferings of *saṁsāra*, caused by ignorance (*avidyā*) concerning the true nature of reality.

Hindu philosophies are immensely sophisticated, often anticipating questions that only now are being raised in Western philosophy. The hundreds of works that have been written by Hindu philosophers over the past thousand and more years deserve the attention of the best minds.

Political Hinduism and Hindu *jagaran*

The ancient and medieval realms of Hindu kings were Hindu kingdoms, i.e. Hinduism was also their political system. When India became a Muslim country and then a British colony, Hinduism largely turned inwards and retreated into piety and spirituality. However, there always remained some individuals like Śivajī and some groups of militant Nāgas who attempted and partially succeeded in reaffirming political power for Hinduism.

The first modern Hindu political party was founded in 1909 by Pandit Mohan Malaviya, a prominent member of the Ārya Samāj: the Hindū Mahāsabhā, as it was called, in reminiscence of classical Hindu assemblies, demanded for Hindus the right to govern themselves by Hindu laws.

The call for a Hindu *rāṣṭra*, a Hindu state, was also reiterated by the later Hindu parties, the Jana Sangh (established in 1950), the Janata Party (established in 1977) and the Bhāratīya Janatā Party (established in 1980), which eventually became the ruling party at the centre in New Delhi and in several Indian states.

Hindu *jagaran*, a great awakening of Hindu consciousness, was proclaimed by non-political, 'cultural' organizations such as the Rāṣṭrīya Svayamsevak Sangh (RSS; founded in 1926) and the Viśva Hindū Pariṣad (VHP; founded in 1964). There are many indications that the Hindu awakening has been successful and it remains to be seen how far the notion of India as a Hindu nation will be carried.

The exercise of political power by Hindus in a contemporary democratic setting may not only transform India but also Hinduism. For the first time in several hundred years Hindus might be able to convene a *dharmapariṣad*, a council empowered to bring about changes in religious law and practice. It will be a chance to modernize Hinduism and to find out how valid the claims voiced by Hindus over the past hundred years are that Hindu solutions to India's problems are better than Western ones.

Conclusion

It is hard to describe a phenomenon like Hinduism, with its thousands of years of history and its myriad forms of expressions. Hinduism is not only a historic phenomenon but also a living reality. There is no way to understand contemporary Hinduism without knowing its past. And there is equally no way of deriving modern interpretations of Hinduism from a study of the ancient documents alone.

While it is absolutely necessary for a student of Hinduism to read the ancient Sanskrit sources, the Vedas, the epics, the Purāṇas, the Āgamas, it is equally important to listen to contemporary expositions of Hinduism in the modern vernaculars of India. Hinduism is the living religion of the many millions of Hindus, not the result of the analysis of literary sources by detached scholars of religion. The apparently bizarre and idiosyncratic is as much part of 'real' Hinduism as the reasonable and conventional, which relies on ancient tradition and common sense. In the end it is Hindus alone who determine what Hinduism is and what it is not. The Hindu community is large and diverse and has room for many different individuals and schools of thought.

Notes

1. This short introduction to the *Concise Encyclopedia of Hinduism* is not intended to replace somewhat more extensive works like the author's *A Short Introduction to Hinduism*, Oneworld Publications 1998, or full-length studies like the author's *A Survey of Hinduism*, State University of New York Press, 1994 (2nd edn), which, in addition to a fuller treatment of the points dealt with here, offers ample documentation from sources and scholarly literature. See also the titles in the opening section of the bibliography.
2. Early Indian history has emerged as one of the most contentious and emotionally charged issues in contemporary Indian scholarship. While the majority of Western Indologists followed Max Müller who assumed that nomadic groups of 'Vedic' Āryans invaded north-western India around the middle of the second millennium BCE and proceeded to conquer the rest of India, traditional Indian scholars always assumed an indigenous development of the Veda and Vedic civilization. Max Müller's chronology was not only countered by traditional Indian claims for a much higher age of the *Ṛgveda* but also by some prominent Western scholars such as Moriz Winternitz and Frederick Eden Pargiter. Recent archeological and palaeo-geographical findings, supported by satellite photography of the former Sarasvatī riverbed, suggest a revision of early Indian history along the lines mentioned here. I do not wish to link my presentation to political and ideological stances that some proponents of the 'new chronology' may maintain.

A

abhāva ('non-being')

Absence of reality, a category in NYĀYA.

Abhinav Bhārat Society

'Young India Society', founded by Vinayak Damodar SAVARKAR and his brother Ganesh Savarkar in the 1930s 'to take up the sword and destroy the Government because it is foreign and oppressive'.

Abhinavagupta (12th century CE)

Representative of KASHMIR ŚAIVISM and one of the most prolific thinkers and writers of Hinduism. Author of the multi-volume *Tantrālokā*.

abhiniveśa
('attachment' [to bodily life])

A form of AVIDYĀ (ignorance) and a cause for suffering and rebirth according to PATAÑJALA YOGA.

Ābhīras

Ancient and populous clan of semi-nomadic cattlebreeders in northern India often mentioned in ancient Indian literature in connection with KṚṢṆA.

abhiṣekha ('aspersion')

Anointment, consecration of either a king or an image.

ācamanīya

The offering of water to a deity during worship for rinsing the mouth.

ācāra ('behaviour')

Rules of life for specific castes, orders or religions, laid down in texts such as *Ācāra-dīpa*.

ācārya ('master')

Honorific title of recognized teachers.

ācāryā

A female teacher.

acyuta ('the unfallen')

Name of VIṢṆU (and KṚṢṆA), either indicating that he did not fall down from heaven (as other minor deities did) or that he is imperishable.

adbhuta ('wonderment')

One of the eight RASAS (sentiments, emotional experiences) of Indian aesthetics.

adharma ('unrighteousness')

The opposite of DHARMA and the cause of the breakdown of law and order. Kṛṣṇa says in the *Bhagavadgītā* that whenever *adharma* threatens to eclipse *dharma* he will appear as an AVATĀRA to save the righteous and destroy the wicked.

adhidaivata
('relating to the gods [*devas*]')

A mode of interpretation of Vedic HYMNS (alternatives: adhiyajña, ADHYĀTMA).

adhikāra ('qualification')

Requirements for commencing study or for becoming a member of a particular school or sect.

adhvaryu

Class of Vedic priests whose task it was to construct the ALTARS and recite the HYMNS at SACRIFICES.

adhyāsa ('superimposition')

A central concept in ŚAṄKARA's ADVAITA VEDĀNTA explaining the congenital and universal illusion that makes one confuse REALITY with UNREALITY.

adhyātma
('relating to the self [*ātman*]', 'spiritual')

A recognized mode of interpreting sacred texts.

Adhyātma Rāmāyana
('Spiritual Rāmāyana')

A 12th-century re-rendering of the RĀMA story in which Rāma from the very beginning appears as divinity incarnate.

Ādi Samāj ('First Association')

Branch of the BRAHMO SAMĀJ led by Debendranath TAGORE after its breakup due to innovations introduced by Keshub Chandra SEN in the 1880s.

Ādiśaṅkarā(cārya) (788–820 CE)

'First, or Original, Śaṅkara', title of the founder of ADVAITA VEDĀNTA to distinguish him from his successors, who also carry the title Śaṅkarācārya.

Aditi

Vedic goddess, mother of the ĀDITYAS.

Ādityas

A group of Vedic deities, sons of Aditi. Initially there were eight of them, but Aditi abandoned Mārttāṇḍa, the sun. Thus the Vedas speak of the 'seven Ādityas', among whom VARUṆA was the foremost, and he is often called 'the Āditya'. In post-Vedic times there were 12 Ādityas, personifying the 12 months. They are the eternal sustainers of light and life.

ādivāsis
('First or Original Inhabitants')

Epithet given to members of indigenous (Indian) tribes.

adṛṣṭa ('unseen')

An important category in MĪMĀṂSĀ and VAIŚEṢIKA: the invisible (but real) fruit of a religious act that adheres to a person and which becomes actualized after death.

Advaita Vedānta

A school of VEDĀNTA, founded by ŚAṄKARA, which teaches 'non-duality', i.e. ultimate identity of BRAHMAN and ĀTMAN.

ādya-prakṛti ('primeval matter')

A title of ŚAKTI, expressing her fundamental importance for everything.

Adyar

Suburb of Cennai (Madras), world headquarters of the Theosophical Society, with an excellent research library containing a large collection of manuscripts, and a publishing house.

afterlife

Belief in life after death is universal among Hindus. However, the forms in which it is envisaged have changed over times and differ from one SAṀPRADĀYA to the next. The Veda explicitly affirms belief in afterlife: the ancestors are enjoying a blissful existence on the moon; the *mṛtyu saṁskara* (ceremonies in connection with death and cremation) is meant to transform the gross dead body into a subtle existence that can continue. With the rise of belief in rebirth (emerging as a universally accepted fact in the Upaniṣads) life after death comes to mean either being reborn in a body (plant, animal, human or god) or finding liberation (*mukti*, *mokṣa*) from the cycle of birth and death. The latter is understood either as a complete merging of the individual soul (ĀTMAN) with the world soul (BRAHMAN) or the transformation of the individual into an immortal being living in the company of an eternal personal god in a specific heaven (Viṣṇu's VAIKUṆṬHA; Śiva's KAILĀSA; DEVĪ's MAṆIDVĪPA).

The souls of persons who have committed sins and die without having atoned for them are punished for appropriate periods in hells (NĀRAKAS) after death. People for whom the appropriate rituals have not been performed are condemned to roam the earth as ghosts (PRETAS) after death and are released from this existence only through the performance of special rituals.

Individual *saṁpradayās* have very concrete notions of afterlife and some of the sectarian works offer vivid descriptions of the passage of souls from earth to heaven, detailing the shape of things to come to the faithful, and prescribing rites (SĀDHANA) to avoid bad afterlife experiences.

Āgama ('scripture')

Used both as a generic name for revealed books and a specific designation of voluminous works of a sectarian nature such as the (canonical) 28 ŚAIVITE ĀGAMAS.

Agastya

(*c.* 10,000 BCE)

Legendary sage who is credited with having introduced Vedic religion to South India and the authorship of the *Agastyam*, the first grammar of the Tamil language.

ages of the world

see TIME, DIVISIONS OF.

Aghori

Member of a ŚAIVA sect that worships the goddess of death and darkness. Aghoris eat and drink whatever is given to them and are said to indulge in cannibalism. They besmear themselves with excrement which they also eat.

Agni ('fire')

Prominent deity in VEDIC RELIGION, where he is called 'the first priest', because of his ability to transform material goods in the sacrifice into a substance through which the gods (DEVAS) are nourished. The first HYMN in the *Ṛgveda* is dedicated to Agni.

Part of the marriage ceremonies consists of lighting the hearth of the new family; this fire was never to be allowed to die out, and was constantly attended throughout a couple's married life.

Agnicayana ('fire offering')

One of the most solemn of the Vedic sacrifices recreating the cycle of birth–life–death of the universe, the regeneration of the seasons and the rejuvenation of the sacrificer. Its preparation was lengthy: a suitable ground had to be found and prepared, a large number of bricks had to be burnt, a great many specialists had to be involved. The number of bricks (10,800) symbolized the number of hours in the year, the five layers in which they were piled symbolized the five seasons, the totality of the ALTAR (in the shape of a falcon) represented PRAJĀPATI, the creator: his hair, skin, flesh, bone and marrow.

Agnihotra

Fire sacrifice, the most common form of Vedic sacrifice.

Agnihotri, Satyānanda (1850–1929)

Also known as 'Dev Ātma'. A social and religious Hindu reformer, he spoke out against child marriage and denounced caste, ritualism, transmigration and belief in AVATĀRAS. In protest against Keshub Chandra SEN's marrying off his underage daughter he left the BRAHMO SAMĀJ and founded the 'Dev Samāj' (1887). He considered himself unique among humans and demanded from his followers strict compliance with rigorous ethical rules. He taught that the only reality was nature and introduced the practice of thanksgiving to humans, animals, plants and inanimate nature. His teachings are contained in *Dev Anusthān Vidhi* (1892) and *Dev Shāstra* (1910).

Agni Purāna

One of the MAHĀ-PURĀṆAS said to have been revealed by AGNI, in which ŚIVA figures prominently.

Ahalyā

Wife of the Vedic ṚṢI GAUTAMA (2). There are many conflicting stories about her. According to one she was the first woman created by Brahmā, and was given in marriage to Gautama. She was seduced by Indra, rejected by Gautama, and turned into a stone. The touch of Rāma restored her to her own form. She is also one of the five pure women whom every Hindu woman is supposed to invoke every morning.

Ahalyā Bāī (1735–95)

After her husband was killed in battle, she became ruler of Indore (1765). She was so highly respected for her piety, her charity and her righteousness that people held her to be an AVATĀRA.

ahaṁ-kāra ('egoity')

Principle of individuation according to the SĀṀKHYA system and generally considered the main hindrance to liberation.

ahi, also ahirbudhnya ('serpent', 'serpent from the depth')

One of the names of VṚTRA, INDRA's chief enemy in the *Ṛgveda*.

ahiṁsā ('non-killing')

The first of the virtues (YAMAS) to be practised by a Hindu, forbidding the taking of life (except in the context of a Vedic SACRIFICE, where it is prescribed and sanctioned); interpreted by GANDHI as 'non-violence' in a universal sense and elevated to the foremost human quality.

Ahirbudhnya Saṁhitā

One of the most important treatises of the PĀÑCARĀTRA school containing philosophical and liturgical materials.

Aihole

Site in Karṇātaka with important rock-cut architecture and ancient temples (sixth to eighth centuries CE).

Aikṣvāka dynasty

The solar dynasty, founded by ĪKṢVĀKU (1), son of Ila and grandson of MANU (2), residing at AYODHYĀ; its most important member-to-be was RĀMA.

Airāvata, Indra's vahana *(vehicle), a four-tusked white elephant.*

Airāvata

A four-tusked white elephant produced from the CHURNING OF THE OCEAN and appropriated by INDRA as his VAHANA. Guardian of the east. (*See also* DIG-GAJA; LOKA-PĀLA.)

aiśvarya ('lordship')

One of the six transcendental attributes of VIṢṆU according to RAMANUJA.

Aitareya Brāhmaṇa

One of the most important compendia of Vedic lore and ritual ascribed to the Vedic seer Mahidasa Aitareya (*See also* BRĀHMAṆA (1).)

Aitareya Upaniṣad

One of the principal UPANIṢADS; part of the *Aitareya Āraṇyaka*. Ascribed to the Vedic sage MAHĪDĀSA.

Ajantā

One of the most celebrated sites of India, situated in Mahārāṣtra, famous for its numerous painted rock-carved temples (mostly Buddhist).

ajñā ('order, authority')

During the investitute ceremony (ABHIṢEKHA) a priest from the local shrine of the Goddess would confer *ajñā* (identified with ŚAKTI) on the new ruler.

ākāśa ('sky, ether')

one of the five elements of which everything is made and into which everything dissolves; according to the VAIŚEṢIKA school it is the only eternal element.

Akbar ('The Great', 1556–1605)

The most important Mogul ruler. He was sympathetic to Hinduism and tried to establish a new universal religion with large borrowings from Hinduism.

akhāḍā ('division')

Unit of armed Hindu SĀDHUS, whose function was to protect SAMNYĀSIS from attack. Since *samnyāsis* had to renounce violence and were not allowed to carry weapons, they could not defend themselves against either rival sects or ordinary robbers. They therefore organized bands of auxiliaries, who underwent military training and carried weapons (usually the traditional *triśula* [trident]) and lived together in designated centres.

Akhaṇḍ Bhārat ('Undivided India')

India before the 1947 partition; the aim of reunification of India sought by Hindu nationalists.

Akhil Bhāratīya Sādhu Samāj

('All India Association of Monastics')

An organization created by then interior minister Gulzarilal Nanda in 1962 to educate and organize the millions of independent and often ignorant renouncers. (*See also* SAMNĀYSI.)

Akhil Bhāratīya Sant Samitī

('All India Saints' Association')

An organization created by Swami VĀMA-DEVA (4) in 1986 to work for the restoration of Hindu political power in India.

Akhil Bhāratīya Vidyārthi Pariṣad

('All India Students' Council')

An organization for students created by the Rāṣṭrīya Svayamsevak Sangh to mobilize students on behalf of Hindu political parties.

Akka Mahādevī (12th century)

An unusually modern medieval women saint. Born to pious Śaivite parents in Uḍutadi (western Karnāṭaka) she began as a young child to worship Śiva as 'lovely Lord, white as Jasmine' and was initiated by an unknown *guru*. The Jain king Kauśika fell in love with her and wanted to marry her. In order to protect her parents from possible reprisals she agreed under condition that she could continue worshipping Śiva, whom she considered her true husband, without any hindrance. When Kauśika broke his promise, Akka divested herself of all the robes that he had given her and left the palace naked. She arrived at Kalyāṇa, a Liṅgāyat centre. After being tested by the religious authorities she began to teach as Jaganmathe (Mother of the World). She became a leading spiritual personality at Kalyāṇa. After about five years she left for Śrīśaila, in the Himālayas, in order to become one with Śiva. She died probably at the age of 25. Contemporary Liṅgāyats celebrate her as a symbol for the EQUALITY OF WOMEN in religion and consider her an early exponent of women's emancipation.

akṛti ('uncreated')

In Mīmāṁsā, the uncreated idea that stands behind every audible word and gives it (permanent) meaning.

akṣara (1) ('imperishable')

A designation of the mantra AUM.

akṣara (2)

In grammar, the individual letter of the alphabet, deemed to be the indestructible, ultimate unit ('atom') of language.

Alberuni

See BĪRŪNĪ, AL-.

Allahābad

Site of the ancient city Prāyāga, a famous place of pilgrimage at the confluence of the YAMUNĀ and GAṄGA (and the invisible SARASVATĪ), renamed by Muslims the 'City of Allah'. One of the four sites for the KUMBHAMELA held every twelve years (the others being HARDWAR, UJJAINĪ and Nasik).

altar

Public Vedic sacrifices were offered on an altar, called VEDI. The fully developed ŚRAUTA (2) sacrifice, performed by professional priests, required three altars: a circular *gārhapatya* altar in the west (symbolizing the earth and fire), a quadratic *ahavanīya* altar in the east (symbolizing the sky and its four directions) and a semicircular *dakṣina* altar in the south (symbolizing the atmosphere between earth and heaven). AGNI thus was present in his terrestrial, celestial and atmospheric form.

In more elaborate rituals, such as the AGNICAYANA, a special altar was built with a specified number of bricks, laid out according to a prescribed plan, and demolished after the performance.

In Purāṇic PŪJĀ no altar properly speaking is used; the object of worship is the IMAGE (*mūrti*) of the deity, usually on a pedestal, and close by the implements of worship and the food to be offered are arranged on an altar-like table.

almsgiving

See DĀNA.

Āḷvārs ('those who dive into God')

A group of twelve poet-saints of South

India (sixth to ninth centuries CE), devotees of Māl (the Tamil form of KṚṢṆA and of VIṢṆU Nārāyana) whose hymns are collected in the *Nalayira Divyā Prabandhaṁ*, the book of 4,000 verses. It is divided into 23 separate works, arranged in four sections, among which the *Tiruvaymoli* by NAMMĀḶVĀR is the most extensive. The *Prabandhaṁ* is widely used in temple worship in South India even today and the ideas expressed by the *Ālvārs* were the foundation on which later ŚRĪVAIṢṆAVISM developed. The greatest of the *Āḷvārs* are NAMMĀḶVĀR, also called Śathakopan (seventh century), and ANṬĀL, also called Goḍā (eighth century), the only female *Āḷvār*. Her one desire was to be married to Viṣṇu and, according to tradition, she vanished into the Viṣṇu image at ŚRĪRAṄGAM. The *Āḷvārs* have lately been the object of extensive scholarly study.

Ambā, also **Ambikā** ('Mother')

Epithet of DURGĀ, formed out of the combined energies of all gods to destroy the buffalo demon.

Ambedkar, Bhimrao Ramji
(1891–1956)

A member of the Māhār (untouchable) CASTE, who succeeded in obtaining a scholarship to study law and who was one of the main architects of independent India's constitution. He had a serious disagreement with GANDHI about the future status of the untouchables. While Ambedkar favoured the abolition of caste, Gandhi wanted the 'HARIJANS' to be admitted to the caste system, by joining the śūdras, the lowest social unit (*varṇa*) within the system. Unhappy also with the continuing casteism within the ruling Congress Party, he left Nehru's cabinet and publicly renounced Hinduism. Several million of his fellow Māhārs became Buddhists with him in 1953. (*See also* ASPṚŚYA; CASTE; OUTCASTE; SOCIAL ORDER.)

amṛta ('nectar')

A liquid that the gods churned out from the milk ocean at the beginning of the world and which gives immortality. (*See also* CHURNING OF THE OCEAN.)

anāhaṭa ('not beaten')

A mystical sound that poet-saints describe as arising spontaneously from within the body, signalling enlightenment.

anahaṭa-cakra

The fourth CAKRA (3) of the body in tantrik theory. (*See also* TANTRA (2).)

Ānanadamayī Mā
(1896–1983)

A famous female guru from Bengal with a large following and numerous ashrams in many places in India, credited with many miracles.

ānanda ('bliss')

A key concept in the UPANIṢADS, the cessation of suffering. VEDĀNTA (2) assumes that human beings are essentially blissful but prevented from recognizing their inherent ānanda nature by mental blindness and involvement in mundane matters.

Ānand(a) Mārg(a)
('Path of Bliss')

A modern Hindu sect, founded in 1955 by Ānand Mūrti (Prabhat Rajan Sarkar), who claimed to be an incarnation of God, with the aim to 'establish God's dicatorship' over India; linked to acts of violence and terrorism in India and abroad. The Ānand Mārg achieved a certain notoriety when eight members took their lives by self-immolation and Ānand Mūrti was accused by his wife of murdering some members of the sect.

Ānanda Tīrtha

See MADHVA.

ananta ('infinite')

An attribute of the supreme.

Ananta

Name of the world-snake (ŚEṢA) upon which VIṢṆU rests, symbolizing infinite time.

aṇava ('atomicity', 'smallness')

Used as a technical term in ŚAIVA SIDDHĀNTA to designate the beginningless bondage of the unredeemed soul, preventing it from being its true self.

ancestors

Important in Hinduism from ancient times. The Hindu funerary ritual is designed to transform a deceased person from a PRETA (ghost) into a PITṚ (father, ancestor). It lasts for a year and its correct execution is a matter of great importance for the family. Many holy places promise rewards not only for the person performing an act of piety but also for the ancestors.

Andhaka ('blind man')

A demon, son of KAŚYAPA and DITI, endowed with a thousand arms and heads, two thousand eyes and feet, who walked like a blind man, although he could see very well. He was killed by INDRA when he attempted to steal the PĀRIJĀTA tree from heaven.

Aṅgiras

One of the seven great vedic ṚṢIS to whom many hymns of the ṚGVEDA are attributed. He is also one of the ten PRAJĀPATIS, the progenitors of humankind, known as lawgiver and as a writer on astronomy. He is identified with BṚHASPATI, the presiding deity of the planet Jupiter. He is called 'lord of the sacrifice'. His wives were Smṛti ('memory'), Śradhhā ('faith'), Svadhā ('oblation') and Satī ('truth'). His daughters were the Vedic hymns, his sons the Havismats (possessors of sacrificial oblations).

Āṅgirasa

Descendants of AṄGIRAS or of AGNI, who is called the first of the Āṅgirasas. They became personifications of light and of luminous bodies, as well as of fire on special occasions, and as the phases of the moon.

aṇimā ('smallness')

In Yoga, the capability of reducing oneself to minute dimensions.

animals

Hinduism assumes a difference only in degree, not in nature, between human and animal (and plant) life: humans can be reborn as animals, animals as humans or gods. Certain animals, such as the COW, enjoy an exceedingly high status. Among the divine AVATĀRAS there are several animals such as the tortoise, the fish, the boar, and the half-man half-lion NĀRASIMHA, who are represented in IMAGES and are worshipped. The most famous animal deity is HANUMAN, the leader of the troops of monkeys who helped Rāma regain the abducted Sītā. In some parts of the country rats, snakes, PEACOCKS, ELEPHANTS and other animals enjoy special religious attention. Each of the major gods of Hinduism has an animal as a VAHANA (vehicle): thus the bird GARUḌA is associated with Viṣṇu, the bull NANDI with Śiva, the peacock with Sarasvatī (1) and with Kārttikeya, and the lion with Durgā.

animal sacrifice

See SACRIFICE.

anna

See FOOD.

annihilation (*saṁhāra, pralaya*)

One of the three divine cosmic functions. According to a fairly common Hindu belief, the universe is annihilated after each KALPA, and remains in a state of potentiality for the duration of a *kalpa*. Within the *trimūrti* (Brahmā–Viṣṇu–Śiva) Śiva is called the 'destroyer'. (*See also* CREATION; SUSTENANCE.)

anṛta ('violation of the law')

The opposite of ṚTA, the moral law.

Anṭāl, also **Goḍā** (725–55 CE)

The only female among the ĀḺVĀRS. Her original name was Kotai and she grew up in the shadow of the temple of Śrīvilliputtur, now boasting the tallest GOPURA in India, built in her honour. Without the knowledge of her father (a temple priest) she draped the garland intended for worship of the IMAGE around her, posing as God's bride. She spent her days in worship, composing hymns and refused to accept anyone but Viṣṇu as her husband. A festive ceremony was arranged to marry her to Viṣṇu at ŚRĪRAṄGAM. When she approached the image, she mysteriously disappeared into it. A temple was built in her honour at Śrīvilliputtur where her songs are sung daily.

antar-ātman ('the self within')

Spirit, innner feelings, heart.

antaryāmi ('the inner ruler')

According to VAIṢṆAVA theology, the form of the deity that dwells in the human heart and guides it, and accompanies it through the experiences of heaven and hell.

antyeṣṭi

See ŚRADDHA.

aṇu ('atom')

According to VAIŚESIKA the smallest unit of matter, the fourth part of a *mātrā* (the diameter of a speck of dust visible in a ray of sunshine).

anugraha ('favour')

God's saving grace.

anumāna ('inference')

One of the PRAMĀṆAS (valid means to find truth) accepted by most Hindu schools of thought.

anurāga ('passionate love')

One of the (higher) forms of BHAKTI.

apara jñāna ('lower knowledge')

A kind of cognition that is still associated with objects and therefore not capable of liberating its practitioner.

aparādha ('fault')

Sin, breach of an injunction which requires penance.

aparigraha ('not grasping')

Freedom from greed, one of the 10 virtues recommended by the YOGA-SŪTRA as preparation for meditation; a key word for Mahatma GANDHI, who interpreted it as meaning total dependence on God's providence.

Āpasmāra

Demon-dwarf, symbol of ignorance and forgetfulness, crushed under Śiva's right foot in his cosmic dance.

Āpastamba

Ancient writer on ritual and law and author of the *Āpastamba Dharmasūtra*. He is often quoted by later writers.

apauruṣeya ('impersonal')

Not originated either by a human or a superhuman person. According to the MĪMĀṀSAKAS the VEDA is *apauruṣeya*, i.e. it has no author but always existed by and of itself.

Appar (eighth century CE)

One of the 63 NĀYAṆMĀRS, poet-saints of ŚAIVISM. Appar was a convert from Jainism and had to suffer persecution for his change of faith, but became instrumental in converting the King of MADURAI and his court.

aprakṛta śarīra
('immaterial body')

VAIṢṆAVAS believe that God possesses an immaterial, indestructible body and that his devotees would also receive one in VAIKUṆṬHA, Viṣṇu's heaven.

Apri(s)

Propitiatory invocations during the fore-offerings of vedic animal SACRIFICES.

apsaras ('nymphs')

Semi-divine female beings, whose beauty is praised in early Vedic literature and who are often sent by the gods, afraid of the power accumulated through self-mortification, to seduce ascetics. Epics and PURĀṆAS contain many stories of *apsaras* marrying humans and the complications arising therefrom.

apūrva ('not before')

A term coined by the MĪMĀMSAKAS to denote the not yet realized, but fully accomplished, fruit of a SACRIFICE, which becomes available to the sacrificer after death.

Āraṇyakāṇda ('Forest part')

The third book of the RAMĀYAṆA, dealing with the forest exile of RĀMA and his entourage.

Āraṇyakas ('forest treatises')

The third section of the VEDA, sometimes joined with the (succeeding) UPANIṢADS, dealing with mystical interpretations of rituals and Vedic sayings.

Āraṇyaparvan ('Forest chapter')

The third book of the MAHĀBHĀRATA, describing the adventures of the exiled PĀṆḌAVAS in the forests in which they had to live for twelve years.

ārati

Worship of an IMAGE or an honoured person by moving lighted camphor or oil lamps in a circular way on a plate in front of the image.

arcana

Worship of the IMAGE of a deity. One of the duties of a devotee of Viṣṇu.

arcāvatāra ('worship descent')

The form of the deity (Viṣṇu) that makes itself available to humans for worship in the form of an IMAGE.

architecture

Assuming that the Indus civilization was a late Vedic development, Hinduism possesses one of the oldest architectural traditions on earth. The Vedic *Śulva* SŪTRAS offer a practical geometry for the construction of complex ALTARS and large structures. Some of the ruins of Mohenjo Daro have been interpreted as remnants of a temple compound and of a temple tank. Most of Vedic architecture was probably embodied in wooden structures that have not survived. Buddhist architecture, largely consisting

The Lakṣmī Nārāyaṇa Temple, New Delhi: Built in the 20th century by the wealthy Birla family (it is also known as 'Birla-Temple'), it uses the canons of architecture determined in the ancient Hindu Śilpa-śāstras.

of *stūpas, caityas* and caves (often richly ornamented and provided with architectural embellishments) in all probability made use of older Hindu models.

Hindu TEMPLE architecture came into its own during the GUPTA renaissance. Around 400 CE the first brick or stone temples appeared, built according to a Roman–Syrian model: a cubicle housing the IMAGE of the deity, a portico for the worshippers in front of it, surrounded by a gallery supported by pillars, with a flat roof, and surrounded by a terrace. Later on, typical Indian (Hindu) models of temple architecture developed, which for convenience may be classified into Northern, Eastern and Southern.

The Northern or *nāgara* style is characterized by a fairly tall and steep *śikhara* (steeple) on top of the *garbhagṛha* (the cella where the image of the deity is housed). The porch in front of it serves as a kind of audience hall for the worshippers. They come individually and circumambulate the image in a clockwise direction. The Eastern or *vessara* style features a more rounded tower and often a more elaborate set of buildings, including a hall for performing musicians and dancers. The Southern or *drāviḍa* style is characterized by multi-storeyed *gopuras*, towering structures over the entrance gates to the temple complex: the sanctuary itself is usually a fairly low and unobtrusive structure, housing only the image of the deity. The temple complex usually contains a number of additional buildings, a tank and other facilities. In South India especially temples developed into veritable holy cities, often built in concentric rectangles, each with its own specific function in the whole.

The architect enjoyed high prestige and was expected to be an all-round expert: not only had he to draw up the plans for the buildings according to traditional specifications, he had to oversee the procurement of suitable materials, to supervise the day-to-day activities and to sculpt the main sculpture of the new temple. Principles of traditional Hindu architecture are found in several Purāṇas and Āgamas; the principal texts are the *Śilpaśāstras*, or *Vāstuśāstras*, of which one is attributed to VIŚVA-KARMA (2), the architect of the gods, and one to MAYA, the architect of the demons.

The main function of the Hindu Temple is to provide an abode for the image of the deity believed to dwell within it.

ardhanārī ('half-woman')

IMAGE of ŚIVA with the left half showing female attributes, the right one male.

One story explains its origins thus: an ardent devotee of Śiva, who refused to worship PĀRVATĪ, his consort, tried to avoid CIRCUMAMBULATING the pair by slipping between their feet. Śiva, resenting this, became one with Pārvatī, so that the devotee could not but also circumambulate the goddess.

arghya

Water to rinse hands and mouth before worship and meals.

Arjuna ('white')

The third of the PĀṆḌAVAS, a brave warrior. KṚṢṆA's partner in the *Bhagavadgīta*, in which he receives the new teaching of salvation through devotion to Kṛṣṇa and the revelation of Kṛṣṇa's VIŚVA-RŪPA (universal form of God). He was asked to perform the funeral rites for Kṛṣṇa in his capital city Dvāraka, and then retired into the Himālayas.

ārṣa ('relating to, or made by, ṛṣis [sages]')

Sayings of (Vedic) sages, or images consecrated by them.

art

The traditional 64 arts (*kalā*) comprise a wide variety of skills, crafts and various artistic activities, such as playing an instrument, flower arranging, dancing, painting, sculpture, architecture, producing perfumes, creating colourful patterns, applying cosmetics, weaving, stitching, basket making, ceramics, singing, woodworking, playing tops, planting gardens, caring for trees, stringing beads, refining diamonds, reading, writing, cooking etc. Their great variety and the inclusion of practical skills and useful crafts is indicative of the Hindu approach to art as part of everyday life rather than the occupation of some individuals for the sake of the aesthetic pleasure of a refined minority.

The endeavour to perfect each of these arts has led to the production of a great many *śāstras* ('sciences') in many areas that have become acknowledged as authoritative. Thus *Nāṭyaśāstra* texts teach music and dance, *Śilpaśāstra* is concerned with architecture and sculpture (including a study of the materials required). The skill of Indian craftsmen was proverbial even in antiquity. The fact that most arts were practised by members of special castes provided India with a large pool of skilled hereditary artists and craftsmen. The fine arts in the modern Western sense, such as painting, sculpture, composing, playing instruments, singing, dancing and performing on the stage were cultivated at all levels. In both the residence towns of Indian rulers and in small towns and villages one can often find exquisite temples, beautiful sculptures and highly skilled craftsmen. Many Hindu housewives in the south decorate the entrance to their homes every morning with beautiful coloured patterns made with riceflower (*raṅgolī*), and the daily rituals of worship performed by ordinary men before the IMAGE of the god in their homes are a sophisticated form of art.

A great deal of art was created in the service of religion: construction of temples, carving of sculptures, producing of brass images and singing and dancing in honour of the deity were part of the service owed to the deity.

artha (1) ('wealth')

One of the four PURUṢĀRTHAS (legitimate human goals).

artha (2)

In grammar, meaning (of words or sentences); object.

artha (3)

In statecraft, acquisition and preservation of wealth. (*See also* ĀRTHA-ŚĀSTRA.)

Ārtha-śāstra
('the science of acquiring wealth [and power]')

A class of writings dealing with economics and politics. One such work, the *Kauṭilīya Ārtha-śāstra*, ascribed to the time of the MAURYAS, has been preserved and widely studied.

Arunācala ('Red mountain')

A large hill in South India sacred to Śiva, next to Tiruvannamalai, an ancient place of pilgrimage. It became well known through RAMANA MAHARṢI who went there as a young boy and established an ashram that attracted many devotees from India and abroad.

Āryans (from *ārya*, 'noble')

The self-designation of the Vedic people as distinct from the *anārya*, the unfree and the tribals. Their rules were called *ārya dharma*; acting contrary to these was *anārya*, 'ignoble'.

Āryabhaṭṭa (fifth century CE)

The earliest known Indian mathematician and astronomer, author of the famous *Āryabhaṭṭīya* and the *Āryasiddhānta*. He is also reputed to have introduced the decimal-place value system.

Ārya Samāj ('Āryan Society')

A reform movement founded in Bombay in 1875 by Swami DĀYĀNANDA SARASVATĪ (1824–83) from Morvi (Gujarat). Dāyānanda considered popular purāṇic Hinduism a corruption of the Vedic tradition and wanted Hindus to return to the original Vedic DHARMA. He abolished all PŪJĀS and all devotional paraphernalia, reintroduced the Vedic fire sacrifice (AGNIHOTRA) and aimed at re-converting Indian Muslims and Christians to (reformed) Hinduism.

The basic teachings of Dāyānanda Sarasvatī are contained in his *Satyārtha Prakāśa* (Splendour of the True Meaning (of the Veda), or 'Light of Truth'), the rituals are laid down in his *Pañca-mahā-yajña-vidhi* and the domestic rites are described in the *Saṃskāra-vidhi*. The VEDA alone is accepted as unconditionally true. He wished to make the Veda available to everyone, including women and people from low CASTES. Engagement on behalf of society at large and improvement of living conditions was also central to early Ārya Samāj practice.

The Ārya Samāj established schools following the traditional GURUKULA system with SANSKRIT as medium of instruction and traditional subjects as content. The Ārya Samāj split into two branches, one of which aimed at offering modern English medium instruction. There are numerous DAV (Dayananda Anglo Vedic) colleges in India. Some members of the Ārya Samāj also became instrumental in the establishment of Hindu nationalist organizations that are working for a transformation of India into a Hindu state, such as the RSS (RĀṢTRĪYA SVAYAMSEVAK SANGH), the JANA SANGH party (later merged into the JĀNATĀ PARTY and into the BJP (BHĀRATĪYA JĀNATĀ PARTY), the VIŚVA HINDŪ PARIṢAD and others.

Today the Ārya Samāj has centres in all cities and towns of India and in many cities abroad and claims a membership of over a million.

asat ('non-being')

A condition of non-differentiation, assumed to exist before creation.

asceticism

Hindus were famous from antiquity for their asceticism. Ascetic practices (TAPAS) were assumed to create powers that are irresistible. Self-control and observation of a strict regimen were part of general ethics. A Hindu was expected to become more and more detached from self-indulgence as he progressed through life. A brahmin's life was to end in SAMNYĀSA, total renunciation. Those who had renounced enjoyed high social status. Apart from reducing one's wants to a minimum and practising sexual continence (BRAHMACARYA), *samnyāsis* developed a great variety of forms of *tapas*, ranging from different forms of abstention from food and drink and other sense gratifications, to lying on a bed of nails, standing for prolonged periods in water, looking into the sun, lifting an arm up till it withered. One of the more widespread forms of self- mortification was the 'Five-fires-practice' (*pañcāgni tapas*): the ascetic sat in the centre of a square which was formed by four blazing fires, with the sun overhead as the fifth fire. Renunciation was held to be the precondition for higher spiritual development, and the practice of asceticism in one form or other is expected of every Hindu.

ashes (*bhasma*)

Sacred ashes play a great role in Hinduism. ŚAIVITES besmear their bodies with ashes. The famous SATHYA SAI BABA creates and distributes ashes which are said to be efficacious in healing all kinds of diseases of body and mind.

ashram *See* ĀŚRAMA (1).

āśirvāda ('blessing', 'benediction')

A ritual performed in temples on visitors by the officiating priests.

āsmitā ('I-ness', egoism)

One of the forms of AVIDYĀ, which has to be eradicated before one can make spiritual progress. (See also AHAMKĀRA.)

aspṛśya ('untouchable')

A class of people ranking below the ŚŪDRAS. Physical contact of any kind was supposed to pollute members of the three upper castes ritually. They were not allowed to use common facilities in villages such as wells and had to live in a separate area outside the villages. They often earned their living by performing dirty and degrading work such as removing carcasses, preparing corpses for cremation, removing night soil from latrines. Mahatma GANDHI fought for their rehabilitation; he called them *Harijan*, 'God's people', and tried to educate and integrate them. The Indian constitution of 1950 abolished untouchability and made it punishable to disadvantage people on this ground. Measures to grant them more access to positions in public service and to schools have met with much resistance, often violent, in recent years.

āśrama (1) ('work place'), also **ashram**

Monastery, abode of as ascetics. *Āśramas* have played an important role in Indian history. Epics and Purāṇas report the visits of their main protagonists to the *āśramas* of famous sages. The *Mahābhārata* offers a veritable guidebook of such places, and it became fashionable for religious teachers to visit the most famous of these. The *āśrama* tradition is still alive in India. Mahatma GANDHI founded an *āśrama* to train his co-workers, and it is quite common today for Hindus to spend some time in an *āśrama*, performing religious exercises.

āśrama (2)

Stage in life, of which according to the VARṆĀŚRAMA DHARMA there are four: BRAHMACARYA (early youth), GṚHASTYA (life of householder), VĀNAPRASTYA (life in forest), and SAMNYĀSA (life of renunciation, homelessness).

The four stages of life: a. Brahmacarya (early youth), b. Gṛhastya (life of householder); c. Vānaprastya (life in forest); d. Samnyāsa (life of renunciation).

Aṣṭādhyāyī ('eight chapters')

Title of the celebrated SANSKRIT grammar by PĀṆINĪ (6th century BCE?) which has been hailed as one of the greatest intellectual achievements of all times. In it Pāṇinī attempts to reduce the entire Sanskrit language to about 800 roots and their derivations, governed by about 4,000 rules. Pāṇinī's grammar became the standard for classical Sanskrit.

aṣṭākṣara ('eight syllables')

The famous mantra: *Om Namah Nārāyanāya*, repeated thrice daily by many VAIṢṆAVAS to obtain liberation. (*See also* MANTRA (3).)

aṣṭa-maṅgala ('eight auspicious objects')

These are required for important official occasions. Their composition varies; one list mentions lion, bull, elephant, water-jar, fan, flag, trumpet, lamp; another has brahmin, crow, fire, gold, ghi, sun, water, king.

aṣṭamūrti ('eightfold image')

The presence of ŚIVA in the five elements, the sun, the moon and in sentient beings, associated with the eight names of Śiva under which he is worshipped (RUDRA, ŚARVA, PAŚUPATI, Ugra, Aṣani, BHAVA, MAHĀDEVA, ĪŚĀNA)

aṣṭāvaraṇa ('eightfold armour')

The eight commandments that VĪRA ŚAIVAS have to observe, namely: obedience towards the GURU, wearing a Śiva linga (*see* LIṄGA (3)), worshipping Śaivite ascetics as incarnations of Śiva, sipping water in which the feet of the guru have been bathed, offering food to a guru, smearing ashes on one's body, wearing a string of RUDRĀKṢA beads, reciting the mantra *Śivāya namāh* (*see also* MANTRA (3)).

asteya ('not-stealing')

One of the basic commandments of Hindu ethics. *Steya* (stealing) was considered a grave sin (MAHĀ-PĀTAKA) only when it involved a large amount of goods (especially gold) stolen from a brahmin. The penalty for this was death. Taking food and other necessities of life was not considered theft.

āstika

Literally, someone who affirms 'it is', i.e. one who accepts the VEDA as normative, an adherent of one of the so-called 'orthodox six systems', namely: NYĀYA, VAIŚEṢIKA, SĀṂKHYA, YOGA, PŪRVA MĪMĀṂSĀ and VEDĀNTA (2)). (See also NĀSTIKA.)

astrology

(*jyotiṣa*, literally 'light-science')

Astrology, which also includes astronomy, considered a science, has played a great role in Hinduism since ancient times. References to eclipses found in the *Ṛgveda* have been used to date the texts to the fourth millennium BCE. One of the VEDĀNGAS (auxiliary sciences of the Veda) is devoted to determining the right time for Vedic SACRIFICES. At birth a horoscope is established for every child by a professional astrologer, which provides the basis for determining auspicious and inauspicious dates for major events like the beginning of schooling, marriage, major business transactions etc. There is a *jyotiṣī* department at Benares Hindu University which annually produces the official astrological calendar (PAÑCĀṄGA) which serves to determine the exact dates for sacred days and to find out auspicious times for public functions, such as the opening of parliament. (*See also* NAKṢATRA.)

asura ('demon')

Class of superhuman beings hostile to the DEVAS (gods). While usually engaged in battles with the *devas*, the *asuras* are not without noble qualities: they are often described as brave, chivalrous, generous and loyal. Among the most famous *asuras* are RĀVAṆA, King of Laṅkā, who abducted Rāma's wife Sītā, BALI, who invited Viṣṇu in the form of the dwarf to his banquet and surrendered his realm to Viṣṇu, and Mahiṣa, the buffalo-demon, whose defeat by the Goddess is celebrated in the yearly Durgāpūjā festival. The linguistic affinity of *asura* with the Zoroastrian high god Ahura (Mazda) has led to the suggestion that *asura* might initially have been the Indian designation for the deity, the term *sura* (gods) being an artificial creation after the split between the Indian and Persian populations. (See also DAITYAS.)

aśva-medha ('horse sacrifice')

See SACRIFICE.

Aśvins ('possessed of horses')

The two physicians of the gods, represented as twin sons of the Sun by a nymph in the form of a mare, harbingers of the dawn, frequently invoked in the *Ṛgveda*. As a constellation they are Gemini (Castor and Pollux).

Atharvan

Name of a famous Vedic sage, eldest son of BRAHMĀ, who learned from

Brahmā and communicated BRAHMA-VIDYĀ; he is believed to have been the first to bring fire down from heaven, offer SOMA and recite MANTRAS (3).

Atharvaveda

The fourth of the vedic SAṂHITĀS (collections of hymns) and the last to be recognized as such. Besides hymns to Vedic DEVATĀS it contains oracular sayings, incantations and imprecations.

athiti ('guest')

Hospitality was a duty in Vedic India and a guest had to be honoured. Neglecting a guest brought misfortune.

Atiśūdra

'below the ŚŪDRA', i.e. OUTCASTE, untouchable.

ātma(n) ('self')

One of the central notions of VEDĀNTA. Assuming that ordinarily persons do not have a correct and adequate notion of the true self, but mistake external attributes such as bodily appearance, sensual experiences, relationships, activities etc. for the self, the UPANIṢADS teach ways for self-finding, culminating in the realization of the self as pure (objectless) experience of consciousness. This self- experience is then identified with the experience of the ground of all things (BRAHMAN) and considered the very purpose of existence, identical with eternal bliss. Vedānta systems variously interpret the nature of the self as either ontically identical with the supreme being (ADVAITA), or as being in close affinity with it, but ontically separate (VIŚIṢṬĀDVAITA, DVAITA). (*See also* SELF.)

Ātmabodha ('self-knowledge')

Title of a short Vedāntic treatise ascribed to ŚAṄKARA (2), teaching how to reach identity of self with BRAHMAN.

ātmakuṭa ('self-intention')

A notion developed by the MĪMĀṂSAKAS, who assumed that scriptural injunctions produce an impulse in a person to do voluntarily what has been prescribed, together with an insight into the appropriateness of the command.

atonement

The consciousness of failure in the observance of moral and ritual laws led early on in Vedic India to the development of a theory and practice of atonement (PRAYAŚCITTAS) through which ritual and moral purity could be re-established. The appropriate sections in the lawbooks (DHARMA-ŚĀSTRAS) provide detailed information on the kind of atonement required for specific breaches, relating not only to the gravity of offence but also to the status of offender and offended. Some of the most frequently practised atonements are ablutions, repetition of MANTRAS (3), fasting (*see* UPAVĀSA), PILGRIMAGES, almsgiving and donations to temples (*see* DĀNA). The most severe offences (MAHĀ-PĀTAKAS) can only be atoned for by death.

Atri ('devourer')

Name of a famous Vedic sage, author of many Vedic hymns as well as of a lawbook, the *Atri-smṛti*. His wife was Anasūyā. He is one of the SAPTARṢIS and represented in one of the stars in Ursa major. He produced the MOON (Atrija) from his eye during meditation.

attachment (*rāga*)

This is viewed as morally objectionable and spiritually harmful. It is one of the manifestations of AVIDYĀ (ignorance) and one ought to give up attachment to oneself, to one's family and one's possessions in order to gain freedom and release.

Aughara

A branch of the Nāṭhapanthis, the followers of GORAKHNĀṬHA, a section of yogis, followers of ŚIVA.

AUM

Also written OM, called the *prāṇava*, the mystical syllable containing the universe. It is explained as consisting of the first (a) and last (u) vowel and the last consonant (m) of the Sanskrit alphabet and therefore encompassing all words (which consist of vowels and consonants). The MĀṆḌUKYA UPANIṢAD identifies it with the four stages of consciousness (a = waking consciousness; u = dream consciousness; m = deep sleep; aum = fourth state). AUM/OM is used to introduce and conclude a religious work, an act of worship, an important task. It is supposed to be auspicious and its prolonged intonation is associated with the creative sound through which the universe came into existence.

Aurobindo Ghose

(1872–1950)

After receiving a completely Western, classical education in England (1879–92) and preparing for a career in the Indian Civil Service, Aurobindo Ghose returned to India with strong sympathies for the Indian nationalist movement. While serving in various official capacities, he wrote and spoke for Indian independence. Arrested in connection with the Alipore Bomb case, he spent a year in jail where he heard Kṛṣṇa exhorting him to devote his life for the spiritual upliftment of India and the world. Fleeing to the French colony of Pondicherry after his release he devoted his life to YOGA and to writing spiritual literature. His ashram under the leadership of 'The Mother' (Mirra Alfasa, who had joined the ashram in the early 1920s), soon attracted people from India and abroad. Aurobindo's attempt to work out an 'Integral Yoga' which combines traditional Hindu spirituality with engagement in the world and modern ideas excited great interest among intellectuals and artists. Aurobindo never left Pondicherry and hardly ever left his room, spending an increasing amount of time in meditation. His work was continued by 'The Mother' and his numerous associates who planned to develop Auroville into a model city for the modern world, combining intellectual and literary work with crafts and practical engagement.

Aurobindo was convinced that the whole universe was the manifestation of consciousness in a process of evolution from matter through mind to supermind and that it was the task of humans to facilitate this evolution by dedicating themselves to the highest ideals.

auspicious (*śubha*)

A very important concept for Hindus, who tend to distinguish almost everything along the lines auspicious/inauspicious. Symbols such as AUM and ŚRĪ are auspicious; they appear on first pages of books and ledgers, on buildings and cars. There are auspicious and inauspicious times during each day, week, month and year which one has to know. There are auspicious and inauspicious sights and sounds. Various methods exist to protect oneself and one's loved ones from inauspicious events.

austerities

See ASCETICISM; ATONEMENT; TAPAS.

āvāhana

Invitation to the deity to appear for worship.

avatāra ('descent')

Mostly used in connection with the bodily appearance of VIṢṆU. The most famous of Viṣṇu's *avatāras* are RĀMA and KṚṢṆA, around whom major branches of Hindu religion have developed. Among the *daśāvatāras* (ten descents), the number most frequently employed, are the tortoise, the boar, the fish and the man-lion, as well as the BUDDHA. The future and last *avatāra* is to be KALKI, who will bring to an end the present KALI YUGA. In the BHAGAVAD-GĪTĀ Kṛṣṇa explains the reasons for God's descent: 'Whenever DHARMA has become weak and ADHARMA has waxed strong I am descending to destroy the wicked and to relieve the good.' *Avatāras* have 'apparent bodies', not real bodies; they are not really born and do not really die. Many schools of Hinduism rule out the possibility of *avatāras*. It is, however, not infrequent even today, for Hindus to regard a living GURU as an *avatāra* of the godhead.

avidyā ('ignorance')

The native lack of knowledge of one's real nature, the root cause of involvement in the cycle of birth and rebirth. All Indian religions consider *avidyā* the ultimate reason for suffering and strive to teach VIDYĀ (wisdom). The Upaniṣads consider Vedic rituals *avidyā* because of their ineffectiveness to liberate from rebirth; ŚAṄKARA (2) identifies PRAKṚTI (nature) with *avidyā*, since it it is the very opposite to spirit. RĀMĀNUJA sees *avidyā* in the 'forgetfulness' of dependence on Viṣṇu. *Avidyā* manifests itself in egotism, attachment, aversion and clinging to physical life and enjoyment.

avyakta ('unmanifest')

The condition of reality before individuation by means of *nāma-rūpa* ('name and form') and after the reabsorption of all individuality in PRALAYA (universal dissolution).

Ayodhyā ('Free from strife')

City in eastern Uttar Pradesh (population *c.* 50,000), one of the seven ancient holy cities of India, the others being Vārāṇasī, Mathurā, Hardwar, Dvāraka, Kāñcīpura and Ujjainī. It has been associated since antiquity with Rāma's capital. A place of pilgrimage and of monastic Hindu establishments, it gained notoriety through the demolition of the Babri Masjid by Hindu activists in December 1992, which provoked the worst Hindu–Muslim rioting since independence all over India as well as in Pakistan and Bangladesh.

ayurveda ('life knowledge')

The system of indigenous Indian medicine. The main texts are *Suśruta Saṁhitā* and *Caraka Saṁhitā*, offering systematic diagnosis and treatment for a great many diseases. Since its medications are largely herbal, *ayurveda* has increasingly found adherents in the West. In India it is officially promoted as a parallel to modern Western medicine.

The underlying assumption of *ayurveda* is that all sickness is due to an imbalance of the three bodily humours (*tridoṣa*): *vaṭa* (wind), *pitta* (bile), *kapha* (phlegm) and that by changing a patient's diet, habits and thoughts the proper balance can be re-established.

B

Bādāmi

Ancient temple site in the Deccan, home to the famous Malegitti Śivālaya temple (seventh century) and others.

Bādarāyaṇa

Legendary author of the BRAHMA-SŪTRAS (also called *Vedāntasūtras*) which systematize the content of the Upaniṣads in 550 SŪTRAS. Dates suggested for the compilation of the *Brahmasutras* vary from 300 BCE to 300 CE.

Badrīnāth

Famous place of pilgrimage in the Himālayas, close to the source of the Ganges.

Bahiṇabāī (1628–1700)

A Mahārāṣṭrian poet-saint, whose *abhaṅgas* (hymns) are very popular to this day. Born into a poor brahmin family in Deogaon (Mahārāṣṭra) she was married at age five to a 30-year-old widower. In her autobiography, *Ātmanivedan*, she describes him as a man of a very angry disposition, who severely beat her, out of jealousy. After the family moved to Dehu, where Tukārām had started the Vārkarī movement, Bahiṇābāī enjoyed more freedom to participate in religious activities in honour of Viṭhobā. She continued both her family life (she had a son and a daughter) and her composition of religious lyrics, which were highly appreciated.

Baladeva, also Balarāma

In North Indian traditions he is the elder brother of Kṛṣṇa; in Tamil mythology he is the elder brother of Viṣṇu, also called VALIYON. Sometimes listed as the eighth AVATĀRA of Viṣṇu, sometimes as an *avatāra* of Śeṣa, the subject of many stories in the *Harivaṁśa* and in Vaiṣṇava Purāṇas, especially the Bhāgavatam. (*See also* KAṀŚA.)

Bāla-kāṇḍa ('Book of Childhood')

The first section of the RĀMĀYAṆA describing the childhood and youth of Rāma.

Bali

A pious DAITYA king, grandson of PRAHLĀDA. His good deeds earned him rulership over the three worlds. The gods implored Viṣṇu to restore their realms. Viṣṇu, in the form of the dwarf Vāmana, asked Bali for a boon: as much land as he could cover with three strides. Bali agreed, and then Viṣṇu stepped with two strides over heaven and earth. Bali offered his head as a rest for Viṣṇu's third stride. Out of consideration for his kindness and Prahlāda's devotion Viṣṇu left the netherworlds to Bali. His capital was MAHĀBALIPURA.

bali

See PIṆḌA.

Banaras (Benares)

Anglicized form of VĀRĀṆASĪ.

Bande mātārām

('I worship you, Mother')

First words of a poem by Bankim Chandra Chatterjee, in which he hymns India as Goddess. It later became the anthem of the Indian National Congress and the Freedom Movement. In the original setting the text appears in the novel *Ānanadamaṭha* as a hymn sung by the patriotic SĀDHUS of Bengal, who rose against the Muslims and the British, to regain their freedom.

bara sthāna ('big place')

Designation of the headquarters of RĀMĀNANDI nāgas.

Basava (12th century)

Minister of a Jain king and founder-reformer of the LIṄGĀYATS, a Śaivite sect which has many followers in Karṇatāka. Basava affirmed the equality of women, wished to abolish caste and exhorted his followers to be always engaged in useful activities.

Basham, Arthur Llewellyn

(1914–1986)

As author of *The Wonder that was India* (1985), which went through many editions and translations, he became probably the best-known Indianist of his generation. Basham was for many years Professor of history of South Asia at SOAS (University of London) before accepting an invitation to become head of the Department of Asian Studies at the Australian National University in Canberra. Contributor to many prestigious publications, recipient of many academic honours, e.g. 'Vidyavaridhi' (1977) by Nalanda University in India, visiting professor in India, Sri Lanka, USA, Mexico, Canada.

Belur

A famous temple site in South India.

Belur-math

A temple near Calcutta where RAMAKRISHNA 'PARAMAHAMSA' officiated as priest and which has become a popular place of pilgrimage under the management of the Ramakrishna Mission.

Besant, Annie, née Wood

(1847–1933)

Social reformer, theosophist and Indian independence leader. Born in England, she married Rev. Frank Besant, but growing doubts about the tenets of Christianity made her leave her husband and the church, becoming a member of the Fabian Society. After meeting with Helena Petrovna BLAVATSKY she joined the Theosophical movement and made India her home (in 1893). She was elected president of the Theosophical Society in 1907. She also supported the Indian Independence Movement and in 1917 was elected president of the Indian National Congress. The Hindu college she founded in Vārāṇasī (Benares) became the nucleus of the Benares Hindu University. She was a prolific writer and also wrote an autobiography.

Bhadrakālī ('propitious Kālī')

Name of the goddess DURGĀ.

Bhagavad-gītā

('Song of the Lord')

A famous philosophical and spiritual poem, often considered the epitome of Hinduism. A dialogue between KṚṢṆA and ARJUNA, just before the beginning of the great Bhārata war, it forms chapters 23 to 40 of the *Bhīṣma Parvan* of the *Mahābhārata*. Much commented upon by hundreds of Indian authors since ŚAṄKARA (2) (eighth century) and translated into all major languages of the world, it is the best-known Hindu scripture worldwide.

Bhāgavata Purāṇa

Although of comparatively recent origin (12th century?) it is one of the most popular and most important scriptures of Hinduism. Its central theme is KṚṢṆA and his exploits. It is frequently recited publicly and has been commented upon by classical and modern authors.

Bhāgavata saṁpradāya, also Bhāgavatism

See VAIṢṆAVISM.

Bhāgīrathī

A section of the Ganges. According to an old legend, King Bhāgīratha of the solar dynasty subjected himself to austere penances for a long time to bring the celestial river GAṄGĀ down from the heavens to purify the ashes of his 60,000 ancestors. To honour his memory one of the three main branches of the Gaṅgā was called Bhāgīrathī.

Bhairava ('the frightening one')

One of the eight forms of Śiva (AṢṬAMŪRTI), worshipped especially by sects such as the Kālamukhas. Bhairava is often depicted riding on a dog and is therefore called Śvāśva, '(one) whose horse is a dog'. There are eight manifestations of Bhairava: Asitāṅga (black limbed); Sanhāra (destruction); Ruru (dog); Kāla (black); Krodha (anger); Tamracūḍā (red-crested); Candracūḍā (moon-crested); Mahā (great).

bhajan ('song')

Especially religious songs that are sung by groups of devotees, a very popular and widespread custom among Hindus.

Bhakti (devotion) to Kṛṣṇa.

bhakti ('devotion')

A central feature of Hinduism, especially in the BHAKTI-MĀRGA, the 'path of devotion'. It is set off over against KARMA/*karma-mārga*, the 'path of ritual (action)' and JÑĀNA/*jñāna-mārga*, the 'path of knowledge'. It consists in outer and inner acts of worship of a personal deity, often embodied in an IMAGE. It characterizes popular Hinduism but has also been elaborated into a sophisticated theological and liturgical system by authorities such as RĀMĀNUJA, MADHVA, RŪPA GOSVAMI, Jīva Gosvami and many others. *Bhakti* was promoted in South India by the ĀLVĀRS between the sixth and the ninth centuries CE; in North India by a large number of SANTS from the 12th to the 16th centuries.

bhakti-mārga ('path of devotion')

One of the three traditional methods of finding spiritual fulfilment. The various teachers advocating it have different understandings of its precise content. Some seem to favour a spiritual interpretation, i.e. an inner surrender to God; others adopt a more ritualistic understanding, an insistence on a routine of rituals performed daily in front of a consecrated image, pilgrimages to holy places and such like. Within *bhakti-mārga* the importance of the spiritual master (GURU) is generally stressed as mediator of God's saving grace. With the growth of the theistic traditions in India (VAIṢṆAVISM, ŚAIVISM, ŚĀKTISM and others) the *bhakti-mārga* became the predominant path in Hinduism.

Bhāmatī

Commentary on Śankara's BRĀHMA-SŪTRABHĀṢYA by VĀCASPATI MIŚRA.

Bhandarkar, Ramkrishna Gopal (1837–1925)

One of India's foremost early 'modern' Indologists, trained both in the Hindu pandit tradition and at Western universities. He had a brilliant academic and public career as professor of Sanskrit at Elphinstone College in Bombay, the Deccan College in Poona, a member of the syndicate and later vice-chancellor of the University of Bombay, member of the Viceroy's Legislative Council, knighted in 1911. At the occasion of his 80th birthday in 1917 the Bhandarkar Oriental Research Institute was officially inaugurated. It became home to the critical edition of the *Mahābhārata*, the largest editorial enterprise ever undertaken. His collected works comprise over 2,000 pages, containing text editions, translations, textbooks and monographs such as his celebrated *Vaiṣṇavism, Śaivism and Minor Religious Systems* (1913). He was also an active member of the PRĀRTHANA SAMĀJ, a religious and social reformer, supporting the remarriage of widows and arguing that many orthodox customs had no basis in Hindu tradition.

Bhāradvāja (4000 BCE?)

A vedic ṚṢI to whom many hymns are attributed. Son of BṚHASPATI and father of DRONA, the teacher of the PĀṆḌAVAS. There are many stories connected with his life in epics and Purāṇas.

Bharata (1)

In the ṚGVEDA, hero and king of the warlike Bhāratas.

Bharata (2)

An ancient king who, while living as a SAMNYĀSI, became attached to a fawn and was reborn as a deer. In a further rebirth as a brahmin he served as palanquin bearer and amazed the king with his wisdom.

Bharata (3)

Son of Daśaratha by his wife Kaikeyī; half-brother of Rāma, he ruled the country during Rāma's absence on his behalf.

Bharata (4)

The son of Duṣyanyta and Śakuntalā, who became a universal monarch: India was called *Bhārata-varṣa* after him. He was a remote ancestor of both PĀṆḌAVAS and KAURAVAS. The Pāṇḍavas were also called Bhāratas: hence the (Mahā-) Bhārata war and the eponymous epic.

Bharata (5), also Bharata Muni (second century BCE)

Author of the *Nāṭyaśāstra*, the earliest treatise on music and dance.

Bhāratī

One of the names of SARASVATĪ (1).

Bhāratīya Jānatā Party ('Indian People Party')

Formed out of sections of the former

Jānatā Party in 1980, with the aim of transforming India into a Hindu state. Its leader Lal Krishna Advani became a popular hero through effectively staged events such as the Rām-śila-yātrā (collecting bricks for a Rāma temple in AYODHYĀ) in 1991, the Ektā-yātrā (Unity Pilgrimage) in 1992, and finally the destruction of the Babri Masjid in Ayodhyā in December 1992, which attracted worldwide attention and led to major Hindu–Muslim riots throughout India.

Bhārgavas

Descendants of the Vedic sage Bhṛgu, one of the PRAJĀPATIS. The Bhārgavas earned fame as a family of scholars/editors. The final redaction of the MAHĀBHĀRATA is ascribed to them.

Bhartṛhari (450–510 CE)

Celebrated grammarian and poet, whose *Vākyapadīa* is the most important work in the area of Indian philosophy of language. He is also credited with the composition of 300 didactic verses contained in the *Śṛṅgāra Śataka* (dealing with erotic matters); *Nīti Śataka* (dealing with polity and etiquette); and *Vairāgya Śataka* (dealing with renunciation).

Bhāsa (third century CE)

Famous classical Indian dramatist, author of *Svapna-vasava-datta* and 12 other plays.

Bhāskara (1) (11th century)

A celebrated mathematician and astronomer, author of the *Bījagaṇita* on arithmetic, the *Līlāvatī* on algebra, and the *Siddhānta Śiromaṇi* on astronomy.

Bhāskara (2)

A Vedāntic teacher, professing a kind of ADVAITA VEDĀNTA.

bhasma

See ASHES.

bhaṭṭa

Honorific title for a learned BRĀHMAṆA (2).

Bhava

A Vedic deity connected with Śarva, the Destroyer; also one of the eight names of Śiva. (*See also* RUDRA.)

bhāva

('feeling', 'condition', 'sentiment')

An important concept in Hindu aesthetics.

Bhave, Vinoba (1895–1982)

Close collaborator of Mahatma GANDHI, and his successor. In a historic *padyātrā* (pilgrimage on foot) he traversed India asking landowners to make a gift of land (*bhū-dān*) for the landless. His aim was to collect and distribute 50 million acres. He shared Gandhi's conviction that India's salvation had to come from the villages and worked for *grāmsvarāj* (village self-rule). He also initiated the Sarvodaya ('universal welfare') movement and created the Sarva Seva Sangh (universal service association). Throughout he emphasized the religious dimension of his activities and his intention to change hearts rather than bring about an economic revolution.

Bhaviṣya Purāṇa

('Future Purāṇa')

A PURĀṆA presented as written in the fifth century and purporting to deal with future events of the Indian Middle ages, including the Muslim invasion. Estimates of the date of its composition range from the 12th to the 19th centuries.

bhaya ('fear')

A basic emotion dealt with in Indian

aesthetics, personified as grandson of Adharma (unrighteousness) and Hiṁsā (violence), and father of Mṛtyu (death).

bhedābheda ('difference and non-difference')

Designation of several schools of Vedānta that both affirm and deny difference between ĀTMAN and BRAHMAN.

Bhīma (1) ('The terrible')

One of the eight forms of RUDRA or Ugra (frightening) Śiva.

Bhīma (2), also **Bhīmasena**

One of the five PĀṆḌAVAS, son of VĀYU. Described as of giant proportions, given to wrath, and a valiant warrior as well as a great eater. He had the nickname Vṛkodara, 'wolf's belly'. Many heroic deeds are ascribed to him in the MAHĀBHĀRATA. Because he violated the code of warriors by striking a foul blow he was called Jihma-yodi, 'unfair fighter'.

Bhimbhetka

Place in Central India where prehistoric (30,000 BCE) cave paintings were found.

Bhīṣma ('the terrible')

The son of King Śāntanu and the river goddess GAṄGĀ, also called Śāntanava, Gāṅgeya, Nadija (river-born). He became one of the main protagonists in the MAHĀBHĀRATA as general of the KAURAVAS and as author of a set of conventions for chivalrous warfare. Mortally wounded by ARJUNA, he survived 58 days, during which time he delivered many teachings. He is considered a model of loyalty and selfless service.

Bhīṣma Parvan

The sixth part of the MAHĀBHĀRATA, which also contains the BHAGAVAD-GĪTĀ.

bhojana ('eating', 'meal')

Surrounded with rituals and also part of the daily temple ritual: the feeding of the image of god is a main ingredient of *mūrti-pūjā*.

Bhṛgu

See BHĀRGAVAS.

bhū, also **bhūmi** ('the earth')

name of one of Viṣṇu's consorts.

bhukti ('[sensual] enjoyment')

Normally seen as the opposite to *mukti*, (spiritual) LIBERATION. However, Śāktism promises both *bhukti* and *mukti* and denies an opposition between them.

bhūr, also **bhūrloka**

The earth.

bhūtas ('spirits', 'ghosts')

Belief in *bhūtas* is widespread in India and there are many ceremonies designed to free a person from their influence. (*See also* PRETA).

Bhuvaṇeśvara ('Lord of the earth')

Title of ŚIVA, name of famous temple city in Orissa with some of the largest Hindu temples such as the 11th-century Liṅgarāja temple.

bhuvar, also **Bhuvarloka**

The firmament, the middle region between earth and sky.

bibhatsa ('loathing')

One of the basic sentiments of Hindu aesthetics. It is used in a purely aesthetic sense, and indicates a strong emotional experience. In GAUḌĪYA VAIṢṆAVISM, for example, it is said that to 'loathe' Kṛṣṇa may be preferable to indifference, because it is at least a reaction to his presence.

bīja-mantra ('seed-mantra')

Single syllables believed to be the sonic equivalent of certain divine powers. They are especially used by Tantrikas. (*See also* TANTRA (2).)

bilva

Tree, sacred to Śiva. Its leaves are offered in worship.

biṁba-pratibiṁba
('image and reflection')

MADHVA's description of the relationship between the supreme and the human. While rejecting the Advaitins' assumption of the identity of ĀTMAN and BRAHMAN, he nevertheless admits to a concept of the human being as 'reflecting' certain features of *brahman*.

biṇḍu 'drop' (1)

A coloured spot in the middle of the forehead of a woman, indicating her married status.

biṇḍu (2)

Name for moon.

biṇḍu (3)

In the title of a book, a very short summary of a longer text.

birth

The birth of a child is surrounded by a great many rituals and festivities, such as establishing a HOROSCOPE, giving a NAME, feeding brahmins etc. Hindus speak of a 'second' birth which is accomplished through UPA-NAYANA by which a person becomes a full member of the Hindu community. Some also talk about a 'third birth', i.e. the birth of one's own child, in which the father is 'reborn'.

Bīrūnī, al- (973–1051)

Persian Muslim scholar, scientist and diplomat who travelled through India from 1030 to 1042. He learned Sanskrit and was the first foreigner to give extensive and correct descriptions of the major branches of Hindu learning and summaries of important Hindu writings. His *al-Hind* became the single most important source of information about India and Hinduism for centuries to come.

Blavatsky, Helena Petrovna
(1831–1891)

Born Helena Petrovna Hahn-Hahn in Ekaterinoslav (Russia), she developed occult powers early on. Married at 17 to a much older man, whom she soon left, she travelled through Europe, America, Egypt, India and Tibet, where she claimed to have met the 'Master' she had seen long before in her dreams. Settling in New York in 1873 and joining the spiritual movement she became acquainted with Colonel Henry S. Olcott with whom she formed the Theosophical Society in 1875. She became widely known through her occult writings, especially *Isis Unveiled* (1877) and *The Secret Doctrine* (1888). She moved to India in 1878, transferring the headquarters of the Theosophical Society to ADYAR (Madras), and founding a journal, *The Theosophist*, dedicated to uniting Eastern spirituality and Western science. The day of her death, 8 May 1891, is celebrated as 'White Lotus Day' by the members of the Theosophical Society.

bliss

See ĀNANDA.

bodha ('understanding')

Personified as son of Buddhi, one of the daughters of DAKṢA.

Bodhāyana

Author of a (lost) gloss on the *Brahma-sūtras*.

body

Hinduism has an ambivalent attitude towards the body. On the one hand there is a sharp dichotomy between body and spirit and most Hindu systems insist on *viveka* (discernment) through which a person learns to identify with the spirit and to consider the body as 'non-self'. On the other hand, the body is valued as a vehicle of salvation: all acts necessary to obtain liberation require a well-functioning body. Many systems of YOGA aim at maintaining or restoring bodily health. In TANTRA (2) the body acquires even greater importance as the seat of *śakti* and as an indispensable instrument for realizing BHUKTI and *mukti* ([spiritual] LIBERATION) together.

According to Hindu psychology and physiology the human being has three components: the gross body (*sthūla śarīra*); the subtle body (*sūkṣma śarīra*); and the spirit–soul (*ātman*). While the gross body decays at death, the subtle body (roughly equivalent to what is today called the 'psyche'), in which the person's KARMA is stored, lives on and is in due time reincarnated in a new (gross) body. This cycle of death and reincarnation continues as long as the subtle body exists, united with the undecaying and unchanging *ātman*. Hindu strategies of liberation are aimed at annihilating the subtle body, neutralizing the force of *karma* and freeing the *ātman* from its bondage to the (gross and subtle) body. (*See also* NĀḌI.)

bondage (*bandha*)

Hindus believe that due to the influence of immemorial KARMA (2) every human being is born in (spiritual) bondage and that every effort must be undertaken to achieve LIBERATION. Bondage is caused by AVIDYĀ (ignorance, lack of wisdom). It consists of the triad of *moha–lobha–krodha* (delusion–greed–anger) which causes people to commit acts that bind them into the cycle of rebirths. More specifically, each Hindu school of thought defines the causes of bondage in correlation to the view of the nature of liberation. Thus SĀṀKHYA considers the spirit's infatuation with nature as the cause of its bondage; Advaitins identify *avidyā* with the habitual perceiving of plurality; RĀMĀNUJA teaches that 'forgetfulness' (of one's true nature as a child of God) is the root of human bondage. All systems also teach means and practices to become free. (*See also* LIBERATION; REBIRTH.)

Brahmā

In Hindu mythology the creator of the universe; the first member of the *trimūrti* (consisting of Brahmā, Viṣṇu and Śiva). He is represented as four-faced. Originally he had five heads; the loss of the fifth head is explained variously by different myths. In iconography he is represented with four arms, holding a sceptre, a ladle, a string of beads and the book of the Veda. His consort is SARASVATĪ, the goddess of learning. His vehicle (VAHANA) is a swan. There are only a few Brahmā temples left in India, the most famous in Puskār (Gujarat). The BRAHMĀ PURĀṆA contains a large amount of mythology concerning Brahmā.

Brahmā Kumāris ('Daughters of Brahmā')

A religious order of celibate women, founded in 1937 by a Sindhi businessman, Dada Lekhraj (1876–1969). Their headquarters are on Mount Abu; they have centres in all major Indian cities and in some cities outside India. They claim a following of over 100,000 worldwide and are active in YOGA education. Dada Lekhraj had visions of

Viṣṇu and received prophecies about the end of the world, which was to be followed by an earthly paradise.

Brahmā Purāṇa

The first in the list of the 18 *Mahā-purānas*, also called *Ādi-purāna*, describing the origin of the universe. It has major parts devoted to a description of the holy places of Orissa.

Brahmā saṁpradāya

One of the four sections of VAIṢṆAVISM, also called Madhva *saṁpradāya*, following the teachings of DVAITA VEDĀNTA. Its centre is in UḌIPĪ (Karṇātaka).

brahmacāri

One who leads the brahman life, i.e. lives in strict celibacy.

brahmacarya

('way of life of brahman')

The first stage in the life of a brahmin, 'studenthood', where strict sexual continence and service to one's GURU is obligatory. Some opt for lifelong *brahmacarya* and become SAMNYĀSIS without going through the *gṛhastya* (householder) stage.

Brahma-loka

Also Sarvaloka ('all places') and Satyaloka ('sphere of truth'), the abode of BRAHMĀ, the highest point in the traditional Hindu universe, from which there is no return.

brahman

The supreme being, universal consciousness, the highest reality. Derived from the Sanskrit root *bṛh* (to grow, to become large), it denotes greatness *per se*. It is a key concept in the Upaniṣads and in the Vedānta systems. *Brahman* is SACCIDĀNANDA, i.e. it is characterized by consciousness, infinity, omnipotence, eternity, immanence in all things, blissfulness and unfathomableness. It is unborn and uncreated, and the source and ultimate destiny of everything.

Brāhmaṇa (1)

The second part of the VEDA, a class of voluminous writings that was intended to guide the BRĀHMAṆAS (2) in their rituals. They also contain short versions of myths which are found expanded in the Purāṇas. The oldest Sanskrit prose texts, they are divided into four groups, according to the division of the Veda. *Ṛgveda*: *Aitareya* and *Kauśītakī Brāhmaṇas*; Black Yajurveda: *Katha* and *Taittirīya Brāhmaṇas*; White Yajurveda: *Śatapatha Brāhmaṇa*; Sāmaveda: *Pañcaviṁśa*, *Ṣadviṁśa* and *Jaiminīya Brāhmaṇas*; Atharvaveda: *Gopatha Brāhmaṇa*.

Brāhmaṇa(s) (2), also brahmin(s)

The first and highest VARṆA, created to recite the Veda, to perform rituals and to teach the rest of the people by word and deed the true nature of DHARMA. Due to their descent, their education and their influence they enjoyed high status throughout Indian history.

brahmānda

See WORLD EGG.

Brahmānda Purāṇa

Purāṇa containing a detailed account of the development of the *brahmāṇḍa* (WORLD EGG) as well as prophecies about the future.

Brahmāṇī

The female form or the daughter of BRAHMĀ, also known as ŚATARŪPĀ (hundred forms).

brahma-randhra
('Brahma's crevice')

Aperture at the crown of the head, identified by the ŚIKHA, the small tuft of hair kept unshaven. According to popular Hindu tradition it is the opening through which the soul of a good person leaves the body at the time of death. Bad souls are forced downwards through the excretionary channels.

Brahma-rekha ('Brahmā's line')

According to popular Hindu belief BRAHMĀ inscribes a child's destiny on its forehead on the sixth day after its birth.

brahmāstra ('Brahma's weapon')

An unfailing device, mentioned in the epics.

Brahma-sūtra

Also called *Vedāntasūtra*, a collection of 550 aphorisms. It is arranged in four *pādas* (parts), subdivided into four *adhyāyas* (chapters), each containing a number of *sūtras* (aphorisms) purporting to summarize the content of the UPANIṢADS. The present *Brahmasūtras* are ascribed to BĀDARĀYANA, although the names of former authors of such works (all of them lost) are mentioned. The *Brahmasūtras* have become the most important text of the Vedānta systems: its brevity necessitates lengthy commentaries (*bhāṣyas*) which have become the main sources of the various systems. Each of these has a proper name: Śaṅkara's commentary is called *Śarīrakabhāṣya*, RĀMĀNUJA's *Śrībhāṣya* and MADHVA's *Aṇubhāṣya*.

brahma-vādinī

A class of women mentioned in the HARITA-SMṚTI, who remained celibate and devoted themselves to study and ritual.

Brahma-vaivarta Purāṇa

A rather late Vaiṣṇava Purāṇa which relates in great detail the story of KṚṢṆA and RĀDHĀ.

brahmāvarta
('The country where brahmins dwell')

The Hindu heartland, considered the ideal living space for Brahmins. Brahmins living in *brahmāvarta* were held up as exemplars to the others.

brahma-vidyā
('brahman knowledge')

The highest kind of knowledge, knowledge that liberates: 'Those who know brahman become brahman.' To attain it a person has to practise SADHANAS and fulfil a variety of conditions (ADHIKĀRAS).

brahmin
See BRĀHMAṆA (2).

Brahmo Samāj
('Brahman Association')

A reformist Hindu movement founded by Ram Mohan ROY in 1828 as 'Brahmo Sabhā' and in 1843 restructured and renamed 'Brahmo Samāj' by Debendranath TAGORE. It aimed at purifying Hinduism and developing a strong ethical consciousness among Hindus.

Braja, also **Brajbhūmi, Vraja**

The district around Mathurā, Uttar Pradesh, associated with Kṛṣṇa. It comprises, besides Mathurā, the birthplace of Kṛṣṇa, Gokula, the hometown of his foster-parents, where he grew up, Vṛndāvana, the place where he frolicked with the GOPIS, Govardhana, where he sheltered the shepherds from torrential rains, and many other forests and ponds associated with his exploits. Revived in the 16th century by the followers of CAITANYA, Brajbhūmi is the destination of many millions Hindu pilgrims every year and a preferred place of retirement for many pious VAIṢṆAVAS. The local language, Brajbhāṣa, a dialect of Hindi, is a major literary language especially for devotional works.

breath control

See PRĀṆAYAMA.

Bṛhad-āraṇyaka Upaniṣad

One of the oldest major UPANIṢADS, the longest of all, extensively used by Vedāntins. It is the last part of the *Śatapatha Brāhmaṇa* and combines both ĀRAṆYAKA and Upaniṣad. (*See also* BRĀHMAṆA (1).)

Bṛhad-devatā

An ancient vedic work (fifth century BCE) containing a systematics of the deities that are addressed in the Vedic HYMNS.

Bṛhaspati

This name is frequently encountered in Hindu literature, with a variety of connotations. In the Vedas he is a deity, the priest of the gods. In later times he is a ṚṢI. The *ṛṣi* Bṛhaspati was the son of the *ṛṣi* ANGIRAS, and is also called Āngirasa. His wife, TĀRĀ, was carried off by Soma (the moon); this led to a war, after which Tārā was restored to Bṛhaspati. She subsequently bore a son, BUDHA, who was claimed by both Bṛhaspati and Soma. Soma was declared the father. Bṛhaspati is also the presiding deity of the planet Jupiter, and a day of the week, Bṛhaspativāra (Thursday), is named after him.

Bṛhat-saṁhitā

A famous work by Varāha Mihira (sixth century) containing information on astronomy/ASTROLOGY, the making of IMAGES and TEMPLES, and other matters of importance in connection with worship.

Buddha (sixth century BCE)

Gautama Buddha, founder of Buddhism, often described in Hindu writings as the worst enemy of Hinduism; also listed as the ninth AVATĀRA of VIṢṆU who descended to earth in order to lead astray people who were destined not to be saved by Viṣṇu.

Buddha, the founder of Buddhism, depicted as the ninth avatāra of Viṣṇu.

buddhi

(Sense-related) mind, *sensus communis.* (*See also* MANAS.)

Buddhism

At the time of Gautama Buddha (sixth century BCE) there were many different schools of thought and many teachers of practices that claimed to lead to emancipation. When Prince Siddhārtha left his home in search of enlightenment he underwent the usual training of a SAMNYĀSI and practised severe forms of self-mortification (TAPAS). After gaining enlightenment and becoming a Buddha, an enlightened one, he first approached his former companions in a grove near Vārāṇasī to announce to them the good news of the finding of deathlessness and freedom from suffering. It was only in the course of time that Buddha's teaching, which de-emphasized caste and ritual, and taught liberation through an ethical life and meditation only, was considered heterodox and his followers were deemed outside the Hindu community.

In later centuries, when Buddhism became the predominant religion in India, Hindus considered it (together with JAINISM) the paradigm of a *nāstika* (heterodox) system, a DARŚANA (2) that did not recognize the Veda as supreme authority and precluded membership in SANĀTANA DHARMA. From the eighth century CE onwards, beginning with Kumārila Bhaṭṭa's *Ślokavārttika*, a major Hindu polemic against Buddhism developed, which found expression in hundreds of literary works as well as in the occasional persecution of Buddhists. In modern India there is a tendency to consider Buddhism as one of the forms of Indian religiosity that in course of time was reabsorbed by Hinduism.

budha ('wise, intelligent')

The planet Mercury; son of Soma (moon), by TĀRĀ (star), wife of BṚHASPATI.

Bühler, Georg (1837–98)

A gifted linguist (he studied Latin, Greek, Arabic, Persian, Zend, Armenian and Sanskrit), he spent many years in India as professor of oriental languages at Elphinstone College, Bombay, and was officially entrusted with the collection of Sanskrit manuscripts in the Bombay Presidency. He produced valuable catalogues of manuscripts, edited texts and produced translations of Sanskrit and Prakrit texts. He specialized in Indian law and contributed a translation of the MANU-SMṚTI with an extensive introduction of his own to the Sacred Books of the East series. He later occupied the chair of Sanskrit at Vienna and became co-founder of the Oriental Institute of Vienna and its journal.

Burnouf, Eugéne (1801–52)

He studied Sanskrit with his father, Jean-Louis Burnouf, and with L. de Chézy, the first occupant of a chair in Sanskrit at a European university. While his main interest was in Buddhist texts, he contributed to the study of Hinduism through his translation of the entire *Bhāgavatam* into French (1840–8). He persuaded Max MÜLLER to undertake the first critical edition of the ṚGVEDA (1849–73).

C

caitanya

See CONSCIOUSNESS.

Caitanya, also **Kṛṣṇa Caitanya** ('Kṛṣṇa Consciousness') (1486–1533)

Born Viśvambhara Miśra, the second son of a VAIṢṆAVA brahmin family, at Nadia (Navadvip, Bengal) he married Lakṣmīprīyā at the age of 19, and, after her death, Viṣṇuprīyā. He began teaching secular literature. At the age of 22 he went to Gayā to perform ŚRADDHA for his deceased father and his first wife. Suddenly overcome by a strong emotional attraction to Kṛṣṇa, he was initiated by Īśvara Pūrī and became the spiritual leader of the Vaiṣṇavas of Nadia. In 1510 he took SAMNYĀSA from Keśava Bhārati and began travelling throughout India proclaiming Kṛṣṇa's name. In 1516 he settled in Purī, regularly worshipping at the JAGANNĀTHA temple and instructing disciples. He died in 1533, when walking in a trance into the sea. His life has been described by his followers Vṛndāvanadāsa (*Caitanya-bhāgavata*) and Kṛṣṇadāsa Kāvirāja (*Caitanya-caritāmṛta*).

His school, which became known as Gauḍīya Vaiṣṇavism, is characterized by its strong emotional Kṛṣṇa BHAKTI and its devotion to RĀDHĀ, Kṛṣṇa's beloved. By his followers he was regarded as an incarnation of both Kṛṣṇa and Rādhā. While only a short poem of eight verses is ascribed to him (*Śīkṣāṣṭaka*), his immediate followers, the six Gosvāmis, who revived VṚNDĀVANA as a centre of Kṛṣṇa worship in the 16th century, produced under his inspiration and command voluminous literature in which the teachings of Gauḍīya Vaiṣṇavism are laid out. The most important of these are RŪPA GOSVĀMI's *Bhakti-rasāmṛta-sindhu* and *Ujjvala-nīlāmaṇī* and Jīva Gosvāmi's *Ṣat-sandarbha*.

Gauḍīya Vaiṣṇavism was revived in Bengal in the late 19th century by Thākura Bhaktisiddhānta (1838–1914). His son, Bhaktivinode Thākur (1874–1937), organized the Gauḍīya Math, consisting of a number of temples and ashrams dedicated to teaching and publishing. One of his disciples, Abhaycaran De, a Calcutta businessman, better known under his monastic name Swami A. C. Bhaktivedanta, founded the INTERNATIONAL SOCIETY FOR KRISHNA CONSCIOUSNESS (ISKCON; 'Hare Krishna Movement') in New York in 1966 and gave the Caitanya movement a worldwide following.

cakra (1) ('wheel', 'discus', 'circle')

One of the weapons of Viṣṇu.

cakra (2)

Symbol for the whole earth: a Cakravartin is a universal ruler.

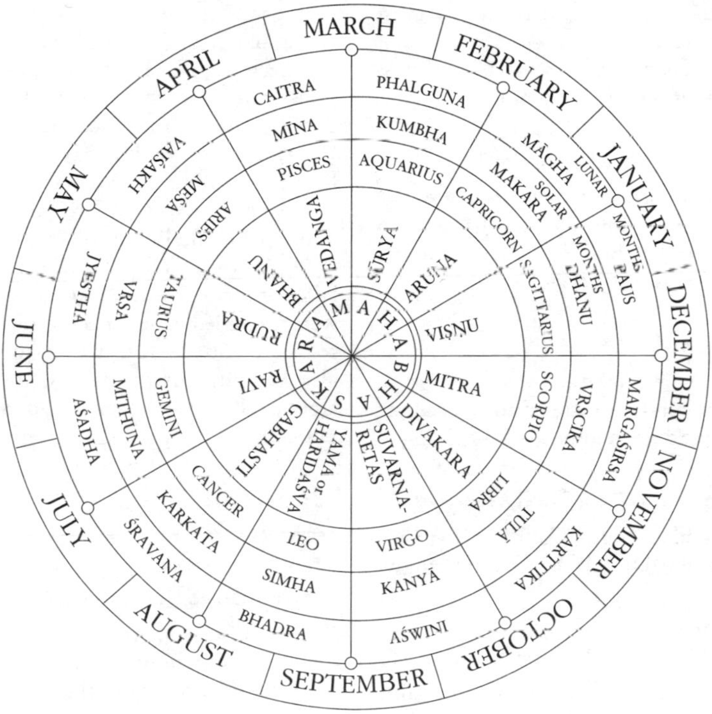

The Hindu calendar: The solar and lunar months are shown with the signs of the Zodiac in relation to the months of the Western (Gregorian) calendar.

cakra (3)

In TANTRA (2), six (to nine) nerve centres in the subtle body through which the spiritual energy is channelled. (*See also* BODY.)

calendar

Calendars were always important in Hinduism for the exact determination of the time for SACRIFICES and feast days, as well as for providing basic information for establishing HOROSCOPES. The Hindu calendar is a solar–lunar calendar, requiring regular adjustments. The printed calendars (PAÑCĀṄGA) contain the astronomical tables for each fortnight as well as other information important for astrological calculations. (*See also* FESTIVALS.)

camphor

The burning of camphor is part of the daily ritual of IMAGE worship; it is believed to keep away ghosts and demons.

Cāmuṇḍā

An aspect of the goddess DURGĀ, created to destroy the demons Caṇḍa and Muṇḍa.

Cāṇakya (fourth century BCE?)

Also called Kauṭilya, author of the famous *Cānakya Sūtra* or *Kauṭilīya Ārthaśāstra*. According to tradition he was a brahmin responsible for the downfall of the NANDAS (2) and the elevation of Candragupta, the founder of the MAURYA dynasty. His work is famous for its realistic, almost Machiavellian tone. It gives a very valuable detailed description of the administration of the Maurya empire.

caṇḍāla ('wicked or cruel')

A generic designation of people of the lowest CASTE, someone who has a Śūdra father and a brahmin mother, and is therefore an OUTCASTE.

caṇḍana

Sandalwood, used in many forms of worship and also valued for its cooling properties when applied as a paste.

Caṇḍī, also **Caṇḍikā, Caṇḍā**

The goddess Durgā (Ambā) in the form she assumed to kill the demon Mahiṣa.

Caṇḍīdāsa

('Caṇḍī's slave') (15th century)

Medieval author of poetry celebrating the loves of KṚṢṆA and the GOPĪS.

Candra

The moon, as both planet and deity.

Caraka (first century CE)

A writer on medicine who is reputed to have lived in Vedic times. Author of the *Caraka Saṁhitā,* one of the most important texts of Indian medicine through the ages. (*See also* AYURVEDA.)

Cārvākas

The followers of an ancient materialistic system of philosophy, which denies the validity of Vedic rites and encourages a hedonistic lifestyle. Hindus have always condemned it as the most objectionable of all NĀSTIKA systems.

caste

The word 'caste' is derived from the Portuguese *casta*: 'pure, clean', designating purity of descent. Hindu society has been characterized by caste divisions from time immemorial. The four classes (*catur varṇa*) mentioned in the VEDA, namely Brahmanas (teachers), Kṣatriyas (soldiers), Vaiśyas (traders) and Śūdras (servants) are subdivided into a great multitude of *jātīs*, 'birth-groups', or castes proper. A large number of people who for various reasons were excluded from these formed the so-called OUTCASTES, who, however, also maintained caste-like ranking among themselves. (*See also* SOCIAL ORDER.)

cat school

See TEṄGALAI.

caturmāsya (1) ('four months')

The rainy season, when ASCETICS were obliged to stay in one place. Viṣṇu was believed to be resting during this time.

caturmāsya (2)

A feast observed at the beginning of each four-month period into which the Vedic year was divided.

catur-varṇa-āśrama-dharma

Comprehensive designation of the Hindu SOCIAL ORDER dividing society into four (*catur*) classes (VARṆA); whose life is to be regulated by four stages: *brahmacarya* (studenthood), *gṛhastya* (householder stage), *vānaprasthya* (forest-dweller stage), and *samnyāsa* (stage of renunciation, homelessness). (*See also* CASTE.)

cauḍa

Tonsure of the whole head before initiation (*upanayana*), leaving only a little tuft at the back (*śikha*). It is repeated every fortnight thereafter. (*See also* SAṂSKĀRA.)

cetana
See CONSCIOUSNESS.

chandas
Verses, metres, one of the six VEDĀṄGAS.

chandoga
A priest or chanter of the Sāmaveda (VEDA of melodies).

Chāndogya Upaniṣad
One of the oldest and largest UPANIṢADS, belonging to the Sāmaveda. It is the most frequently referred to text in Bādarāyaṇa's BRAHMA-SŪTRAS.

chāyā (1) ('shade', 'shadow')
Mythical handmaid of the SUN.

chāyā (2)
Term used to designate an aid in understanding a text.

child marriage
See MARRIAGE.

children
To have children, especially sons, was the purpose of Hindu MARRIAGE from early on. An often-used marriage ritual closes with the blessing of the bride: 'May you be the mother of a hundred sons.' Children were important not only for the continuation of the family lineage but also for the performance of the last rites for their parents (besides being expected to contribute to the maintenance of their parents in old age). Limiting the number of children or practising birth control (especially abortion) has been condemned by classical Hindu ŚĀSTRAS as well as by contemporary Hindu leaders.

Chinmoy (1931–)
Kumar Ghosh, a disciple of AUROBINDO GHOSE. He called himself 'Made of Mind', settled in the USA in 1964 and has formed meditation groups at the UN in New York. The main technique is interiorization of the GURU by the disciple.

Chinnamaṣṭā ('the beheaded')
A form of DURGĀ, carrying her own decapitated head under her right arm; one of ten tantrik DAŚA VIDYĀS.

Chitragupta
YAMA's secretary in the netherworlds, recording the good and evil deeds of people. (*See also* AFTERLIFE, PĀTĀLA.)

choti ('small')
See ŚIKHA.

chronology
It has always been extremely difficult to establish a chronology of Hinduism before the time of the Buddha (sixth century BCE). Widely accepted chronologies devised in the late 19th century, assuming an invasion of the Vedic ĀRYANS around 1500 BCE and the development of the Veda between 1200 and 600 BCE, have been challenged and are no longer tenable. The 'new chronology', supported by astro-archaeology, satellite photography and archaeo-climatology, rejecting the 'Āryan invasion theory', sets the beginning of the Vedic age at around 4000 BCE and its end at around 2000 BCE.

churning of the ocean
(*samudra manthana*)
An ancient story, often depicted in Indian art, concerning the attempt made by DEVAS and DAITYAS at the beginning of time to obtain AMṚTA, the nectar of immortality. They used Mount MAṆḌARA as a churning stick, put it upon the

The Churning of the Ocean: Devas and asuras churn the ocean from which wonderful objects such as the elephant Airāvata, the wish-fulfilling tree, the vessel of ambrosia, and many more are obtained.

TORTOISE, a form assumed by Viṣṇu, took the king of snakes, Vasuki, as a rope and successively obtained the fiery poison HALĀHALĀ, the heavenly elephant AIRĀVATA, and DHANVANTARI with a pot filled with the nectar of immortality. To prevent the *daityas* from gaining immortality, Viṣṇu appeared in the form of Mohinī (seductress) and distracted their attention while the *devas* shared *amṛta*.

Cidambaram

Famous temple city in Tamilnāḍu, South India, sacred to ŚIVA. Śiva is believed to have first performed the TAṆḌAVA dance at Cidambaram, which is repeated daily in his honour by professional temple dancers.

Cinmayananda, Swami (1915–97)

Founder of Sandipani Hindu Mission and instrumental in founding the VIŚVA HINDŪ PARIṢAD in Bombay in 1964.

circumambulation, also **parikrama, pradakṣiṇa**

Ritually walking around a person, an IMAGE, a place, keeping the venerated object to one's right; a widespread Hindu custom showing respect. Besides the circumambulation of an image in a temple, or the temple complex itself, circumambulation of sacred cities such as Vārāṇasī or Vṛndāvana, or a district such as BRAJA, takes place. The circumambulation of the river NARBADĀ or of the whole of India is a custom still practised by many SĀDHUS today.

cit

See CONSCIOUSNESS.

citra nāḍī

One of the inner vessels of the subtle body according to KUṆḌALINĪ YOGA. (*See also* BODY.)

Cokamela (1293–1338)

HARIJAN saint from Mangalredha (Mahārāṣṭra), a devotee of Viṭṭhal (a Mahratti form of Viṣṇu); he had to pray outside the shrine because of his OUTCASTE status, and suffered many humiliations, but was also recognized for his piety and his inspired songs. After his death he was interred at PANDHARPUR beside NĀMADEVA. He is the author of many popular devotional songs (*abhangs*) in Marathi.

Colas

Prominent dynasty in South India (*c.* 319–1297). The Colas were mostly adherents of ŚAIVISM; they patronized the arts and religion. They also built, over the centuries, extensive irrigation systems that are still functional. Famous temples such as the Rajeśvara temple in TANJORE owe their existence to Cola munificence. Cola bronze images, especially of Śiva NĀṬARĀJA, are famous for their craftsmanship and high artistic quality.

confession

Confessing breaches of the moral code is one of the ways of atonement (PRAYAŚCITTA) for most lighter infringements.

consciousness, also **caitanya, cetana, cit**

One of the key concepts in Hindu thought. Advaitins identify the very essence of the person with consciousness, others consider it an essential attribute. BRAHMAN is often defined as *sat–cit–ānanda* (being–consciousness–bliss). The Upaniṣads teach four stages of consciousness, corresponding to different perceptions of reality: *jāgarita sthāna* (waking state: corresponding to the perception of multiple entities different from the perceiving subject); *svapna sthāna* (dream state: perception of mind-generated objects, different from the subject); *suṣupti* (dreamless deep sleep: no perception of difference between object and subject); *turīya* ('the fourth state', lucid trance, awareness without any subject–object split).

Coomaraswami, Ananda (1877–1947)

Born in Ceylon (Śrī Laṅka) to a Ceylonese father and a British mother, and trained in London as a geologist, Coomaraswami became best known as a rediscoverer of Indian art, especially of ancient and classical Indian painting. He wrote *Indian Drawings* (1910); *Indian Drawings: Second Series* (1912); *Rajput Painting* (1916). He developed broad interests in Indian culture in general, evident in a great number of essays dealing with Indian mythology and history (*The Dance of Śiva*, 1918, *Why Exhibit Works of Art?*, 1943) and a monumental *History of Indian and Indonesian Art* (1927).

cosmology

Hinduism does not possess a uniform and commonly accepted cosmology. Cosmology, however, was always very important. In the Vedas we find a tripartition of the universe into an upper, middle and lower sphere: to each were assigned eleven deities. The moon was believed to be the resting place for the deceased ancestors. In the Purāṇas we find an elaborate division of the universe into a series of concentric continents surrounded by oceans – all of immense size. The Purāṇas also speculate that besides the universe inhabited by us there are countless other universes. The world we inhabit is not seen as the best of all worlds but as the only place where people can work out their salvation. Hindus also operated with immense time-frames in the context of a periodic creation and annihilation of the physical universe. (*See also* TIME, DIVISIONS OF.)

cow (*go*, *gomātā*)

'Mother Cow', held sacred by Hindus as the seat of many gods. Killing a cow was considered one of the most heinous crimes and was heavily punished. Many contemporary Hindu political movements agitate for a complete ban on cow slaughter, which is forbidden in many Indian states. Affluent Hindus establish in many places *gośālās*, homes for old cows, who are fed and cared for until they die a natural death. Many ancient rituals involve cows, and the five products of the cow (milk, curds, butter, urine, dung) are highly priced for their purity which they pass on when applied to the human body. Kṛṣṇa, who also is known as Gopāla (protector of cows), is often depicted in the guise of a cowherd, and the cowherd girls (GOPĪS) are considered the best models of devotion to him.

creation (*sṛṣṭhi*)

The first of the three divine cosmic functions, often associated with BRAHMĀ. Creation stories figure prominently in the Purāṇas. The Veda has two versions of a creation myth: in the first the mythical human, PURUṢA (1), is sacrificed and out of his body the four CASTES are created. In the second the whole universe is fashioned by Vāc (word). Some Purāṇas mention several creations: the first was unsuccessful because of lack of will to procreate among the first creatures. Since creation is a process, it will find an end and the universe will return to its pre-creation state. Hindu theologians emphasize that there was no need for God to create the universe, and that the divine creative activity is more like a game (LĪLĀ). (*See also* ANNIHILATION; SUSTENANCE; WORLD EGG.)

cremation (*smāsana*)

The most frequently employed mode of disposal of dead bodies. It is believed that the fire that consumes the body will transform it into a higher form. Cremation follows a set of ancient rules and is usually done in specially chosen places outside towns and villages. Normally only members of the immediate family are allowed to witness cremation. Ancient taboos regarding pollution by being associated with a corpse are still maintained. SAMNYĀSIS are not cremated but buried, because they perform a symbolic self-cremation as part of their rites of initiation. LIṄGĀYATS, a reformist Hindu sect, also bury their dead.

D

Dadhīca, also **Dadhyanc**

Vedic ṚṢI, son of ATHARVAN, frequently mentioned in Hindu literature.

daily rituals

The brahmin's entire daily routine was enveloped by rituals. Many of these rituals cannot be observed in modern city life, but some are followed quite widely, such as the thrice daily recitation of the GĀYATRĪ mantra, the daily worship of IMAGES in the home, and RITUALS on special occasions. Members of particular SAṀPRADĀYAS often practise extended daily rituals at home and in the temple, decorating their bodies with markings designating their affiliation.

daityas ('demons', 'giants', 'titans')

Descendants of DITI and KAŚYAPA, hostile to the GODS and to SACRIFICE.

daiva (1) ('belonging to the gods')

Fate.

daiva (2)

A type of (legally recognized) marriage, in which a young woman was given to an officiating priest in a sacrifice.

Dākinī

Female fiend in the company of KĀLĪ (2), feeding on human flesh. Also called Aśrapa, 'blood drinker'.

Dakṣa also **Prācetas** ('skilful')

Proper name of a son of BRAHMĀ, a PRAJĀPATI. One of his many daughters was SATĪ (Umā), who married ŚIVA against her father's will. Dakṣa excluded him from a great sacrifice he was performing and insulted him in Satī's presence. Satī then took her own life and Śiva wrecked Dakṣa's sacrifice. Śiva decapitated Dakṣa and burned his head, but later restored him to life and gave him a goat's head.

Dakṣa-smṛti

A code of law. Dakṣa was one of the original eighteen lawgivers and is reputed to be author of the *Dakṣasmṛti*.

dakṣinā ('south')

Fee for a brahmin's services, personified as a goddess.

dakṣinācāra ('right-hand way')

One of the branches of TANTRA (2).

Dakṣiṇā-mūrti

One of the *saumya* (auspicious) forms of ŚIVA: Śiva as teacher of various arts, of YOGA and of *mokṣa* (LIBERATION). The images of Śiva NĀṬARĀJA also belong to this category.

Dakṣiṇeśvara

Kālī–Durgā temple near Calcutta built in the 19th century, which became famous through RAMAKRISHNA, who was a temple priest there for many years. Now it is one of the major sacred sites of the Ramakrishna Mission.

dalit ('oppressed')

Self-designation of former OUTCASTES, untouchables, scheduled CASTES. They have formed many organizations according to religious affiliation. Strictly speaking, most *dalits* were not members of Hindu (caste) society, but were considered servants for impure and degrading work. *Dalits* today strive for emancipation and equal opportunities.

damaru

Śiva NĀṬARĀJA's drum, shaped like an hourglass.

Dāmodāra

A name given to KṚṢṆA on account of his foster-mother's attempt to tie him to a pillar with a rope (*dāma*) around his belly (*udāra*).

dāna ('gift', 'charity')

A major concern in traditional Hinduism. Charity was enjoined on the rich on behalf of the poor, and on sacrificers to brahmins. It was regulated by numerous laws. Major donations of land or villages were often recorded on copper plates and stored either in temples or in palaces. Reneging on pledges made legally was considered a major sin for which punishments in hell were foreseen.

Dānavas

Descendants of Danu, one of the daughters of Dakṣa, and Kaśyapa. Like the DAITYAS they were giants who fought against DEVAS and SACRIFICE.

dance

Ritual dance seems to have been part of the Hindu traditions from the earliest times, as the dancing figurines from the

Bhils dancing in the forecourt of the palace, Udaipur Festival.

Indus civilization indicate. Creation was often described in terms of a cosmic dance (LĪLĀ). One of the most famous representations of ŚIVA is that of NĀṬARĀJA (king of the dance). KṚṢṆA performed a dance on the heads of KĀLIYA and his favourite pastime was the *rasa-līlā*, the round-dance with the GOPĪS of Vraja. The goddess is often represented in dance. Temple dancing, both spontaneously done by devotees and organized by professionals, is one of the routine forms of temple worship. The *Naṭya-śāstra*, attributed to BHĀRATA (5), is the most important text dealing not only with dance, but with drama and the principles of aesthetics. Dance, especially the re-enactment of scenes from the PURĀṆAS, is seen as a means to gain LIBERATION. In some major Hindu temples groups of professionals regularly perform ritual dances in honour of the deity, e.g. in the Śiva temple at CIDAMBARAM (TAṆḌAVA), or the Kṛṣṇa temple of Guruvayur (Kṛṣṇattam).

daṇḍa ('rod', 'punishment')

Insignia of YAMA, the god of death and of kings, whose duty it was to punish evildoers and protect society from them.

daṇḍa nīti ('science of punishment')

Administration, government.

Dandin (seventh century)

Classical (Sanskrit) writer, author of *Daśa-kumāra-carita*, the story of the ten princes who went out to find fulfilment of their desires.

Dārā Shukoh (1613–1659)

Son of Mogul emperor Shah Jahan, who took a great interest in Hinduism. In 1657 he produced the first translation of some of the Upaniṣads into Persian, a Latin translation of which (made by Anquetil Duperron in the early 19th century) reached the West and was enthusiastically received by the German philosopher Arthur Schopenhauer (1788–1860 CE). Dārā Shukoh was executed by his brother Aurangzeb after having participated in a failed rebellion against him.

darśana (1)

('seeing', 'demonstration')

The respectful or worshipful beholding of a divine image or a venerable person, a central religious activity of Hindus.

darśana (2)

('theory', philosophical system')

Especially one of the *ṣaḍ-darśana* ('six orthodox systems': SĀṀKHYA, YOGA, ṄYĀYA, VAIŚEṢIKA, Purva MĪMĀṀSĀ and Uttara Mīmāṁsā or VEDĀNTA).

dāsa ('slave')

Caste name of a ŚŪDRA; from the Middle Ages on, many VAIṢṆAVAS used it also as an affix to express their devotion (e.g. Viṣṇudāsa, Kṛṣṇadāsa, etc.).

Daśabodha

Famous religious work (in Marathi) by Samārtha Guru Rāmadāsa (written *c*. 1659).

dāsa-mārga ('the slave's way')

The lowest stage in ŚAIVA SIDDHĀNTA, consisting of activities such as cleaning a temple, weaving garlands, lighting temple lamps, offering one's services to other Śiva devotees.

daśa-nāmis ('ten names')

Ten orders of *samnyāsis* (sects) reputedly founded by ŚANKARA in the ninth century and attached to one of the MAṬHAS established by him. They enjoy a high reputation for their asceticism and scholarship. One of these names is attached to the title of every member of one of the orders: Āraṇya, Vāna, Giri,

Pārvata, Sāgara, Tīrtha, Āśrama, Bhārati, Pūrī, Sarasvatī.

Daśa-padārtha Śāstra
('science of ten word meanings')

Title of a sixth-century text explaining the tenets of VAIŚEṢIKA, one of the six orthodox systems of Hindu philosophy.

Daśa-ratha ('ten chariots')

A prince of the solar dynasty, king of AYODHYĀ, father of RĀMA, a major figure in VĀLMĪKI'S RĀMĀYAṆA.

daśāvatāras

See AVATĀRA.

daśa vidyās ('ten wisdoms')

Ten forms of the Goddess worshipped by Tantrikas: Kālī, Tārā, Ṣoḍaśī, Bhuvaneśvarī, Bhairavī, Chinnamaṣṭā, Dhūmāvatī, Bagalā, Maṭaṅgī, Kāmalātmikā. (*See also* TANTRA.)

Dasgupta, Surendranath
(1885–1952)

One of the foremost modern scholars of Hinduism, author of the authoritative five-volume *A History of Indian Philosophy* (1921–55), the unsurpassed standard work of its kind. He had a distinguished career as an academic teacher in Chittagong College, Calcutta Presidency College, Government Sanskrit College, and the University of Calcutta, and was the recipient of many honours and awards.

dasyus

Described in the Vedas as the enemies of the ĀRYANS, dark-skinned and evil. Their identity is disputed.

Dattātreya (1)

A deity, one of the forms of Viṣṇu, partaking of the nature of Brahmā, Viṣṇu and Śiva. Represented as a wandering mendicant followed by four dogs (the four VEDAS). His places of worship are called Datta-*maṇḍiras*. Popular in Mahārāṣṭra as 'Dattobā'. The Dattātreya SAṀPRADĀYA is quite strong in Mahārāṣṭra; it is engaged on behalf of peace and mutual tolerance.

Dattātreya (2)

A brahmin saint, son of ATRI and ANASŪYĀ, considered an incarnation of Viṣṇu and Śiva.

Dattātreya (3)

A philosopher, the sixth AVATĀRA of Viṣṇu. According to the *Bhāgavata Purāṇa* he achieved liberation by following the advice of twenty-four GURUS in the form of forces of nature.

Dāyānanda Sarasvatī
(1824–83)

Influential Hindu reformer, founder of ĀRYA SAMĀJ. Born Mūla Śaṅkara in Morvi, Gujarat, into a pious Śaivite family, Dāyānanda rejected IMAGE worship and went in search of a GURU. After fifteen years of wandering through India, moving from teacher to teacher, he finally settled down in Mathurā with Virājānanda Sarasvatī, a blind and temperamental ultra-orthodox Vedic teacher. After three years of humiliations and grammar study Virājānanda dismissed his student with instructions, to teach the true ŚĀSTRAS in India again and to dispel the darkness that the wrong faith had engendered.

His teachings, contained in *Satyārtha Prakāśa* ('Light of Truth'), rely on the infallibility of the Veda: all accretions to Hinduism of later times (epics, Purāṇas, Āgamas) were rejected as corruptions. Dāyānanda believed he had a mission to lead India back to its original, pure Vedic religion. He reintroduced Vedic HOMA (*see* GHĪ). Socially he was progressive: he rejected casteism, promoted the equality of women and men, and insisted on social service and altruism as expressions of true DHARMA.

death

A major preoccupation of Hinduism, as of all religions. Hindus generally believe in life after death and most believe in rebirth (and re-death) of those who have not found emancipation. It is surrounded by many rituals, and many scriptures describe the fate of persons after death. Since physical death is not considered final, the *Bhagavadgītā* compares it with the changing of worn-out clothing and exhorts not to grieve for those who have died, because they are bound to return in a new body. (*See also* AFTERLIFE; MṚTYU-SAṂSKĀRA.)

demons

Hinduism knows many kinds of demons, or antagonists of the gods. Not all of them are wicked; some are described as righteous rulers and good kings. (*See also* ASURA; BALI; DAITYAS; DĀNAVAS; RĀKṢASA.)

Deussen, Paul (1845–1919)

'Devasena', as his Indian friends called him, an expert in Sanskrit and in philosophy. He held university appointments in Berlin and Kiel. In his six-volume *General History of Philosophy* he devoted the first three volumes to India, including translations of hitherto unknown texts. He translated sixty Upaniṣads from Sanskrit into German, Śaṅkara's complete commentary on the *Brahmasūtras*, as well as major portions from the *Mahābhārata* (including the *Bhagavadgītā*) and wrote a monograph on *The Philosophy of the Upaniṣads* (1899).

deva, also devatā ('shiny')

Generic name of higher beings, usually translated as 'god' (etymologically related to Latin *deus*, Greek *theos*, from which French *dieu*, Italian *dio*, Spanish *dios*, English *divine*). Their number is given in the Vedas as thirty-three, in later Hinduism as virtually infinite. (*See also* GOD AND GODS.)

deva-dāsī

('female servant of the deity')

A woman who was dedicated to temple service, professional dancer, often kept as temple prostitute.

Devakī

Wife of VASUDEVA, mother of Kṛṣṇa.

Devī ('goddess')

Used generically as well as more specifically for the wife of Śiva, or the highest principle, imagined as female. She has many names, expressing her many functions. Goddess worship is almost universal in Hinduism.

Devī Mahiṣamārdinī: The goddess who slays the buffalo demon; an object of devotion at the time of Dūrgā Pūjā.

Devī Bhāgavata Purāṇa

An *Upa-Purāṇa*, by some considered one of the 18 *Mahā-purāṇas* (replacing the Vaiṣṇava *Bhāgavatam*) eulogizing ŚAKTI.

Devī Māhātmya

('The Glorification of the Goddess')

A section of the MĀRKAṆḌEYA PURĀNA, narrating the victory of the Goddess over the buffalo-headed demon (Mahiṣamārdinī). It is recited daily in Śākta temples and often publicly read out during *Dūrgapūjā* (*see* DURGA) celebrations.

Dhanvantari

The physician of the gods, teacher of medicine, author of a text on AYURVEDA.

dhārana ('concentration')

One of the stages of PATAÑJALA YOGA.

dharma ('law')

Cosmic and social order and the rules pertaining to it. It is the central concern of Hinduism, which defines itself as SANĀTANA DHARMA, eternal law. In the *Bhagavadgītā* Kṛṣṇa says that he is assuming a human form for the sake of upholding *dharma*, whenever it is threatened. *Dharma* comprises general morality (SADHĀRANA DHARMA) as well as specific rules for members of castes (*viśeṣa dharma*). The former consists of five injunctions (*yama*) and five prohibitions (*niyama*), namely firmness (*dhṛti*), forgiveness (*kṣamā*), charity (*dāna*), purity (*śauca*), not stealing (*aṣteya*), sense-control (*indriya nigraha*), prudence (*dhī*), wisdom (*vidyā*), truthfulness (*satya*), freedom from anger (*akrodha*). The latter comprises the very detailed and specific injunctions of *varṇāśramadharma*. Over and above these, there are regulations for members of religious communities (*saṁpradāyas*) such as the *Vaiṣṇavadharma*, which prescribe the mode of worship, the kind of dress and diet etc. a member of such a community has to follow. While for many centuries Hindu *dharma* was supposed to be unchanging, in our time voices are being heard that attempt to modernize *dharma* and to use *dharma* as a political programme for the creation of a Hindu rule in India.

As sources of *dharma* the *Manusmṛti* identifies the Veda in its entirety, established traditions in the heartland of Hinduism (*Āryavārta*), the behaviour of exemplary citizens, and one's own conscience (*ātmatuṣṭi*).

Dharma-rāja ('King of the Law')

Title of YAMA, the god of the dead, and of YUDHISṬHIRA, his son.

Dharma-śāstra

The Hindu code of law in general, or a specific work on law, such as *Manusmṛti*, *Yājñavalkyasmṛti* and others. These deal generally with three major areas: rules of conduct (ĀCĀRA); civil and criminal law (VYAVAHĀRA); punishment and penances (PRAYAŚCITTA). The number of works on *dharmaśāstra* is very large, and since it covers both secular and religious law, it has always been very important for the practice of Hinduism.

Dhenuka

A demon in the shape of an ass, killed by BALADEVA, who swung it round by its legs and smashed it against a tree.

Dhṛta-rāṣṭra

('whose kingdom is well established')

A major figure in the MAHĀBHĀRATA story: the eldest son of Vicitravīrya, brother of Pāṇḍu, had a hundred sons, of whom Duryodhana was the oldest. Dhṛtarāṣṭra was blind and renounced the throne in favour of his brother

Pāṇḍu. He too renounced the throne because of a leprous affliction and this led to a conflict between their sons, culminating in the Great War.

Dhruva ('firm')

The pole star. A story in the *Viṣṇu Purāṇa* records that as a child Dhruva was humiliated, became a hermit and obtained the favour of Viṣṇu who raised him to the sky as pole star for all to see.

dhūma-ketu ('smoke-bannered')

An epithet of DEATH (represented as a god).

dhyāna ('trance')

One of the stages of PATAÑJALA YOGA.

dig-gaja, also **dik-pāla** ('supporters of the regions')

Eight elephants who support the points of the compass: AIRĀVATA, Puṇḍarīka, VĀMANA, Kumuda, Anjana, Puṣpadanta, Sarvabhauma, Supratīka.

dig-vijāya ('conquest of the regions')

The practice of major teachers of challenging exponents of other religions and schools of thought and claiming victory over all. Described in works such as the *Śaṅkara Digvijāya* by MĀDHAVA (2).

dīkṣā ('initiation')

Especially into a monastic order or a specific SAṀPRADĀYA. It is a very important step for a Hindu and implies a lifelong commitment to the mode of life of the community. Usually it consists of a number of rituals, often the complete stripping of the candidate and a symbolic self-cremation, the taking of a new name and the transmission of a secret MANTRA (3). The *dīkṣa guru* has to come from an acknowledged line of teachers (*guru paraṁparā*) and remains in touch with those initiated by him.

dīpa ('lamp')

Usually fed with *ghī* (clarified butter); a lamp is required in almost all forms of PŪJĀ.

Dīpāvalī, also **Divālī** ('feast of lamps')

The most popular Hindu celebration, celebrated in the second half of Aśvina, when Hindus put up countless little lamps on houses and temples and on rivers, celebrating the homecoming of Rāma and Sītā to AYODHYĀ after their exile had ended. People offer jewels and food to Lakṣmī and wear new clothes. Dipāvālī has in today's India acquired among Hindus the commercial status of Christmas in Western countries, with the exchange of gifts and family celebrations.

Diti

Vedic deity, sometimes regarded as counterpart, sometimes as complement of ADITI; frequently referred to in epics and Purāṇas. She is described as daughter of DAKṢA and wife of KAŚYAPA, the mother of the DAITYAS and of HIRAṆYAKAŚIPU.

Divine Life Mission

See ŚIVĀNANDA, SWAMI.

Divine Light Mission

Founded in India in 1960 by Guru Mahārāj Jī (Gurujī), a youthful hereditary teacher in the tradition of Vallabha's PUṢṬIMĀRGA. It spread rapidly in the West in the seventies, but faded after Gurujī had been accused of some improprieties and returned to India.

divine qualities

According to VAIṢṆAVAS God is *saguṇa*, i.e. exhibits six qualities that define his essence: *jñāna* (knowledge), *bala*

Dīpāvali (Divālī) celebrations in Manchester, England.

(strength), *aiśvarya* (lordship), *vīrya* (heroism), *śakti* (power), *tejas* (splendour).

Divodāsa (1)

A pious king in the *Ṛgveda*, for whom INDRA demolished a hundred stone fortresses.

Divodāsa (2)

A brahmin, twin brother of AHALYĀ, called 'Atithigva' because of his generosity toward guests (*atithi*)

Divodāsa (3)

A king of Kāśī (VĀRĀṆASĪ), celebrated as a physician, identified with DHANVANTARI.

domestic rites

The Hindu home, usually the dwelling place of an extended family, plays a central role in Hinduism. The family is the basic unit of Hindu society and from the earliest times essential rituals could only be performed in a family setting. The Veda prescribes a number of ceremonies that a brahmin has to perform daily in his home. They are codified in a number of *Gṛhya Sūtras*. The SAṀSKĀRAS, for example initiation, marriage and funeral rites, are also performed in the home. Every Hindu home has either a room or part of a room reserved for worship, and members of the family often spend a considerable amount of time doing PŪJĀ at home. Many Hindu homes are adorned with pictures of deities and saints. In VAIŚṆAVA homes a TULASĪ plant is usually kept in the courtyard and regularly tended and worshipped. Vaiṣṇavas also routinely offer their meals to the deity in their worship room before beginning to eat, considering their meal the *prasāda* ('grace', leftovers) of the deity's. The Hindus' daily and yearly domestic religious routine is strongly shaped by the rituals and festivities of the communities to which hey belong and by specific family traditions.

donkey

An animal that was not considered fit for Vedic sacrifice because it lacked MEDHA.

Draupadī

Daughter of King Drupada and wife of the five Pāṇḍava brothers. A major figure in the MAHĀBHĀRĀTA. Her humiliation by the KAURAVAS eventually brought about the great war.

Drāviḍa (1)

South India, where Dravidian (non-Sanskritic) languages are spoken (Tamil, Tulu, Telugu, Malayalam) and everything connected with it.

Drāviḍa (2)

South Indian style of architecture.

Drāviḍa Prabandham

Collection of (Tamil) hymns composed by the ĀḶVĀRS, especially by NAMMĀḶVĀR, undertaken by NĀṬHA MUNĪ and considered on par with the VEDA in worship; the 'Tamil Veda'.

Drona ('bucket')

A brahmin who according to legend was generated by his father, BHĀRADVĀJA, in a bucket. He was the teacher of military arts to both the PĀṆḌAVAS and the KAURAVAS. In the Great War he sided with the Kauravas and, in spite of being a brahmin, became commander-in-chief after Bhīṣma's death. He was killed by Dṛṣṭadyumna, Drupada's son, whom Drona had slain earlier in battle. (*See also* Mahābhārata.)

Dṛṣadvatī

River referred to in the Ṛgveda, constituting the eastern and southern border of BRAHMĀVARTA.

Durgā ('difficult of access')

A name of the Goddess (DEVĪ), especially in her fierce form. Seen either as one of the forms of PĀRVATĪ, the consort of Śiva, or as the combined ŚAKTI of all the deities, she is one of the major figures in the Hindu pantheon. In her role as *Mahiṣamārdiṇī* (slayer of the buffalo demon), Durgā is honoured every year during *Durgāpūjā* as the saviour of the world from evil. Durgā celebrations are especially elaborate in Bengal, where her images are set up in homes and public places and worshipped for a period of nine days (*Navarātrī*).

Arjuna has a vision of Durgā the night before the battle and invokes her at the beginning of the Great War. The major text dealing with Durgā is the *Devīmāhātmya* of the MĀRKAṆḌEYA PURĀṆA.

The goddess Durgā riding on her vahana *(vehicle), the lion.*

Durvāsas ('ill-dressed', 'naked')

A sage, son of ATRI and Anusūyā, noted for his irascibility. He cursed ŚAKUNTALĀ for keeping him waiting at the door and thus caused her separation from King Duṣyanta. His blessing caused Kuntī to become the virgin mother of KARṆA by the sun. He also cursed Kṛṣṇa for a minor fault and foretold for him the manner of his death.

Duryodhana ('hard to conquer')

Eldest son of Dhṛtarāṣṭra and leader of the KAURAVAS in the Great War of the *Mahābhārata*.

dūta ('messenger', 'envoy')

Messengers play a great role in classical Sanskrit drama. See, for example, the famous poem by KĀLĪDĀSA, *Meghadūta*, ('The Cloud-Messenger').

duties

The Hindu ethic is an ethic of duties rather than rights. According to Vedic tradition a human is born with five 'debts' (*ṛṇa*) or duties which he has to redeem during his life: duties towards the gods, parents and teachers, guests, other human beings and all living beings. Each VARṆA has specific duties as well. Most Hindus believe that they have a lifelong duty to perform formal worship and to recite certain religious texts or formulae. Membership in particular SAṀPRADĀYAS also entails specific duties with regard to worship, mode of life, relation to fellow members. (*See also* DHARMA.)

Dvaita Vedānta ('Dualistic Vedānta')

A school of Vedānta founded by MADHVA, which emphasizes the non-identity of humans and the ultimate. Developed in direct opposition to ADVAITA, Dvaita teaches 'five differences' (*pañca bhedā*): the difference between God and humans; between nature and God; between individual humans; between humans and inanimate objects; and between one inanimate object and another.

dvandvas ('pairs of opposites')

For example, hot–cold, bright–dark, which characterize the world of change and impermanence, in contrast to the all-oneness of the ultimate.

Dvāpara Yuga

The third of the four world ages, preceded by Kṛta Yuga and Treta Yyuga, and followed by Kali Yuga.

Dvāraka

Famous ancient city on the west coast of India, one of the seven ancient holy cities of India, Kṛṣṇa's capital. It was submerged in the ocean but has recently been partially excavated.

dvi-jāti ('twice-born')

Appellation of the three higher CASTES (Brahmin, Kṣatriya, Vaiśya), whose initiation (*upanayana*) is seen as 'second birth', which entitles them to participate in ritual activity. (*See also* SAṀSKĀRA.)

dvīpa ('island', 'continent')

In Hindu cosmography the continents (*dvīpas*) stretch out like the leaves of a lotus from the centre occupied by Mount MERU and are separated from each other by distinct circular oceans. There are seven such *dvīpas* separated by seven oceans consisting of different liquids: Jambu-dvīpa, surrounded by *lavana* (salt water); Plaksa-dvīpa, surrounded by *īkṣu* (sugarcane juice); Śālmala-dvīpa, surrounded by *suṛā* (wine); Kuśa-dvīpa, surrounded by *sarpis* (clarified butter); Krauñca-dvīpa, surounded by *dadhi* (curds); Śāka-dvīpa, surrounded by *dudgha* (milk); Puṣkara-dvīpa, surrounded by *jala* (sweet water).

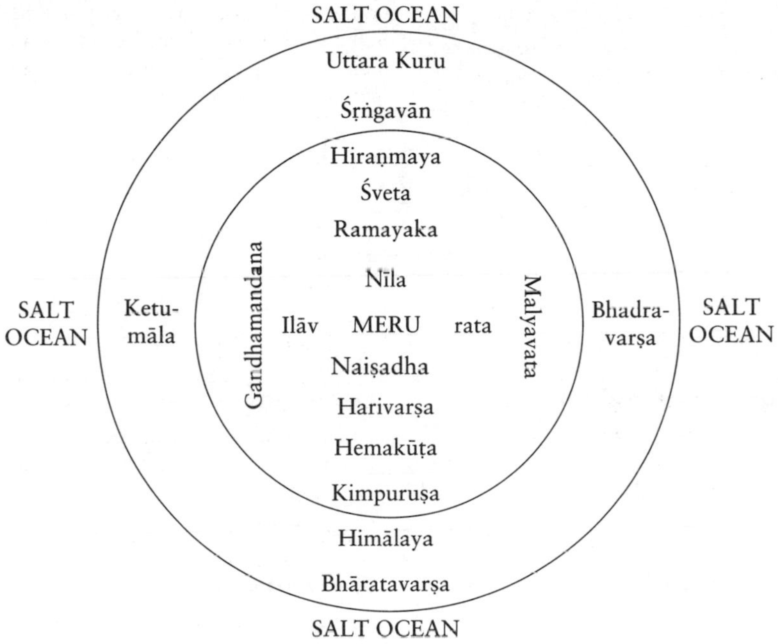

A Puranic model of Jambu-dvīpa. In its centre rises Mount Meru.

Jambu-dvipa contains nine *varṣas* (countries), the foremost of which is Bhārata (India). Bhārata, again, is subdivided into nine *dvīpas*, or sections, of which Indra-dvīpa is the foremost.

Dyaus ('sky', 'heaven')

In the Vedas a male deity, called Dyaus-pitṛ, 'heavenly father', the earth (PṚTHIVĪ) being regarded as mother. Father of UṢAS, the dawn. Dyava-pṛthivī are the universal parents.

E

Edgerton, Franklin (1885–1963)

Orientalist, teacher of Sanskrit at Yale University, translator of the *Bhagavad-gītā*.

Eidlitz, Walter (1892–1976)

Austrian diplomat who, while posted in India, developed a deep interest in GAUḌĪYA VAIṢṆAVISM. Author of *Bhakta – eine indische Odysee* (1951), *Die indische Gottesliebe* (1955), *Der Glaube und die heiligen Schriften der Inder* (1957), and *Kṛṣṇa–Caitanya: Sein Leben und Seine Lehre* (1968), an authoritative work with many translations from Sanskrit and Bengali sources.

ekadaṇḍi ('one-staffed')

Appellation of certain orders of SAMNYĀSIS, who carry a single staff (in contrast to the *tri-daṇḍi*, who carry three staffs bundled together.

ekagratā ('one-pointedness')

The aim of PATAÑJALI YOGA.

Eka-nāṭha (1533-1598 CE)

Famous Mahratta poet-saint, author of a commentary on Book XI of the *Bhāgavata Purāṇa*, *Bhavārtha Ramāyaṇa*, and numerous *abhaṅgas* (hymns), as well as the editor of JÑĀNEŚVARA's *Jñāneśvari*.

Eka-śṛṅga (1) ('one-horned')

One of the early AVATĀRAS of Viṣṇu (often depicted as a fish with a protruding horn) who saved MANU (2) during the Great Flood.

Eka-śṛṅga (2)

Name of a recluse who had grown up without having seen women, and let himself be seduced by courtesans in the context of a ritual designed to end a long-lasting drought.

ekoddiṣṭa

A special ŚRADDHA, performed at each new moon, designed to secure the admission of the deceased into the company of the forefathers, transforming him from a PRETA (ghost) into a PITṚ (ancestor).

elephant

Elephants, both mythical and real, play a great role in Indian religious lore, from AIRĀVATA, Indra's mount and the other DIG-GAJAS, to the king of the Elephants, saved by Viṣṇu from the clutches of a crocodile (*Gajendra-mokṣana*), a scene often described in literature and portrayed in art. Elephants were a royal prerogative, and every temple had to keep at least one elephant for ceremonial purposes. Elephants were also extensively used in warfare. They are a favourite with Indian sculptors and painters.

Eliade, Mircea (1907–86)

Historian of religion and author of many well-known books. General editor of the 16-volume *Encyclopedia of Religions*. His early studies of Hinduism culminated in his *Yoga: Immortality and Freedom* (1930).

Ellora, also Elurā

Famous site in *Mahārāṣṭra*, near Aurangabad, with Buddhist, Jain and Hindu caves. The best-known monument, however, is the eighth/ninth century Kailāsanāṭha Śiva temple, the world's largest monolithic structure. It is carved out of the mountainside with numerous sculptures relating to Śiva mythology. The work started under the Rastrakuta king Krishna I and took about a century to complete.

Emerson, Ralph Waldo (1803–82)

Popular American writer and philosopher, one of the first to show serious interest in Indian thought, especially Vedānta.

emotions

See BHĀVA, RASA.

environment

Vedic Hinduism was very environmentally conscious: pollution of land and water was forbidden and care was taken to preserve the natural fertility of the environment. Purāṇic ideas such as the concept of the material world as God's body sharpened the awareness of the sacredness of nature. Many large tracts of land were kept in pristine condition as places for the gods to inhabit. With the Islamic conquest, and later with European colonial administration, that tradition waned and the country became increasingly exploited. Overuse of grazing areas, deforestation, salinization of the soil due to poor irrigation methods and overexploitation of fertile land led in many areas of India to serious problems long before the industrialization of the country. Modern India has very serious environmental problems caused by overcrowding, pollution, irresponsible industrial development, neglect and overuse of land. Many agencies are trying to deal with the problem, rediscovering in the process some ancient ecological wisdom.

epics

See MAHĀBHĀRATA; RĀMĀYAṆA.

epistemology

The age-old Indian equation of emancipation with knowledge and understanding led very early to questions of epistemology, especially an attempt to define the criteria of proofs for truth (PRAMĀṆAS). Hindus, basing their tradition on the Veda, accepted ŚRUTI as 'true', and Vedic propositions as proof-texts. An early controversy arose between the MĪMĀṀSAKAS, who accepted only injunctions (*vidhi*) as 'revealed', and the VEDĀNTINS, for whom the purpose of the Veda was ultimate knowledge (VIDYĀ). In debates with non-Vedic systems, such as those of the various schools of Buddhism and Jainism, Hindus developed their own epistemology. The NYĀYA (1) school especially investigated questions of logic and epistemology. From the early Middle Ages it became customary for Hindu scholarly writers to preface their works with a statement detailing which *pramāṇas* they embraced: all accepted *śabda* (the word of scripture) and *pratyakṣa* (direct perception); some used in addition *upamāna* (analogy), *anumāna* (inference), *arthapatti* (presumption) and *abhāva* (absence). As a result of debates between different schools, major works on epistemology were written by several authors who attempted to refute other opinions and to establish their own conclusions on rational grounds.

equality of women

Women and men were considered equal during early Vedic times: women appear as composers of Vedic HYMNS (*ṛṣis*), as vedic teachers (ĀCĀRYĀS) and as companions in rituals. With the increased specialization of brahmanic ritual and the rise of urban culture the status of women has diminished. The influential MANU-SMṚTI (sixth century BCE?), while giving lavish praise to the mother in the home, advises that a woman should never be without male supervision. In childhood she was to be under the authority of her father, in marrriage under the rule of her husband, in widowhood under the supervision of her son. Ritually also women were disadvantaged: they no longer received UPANAYANA, they could not study the Veda, they were excluded from most religious activities. BHAKTI movements attempted to readmit women to religious practices, sometimes even placing women higher than men, as did the GAUḌĪYA Vaiṣṇavas, who considered the GOPĪS superior to male devotees. In ŚĀKTISM women were given an exalted position in rituals as embodiments of the Goddess. With the Muslim conquest of India, restrictions on the movement of women increased: Hindus adopted the Muslim custom of *purdah* and did not allow women to leave their assigned quarters without special permission. Many Hindu reformers of the 19th and early 20th centuries fought for women's rights and women's education. Mahatma GANDHI accepted women as equal partners in the struggle for independence, and expressed the wish to see a *Harijan* woman as the first president of independent India. Since the 1960s Indian womens' movements have grown in importance and influence. The HINDU MARRIAGE ACT of 1956 established the equality of men and women in most matters on a legal basis. In spite of all these efforts old attitudes towards women continue. Although the giving and taking of dowries is outlawed, it is still widely practised, and frequently leads to criminal abuses. The so-called 'dowry deaths' are the result of failed attempts to blackmail brides' parents into providing more dowry; the often open-ended agreements concerning dowries expose brides to threats and abuse. (*See also* FEMALE INFANTICIDE.)

eternity

Concepts premised on eternity (*nitya, ananta, amarta*) are central to Hinduism. It was always assumed that the ultimate principle, the supreme reality, the highest God, was eternal, i.e. without beginning or end. Attempts to win immortality are described in Hindu literature from the Vedas through the epics to the Purāṇas. With the Upaniṣads the notion arose that the soul (*jīvātma*) was eternal, uncreated and indestructible. As long as it was not emancipated from its bodily desires, it had to transmigrate from one corporeal existence to the next. The ultimate destiny was immortality and eternity.

ethics (*śīla*)

The definition of Hinduism as DHARMA clearly indicates the primacy of ethics: while beliefs and doctrinal formulations were largely left to individual choice, conformity with the rules of behaviour, including ritual, was mandatory and the single most important criterion of membership in Hindu society.

evil

The conflict between good and evil is represented in Hindu tradition in a variety of images and notions: in the Veda INDRA represents 'good', VṚTRA 'evil'; the DEVAS are opposed by the ASURAS; the Āryas fight the DAITYAS. In the Purāṇas Viṣṇu appears in a series of AVATĀRAS to combat evil: NĀRASIMḤA kills HIRAṆYAKAŚIPU to save PRAHLĀDA; Kṛṣṇa kills KAṂŚA to save his people in Vraja; Rāma kills RAVAṆA. Śiva drinks the poison HALĀHALĀ to save humankind. Durgā kills the buffalo demon to save the three worlds from demon rule. On the level of ethics the opposition between good and evil is manifested in following/not following the duties imposed by one's VARṆA, and in the sets of virtues/vices developed especially by the Nyayaikas (*see* NYĀYA). True to the holistic bent of Hindu thought, however, the opposition between good and evil is not seen as a metaphysical split in reality: the categories good/evil are within the realm of *dvandvas*, pairs of opposites in the finite sphere, ultimately to be overcome. Hinduism does not acknowledge an eternal hell or eternal damnation as punishment for evil actions. Even the demons are eventually saved from their evil nature, after having served a cosmic purpose.

experience

Hindus have always endeavoured to experience the ultimate rather than conceptualize it. Upaniṣadic techniques aim at an experience of the oneness of ĀTMAN, and BRAHMAN and Vedāntic teachers amplify and refine these methods. ŚAṄKARA (2) insists that *anubhava* (experience), rather than intellectual understanding, can bring about LIBERATION. Theistic Hindu traditions aim at SĀKṢĀTKĀRA (a direct visual experience of God), which many Hindus claim to have had.

F

faith (*viśvāsa, śraddhā*)

In a general sense 'faith' plays a central role in Hinduism: the acceptance of ŚRUTI as 'revealed word' requires faith. Faith is also demanded from the disciple towards his teacher, an acceptance of the teacher's authority. Pilgrims travelling to temples to find relief from their suffering or help in their needs also exhibit a great amount of faith. The crowds surrounding living manifestations of the deity, such as ĀNANDAMAYĪ MĀ or SATHYA SAI BABA, exhibit tremendous faith. In a more specific, theological sense, faith plays a much smaller role in Hinduism than in biblical religions. It is seen important only as an early stage in one's spiritual development, not as an end in itself. Faith as such is not the cause of LIBERATION, but only a preparatory phase, to be superseded by direct experience.

Farquhar, J. N. (1861–1929)

Scottish missionary. He worked in India (mainly in Calcutta) from 1891 to 1923, initiated serious study of Hinduism among Protestant missionaries, and is the author of such standard works as *A Primer of Hinduism*, *Modern Religious Movements in India*, *An Outline of the Religious Literature of India*, *The Crown of Hinduism*, *Hinduism, its Content and Value.*

fasting

See UPAVĀSA.

female infanticide

The religious need for a male heir, and the great expense of marrying off a daughter, led in former times to widespread female infanticide among Hindus, especially in Bengal. Female babies were either offered to Goddess GAṄGĀ or exposed in fulfilment of a VRATA. While not as prevalent today, there are still cases of female infanticide, very often following determination of the female gender of the foetus through amniocentesis.

festivals

Hinduism is rich in festivals. Besides the local temple feasts, which often attract millions of visitors to famous places of pilgrimage, such as the *ratha-yātrā* at JAGANNĀTHA PURĪ, there are some feasts that are celebrated all over India or in large areas. Among these the following stand out:

Kṛṣṇa-jayanti, Kṛṣṇa's birthday, celebrated on the eighth KṚṢṆA-PAKṢA of the month *Śravana* (July–August) in commemoration of Kṛṣṇa's birth at midnight in the prison of Mathurā. It is a national holiday in India.

Śiva-rātrī, Śiva's night, celebrated on the thirteenth *kṛṣṇa-pakṣa* in the month *Māgha* (January–February), the principal feast of Śaivas, but also observed by Vaiṣṇavas, who consider Śiva the first devotee of Viṣṇu. The LIṄGA (3) is decorated and bathed in honey and milk.

Dassera, 'ten days', celebrated in the first half of the month *Āśvina* (September–October), is a string of festivals during the beautiful time after the monsoon. The first nine days, *Nava-rātrī*, is also the time of the famous *Durgāpūjā* in Bengal.

DĪPĀVALĪ or *Divālī*, 'the feast of lights', is celebrated in the second half of *Āśvina*, with the lighting of countless lamps on rivers and houses.

Holi, celebrated in ŚUKLA-PAKṢA of the month *Phalguṇa* (February–March), is a celebration of spring resembling a Western carnival. It is also New Year's day.

Ganeśa-catūrthi, celebrated on the fourth *śukla-pakṣa* of *Bhadra* (August–September), is the major feast in *Mahārāṣṭra*: figures of GAṆEŚA are displayed in public places and homes, and after a festive procession through town immersed in the sea.

Nāgapañcamī, a celebration in honour of cobras, is very popular in the south.

Filliozat, Jean (1906–82)

French Indologist. Founder of the Institut Française d'Indologie at Pondicherry (1955), initiator of studies in Śaivite ĀGAMAS, author of *Les relations extérieures de l'Inde* (1956), translator of *Ajitagāma*, *Yogabhāṣya*, *Yogaśataka*.

fire

See AGNI.

flood

Hindu tradition has tales of a universal flood (the Great Flood) that exterminated all of humankind, excepting MANU (2) and his family. It was preceded by the appearance of Viṣṇu in the form of a fish (MATSYA) whom Manu caught and reared and released into the ocean. Before parting he instructed Manu about the coming disaster. When the whole world was flooded, Viṣṇu EKAŚṚṄGA (1) appeared and brought Manu to safety. Manu, being the only survivor, became both the progenitor of the new human race and the first lawgiver. (*See also* MANUSMṚTI.)

food (*anna*)

Food plays a major role in Hinduism. All SACRIFICES involved food, and only the best was deemed fit for the gods. The Upaniṣads interiorize the role that food plays: everything is seen as arising from food and becoming food again. Preparing and consuming food is regulated by a host of rules. Many CASTE regulations concern commensality. While Vedic Indians seem to have had few, if any, restrictions with regard to food (apparently the animals that were unfit for sacrifice, such as donkeys and camels, were also unfit for eating), later Hinduism developed many such taboos, which were further hightened by sectarian regulations. With the ascendancy of Buddhism and Jainism, most Hindus, especially the brahmins, seem to have adopted VEGETARIANISM. VAIṢṆAVAS in particular developed a whole theology of food: categorizing all foods according to the three GUṆAS, they advised the taking of *sāttvik* food (milk and milk products, most grains, fruit and vegetables) and the avoidance of *rājasik* food ('exciting' foods such as garlic, eggs, red-coloured vegetables and fruit) and *tāmasik* ('foul' foods such as meat and intoxicating substances). ŚAIVAS and ŚĀKTAS observe few restrictions with regard to food. (*See also* MEAT EATING.)

Frauwallner, Erich

(1898–1974)

Professor of Indian and Iranian studies at the University of Vienna. His contributions to the study of Hinduism are mainly in the areas of SĀṀKHYA and MĪMĀṀSĀ. He had planned to write a five-volume history of Indian philosophy, of which only two volumes appeared, containing valuable information on Sāṁkhya, YOGA and VAIŚEṢIKA.

freedom (*mokṣa*, *mukti*, *vimukti*)

A central notion in Hinduism. It presupposes the condition of BONDAGE, whose most conspicuous manifestation is the existence in SAṀSĀRA and the KARMA(2)-induced necessity of bodily REBIRTH. All Hindu systems are paths to freedom, which is understood as the proper condition of the soul. A major difference concerns the understanding of the relationship between bondage and freedom and the paths leading from bondage to freedom. ADVAITA VEDĀNTA holds that freedom results from divesting oneself of ĀVIDYĀ; Theistic VEDĀNTA (2) considers freedom a gift of God's grace and an enhancement of the natural condition.

Political freedom fighters in the 19th and 20th centuries adopted some of the Vedāntic notions and transferred them to the socio-political arena. Thus GANDHI considered colonial rule 'sinful' and liberation from it an act of (religious) salvation.

funeral rites

See ŚRADDHA.

G

Gaja-Lakṣmī ('Elephant-Lakṣmī')

A portrayal of LAKṢMĪ being doused by two elephants, one on each side, a favourite motif in Hindu sculpture.

Gandharva (1)

In the VEDA, Gandharva is a deity who knows and reveals the secrets of heaven.

Gandharva (2)

Heavenly musicians who were fond of women.

Gandharva (3)

A form of (legitimate) marriage designating a love union.

Gandharva Veda

Treatise on music and song, including drama and dancing. Its author is BHĀRATA MUNI and it is an appendix to the Sāmaveda.

A commemorative stamp showing the head of Gandhi.

Gandhi, Mohandas Karamchand (Mahatma) (1869–1948)

Indian nationalist leader, pioneer of passive resistance and advocate of non-violence. Gandhi was born in Porbandhar, Gujarat. His father and his grandfather had been premiers in small princely states in Kathiawar. His mother was a devout VAIṢṆAVA and as a youth he befriended a Jain, who had a major influence on his character. After studies in England he practised law in South Africa where he played an important part in the contribution of the Indian community to the struggle against apartheid, developing concepts such as *satyāgraha* (truth-grasping) and techniques such as *ahiṁsā* (non-violent resistance).

Returning to India in 1915 he joined the freedom movement and quickly rose to be one of its leaders. He organized mass civil disobedience events, marches and protest movements. He founded an ashram at Wardha near Ahmedabad to train his co-workers in *ahiṁsā* (non-violence) and *satya* (truthfulness), believing that non-violence and truth would prevail. To give emphasis to his demands, both for concessions from the British government and for peace between warring groups of Muslims and Hindus, he undertook lengthy fasts. He was a deeply religious man and convinced that in order to do God's work he had to discipline himself and earn God's grace. He was unable to prevent the partition of the country which led to widespread bloodshed. Accused by some of having done more for Muslims than for his fellow Hindus, he was shot on 30 January, 1948 by Nathuram GODSE, an extremist Hindu, during a prayer meeting at Birla house in New Delhi.

Gandhi not only helped to bring about India's independence from Britain, he also did much for the uplift-ment of the former untouchables (whom he named HARIJAN, 'God's people') and for the equality of women. He developed an economic programme for India, based on his principles of *ahiṁsā* and *satya* and emphasizing the human element, the need to give mean-ingful work to everyone and respect for nature.

Gandhi considered himself first and foremost a religious and moral reformer, and hoped to further the *Rāmarājya*, which he understood as the kingdom of God, through his social and political activities.

Gaṇeśa, also **Gaṇapati**

('Lord of the *gaṇas* [the hosts of minor Vedic deities]')

Son of Śiva and Pārvatī, with a human body and an elephant's head. He is worshipped as god of wisdom and remover of obstacles (Vināyaka), and invoked before the beginning of any major undertaking. He is VYĀSA's secre-tary and wrote, at his dictation, the *Mahābhārata*. His VAHANA is a rat. He is very popular with students, clerks, writers and business people, and there are numerous temples in his honour. His festival, *Gaṇeśa catūrthi*, is cele-brated very lavishly especially in Mahārāṣṭra, with displays of Gaṇeśa images on public places and in homes and processions through the streets. There are many stories explaining how he came to have an elephant's head.

Ganeśa, the popular elephant-headed god, patron of scholars and scribes.

Gaṅgā, also **Ganges**

India's most holy river. Mentioned only twice in the *Ṛgveda*, it became a promi-nent subject of praise in the Purāṇas. Originally a heavenly river, it was brought down to earth by the prayers of

Bhāgīratha to purify the ashes of the 60,000 sons of his ancestor King Sagara, who had been burnt to death by the anger of the sage Kapila. Originating from Viṣṇu's toe, its turbulence, which would have destroyed the earth, was stopped by the matted hair of Śiva, who therefore has the title 'Gaṅgā-dhāra'. The river has different names in different sections: first it is called Bhāgīrathī, then Gaṅgā, further down it splits into many branches, each of which has a different name, for example Jāhnavī, Mandākinī. As a goddess Gaṅgā is the eldest daughter of Himavat (the personificiation of Himālaya) and Menā; her sister is Umā. She married King Śāntanu: her son BHĪṢMA is also known as Gāṅgeya. She is called by many names in numerous hymns addressed to her. Her water is believed to be always pure and purifying, and pilgrims take flasks of Ganges water with them for use especially in the last rites.

Gaṅgeśa (12th century)

Celebrated author of the *Tattvacintāmaṇi*, the main work of Nava Nyāya.

garbha-gṛha ('womb-house')

The innermost cell and most sacred part of a temple, where the IMAGE is housed.

Gārgī

Upaniṣadic sage, wife of YAJÑAVĀLKYA, with whom she conducted debates.

Garuḍa

Viṣṇu's VAHANA, half vulture, half man, the king of birds and the enemy of serpents. Many Purāṇic stories recount his ventures. He is known by many different names. Each Viṣṇu temple in South India has a *Garuḍastambha*, provided for Garuḍa to alight upon when bringing Viṣṇu down to earth.

Gauḍapāda (eighth century?)

Śaṇkara's *parama guru* (GURU's *guru*); author of the famous *Gauḍapāda Kārikās*, a commentary on the MUṆḌAKA UPANIṢAD, the first exposition of Advaita Vedānta, upon which ŚAṄKARA (2) commented.

Gauḍīya Vaiṣṇavism
('Bengal Vaiṣṇavism')

The term comes from Gauḍa, an ancient name for Bengal. It is frequently used as synonymous with CAITANYA's 16th-century revival of Vaiṣṇavism in Bengal.

Gaurī ('yellow', 'brilliant')

One of the names of Pārvatī, the consort of Śiva.

Gautama (1)

Vedic sage, author of a work on DHARMA-ŚĀSTRA.

Gautama (2), also **Gotama**
(*c.* 300 BCE)

Author of the NYĀYA SŪTRAS.

gāyatrī

The most sacred verse from the *Ṛgveda*, addressed to Savitṛ, the sun, light, wisdom. Every brahmin must recite it during morning and evening prayers. Its translation is unclear but scriptures recommend repeating it as often as possible because through it the forefathers had achieved long life, honour, understanding and glory. It is supposed to be a summary of the entire Veda.

ghī

Clarified butter, an ingredient of many SACRIFICES and PŪJĀS, such as the Vedic sacrifice *homa*, in which *ghī* is thrown into fire.

Ghoṣā

Daughter of the *ṛṣi* (sage) Kakṣīvat. She was afflicted with leprosy, but the AŚVINS cured her late in life, and bestowed beauty and youth on her so that she could marry.

ghosts

See BHŪTA; PRETA.

gifts

See DĀNA.

Giridhāra

('the upholder of the mountain')

Epithet of Kṛṣṇa, who held Mount Govardhan up high in order to protect the shepherds of Vraja from torrential rains sent by Indra.

Girijā ('mountain-born')

A name of DEVĪ.

gītā ('song')

A religio-philosophical text in the form of an epic poem. The best known is the *Bhagavadgītā*, which is found as an insert in the sixth book of the *Mahābhārata*. Other well-known *gītās* are the *Upagītā*, also found in the *Mahābhārata*, and the *Bhrāmaragītā*.

Gīta-govinda

Famous poem by JĀYADEVA, celebrating the love of Kṛṣṇa and the GOPĪS, influential for the development of GAUḌĪYA VAIṢṆAVISM.

Gītā-rahasya ('secret of the Gītā')

A work by B. G. TILAK interpreting the *Bhagavadgītā* as a 'Gospel of action.'

Glasenapp, Helmut von

(1891–1963)

German Indologist and scholar of religion, who taught mainly at Königsberg and Tübingen, and promoted the knowledge of Indian religions, especially Hinduism, through many scholarly and popular works: *Der Hinduismus* (1930); *Die Religionen Indiens* (1943); *Die Philosophie der Inder* (1949); *Das Indienbild deutscher Denker* (1960).

go

See COW.

goat (*aja*)

The most frequently used animal for Vedic SACRIFICES. Goats are still offered to KĀLĪ (2) on a regular basis. *Aja* also means 'unborn', and many interesting speculations make use of the double meaning of the word.

God and gods

Many outsiders are fascinated to learn that Hindus worship 330 million (thirty-three *crores*) gods. There is no record of the names of all of these, of course, and the figure serves to indicate that the number of higher powers is unimaginably high. There are lists of gods that go into the hundreds and there are litanies of names of major gods, such as Śiva or Viṣṇu, that enumerate a thousand names.

The English word God/gods stands for a great many Hindu (Sanskrit) terms that have clearly differentiated meanings. The most commonly used word is DEVA or *devatā*, generically applicable to all higher powers and also liberally used by Hindus when addressing an important human being, who is honoured by the title 'Deva'. *Deva* is everything that reveals something unusual or uncommon, that exercises power and influence, or that is helpful or harmful. The Vedas speak of 33 gods: 11 assigned to the earth, 11 to the heavens and 11 to the region in between. They address Agni (fire), Sūrya (sun) and Uṣas (dawn) as *devas*; they also contains hymns to Indra, described as powerful protector of the ĀRYAN people, who is exalted above other gods as the one who creates and delivers. There is also the statement that 'although Indra is one, he is called by many names'.

In the Upaniṣads the role of the *devas* recedes into the background: they are not seen as important for reaching the transcendental consciousness in which ultimate fulfilment was seen. Buddhists and Jains too devalued the position of gods to merely innerworldly agents, useless in the pursuit of *nirvāṇa* or *kaivalya*.

During the GUPTA renaissance, and with the rise of Purāṇic Hinduism, some gods emerged as major figures: Brahmā, Viṣṇu and Śiva (the TRIMŪRTI), representing the cosmic forces of creation, sustenance and destruction. Not only were these *īśvaras* ('lords') seen as of the utmost importance for the existence of the universe and the protection of their worshippers, they also were seen as *muktidātā*, i.e. givers of LIBERATION/salvation. Worship of gods (PŪJĀ) became an integral part of Hindu religion. With the construction of genealogies of gods and the developing belief in multiple bodily descents (AVATĀRAS) the number of gods and goddesses increased dramatically.

Along with the officially sanctioned worship of a great variety of manifestations of Viṣṇu, Śiva and Devī, at the village level the worship of autochthonous deities continued and was augmented by the worship of local gods and goddesses, often the spirits of departed members of the village community who had revealed some extraordinary powers.

Most Hindus choose one of the deities as their *iṣṭa devatā*, their 'wish-god' or personal deity, who becomes the focus of their piety and worship. The fact that different people choose different *iṣṭas* makes for a unique kind of polytheism: while remaining loyal to the deity of their choice, most are convinced that it is one of many manifestations of the ultimate power (BRAHMAN) and that ultimately there is only one Supreme God, whose true nature is beyond human powers to comprehend. Most Hindus are worshippers of one God, whom they consider creator, sustainer and redeemer and to whom they address their petitions and prayers. They usually respect other gods, often considering them a manifestation of their own God. They will repeat MANTRAS to a great many *devatās*, whom they believe to be the guiding and presiding powers of natural and cultural phenomena.

Godāvarī

Major river in South India, whose banks contain many sacred places.

Godse, Nathuram (1912–49)

Former member of the RĀṢṬRĪYA SVAYAMSEVAK SANGH, who assassinated Mahatma GANDHI out of a conviction that Gandhi had been too friendly towards Muslims and was responsible for the great suffering of millions of Hindus after the partition of India in 1947. He was apprehended on the spot, tried, condemned to death and hanged.

Gokhale, Gopal Krishna (1866–1915)

Important early Hindu reformer and promoter of religious nationalism. At the age of 19 he joined the Deccan Education Society in Poona, taking a vow of poverty for 20 years in order to devote himself to educating his fellow countrymen, at the Fergusson College, established by the society. In 1905 he founded the Servants of India Society, devoted to social and economical support of the lower classes. At the age of 30 he became a member of the Imperial

Legislative Council, working for administratrive and financial reforms. He took great interest in the work of M. K. GANDHI in South Africa, encouraging and advising him.

Gokula

Rural area on the Yamunā, where Kṛṣṇa spent his boyhood with the shepherds of Braja.

Goloka ('the world of cows')

Kṛṣṇa's heaven.

Golwalkar, Madhav Sadashiv (1906–73)

From 1940 to 1973 Sarasanghachalak (Supreme Chief) of the RĀṢTṚĪYA SVAYAMSEVAK SANGH, author of *Bunch of Thoughts* and *Sri Guruji Samagra Darshana*, a seven-volume collection of his speeches in Hindi.

Gonda, Jan (1905–96)

Prolific Dutch Indologist, for many years professor and department head at the University of Utrecht, who wrote on all aspects of Hinduism from Vedic to contemporary. Some of his major works are *Aspects of Early Vaisnavism* (1954), *Die Religionen Indiens* (2 vols; 1960–3), *The Ritual Sutras* (1977), *Vedic Ritual: The Non-Solemn Rites* (1980), *The Indra Hymns of the Rgveda* (1989).

good and evil

What the Veda prescribes (VIDHI) is 'good' and what it forbids (*niṣedha*) is 'evil'. Hindu SAṀPRADĀYAS, relying on specific works that they consider revelations, usually extend the range of good and evil to include sectarian observances with regard to worship, mode of life, contacts with members of one's own and of other communities. For Advaitins the dichotomy of good and evil applies only to the lower sphere of practical life, it is one of the *dvandvas* (pairs of opposites) that have no validity in the ultimate sphere, where those distinctions are meaningless. Nevertheless all Hindus would agree that the PURUṢĀRTHAS encapsulate what is considered 'good' and that *mokṣa* (emancipation) is the supreme good to be aimed at. There is also fairly large agreement that good actions generate good *karma*, and bad actions result in bad *karma*; the future rebirth of a person will be determined by the kind of *karma* she has acquired in her previous lives. (*See also* DHARMA; ETHICS; EVIL.)

Gopāla ('protector of cows')

An epithet of Kṛṣṇa.

Gopāla Bhaṭṭa (16th century)

One of the original six Gosvāmis of VṚNDĀVANA, sent there by CAITANYA to revive the tradition of Kṛṣṇa worship, author of *Haribhaktivilāsa*, a famous work of GAUḌĪYA VAIṢṆAVISM, which describes the proper form of worship.

gopīs

Daughters and wives of cowherds in Braja, whose love for Kṛṣṇa is considered exemplary: they forsook their husbands and neglected their families in order to be with Kṛṣṇa. They are the subject of numerous stories and songs.

The gopīs *of Vṛndāvana, models of highest* bhakti *to Kṛṣṇa.*

go-pūjā ('cow-worship')

Part of the ceremonies performed during *mattupoṅgal* in Tamilnādū. (*See also* POṄGAL.)

gopura ('cow fortress')

Entrance towers to South Indian temples.

Gorakhnātha

(between 900 and 1225 CE)

A great yogi and miracle worker about whom many legends circulate in India; founder of the Nāṭhapanthis, a sect of Śaivas who practise extreme forms of asceticism. One branch, the Kāṇphatas, derive their name from the initiation practice of piercing the ear-lobes with a double-edged knife and inserting an iron ring. They have centres in many towns in North India. Gorakhnātha's teachings are contained in works attributed to him: *Siddha siddhānta-paddhatī*, *Gorakṣaśataka*, and *Gorakhbodha*. All teach Haṭha-yoga. The aim of the practice is to become the equal of Śiva.

Gorakhpur

Town in Uttar Pradesh, named after Gorakhnāṭha, the headquarters of the Nāṭhapanthis. It also is the home of the Gītā Press, established in 1923 by Hanuman Prasad PODDAR, the largest publisher of Hindu religious literature in Hindī and Sanskrit, publishing a Hindī-language religious monthly, *Kalyāṇ*, with a circulation of over 200,000.

gośālā

See COWS.

Gospel of Ramakrishna

English translation of a transcript of discourses and conversations by Paraṁahamsa RAMAKRISHNA recorded by one of his disciples, known as M.

gosvāmi ('Lord of cows')

An honorific title given to the first six disciples of CAITANYA designating their authority as teachers. They were RŪPA and his brother Sanātana, their nephew Jīva, GOPĀLA BHAṬṬA, Raghunātha Bhaṭṭa and Raghunātha Dāsa, who all wrote authoritative works. Their descendants claim ownership of important temples in Vṛndāvana.

gotra ('clan')

Important (smallest) CASTE unit, within which marriages are severely restricted or forbidden. (*See also* JĀTI.)

Govardhana

A mountain in Braja. Kṛṣṇa persuaded the cowherds of Braja to worship Govardhana instead of Indra. Indra, enraged, sent a deluge, which threatened to drown all people. Kṛṣṇa supported the mountain on his little finger for seven days and thus sheltered and saved the people of Braja. Kṛṣṇa is therefore called *Govardhanadhāra*, the 'upholder of Govardhana mountain'.

Govinda ('finder of the cows')

An epithet of KṚṢṆA.

Govinda Bhāṣya

See VIDYĀBHŪṢANA BALADEVA.

grace

See KṚPĀ; ANUGRAHA.

grammar

See VYĀKĀRAṆA.

gṛha praveśa ('entering the house')

A ceremony performed by brahmins when a family first enters a new home.

gṛhastya ('householder')

A brahmin in the second stage of his life-cycle. (*See also* CATURVARṆĀŚRAMA DHARMA; VARṆĀŚRAMA DHARMA.)

Gṛhya Sūtra

Text dealing with the regulations of domestic rites and SAṂSKĀRAS. Several collections of *Gṛhya Sūtras* are in existence, for example *Āśvalāyana Gṛhyasūtras*.

Griffith, Ralph Thomas Hotchkins (1826–1906)

Orientalist and teacher. He was professor of English and principal at Benares College, director of public instruction in the North-West Provinces and Oudh, founder-editor of *Pandit*, a journal dedicated to classical Sanskrit studies, translator of the *Rāmāyana* (1870–5), *Ṛgveda* (1889–92), *Sāmaveda* (1893), *Atharvaveda* (1895–6), and the *White Yajurveda* (1899).

Gudimally

Temple town in South India with what is reputed to be the oldest Śiva LIṄGA (3) worshipped, dating from the second century BCE.

Guenon, René (1886–1951)

Widely appreciated writer on spirituality and religious traditions. Although Guenon became a Muslim in early adulthood and spent much of his life in Egypt (under the name of Shaikh Abd'al Wahid Yahya) his universal interests in religious traditions also included Hinduism, and his *Introduction générale à l'étude des doctrines hindoues* (1921) is considered a seminal work, which still influences the understanding of Hinduism in the West.

guṇa ('quality')

Used in a very general sense, also 'virtue'; more specifically used by the SĀṂKHYA system to designate the three principles of all material beings: *sattva* (light), *rajas* (excitement) and *tamas* (darkness).

Gupta

A dynasty of rulers of MAGADHA (319–415 CE) under whose reign Hinduism experienced a cultural renaissance and royal support. It was a golden time for the arts and the traditional sciences.

guru ('elder')

Teacher, especially of sacred lore and meditation, spiritual master, who initiates and guides disciples in a particular tradition.

guru-dīkṣā

Tantrik ceremony of initiation for a religious preceptor (both women and men can receive it).

gurukula

The *gurukula* system is built on a close relationship between teacher and student. In Vedic times the student spent twelve years in the home of his teacher, serving him and learning from him. During this time the student maintained strict celibacy (BRAHMACARYA), and was to show lifelong respect for his teacher.

H

Hacker, Paul (1913–79)

Eminent Indologist. He taught at Bonn and Münster. His main contribution was the study of early ADVAITA, where he attempted to develop criteria to establish the authentic writings of ŚAṄKARA (2). In a number of papers he examined larger concepts such as *Śraddha* (1963), *Dharma* (1965) and *Vrata* (1973), and brought out a monograph on *Prahlāda* (1959).

Haihaya (1)

Prince of the lunar dynasty, great-grandson of Yadu. (*See also* YĀDAVA.)

Haihaya (2)

Descendants of Haihaya (1), according to the VIṢṆU PURĀṆA.

hair

Many Hindu rituals concern the cutting of hair. Part of the UPANAYANA (initiation) ceremony is the shaving of the head, with the exception of the ŚIKHA, and it remains a religious obligation for brahmins to shave their heads every fortnight. When a man becomes a SAMNYĀSI, the DĪKṢĀ includes the shaving of all hair of the body, including the *śikha*. Similarly, a dead man's hair is to be shaved before cremation. In the famous temple of TIRUPATI pilgrims offer their hair to the deity in fulfilment of vows. Keśin, 'the hairy one', is an epithet of Kṛṣṇa.

hala ('ploughshare')

Symbol of BALADEVA, also called Halabhṛt, 'bearing a plough' and 'Halāyudha', 'having a ploughshare for a weapon'.

halāhalā

The fiery poison that emerged as the first product from the CHURNING OF THE OCEAN by gods and demons at the beginning of the world. It threatened to engulf the world, whereupon Śiva swallowed it. Its power darkened Śiva's throat, and he is since known as NĪLAKAṆṬHA, 'the one with the blue throat'.

Halebid

Famous temple city in Karṇātaka, built by the HOYŚALAS.

Haṁsa avatāra

Viṣṇu's descent in the form of a swan.

Hanuman(t)

Celebrated chief of monkeys, son of Pavana (wind) and Anjanā, a major figure in the RĀMĀYAṆA. He aided RĀMA in the conquest of Śrī Laṅka, RĀVANA's capital. His worship is very popular and many temples were built for him. He is also known as a great scholar and author of a grammar.

Hanuman, the monkey ally of Rāma, conquering Laṅkā and liberating Sītā from Rāvaṇa's captivity.

happiness (*sukha*)

This is the declared aim of all Hindu systems, spurred by the experience of unhappiness (*duḥkha*).

Hara ('the one who takes away')

A name of ŚIVA.

Harappa

An ancient city in the Indus valley, excavated in the early 20th century. While most scholars still consider it as part of a pre-Āryan civilization, some recent findings suggest that it might have been a late Vedic urban settlement.

Hardwar, also **Hari-dvār(a), Hara-dvār(a)** ('gate of Hari/Hara')

Famous place of pilgrimage in North India where the already mighty GAṄGĀ breaks through the last range of the Himālayas and enters the plains. It is filled with ashrams and temples, and is one of the four places where the KUMBHAMELA is held every twelve years. It is also the starting-point for pilgrimages to Kedarnāṭh and Badrīnāth.

Hari ('the yellowish-green one')

A name of VIṢṆU.

Hari-Hara

A combination of Viṣṇu and Śiva in one image.

Harijan ('God's people')

Designation for OUTCASTES introduced by Mahatma GANDHI to emphasize their dignity and human rights.

Hariścandra

An ancient king famous for his piety and righteousness, a paradigm of liberality, the subject of many stories in Purāṇas and dramatic performances.

Harita-smṛti

A lawbook ascribed to the sage Harita.

Hari-vamśa (Purāṇa)

A lengthy appendix to the *Mahābhārata.* Literally the 'genealogy of Hari', the work conists of three parts: (1) creation, patriarchal and regal dynasties; (2) the life and exploits of Kṛṣṇa; (3) future of the world and the end of the KALI YUGA.

Hastinā-pura

The capital city of the KAURAVAS at the Bhāgīrathī (Gaṇgā), about 100 km north-east of modern Delhi, founded by Hastin, a descendant of BHARATA (4), installed on the throne by ṚṢABHA.

hāsya ('laughing')

One of the RASAS of Indian aesthetics.

Haṭha-yoga ('forced yoga')

A system of physical exercises designed to increase bodily strength and health. The *Haṭhayoga pradīpikā* by Svatmarāma Yogīndra is a standard manual.

Haya-śiras (1), also **Haya-śirsa, Haya-grīva** ('horse-head', 'horse neck')

The eighteenth AVATĀRA of Viṣṇu, revealer of sacred lore.

Haya-śiras (2)

A demon who stole the Veda and was slain by Viṣṇu in the form of the MATSYA AVATĀRA.

Hazra, Rajendra Chandra (1905–82)

Professor at Sanskrit College Calcutta, author of many authoritative works on Purāṇas: *Studies in the Puranic Records on Hindu Rites and Customs* (1940); *Studies in the Upapurāṇas* (2 vols, 1958 and 1963).

heart (*hṛdaya*)

The seat of feeling and emotions, of thought and intellectual operations. Metaphorically it designates the best or the essence of a thing. Hindu writings speak of the presence of 'an eternal monitor in the heart', i.e the conscience; of 'heart fetters' or 'heart knots', the hindrance to attaining freedom; of a 'cave of the heart' (*hṛdaya guha*), the place where one encounters the ultimate. The activity most eminently connected with the heart is love. (*See also* BHAKTI.)

heaven

The ultimate human aim, according to the Veda, to be obtained through appropriate sacrifices. This concept was superseded by the Vedāntic notion of *mokṣa*, a completely spiritual emancipation. The Purāṇas, with their sectarian bias, present a different heaven for each of the major gods: Viṣṇu's heaven, for example, is Vaikuṇṭha; Śiva's Kailāsa; Devī's Maṇidvīpa. (*See also* AFTERLIFE; SVARGA.)

Hedgewar, K.V.

See RĀṢTṚĪYA SVAYAMSEVAK SANGH.

hell

See NĀRAKA.

Himālaya, also **Himācala, Himādri** ('abode of snow')

Immense mountain range in the north of India with great religious significance. Śiva is supposed to reside on Mount Kailāsa; Devī is called Pārvatī, the 'daughter of the mountains'. Countless ascetics have withdrawn to the Himālayas since time immemorial and there are famous places of pilgrimage visited by many thousands of pilgrims every year, such as Hardwar, Hṛṣikeśa, Badrīnāth, Kedarnāth. The mountain range is personified as Himavat (husband of Menā, father of Umā and Gaṇga).

hiṁsā

See VIOLENCE.

Hindu jagaran ('Hindu awakening')

Collective designation of efforts that began at the end of the 19th century to 'raise Hindu consciousness'. Persons active in this process were DĀYĀNANDA SARASVATĪ, AUROBINDO GHOSE, Bal Gangadhar TILAK and others. Movements contributing to it were the Ārya Samāj, the Rāṣṭrīya Svayamsevak Sangh, the Viśva Hindū Pariṣad, and political parties such as the Hindu Mahāsabhā, the Jana Sangh and the Bhāratīya Jānatā Party.

Hindu Mahāsabhā ('Great Hindu Assembly')

Political party founded by Pandit Mohan MALAVIYA in 1909 to counteract a perceived pro-Muslim bias in the Indian National Congress. It advocated a Hindu rāṣṭra (rule according to traditional Hindu law) and demanded, after independence, a reunification of divided India. It had in Vir SAVARKAR its most articulate ideologue, whose notion of HINDUTVA has become the mainline policy of the right wing Hindu parties. Savarkar wanted to 'Hinduize politics and militarize Hinduism'.

Hindu Marriage Act

The government of India in 1955 passed the Hindu Marriage Act, which, with several amendments, became official law for Hindus, replacing earlier regulations based on DHARMA-ŚĀSTRAS and regional custom. It unified Hindu marriage law and brought it closer to Western law by recognizing civil marriage and allowing divorce at the request of the wife. Its enactment created a great deal of controversy in India.

Hindutva

('Hindudom', 'Hindu-ness')

A concept created by Vir SAVARKAR, spokesman for the Hindu Mahāsabhā, in the 1930s, to distinguish Hindu culture from *Hindu dharma*, 'Hindu religion'. Hindu Political parties demand that *Hindutva* become the criterion for citizenship in a Hindu nation. It includes an emotional attachment to India as 'holy land' and participation in Hindu culture. It has become a very controversial issue in today's India.

Hiranyagarbha

('golden womb' or 'golden egg')

Principle and lord of all creation, identified with BRAHMĀ; a major motif in Vedas, Upaniṣads and Purāṇas.

Hiraṇyakaśipu ('golden dress')

A powerful demon king, father of PRAHLĀDA, whom he persecuted for his devotion to Viṣṇu. He was killed by Viṣṇu in the form of NĀRASIMHA.

hita–ahita

('wholesome–unwholesome')

Matters relating to LIBERATION and BONDAGE. *Hita* comprises all acts considered a requirement to attain liberation, the way to salvation as outlined by individual masters. *Ahita* designates all contrary acts. (*See also* BHAKTI; JÑĀNA; KARMA; PRAPATTI.)

hlādinī-śakti

('power of enjoyment')

One of the three *śaktis* (powers) ascribed to Kṛṣṇa in GAUḌĪYA VAIṢṆAVISM, the other two being *sandhini-śakti* (power of existence) and *samvit-śakti* (power of consciousness). They collectively correspond to the definition of BRAHMAN as SACCIDĀNANDA.

Holikā

A demoness, who every year demanded a child to devour from a certain town. When the lot fell on a poor widow's only son, the woman consulted a holy man. He advised that all the children should gather, shouting abuse and throwing filth at the demoness, when she came to town. Holikā died of shame and embarrassment, and the children were saved. This incident is remembered at *Holī*, a very popular kind of Hindu carnival celebrated in spring, with everybody squirting coloured water on everybody else, and telling ribald jokes.

horoscope (*janmapatrikā*)

It is an old Hindu tradition to have a horoscope established by a professional astrologer (*jyotiṣa*) shortly after the birth of a child, entering the precise astronomical coordinates. All important events in the life of a person are decided upon after consultation of the horoscope. (*See also* ASTROLOGY.)

hospitality

Offering a meal or shelter for the night to a stranger who asked for it was one of the traditional duties of a Hindu. If a person was refused hospitality he could 'unload' his sins on the unwilling host. Hospitality was especially important towards brahmins and SAMNYĀSIS. On the other hand, hospitality was not to be abused, and strict limits were set. Hindu literature is full of stories about hospitality refused and punishments following, as well as about poor people sacrificing their last possessions for a guest, who turns out to be God in the guise of a poor man (*daridra Nārāyaṇa*) who amply rewards his hosts. (*See also* ATITHI.)

hotṛ

A Vedic priest whose task it was to recite the hymns of the *Ṛgveda*.

Hoyśalas

Dynasty of rulers in Karṇātaka (1006–1346), great warriors and administrators as well as defenders of the Hindu faith and builders of temples distinguished by a unique style, a kind of Indian roccoco (Belur, Halebid, Somnathpur).

Hṛṣikeśa (1) ('lord of the senses')

An epithet of Viṣṇu or Kṛṣṇa.

Hṛṣikeśa (2), also Rishikesh

Mountain and place of pilgrimage 30 km north of HARDWAR.

human sacrifice

See SACRIFICE.

humility (*dainya*)

One of the virtues to be cultivated by a VAIṢṆAVA who, according to an old verse, is supposed to be 'more humble than a blade of grass'. It is further specified as the effort to put oneself down in comparison to others, not to mention one's own merits, to serve one's spiritual master and all other devotees.

hymns

The *Ṛgveda* is a collection of hymns (*sūktas*) that are essential components (MANTRA (1)) of Vedic rituals; they are still used and recited by brahmin priests. Besides these, another genre of hymns, called *stotras* (praise), has become very important in connection with the worship of deities such as Viṣṇu, Śiva and Devī as well as Gaṇeśa, Hanuman and other lesser *devas*, and humans deemed to be manifestations of a deity. Epics and Purāṇas contain many such hymns, and great ācāryas (masters) such as ŚAṆKARA (2), RĀMĀNUJA and MADHVA (2) composed hymns that are used in worship. Most of the works of the poet-saints of the Indian Middle Ages are hymns in vernaculars (Tamil *Prabhanda*, Hindī *bhajans*, Mahratti *abhaṅgas*). Much of popular Hindu religious practice consists of singing such hymns. There are many popular collections, such as the *Stotramālā* and *Stotraratnāvalī*, which contain hymns to many different deities.

I

icchā ('desire', 'wish')

This usually has a negative connotation as longing for some finite object and therefore a hindrance to the ultimate end, which requires desirelessness.

Īḍā, also Īlā

Subject of a number of different stories concerning sex-change either from male to female, or female to male.

ignorance

See AVIDYĀ.

Īkṣvāku (1)

Son of MANU (2) Vaivasvata, descended from the sun, founder of the solar race, who reigned in Ayodhyā in the TRETA YUGA. He had a hundred sons.

Īkṣvāku (2)

Founder of the dynasty of the Purus.

Īkṣvāku (3)

Dynasty that ruled in both North India (Kośala), and South India (Madupūra) as well as in Śrī Laṅka.

Illakumi

Tamil name of goddess LAKṢMĪ, also known as Tiru (ŚRĪ).

image

(*mūrti*, lit. 'embodiment [of God]')

Usually a three-dimensional representation of a specific deity according to an established canon. Worship requires an image of some kind, conceived as the presence of the deity. Image making is governed by a set of rules that determines the material, the way the deity is to be represented, the paraphernalia given to it. A human-made image becomes a vessel for the presence of God through the act of consecration (*pratiṣṭhāpana, abhiṣeka*); either permanently or for the duration of the time of worship. Non-human-made images are those that have been found, usually revealed in a dream which do not need a special act of consecration. If an image suffers major damage, it can no longer serve as an object of worship. Hindu temples are primarily homes for the images of gods, whose worship consists in caring for the needs of the deity by bathing, feeding, clothing and fanning it. Most Hindu homes keep images of gods and regular worship is performed before them.

immortality

The search for immortality is a major theme in Hindu mythology. When the gods and the demons churned the ocean at the beginning of time, one of the most prized items that emerged was a pot with AMṚTA, nectar providing immortality. By a ruse the gods appropriated it and gained immortality thereby. The Upaniṣads also teach a way to immortality, based on the insight into the immortal nature of consciousness (*ātman*). They hold indefinite existence in a body to be an impossibility: everything that is born must die. Purāṇic Hinduism promises bodily immortality to the devotees of Viṣṇu, who after reaching VAIKUṆṬHA are endowed with incorruptible bodies. Some systems of YOGA also aim at making the practitioner physically immortal. (*See also* AFTERLIFE.)

impurity

Ritual impurity is usually caused by contact with what are considered impure substances: generally contact with corpses, with blood (especially menstrual blood) or other bodily fluids, or with 'untouchables' (persons belonging to the *Atiśūdras*, often dealing with carcasses, faeces etc.). This impurity is removed through religious practices such as bathing, repeating mantras and fasting according to a well-established canon.

incarnation

See AVATĀRA.

Indra

The first among the Vedic gods, to whom most of the hymns of the *Ṛgveda* are devoted. He is described as warrior, as fond of SOMA (2), as destroyer of forts and as enemy of the DASYUS. His most important aspect is *vṛtraha*, slayer of VṚTRA. Several hymns are devoted to this event, through which the waters were released, the sky cleared and Indra's supremacy established. Indra has many features of the Supreme Being and his activity is both creative and salvific. Worship of Indra was superseded by worship of Viṣṇu–Kṛṣṇa and Śiva–Devī. In the Purāṇas Indra is often depicted as rival of Kṛṣṇa. Feasts in honour of Indra are still celebrated in Nepal.

Indrajit ('conqueror of Indra')

Epithet of Meghanāda, a son of RĀVAṆA, who captured Indra and brought him to Laṅkā. He refused to surrender to the assembled gods until they had made him immortal.

Indraloka

Indra's heaven. Also known as *Svarloka* or *Svarga*, it is situated north of Mount MERU, and is the epitome of sensual delight, inhabited by *apsaras* (nymphs) and *gandharvas* (heavenly musicians). It is the home of KĀMADHENU, the 'cow of plenty', and of the PĀRIJĀTA tree, which grants all wishes. The capital city is Amarāvatī, which contains Indra's palace, Vaijayanta. Indra's heaven is associated with the highest pleasure and enjoyment of all kinds.

Indrāṇī

INDRA's wife, also called Śacī and Aindrī, mother of Jayanta and Jayantī

Indraprastha

The capital city of the PĀṆḌAVAS, located in what is today Delhi.

initiation

See DĪKṢĀ, UPANAYANA.

International Society for Krishna Consciousness (ISKCON)

A branch of the GAUḌĪYA VAIṢṆAVA tradition, with an international membership, founded by A. C. Bhaktivedanta Swami (Abhay Charan De) in 1966 in New York. It is also known as the 'Hare Krishna Movement' from its

Swami A. C. Bhaktivedānta, called 'Prabhupāda', founder of ISKCON.

public chanting of the Hare-Kṛṣṇa MAHĀ-MANTRA. It is by now established in all Western countries and has a sizeable presence in India. Among the innovations that 'Prabhupāda' Bhaktivedanta Swami introduced is the awarding of brahmin status to all initiates, the accepting of non-Hindus into SAMNYĀSA, and the establishment of a great number of temples under the care of non-Indian devotees. ISKCON is very active in publishing, in relief work and in maintaining authentic traditional image worship.

International Transcendental Meditation Society (TM)

Founded by Mahesh Yogi Maharishi in the late 1950s, it initially attracted a very large number of people in all Western countries by its teaching of Transcendental Meditation, a simplified form of Yoga. Followers of TM claim that it relieves tension and worries. Mahesh Yogi Maharishi also set out to teach SIDDHIS (miraculous higher powers). He established the Maharishi International University in Fairfield, Iowa which aims at integrating modern Western science with ancient Hindu traditions. Mahesh Yogi Maharishi developed various plans to give worldwide coverage to his ideas.

Īśa, also **Īśāna** ('lord')

Title of ŚIVA, 'maheśa' ('Mahā' + 'īsā': Maheśa – Great Lord).

Īśa(vasya) Upaniṣad

The shortest of the principal Upaniṣads, said to contain the essence of all. It is read out to a dying person to ensure a good passage. It has been commented upon by ŚAṄKARA (2) and other Vedāntins.

iṣṭa devatā ('deity of choice')

The form of the divine most appealing to a person and therefore singled out for worship, without denying the existence of others.

īśvara ('Lord')

A generic title given to the creator of the world.

Īśvara Kṛṣṇa (third century CE)

Author of the *Sāṁkhyakārikās.*

Īśvara Muni (tenth century CE)

A great PĀÑCARĀTRA teacher, father of NĀṬHA MUNI, the first of the ĀCĀRYAS of Śrīraṅgam.

itihāsa ('so it has been said')

A generic term for traditional history, specifically applied to the RĀMĀYAṆA and the MAHĀBHĀRATA.

J

jaḍa-patha ('braided text')

A form of recitation of the Veda involving a reverse reading.

jagad-guru ('world teacher')

Title assumed by the *Śaṅkarācāryas*, the ruling heads of the Śaṅkara *maṭhas*. (*See also* ŚAṄKARA (2).)

jaga-mohan

Place of assembly of worshippers at a Hindu temple.

Jagan-nātha Purī

One of the four holiest places of India, on the east coast in the state of Orissa, visited by millions of Hindus every year. A pilgrimage to Purī is believed to liberate a person from the round of rebirths. The focus of attention is the huge Jagannātha ('Lord of the World') temple dedicated to Viṣṇu, built during the reign of Anantavarman Choda Ganga (1076–1148), in which 6,000 priests and attendants serve. The most popular feast is the *ratha-yātrā* in June. A huge canopied car (15 m high, 12 m square) on which Kṛṣṇa is enthroned, is pulled through the streets on thick ropes by hundreds of pilgrims. (The English word 'juggernaut' is a corrupt form of Jagan-nātha.) The feast commemorates Kṛṣṇa's journey from GOKULA to MATHURĀ. The main chariot is followed

The famous ratha *(car) festival in Jagan-nātha Puri: The images of the deities are carried in huge, temple-shaped chariots through the town.*

by two smaller ones, carrying Kṛṣṇa's sister Subhādrā and his brother Baladeva. After seven days Kṛṣṇa returns from his summer house in an equally spectacular procession.

jāgarita sthāna ('waking state')

The first (and lowest) stage of CONSCIOUSNESS according to Vedānta.

Jaimini (*c.* 600 BCE)

A celebrated sage, said to be VYĀSA's disciple. According to tradition he received the Sāmaveda from Vyāsa, which he then taught. He is the author of the Jaimini *sūtras*, also called Mīmāṁsā Sūtras, the basic text of the school of MĪMĀṀSĀ.

Jainism

While claiming prehistoric origins for their first teacher Ṛṣabha (*c.* 30,000 BCE) the Jains acknowledge the last of the 24 Tirthāṅkāras, Mahāvīra (sixth century BCE) to be the historical founder of the form of religion they are following. Jainism does not accept a creator or a saviour god. It holds the universe to be eternal and the task of humans to redeem themselves from entanglement in the material world by strict ascetical practices.

Originally an order of naked ascetics who had no fixed abodes and who lived by what was given to them freely. Jainism developed into a mass religion with lay followers, and became one of the dominant religions of India from the third century BCE onwards. There were famous Jain kingdoms in South India and the Jain leaders enjoyed high prestige. In the first century CE the Jain order split into two groups: Digambara ('heaven-clad', i.e. naked, following the older, stricter tradition) and Śvetāmbara ('white-clad', whose followers wore white dresses, and also made other concessions with regard to asceticism). Jains produced many works of art, were active as scholars in the fields of grammar and lexicography, and established schools and charitable insitutions. By the 13th century the last Jain kingdoms had disappeared and Jains are today a small minority in India, counting only about 2 million followers. Since they are successful in banking and business, they exert considerable influence.

Jamadagni

One of the SAPTARṢIS, author of a Vedic hymn and the subject of stories in epics and Purāṇas.

Jambu-dvīpa
('rose-apple continent')

One of the seven DVĪPAS. It consists of nine parts: Bhārata, Kiṁpuruṣa, Harivarṣa, Īlāvṛta (containing Mount Meru), Ramyakā, Hiraṇmaya, Uttara-Kuru, Bhadrāsva, Ketumāla.

Jana Sangh

Also Bhāratīya Jana Sangh, founded in Bengal in 1950 as 'People's Party of India', in the wake of alleged maltreatment of Hindus in East Pakistan (now Bangladesh), when millions of Hindus fled to India. The founding members were former high-ranking Congress ministers such as Shyamprasad Mookerjea, John Matai and K. C. Neogy. It had a clear anti-Muslim and pro-Hindu orientation. It later merged with other Hindu parties to form the JĀNATĀ Party in 1977.

Janābāī (14th century)

An orphan girl, adopted by a tailor family, she became one of Mahārāṣṭra's most popular composers of *abhaṅgas*, which are recited in *kīrtans* to this day. One of the sons of the family she grew up with was NĀMDEV, who later became one of Mahārāṣṭra's famous poet-saints. Asked by him to help him compose a large number of *abhaṅgas* she excelled in this task. According to legend she was blessed by the company of Viṭhobā, who often came and took his meals with her.

Janaka

Major figure in the RĀMĀYAṆA, King of Videha. He was the father of Sītā, famous for knowledge and good works.

Jānakī

Patronymic of SĪTĀ, the heroine of the RĀMĀYAṆA.

Jana-loka

The abode of BRAHMĀ.

Janamejaya

The king to whom the *Mahābhārata* was recited by Kṛṣṇa VAIŚAMPĀYANA. He was the great-grandson of ARJUNA, and was also known as Sarpasattrin (serpent-sacrificer). After his father PARIKṢIT died from a snake-bite, Janamejaya was determined to exterminate all snakes in a great sacrifice, but was persuaded by the sage Astika to desist when all snakes but one (Takṣaka) had been burnt.

Jānatā Party

Formed in 1977 from a variety of Hindu parties to succeed Indira Gandhi's Congress government which was defeated in elections after the so-called 'emergency'. It fell apart, largely over the question of connections between some of its leaders and the Rāṣṭrīya Svayamsevak Sangh, and the former JANA SANGH formed the BHĀRATĪYA JĀNATĀ PARTY.

Janar-dana ('giver of rewards')

Epithet of VIṢṆU.

Janardana Swami (1504–75)

Militant sage from Mahārāṣṭra, the teacher of EKANĀṬHA.

janëu

The holy thread which members of the three upper CASTES receive at the time of *upanayana* (initiation) and which they have to wear throughout their lives as a mark of distinction. It is made out of three times three strands of cotton fibre and is worn at all times directly on the body.

japa

Repetition of a sacred name or MANTRA (3), one of the most popular religious practices of Hindus. It is often done with the help of a MĀLĀ, a rosary consisting of beads made from the wood of the TULASĪ plant. It can be performed audibly, inaudibly or mentally. It is supposed to bring about a union of the devotee's mind with God, revealed in the name.

jaṭa

Matted hair, a sign of mourning and of renunciation.

Jaṭa-dhāra ('the one with a crown of matted hair')

An epithet of ŚIVA.

jāta-karma

Ritual performed by a father immediately after the birth of a child, before the severing of the umbilical cord, to guarantee long life and health.

Jaṭāyu

King of the vultures, son of GARUḌA, Viṣṇu's VAHANA. As an ally of RĀMA he attacked RĀVAṆA, when he carried away Sītā. Although mortally wounded, he was able to tell Rāma about the incident. Rāma and LAKṢMANA performed his funeral rites and he rose to heaven in a chariot of fire.

jātī ('birth-group')

Lineage, sub-caste. Each *jātī* consists of a number of *gotras* (clans).

jauhar

Group self-immolation in a fire, practised by Rājput women to escape capture by enemies. Several historical instances have been recorded at Chitor from the 14th to the 16th centuries.

Jayadeva (12th century)

Pen name of the author of the *Gītagovinda*, celebrating the love between Kṛṣṇa and RĀDHĀ, which is sung at the JAGANNĀṬHA temple in Purī as part of the daily ritual.

Jayantī

One of the names of the Goddess (DEVĪ).

Jaya-Vijaya ('victory and defeat')

Names of the two gatekeepers in Viṣṇu's heaven.

Jha, Ganganatha
(1871–1941)

Eminent Indian Sanskritist, educated both in the old Pandit tradition and along modern lines, a specialist in Pūrva MĪMĀṀSA. He taught at Muir Central College in Allahābad, served as principal of Benares Sanskrit College and was vice-chancellor of Allahābad University. He translated many major Sanskrit works into English: *Śabarabhāṣya, Ślokavārttika, Tantravārttika*, and his books include *Prabhākara School of Pūrva Mīmāṁsa* (1909), *Pūrva Mīmāṁsa in its Sources* (1942). He was honoured with the title 'Mahāmahopādhyāya' (great teacher).

Jiṣṇu ('victorious')

Epithet of INDRA, ARJUNA and VIṢṆU.

jīva, jīvātma

Individual (finite) living being.

jīvan-mukta
('liberated while alive')

A person who has achieved ultimate emancipation while still in a body.

jīvan-mukti

The state of being liberated while still in a body. Some Hindu schools, such as ADVAITA VEDĀNTA, admit such a possibility, others deny it.

jñāna ('knowledge')

This is especially in the specific sense of spiritual wisdom, insight, realization of one's own true nature. (*See also* VIDYĀ.)

(Jñāna) Sambandhar
(*c.* 750–825 CE)

One of the most prominent NĀYANMĀRS, Śaivite teachers of South India. Author of the *Tevaram*, which ridicules and attacks Jainas.

Jñāneśvara, also **Jñānadeva**
(*c.* 1275–1350)

Poet-saint from Mahārāṣṭra, author of the *Jñāneśvari*, a lengthy commentary on the *Bhagavadgītā*.

joint family

The traditional Hindu family consisted of groups of related families belonging to several generations. It provided security and shelter to all its members and created a strong bond between them. It allowed for little privacy and did not leave much room for individual decisions concerning vital issues. While it is still to be found in rural India, in the Westernized large cities of India the norm today is the nuclear family.

Jones, Sir William (1746–94)

Orientalist and jurist. He studied Oriental languages at Oxford. Appointed judge at the Supreme Court in Calcutta in 1783, he founded Bengal Asiatick Society in 1784 (and remained its president till 1794). He studied Sanskrit, and produced the first translations into English of Kālidāsa's *Śakuntalā, Manusmṛti, Hitopadeśa, Gītagovinda.*

justice

See DHARMA.

Jyeṣṭhā

South Indian goddess, identified with Sītalā, the goddess of smallpox.

jyotir-liṅga ('*liṅga* made of light')

Twelve LIṄGAS (3) in famous places of pilgrimage (e.g. Kedarnāṭh in the Himālayas), said to have come into existence without human agency, manifesting special potency. (*See also* SVAYAMBHŪ.)

jyotiṣa

See ASTROLOGY.

jyotiṣṭoma

A special Vedic SACRIFICE for the deceased.

K

Kabīr (1440–1518)

Famous poet-saint, composer of many hymns used by Hindus, Sikhs and Muslims, author of the *Bijak* and founder of the non-sectarian Kabīr-Panth.

Kādambarī (1)

Daughter of Chitraratha, king of the GANDHARVAS (1) and one of the sixteen sons of KAŚYAPA and Madirā (also called Vāruṅī, the goddess of wine).

Kādambarī (2)

Title of a Sanskrit prose work by Bāna (seventh century CE).

Kaikeyī

A princess of the Kaikeya nation, a major figure in the RĀMĀYAṄA, one of the three wives of Daśaratha, and mother of BHARATA (3). When she nursed Daśaratha back to life after he was severely wounded in a battle, he promised to grant her any two wishes. Prompted by her maid-servant Mantharā, and fearing that Daśaratha's eldest son, Rāma, would kill his rivals, she used this promise to prevent Rāma from ascending the throne, and to send him into a 14-year forest exile.

Kailāsa

Mountain in the Himālayas, Śiva's heaven.

kaivalya ('aloneness')

The ultimate aim of PATAÑJALA YOGA.

Kāla ('time')

A name of YAMA, the king of the dead. (*See also* TIME.)

Kalahasti

Famous Śiva temple in Andhra Pradesh, connected with the story of how an elephant, a spider and a snake gained salvation by worshipping a Śiva LIṄGA (3).

Kālarātrī ('black night')

One of the names and forms of the Goddess (DEVĪ).

Kālī (1) ('the black one')

In the Vedas the name was associated with AGNI, who was represented as having seven tongues to devour butter: *kālī* was his black or terrible tongue.

Kālī (2) ('black [Goddess]')

The fierce aspect of DEVĪ, associated with disease, death and terror. She is usually represented by a black image, with a red tongue protruding from the mouth and a garland of skulls around the neck. In former times she was placated with human SACRIFICES; today she is honoured by the sacrifice of goats, which are decapitated. Kālī and DURGĀ

The ancient image of Kālī being worshipped in the famous Kālī temple in Calcutta.

are treated as synonymous. The main festivity focusing on Kālī–Durgā is Kālī/Durgāpūjā. The major feat associated with her is the killing of the buffalo demon Mahiṣāsura.

Kali Yuga ('age of strife')

The last and worst of the four ages of the world, the one in which we find ourselves at present. It began in 3102 BCE (with the *Mahābhārata* war) and is to last a total of 432,000 years.

Kālidāsa (fifth century CE) ('servant of Kālī')

The greatest of India's classical Sanskrit poets and dramatists, one of the 'nine gems' at the court of King Vikramāditya at Ujjaini. His most famous drama is *Śakuntalā*, one of the first Sanskrit plays translated into English (by H. H. WILSON).

Kālikā Pīṭha

A special place of worship of the Goddess, associated with a limb of the Goddess after she took her life and was dismembered by Śiva. There are 51 such Kālikā or Śakti Pīṭhas in India, the most famous at KĀMĀKHYĀ in Assam.

Kālikā Purāṇa

One of the *Upapurāṇas*, dealing with the Goddess (DEVĪ), differentiating her worship according to the various parts of her body.

Kāliya, also Kāliya nāga

A serpent king possessing five heads, (although he is also described as 'the thousand-headed') who lived in the Yamunā near VṚNDĀVANA together with his retinue. He emitted smoke and poisonous fumes, endangering the entire region of Braja. Kṛṣṇa jumped into the water, danced on Kāliya's heads and threatened to kill him. Kāliya begged for mercy, and was allowed to live, on condition that he move further downstream. The place where this event occurred is marked in Vṛndāvana by a little temple with a sculpture depicting the scene.

Kalki ('the white horse')

The future and last AVATĀRA of Viṣṇu, which will come finally to conquer evil and to save the good at the end of the KALI YUGA.

Kalki Purāṇa

One of the *Upapurāṅas*, describing the (future) KALKI AVATĀRA and events associated with his appearance.

kalpa

A day and night of BRAHMAN, comprising 4,320,000,000 years. Each *kalpa* consists of four *yugas*. (*See also* TIME, DIVISIONS OF.)

Kalpa-sūtra

One of the VEDĀṄGAS, dealing with ritual.

Kāma, also Kāmadeva

The god of love. The *Ṛgveda* states that desire was the first emotion that stirred in the One. According to one tradition, Kāma is the son of Dharma and Śraddhā. He is also sometimes called Aja (unborn). In the Purāṅas he plays a major role: angering Śiva during his meditation, he was burned to ashes by his gaze. When Śiva realized that the whole world was withering away, he resurrected him. His wife is Ratī (lust). He is usually represented as a young man with bow and arrows made of flowers, riding on a parrot, attended by APSARAS. He has many names.

Kāmadhenu also Kāmaduh ('wish-fulfilling cow')

A cow belonging to the sage VAŚIṢṬHA. She emerged from the CHURNING OF THE OCEAN, and granted every wish presented to her. She is also known as Śavalā, Surabhī or Nandinī.

Kāmākhyā

The most famous of the Śakti PĪṬHAS, near Guhāvatī in Assam, where according to tradition SĀTĪ's YONI fell; it is worshipped there in the form of a cleft rock. In former times many human SACRIFICES were offered to her. Self-immolation by self-decapitation was also practised by some devotees.

Kāmakothi Pīṭha

According to a local tradition the place of burial of ŚAṄKARA (2) and the seat of the Śaṅkarācārya in KAÑCĪ-PURA, whose foundation as one of the original Śaṅkara MAṬHAS is however disputed.

Kāma-rūpā

North-eastern Bengal and western Assam.

Kāmeśvarī ('Mistress of Kāma')

A title of the goddess KĀMĀKHYĀ, whose temple is in Kāmākhyā.

Kaṁśa, also Kaṅśa

Tyrant of MATHURĀ, and a cousin of Devakī, Kṛṣṇa's mother. It was prophesied to him that a son born to Devakī would kill him; so he confined Devakī to a prison, taking away all the children she bore and killing them. Her husband, Vasudeva, was not imprisoned and apparently was free to visit her in prison. Baladeva, her seventh, was smuggled out from prison and taken to Gokula. When Kṛṣṇa was born his parents fled with him and he grew up with his foster mother, Yaśodā. Kaṁśa gave orders to kill all young male infants. Later Kṛṣṇa conquered Mathurā and killed Kaṁśa.

Kaṅāḍa (sixth century BCE?)

The founder of the VAIŚEṢIKA *darśana.*

Kāñcī-pura ('the golden city')

City in Tamiḷnādū, 50 km north-west of Madras. It is one of the seven ancient holy cities of India. It was the capital city of the PALLAVAS and later of the COLAS, who lavished their wealth on it. It is sacred to both Viṣṇu (Viṣṇukāñcī) and Śiva (Śivakāñcī) and boasts over a hundred large temples, some of them going back to the ninth century. An abundance of sculptures and paintings illustrate myths associated with Viṣṇu and Śiva. It is also the seat of one of the Śaṅkarācāryas (KĀMAKOTHI PĪṬHA) and a centre of traditional Hindu learning.

Kane, Pandurang Vaman (1880–1971)

One of the most knowledgeable scholars in the area of Hindu law. He was an advocate at the Bombay High Court,

National Research professor of Sanskrit, editor of many Sanskrit works and author of the multi-volume *History of Dharmaśāstra* (1930–75).

Kangri

Place of pilgrimage near Hṛṣikeśa in the Himālayas; site of an ĀRYA SAMĀJ GURUKULA, now Kangri Forest University, a residential traditional Hindu school with Sanskrit as medium of instruction.

Kāṇphata ('hole in the ear')

A sect of Śaiva ascetics whose ears are pierced with a two-edged knife as part of the initiation ceremonies.

Kanyākumārī ('virgin lady')

Epithet of the Goddess (DEVĪ) and name of the southernmost point of India, a place of pilgrimage with a large Goddess temple.

Kapālika ('skull-carrier')

A sect of Śaivites who wear garlands of skulls, from which they also eat and drink.

Kapila (sixth century BCE)

A famous sage, founder of the SĀṀKHYA system.

karma ('action') (1)

In the Veda and Pūrva MĪMĀṀSĀ, a ritual act, SACRIFICE.

karma (2)

In the Upaniṣads and in Vedānta, nonmaterial residue of any action performed by a person, the cause of embodiment and of SAṀSĀRA. Virtually all Hindu schools have developed their own *karma* theories. Some elements are fairly commonly agreed upon, such as the derivation of the word *karma* from the root *kṛ-* to act, and the incompatibility of *karma* and LIBERATION (*mukti*, *mokṣa*). The notion first occurs in the Upaniṣads where *karma* is seen as responsible for enmeshing a living being in the cycle of birth and rebirth. Attainment of VIDYĀ, or *jñāna* (knowledge) is considered the only means to gain liberation from *saṁsāra*. In addition to the *karma* one accumulates from one's own actions in the present life, there is *prārabdha karma* with which a person is born and which has to run its course. The *Bhagavadgītā* teaches that actions performed without selfish desire do not yield *karma*. In the Purāṇas the intervention of God absolves devotees from having to suffer from their *karma* and God's grace nullifies *karma*. On a popular level many Hindus are inclined to attribute everything that happens to them, fortune as well as misfortune, to their *karma*.

karma-mārga ('path of works')

One of the three traditional ways to find spiritual fulfilment. *Karma* in that context means (prescribed) Vedic ritual actions, such as sacrificing an animal or some other object in fire, undergoing the *saṁskāras* (rites of passage), maintaining the routine of prescribed daily, monthly and yearly rituals and performing the ceremonies required in connection with certain events in one's life. In later times a more metaphorical interpretation was adopted. Ritual usually meant ceremonies performed to honour the presence of God in an IMAGE and the 'path of works' was understood to mean selfless and dedicated performance to one's (CASTE) duties.

Karṇa

Son of KUNTĪ by the Sun, before her marriage to PĀṆḌU. Born equipped with arms and armour, he was exposed by his mother on the banks of the Yamunā and found by Nandana, the charioteer of DHṚTARĀṢṬRA, who brought him up as his own child. Later Karṇa became king of Anga (Bengal). In the Great War he fought at the side of the KAURAVAS and was killed by ARJUNA, who only then found out that Karṇa was the half-brother of the PĀṆḌAVAS. (*See also* MAHĀBHĀRATA.)

Karpatriji Maharaj (1898–1973)

VAIṢṆAVA ascetic, founder of the Rāmarājya Pariṣad, a Hindu political party with a nationalist agenda.

Kārṣṇa, also Kārṣṇajinī

A sage, reputed author of a lost BRAHMA-SŪTRA.

Kārtavīrya

Son of Kṛtavīrya, patronymic of ARJUNA.

Kārttikeya, the god of war, son of Śiva and Pārvatī.

Kārttikeya

God of war, the planet Mars, also known as MURUGAN and Skanda. Son of Śiva, in some traditions born without a mother. He is represented as having six heads, riding on a peacock, holding a bow in one hand and an arrow in the other. His wife is Kaumarī or Senā. He is also called Senāpati (lord of the army, or husband of Senā), Siddhasena, Kumāra. In South India he is known as Subrahmaṇia.

Karve, Dhonde Keshav (1858–1962)

Professor of Sanskrit in Poona, social reformer, founder of the Widow Marriage Association, and of the Women's University in Poona.

kārya ('condition of bondage')

A knowledge of this is essential to gain LIBERATION, according to the PĀŚUPATAS.

Kashmir Śaivism

An important school of philosophical Śaivism, which flourished from the 8th to the 12th centuries in Kashmir. Also known as Śiva Advaita, Tṛka, Spaṇḍa-śāstra, Pratyābhijñā. Its most important representative was Abhinavagupta (*c.* 1100), whose main work is known as *Tantrālokā*. Its designation as 'Śiva Advaita' reflects its doctrine that all reality is undivided Śiva; it is called Spaṇḍaśāstra (vibration) because it teaches that every atom in the universe is constantly oscillating; it is known as Pratyābhijñā (recognition) because it holds that Śiva is mirrored in the soul and that recognizing his image brings about LIBERATION. There are few teachers of this tradition left. Its best-known contemporary representative was Pandit Lakṣman Joo.

Kāśī

See VĀRĀṆASĪ.

Kāśīkhaṇḍa

Part of the *Skanda Purāṇa*, giving a detailed description of Śiva temples in and around VĀRĀṆASĪ.

Kaśyapa ('tortoise')

One of the seven Vedic ṚṢIS who married Aditi and twelve other daughters of DAKṢA. He is the father of Indra as well as of Vivasvat, whose son was MANU (2). He is also believed to be the forefather of *nāgas* (serpents), demons, birds, reptiles, and all kinds of living things. He is often called PRAJĀPATI, progenitor.

Kaṭha Upaniṣad

One of the principal UPANIṢADS, famous for its teaching that liberating knowledge cannot be earned or acquired, but is freely given by the Supreme to the 'elect'.

Kathā-sarit-sāgara

('ocean of rivers of stories')

A very large collection of tales by Somadeva Bhaṭṭa of Kashmir (early 12th century).

Kātyāyana (fourth century BCE?)

Famous grammarian, author of *Vārttika*, which provides supplementary rules to PĀṆINI's *Aṣṭādhyayī*. He is also the author of the Kātyāyana *Śrauta Sūtras*.

Kaula

The highest rank in TANTRA (2), a practitioner of the *Kula-ācāra*, one who has overcome all inhibitions based on conventional distinctions.

Kaundiṇya

An ancient sage and grammarian. He was saved from the anger of Śiva, whom he had offended, by Viṣṇu's intervention and was then known as Viṣṇugupta, 'protected by Viṣṇu'.

kaupina

A piece of cloth covering the private parts, tied around the initiate by his GURU as part of DĪKṢĀ.

Kauravas

Descendants of Kuru. Kuru was the son of Saṁvara and Taptī. The Kauravas were the sons of DHṚTARĀṢṬRA and opponents of the PĀṆḌAVAS in the Great War. (*See also* MAHĀBHĀRATA.)

Kauśalya

('belonging to the Kośala clan')

A patronymic of several famous women such as the mothers of JANAMEJAYA, RĀMA, DHṚTARĀṢṬRA and PĀṆḌU.

Kauśītakī (1)

A branch of the ṚGVEDA.

Kauśītakī (2)

A BRĀHMAṆA, an ĀRAṆYAKA and an UPANIṢAD.

Kaustubha

A famous jewel obtained by the gods from the CHURNING OF THE OCEAN and worn on the chest by Viṣṇu or Kṛṣṇa.

Kauṭilya

See CĀṆAKYA.

Kautsa

Author of *Nirukta*, an early etymological lexicon of obscure words in the Veda, one of the VEDĀṄGAS. He considered the Vedas as meaningless and the *Brāhmaṇas* wrong.

Kauverī

Major river in South India on whose banks are many famous holy places. The temple city of ŚRĪRAṄGAM is located on an island in the Kauverī.

kavi (1)

'poet', 'sage'

kavi (2)

The colour of the garment worn by SAMNYĀSIS (ochre orange, saffron).

Kedar(a)-nāṭh(a) (1)

A name of ŚIVA.

Kedar(a)-nāṭh(a) (2)

A place of pilgrimage in the Himālayas, location of one of the twelve JYOTIRLIṆGAS.

Kena Upaniṣad

One of the major Upaniṣads, beginning with the word *kena* (by whom?).

Keśava Miśra (14th century)

Author of the *Tarkabhāṣa*, a popular introductory text to NYĀYA.

Keśī (1)

In the *Mahābhārata*, a demon slain by Indra.

Keśī (2)

In the Purāṅas: a DAITYA who appeared in the form of a horse, and attempted to kill Kṛṣṇa. Kṛṣṇa pulled his jaws asunder and killed him.

khadi

Homespun and homewoven cotton cloth, whose production was encouraged by Mahatma GANDHI to provide work for villagers who had lost their traditional occupations through the importation of foreign, machine-produced textiles. Wearing *khadi* became obligatory for members of the Indian Congress Party to show their solidarity with the people. Gandhi himself took to spinning yarn and promoted it among his fellow party members.

Khajurāho

Former capital city of the Chandella kings (*c.* 650–1150 CE), in Bundelkhand, today's Madhya Pradesh, famous for a group of 85 temples, built between 950 and 1100 CE, which are amongst the finest examples of North Indian temple architecture, such as the Kaṇḍarīya Mahādeo (Śiva) temple. Some of these, such as the Devī Jagadambi (mother of the universe) temple, are profusely decorated with erotic sculptures, probably connected with tantric practices. Most of the temples are dedicated to the major gods of Hinduism, but there are also Jain temples and temples in honour of lesser deities.

kingship

For most of its history India consisted of a number of kingdoms (*rājya*) ruled by hereditary monarchs. Thus the notion of kingship is very important and a major issue in Hindu literature. Hindu tradition has it that in the beginning people were virtuous and followed the DHARMA spontaneously. When they began cheating and exploiting each other, it became necessary to introduce punishment, the main function of the king. The *Mahābhārata* has a long section called *rājadharma* which lays out the duties and rights of a king in classical times. The king's duties comprised protection of the country, the safety of its citizens, support for the socially weak and for scholars. The *Kauṭilīya Ārthaśāstra* describes in great detail the actual administration of an ancient

Indian kingdom. There also was a gradation among kings: a 'great king' (mahārāja or rājādirāja) usually had several lesser kings (rājas) as vassals. (*See also* CĀṆAKYA.)

kinnaras, also **kimpurusas** ('what men?')

Mythical beings with human bodies and horses' heads, celestial musicians and dancers, who live in KUBERA's paradise.

kīrtaṇa

Praising, singing, usually in the context of religious worship, mainly of Viṣṇu–Kṛṣṇa.

kleśa ('affliction')

Used generally and also specifically in the YOGA SŪTRAS to identify the motive for seeking LIBERATION.

knowledge

See JÑĀNA; VIDYĀ.

Koil Olugu ('temple history')

Tamil chronicle of ŚRĪRAṄGAM, describing the vicissitudes of that famous temple since the Middle Ages. It is an important source for the history of ŚRĪVAIṢṆAVISM.

Konārka

Also known as the 'Black Pagoda', a 13th-century Sun temple on the shores of the Bay of Bengal, in Orissa, famous for its architecture (it is conceived as the gigantic chariot of the sun, drawn by seven horses) and its erotic sculpture, probably connected with tantric cults.

Kosambi, Damodar Dharmanand (1907–66)

Mathematician, author of works on early Indian history, editor of BHARTṚHARI's *Śatakatraya*.

Kotai

See ANṬĀL.

krama-pāṭha

A special way of reading the Veda, in which every word is read twice, first combined with the preceding word, and then with the following.

Kramrisch, Stella (1898–1996)

Austrian-born scholar specializing in Indian art and architecture, author of *The Hindu Temple* (1949), and of many groundbreaking essays: *The Presence of Śiva* (1981), for many years curator of the Museum for Indian art in Philadelphia. She influenced a whole generation of Indian art historians.

Krishna Prem (1898–1965)

Born Ronald Nixon in Britain, he was initiated as a Vaiṣṇava VAIRĀGI and lived and taught at a small ashram in Almora. He wrote several popular books on Vaiṣṇavism and became well known in India.

Krishnamurti, Jiddu (1895–1990)

Educated at ADYAR by Annie BESANT, who expected him to be the AVATĀRA of the 20th century, he dissociated himself from the Theosophical Society and became a popular speaker and writer on spirituality in his own right, claiming not to follow any system. Among his works are *Immortal Friend*, *Life, the Goal* and *The Awakening of Intelligence*.

kriyā ('[ritual] action')

Personified as a child of Dharma.

krodha ('anger')

One of the three 'gates to hell', i.e. propensities that have to be overcome if one is to lead a religious life, personified as child of Adharma. (*See also* LOBHA, MOHA.)

kṛpā ('grace', 'pity', 'compassion')

A key term in VAIṢṆAVISM where God's grace is the only saving agent.

Women worshipping Kṛṣṇa.

Kṛṣṇa ('black')

The most popular (eighth) AVATĀRA of VIṢṆU, the subject of major Hindu classics such as the *Bhagavadgītā* and the *Bhāgavatapurāṇa*. He is also called Śyāma. For many of his worshippers he is the (only) full manifestation of Viṣṇu. Traditional history places him at around 3000 BCE and considers him the ruler of Dvāraka on the Arabian Sea. He was a descendant of the YĀDAVA race, an old pastoral tribe living on the Yamunā around VṚNDĀVANA on the western bank, and around Gokula on the eastern. When he was born, KAMŚA had usurped rulership of Mathurā; Kṛṣṇa later killed him. The many exploits of Kṛṣṇa, as narrated in VAIṢṆAVA scriptures, are celebrated in many feasts, especially in VṚNDĀVANA, and have inspired numerous poets, musicians, choreographers, painters and sculptors.

Kṛṣṇā

Personal name of DRAUPADĪ.

Kṛṣṇa Dvaipāyana

See VYĀSA.

kṛṣṇa-pakṣa ('the dark part [of the lunar month]')

The period from the day after full moon to new moon. Indian dating, especially of feasts, always includes such markers. (*See also* ŚUKLA PAKṢA.)

Kṛta Yuga

The first age of the world, also called Satya Yuga, the golden age, when people were virtuous and lived long lives. It lasted for 1,728,000 years.

Kṛttikās

The Pleiades; personified as the six nurses of KĀRTTIKEYA.

kṣamā ('forgiveness')

One of the main virtues of Hindu ETHICS.

Kṣatriya

Member of the second VARṆA, a warrior or administrator.

kṣetra ('field')

Metaphorically used (in the *Bhagavadgītā*) to designate the body.

Kṣirasāgara ('ocean of sweet milk')

One of the oceans separating the DVIPĀS.

Kubera, also **Kuvera**

God of wealth and presiding deity of the north, king of YAKṢAS and KINNARAS. Represented as a deformed dwarf, with three legs, eight teeth and one eye.

Kumāra ('boy', 'prince')

A name of KĀRTTIKEYA.

Kumāra Sambhava ('Birth of the war-god')

Celebrated poem by KĀLIDĀSA.

Kumāras

The four mind-born sons of Brahmā: Sanatkumāra, Sananda, Sanaka, Sanātana. Sometimes Ṛbhu is added as a fifth. They refused to procreate.

Kumārī ('virgin')

A name of the Goddess (DEVĪ).

Kumārila Bhaṭṭa (*c.* 650–725 CE)

Famous exponent of Pūrva MĪMĀṀSĀ, author of the *Ślokavārttika* and the *Tuptīka*, a gloss on the *Mīmāṁsāsūtra*; a staunch opponent of Buddhism.

Kumbha-mela

Major religious gathering (*mela*) when the sun stands in Aquarius (*kumbha*). It takes place every three years and rotates between the holy cities of Hardwar, Prāyāga, Ujjainī and Nasik. It is an occasion for many members of all Hindu SAṀPRADĀYAS to gather and decide on controversial matters or to introduce changes in their routine.

kuṇḍalinī

In TANTRA (2), the energy (*śakti*) of a person conceived of as a snake wrapped around the base of the spine, whose awakening and movement through the CAKRAS brings about bliss and LIBERATION.

Kuntī

She is also called Pṛthā and Pārsnī. One of the wives of Pāṇḍu, mother of YUDHIṢṬHIRA, BHĪMA and ARJUNA.

Kuppuswami, Sethurama Sastri (1880–1943)

'Mahāmahopadhyāya' (great teacher), outstanding Hindu scholar. He was professor of Sanskrit at Madras Sanskrit College, editor of many important texts and collections, founder of the Oriental Research Institute at the University of Madras, originator of *New Catalogus Catalogorum*, founder of *Journal of Oriental Research*, and a recipient of many academic and civic honours. In 1944 a Sanskrit research institute was founded in Madras (Cennai) and named after him.

Kureśa (11th century)

Faithful disciple of RĀMĀNUJA. He stood in for Rāmānuja and underwent interrogation by a hostile Śaivite king, who had his eyes plucked out for not acknowledging Śiva as the greatest god. Rāmānuja's tears miraculously brought back his eyesight.

kūrma ('tortoise')

One of the forms in which Viṣṇu appeared as an AVATĀRA. The tortoise also served as foundation for Mount Maṇḍara which was used as a churning stick when the gods and demons churned the milk ocean. (*See also* CHURNING OF THE OCEAN.)

Kūrma Purāṇa

One of the *Mahāpurāṇas*, dealing mainly with ŚIVA.

Kurukṣetra ('the field of the Kurus')

A plain near Delhi where the MAHĀBHĀRATA war took place.

Kuśa ('happy')

The elder of the twin sons of Rāma and Sītā, brought up by VĀLMĪKI, who taught him to recite the RĀMĀYAṆA. He was made king of Kuśāvatī, and later of Ayodhyā.

kuśa

A variety of grass considered indispensable in many religious ceremonies.

Kuśānas

A dynasty of rulers of Scythian descent whose capital was MATHURĀ (first to second centuries CE). The sculpture produced under their patronage has a certain heaviness.

Kutsa

A Vedic ṚṢI and author of several hymns.

L

lakṣaṇa ('mark', 'characteristic')
In logic, implication.

Lakṣmaṇa
Son of King DAŚARATHA by his wife Sumitrā, twin brother of ŚATRUGHNA and half-brother of RĀMA. He married Ūrmilā, sister of Sītā. He was very attached to Rāma and Sītā and accompanied them on their 14-year forest exile. He is seen as ideal of brotherly love and loyalty. (*See also* RĀMĀYAṆA.)

Lakṣmī, also **Śrī, Tiru**
('good fortune')
Personified as the goddess of fortune, wife of Viṣṇu and mother of KĀMA. She sprang fully developed from the sea at the time of the CHURNING OF THE OCEAN with a lotus in her hand. She is represented as having four arms.

Lakulin, also **Lakuliṣa**
(second century CE)
Legendary founder of the PĀŚUPATA system, a school of Śaivism.

Lalla, or **Lal Ded** (14th century)
A Śaivite woman poet and spiritual teacher from Kāshmīr, whose verses have been published under the title *Lalla-vākyāṇi*. She advocated openness for all schools of thought and religion and rejected ritualism and IMAGE worship. She taught that the way to salvation was the disinterested performance of one's duties.

language
Language was always very important to Hindus, and their greatest cultural achievement is in the area of language. The Veda exhibits great respect for language and treats it as a divine being from which everything originated. The extraordinary care with which the Veda was preserved and transmitted over thousands of years again shows how greatly language was valued. According to Hindu tradition Sanskrit, their sacred language, the 'language of the gods', is eternal. In the course of time Hindus developed a variety of theories concerning the nature of language. One of the early controversies concerned the question whether words (*pāda*) or sentences (*vākya*) were the basic elements of language. The early interest in grammar and etymology, as shown by the VEDĀṄGAS and later scholarly works, again exhibits a religious concern with language. A proper study of language was considered the preliminary to all other disciplines. Cultivation of language skills was always considered the highest aim of education.

Lava

The younger of the twin sons of Rāma and Sītā, later King of Śrāvastī. (*See also* RĀMĀYAṆA.)

liberation (*mokṣa, mukti*)

With the acceptance of the notions of SAṀSĀRA and rebirth, the major preoccupation of Hindus became liberation from the cycle of birth and death. The Upaniṣads call the Vedas 'unsafe boats' because they are unable to carry one to 'the other shore'. The Vedānta and most other systems are primarily concerned with teaching paths to liberation from rebirth. They agree on the necessity to neutralize KARMA (2) and to detach oneself from desire. They differ in the roles ascribed respectively to ritual (*karma*), devotion (BHAKTI) and insight (JÑĀNA). They also disagree on the possibility of reaching liberation while still in a body (*jīvanmukta*) and on the condition of the liberated (*mukta*): while ŚAṄKARA (2) teaches complete loss of individuality in the merging of the liberated with BRAHMAN, RĀMĀNUJA and other theistic Vedāntins speak about an eternal individual existence in the company of the highest God.

life (*ayus*)

Hindus have always considered life as one, making distinctions in degrees only between the various forms of life. Rebirth could take place in any form of life: plant, animal, human or divine. Human life was always considered special as the only form of life in which LIBERATION from rebirth could be gained. As regards the Hindu attitude towards life, there were two contrary opinons: the one, represented by Kṛṣṇa in the *Bhagavadgītā*, devalues physical life as just a garment of the spiritual soul, which can be changed at will. The other, considering *ahiṁsā* (not killing) as the highest duty, would take great care of life in all its forms and consider it sacred. The Hindu life sciences (AYURVEDA) were highly developed and had as their aim the preservation and prolongation of life.

light

the many terms used for light (*jyotis, prabhā, prakāśa, pratibhā, dīpti, kānti, śobhā* etc.) and the appellation of the highest experience as 'enlightenment' indicate the great importance that light and everything connected with it have in Hindu thought. One of the oldest and best-known Vedic prayers asks to be led 'from darkness to light' and the obligatory GĀYATRĪ mantra asks the SUN to illumine the mind. Not only was Sūrya widely worshipped (sun temples used to be quite frequent in the Middle Ages), but Viṣṇu also has a solar background. All the major gods have names that express light, splendour, brightness (*Prakāśātman*, 'self-luminous'; *Bhāskāra*, 'sunlike', *jyotis*, 'light') and the ultimate condition is described in terms of a light-experience.

līlā ('play', 'sport')

The creation of the world by God is described as *līlā* because it does not serve a purpose for God. Kṛṣṇa's dealing with the GOPĪS, especially RĀDHĀ, is called *līlā*, divine playfulness.

liṅga (1)

('sign', 'characteristic', 'token')

In logic, the predicate of a proposition.

liṅga (2)

The male organ.

liṅga (3)

The aniconic symbol under which Śiva is most often worshipped. The twelve JYOTIR-LIṄGAS are supposed to have come into existence without human intervention.

Liṅga Purāṇa

One of the Śaiva Purāṇas, containing many stories about Śiva LIṄGAS (3).

Liṅgāyat(s)

A sect of Śaivas reformed by Basava (12th century), also called Vīra-śaivas (heroic Śaivas), that insists on each of its members always wearing a small LIṄGA (3) on their body to remind them of their innate Śiva nature. *Liṅgāyats* emphasize the equality of men and women, do not recognize CASTE differences and give great importance to productive work and social responsibility. They bury their dead, instead of cremating them, as most Hindus do. They are found mainly in today's Karṇātaka.

lobha ('greed')

One of the three 'root sins' or 'gates to hell', which must be overcome to achieve LIBERATION. (*See also* KRODHA; MOHA.)

loka ('world', 'universe')

The Vedic TRILOKA ('three worlds') consists of earth, heaven and hell. The Purāṇic universe is subdivided into a great many different *lokas*: the upper regions consist of Satyaloka (the realm of Brahmā), Tapoloka, Janaloka and Maharloka; the middle regions, also called 'regions of the consequences of work', are Svarloka (planets), Bhuvarloka (sky) and Bhuloka (earth). The region of the netherworlds is subdivided into eight *lokas*, below which there are 28 NĀRAKAS (hells) in which sinners receive punishment according to their deeds. Over and above these *lokas* the various *saṁpradāyas* (sects) have their own sectarian cosmologies: for Vaiṣṇavas, Vaikuṇṭha is the supreme heaven of Viṣṇu; for Śaivas, Kailāsa is Śiva's abode; Śāktas believe that Devī resides in MAṆIDVĪPA.

Lokāloka ('world and no world')

The outermost ring of mountains, separating the visible world from the sphere of darkness.

loka-pāla

Guardians of the world; the eight deities that preside over the eight points of the compass: Indra (east); Agni (south-east); Yama (south); Sūrya (south-west), Varuṇa (west); Vāyu (north-west); Kubera (north); Soma (north-east). Each of the LOKAPĀLAS has an elephant who assists in the defence of the respective quarter. Indra's elephant is Airāvata. (*See also* DIG-GAJA.)

loka-saṅgraha ('well-being of the world')

Expression used by Kṛṣṇa in the *Bhagavadgītā* to explain the motivation of his activity in this world.

Lomaharṣaṇa, also Romaharṣaṇa

A pupil of VYĀSA who recited several major Purāṇas to ŚAUNAKA.

Lopā, also Lopāmudrā, Kauśītakī, Varapradā

A girl fashioned by AGASTYA from the most beautiful parts of different animals, so as to have the most desirable wife. She grew up as the daughter of the king of Vidarbha. Before consenting to marry Agastya she demanded great wealth which Agastya finally obtained from the demon Ilvala.

M

Macdonell, Arthur Anthony (1854–1930)

Orientalist and Sanskrit scholar. He was born at Muzaffarpur, he was a Taylorian teacher of German at Oxford University (1880–99), and later Boden Professor of Sanskrit. His works as editor and translator include *Sarvānukramaṇika* of the *Ṛgveda* (1886); a Sanskrit–English Dictionary (1892), *Vedic Mythology* (1897), *History of Sanskrit Literature* (1900), and *Sanskrit Grammar* (1901).

macrocosm–microcosm

The *Ṛgveda* assumes a close correspondence between the universe and the individual person: the *Puruṣasūkta* depicts the creation of everything on earth as the result of the sacrifice of PURUṢA, a human-shaped primeval cosmic being. The Upaniṣads not only equate the human ĀTMAN with the cosmic BRAHMAN, but also categorize human properties and cosmic phenomena in corresponding pentads. SĀṀKHYA YOGA is based on the assumption of a thoroughgoing structural parallelism between human and cosmic realities. The VAIṢṆAVA notion of the universe as the body of God, and Viṣṇu as the soul and immanent ruler of the world, gives concrete expression to the microcosm–macrocosm parallelism. Parallels were also drawn between the various components of the human body and the sacred geography of India: the Gaṅgā (Ganges) was equated with the Īḍā, and the Yamunā with the Piṅgalā of the subtle body. Popular Hindu writings expand these parallelisms vastly and base the process of LIBERATION on it.

mada ('intoxication')

Personified as a monster created by the Vedic sage Cyavana, with fearful teeth and long jaws. Intoxication is forbidden by Hindu ethics, but forms one of the 'five ms' of tantric practices. (*See also* TANTRA (2).)

Mādhava (1) ('made of honey')

Name of KṚṢṆA or VIṢṆU.

Mādhava (2), also **Vidyāraṅya** (14th century)

An important teacher in the ADVAITA VEDĀNTA tradition. Brother of Sāyaṅa, a commentator on the Veda. He was prime minister at the court of VIJĀYANĀGARA before taking SAMNYĀSA and becoming ĀCĀRYA of the Śringerī mātha. He is the author of *Sarvadarśanasaṁgraha*, a critical compendium of all philosophical and religious systems, the *Pañcādaśī*, a manual for the study and practice of Advaita Vedānta, and the *Śaṅkara Digvijāya*, a summary of ŚAṄKARA's (2) victorious disputes with proponents of other doctrines.

Madhu

A demon slain by Kṛṣṇa.

madhurasa ('sweet love')

The highest stage of emotional devotion (*bhāvana bhakti*) in the teaching of GAUḌĪYA VAIṢṆAVISM.

Madhusūdana (1) ('slayer of Madhu')

One of the VYŪHAS of Viṣṇu.

Madhusūdana (2)

An epithet of KṚṢṆA.

Madhusūdana (3) (14th century)

A celebrated teacher of ADVAITA VEDĀNTA, author of the *Khaṅḍanakhaṇḍa Khādya*.

madhu-vidyā ('honey knowledge')

A section in the *Bṛhadāranyaka Upaniṣad* ascribed to Dadhīca, which teaches a particular VIDYĀ.

Madhva, also **Ānanda Tīrtha** (1238–1317)

Born in Udipī, Karṇātaka, founder of the school of DVAITA VEDANTA, hostile to Jains, Buddhists and Advaitins, author of numerous works (commentaries on the *Brahmasūtras*, the *Bhagavadgītā*, portions of the *Ṛgveda*, and independent treatises) in which he tries to prove that ŚRUTI, which for him also includes such works as the *Viṣṇupurāṇa* and *Āgamas*, reveals the dual reality of BRAHMAN and ĀTMAN. Madhva was a staunch VAIṢṆAVA. His teaching is also known as *biṁba-pratibiṁba*, 'image and reflection', suggesting that the *ātman* is a mirror image of God. The way to liberation is self-surrender to Viṣṇu through active love which centres on ritual worship of God's image.

Madhya-deśa ('middle country')

Described in the *Manusmṛti* as the land between the Himālayas and the Vindhya mountains, east of Vināśana and west of Prāyāga. It is also called Āryāvarta, the 'land of the Āryas', and its customs were considered models for proper behaviour.

Mādhyandina ('midday')

An important Vedic school, a branch of the Vajasaneyi *śākhā*, connected with the *Śatapatha Brāhmana*. It developed its own approach to astronomy and derives its name from its making noon the starting-point for calculating planetary movements.

Mādrī

Sister of the King of the Madras and second wife of PĀNDU; her twin sons were Nakula and Sahadeva. She chose to become a SATĪ on the funeral pile of Pāṇḍu.

Madurai

Ancient temple city in South India (Tamilnādū), dominated by the famous MĪNĀKṢĪ temple, dedicated to the 'fish-eyed' Goddess and her consort Sundareśvara. Many classical texts sing the glory of Madurai and millions of pilgrims visit the Mīnākṣī temple every year. The major structures of the present temple were built in the 16th century under the patronage of the Nayyakas, successors to the Pāṇḍyas.

Maga

An ancient people, sun-worshippers, associated with the erection of megalithic monuments in India, in the Veda connected with the ŚAKADVĪPA and often alluded to in the epics and the Purāṇas.

The temple at Madurai.

MAYA, the master architect of the ASURAS, who built mighty palaces and also excelled in magic, is supposed to have belonged to the Magas. They are believed to be the founders of MAGADHA.

Magadha

One of the most ancient kingdoms of northern India, occupying part of modern Bengal, Bihār and Orissa. In the *Ṛgveda* it is associated with the (heretical) VRĀTYAS. Later Vedic literature refers to it as a land where only degraded brahmins live. It became the main staging area for Buddhism and Jainism in the sixth and fifth centuries BCE. King Bimbisāra and his son Ajātaśatru were supporters of Gautama BUDDHA. The capital, Pataliputra (Patna), was the place where the first Buddhist Council was held. Magadha was successively ruled by the Nandas (364–22 BCE), the MAURYAS (322–183 BCE), the Śuṅgas (183–72 BCE) and the Kāṅvas (72–28 BCE). Until about the fifth century CE Magadha remained the cultural heartland of Buddhism. Only with the rise of the imperial GUPTAS did Hinduism reassert itself.

Māgha Melā

A yearly gathering of SĀDHUS at the Triveni in Prāyāga during the month of MĀGHA (January/February).

Mahabalipura

('the city of Mahā-Bali')

A place near Cennai (Madras), famous for its architectural monuments (*rathas* from the seventh century, the large relief of the descent of the Gaṅgā and the shore temple).

Mahā-bhārata

('the great [war of the] Bhāratas')

The longest epic ever written, it constitutes a veritable encyclopedia of Hinduism. Its authorship is ascribed to Kṛṣṇa Dvaipayana or VYĀSA, the 'arranger' of the Vedas. The narrative of the Great War, which provided its title, makes up less than a fifth of the entire work. The rest consists of lengthy stories about the main characters of the work, the Pāṇḍavas and the Kauravas, ethical discourses and descriptions of large parts of northern India. It contains a number of fairly independent philosophical/theological treatises, such as the *Bhagavadgītā*, the *Aṇugītā* and others. It is divided into 18 *parvas* whose names are somewhat indicative of their contents: *Ādiparva* (introductory book); *Sabhāparva* (assembly book); *Vana-* or *Āraṇyaparva* (forest book); *Virāṭaparva* (Virāta's book); *Udyogaparva* (effort book); *Bhīṣmaparva* (Bhīṣma's book); *Droṇaparva* (Droṇa's book); *Śalyaparva* (Śalya's book); *Sauptika-parva* (night book); *Strīparva* (women's book); *Śāntiparva* (peace book); *Anuśāsanaparva* (rule book); *Aśva-*

medhaparva (horse-sacrifice book), *Āśramaparva* (hermitage book); *Mausalaparva* (maces book); *Mahāprasthānikaparva* (great journey book); *Svargārohaṇaparva* (ascent to heaven book).

Mahā-bhāṣya ('great commentary')

A lengthy commentary on PĀṆINĪ's grammar, ascribed to PATAÑJALI, in response to KĀTYĀYANA's critique.

Mahā-deva ('great god')

An epithet of ŚIVA.

Mahadevan, T. M. P. (1911–92?)

Prominent Indian philosopher. He was the founder and director of the Radhakrishnan Institute for Advanced Study in Philosophy at the University of Madras, and the author of numerous books and articles, especially on ADVAITA VEDĀNTA: *Gauḍapada – a study in Early Advaita* (1952), *Ten Saints of India* (1961).

Mahā-devī ('great goddess')

An epithet of PĀRVATĪ.

Mahā-kāla ('great time')

An epithet of ŚIVA, as the destroyer.

mahā-mantra ('the great formula')

Also called the 'mantra of sixteen names', an invocation of Viṣṇu (Hari), whose repetition (JAPA) is considered most effective to win God's grace:

Hare Rāma Hare Rāma
Rāma Rāma Hare Hare
Hare Kṛṣṇa Hare Kṛṣṇa
Kṛṣṇa Kṛṣṇa Hare Hare

Mahā-nārāyaṇa Upaniṣad

A late Upaniṣad belonging to the Black YAJURVEDA, the end portion of the *Taittirīya-Āraṇyaka*, containing many details of the daily observances of Hindus. (*See also* TAITTIRĪYA.)

Mahā-nirvāṇa Tantra

An 18th-century text, which attempts to reform certain aspects of TANTRA (2).

mahant

Supervisor of a temple or monastery.

mahā-pātakas ('great sins')

Offences against the moral and social law that are (in theory) unforgivable, or can be atoned for only by death. The five standard *mahāpātakas* are: *brahmaṇahatya* (killing a brahmin; killing an unborn child or a pregnant woman); *sūrapāna* (taking intoxicating substances); *steya* (major theft of gold); *guruvaṅganagana* ('violating the GURU's bed', also interpreted as incest); *mahāpātakasaṁsarga* (association with great sinners). Some sources add specific *mahāpātakas* for KṢATRIYAS (fleeing from a battlefield or meting out unjust punishment), for VAIŚYAS (using false scales and false weights), and for ŚŪDRAS (selling meat, injuring a brahmin, having intercourse with a brahmin woman, drinking milk from a reddish cow). (*See also* UPA-PĀTAKAS.)

Mahā-pralaya ('great dissolution')

The total annihilation of the material universe at the end of a KALPA. Also called *saṁhāra*, *kṣiti*.

Mahā-purāṇa ('great Purana')

There are eighteen *Mahāpurāṇas*, subdivided into *sāttvika* or Vaiṣṇava (*Viṣṇu, Bhāgavata, Nāradīya, Garuḍa, Padma, Varāha*), *rājasika* or Brahmā (*Brahmā, Brahmāṇḍa, Brahmavasivārta, Mārkaṇḍeya, Bhaviṣya, Vāmana*) and *tāmasika* or Śaiva (*Śiva, Liṅga, Skanda, Agni, Matsya, Kūrma*). Their content is supposed to be circumscribed by 'five topics' (*pañcālakṣana*): *sarga* (creation), *pratisarga* (dissolution), *manvantara* (world periods), *vaṁśa* (genealogies), *vaṁśānucarita* (stories about the deeds of the descendants of the dynasties mentioned). In fact they contain a great amount of additional material on the four aims of life (*puruṣārthas*), especially DHARMA and *mokṣa* (LIBERATION), vows (*vratas*), RITUALS, places of PILGRIMAGE (*tīrthas*) and other matters.

Māhār

Member of a (formerly) OUTCASTE community occupied with cleaning.

Maharsi ('Great Ṛṣi')

Honorific title applied to the mythical PRAJĀPATIS and to historical personalities (e.g. RAMANA MAHARṢI).

mahat ('the great one')

According to SĀṀKHYA the first entity produced from the interaction of PURUṢA (2) and PRAKṚTI (spirit and matter), the origin of everything else in the universe. Also identified with *buddhi*, intellect.

mahātma ('great soul')

Honorific for highly meritorious people, such as Mahatma GANDHI.

māhātmya

A class of writings eulogizing a god, a person, a place or a text.

mahā-vākyas ('great sayings')

Four brief statements considered by some Vedāntins to embody the gist of the Upaniṣads and to convey LIBERATION: *tat tvam asi* ('That you are'), Chāndogya VI, 8, 7; *aham brahmāsmi* ('I am *brahman*'), Bṛhadāraṇyaka I, 4; *ayam ātma brahma* ('This self is *brahman*'), Bṛhadāranyaka II, 5, 19); *prajñānam brahma* ('Wisdom is *brahman*'), Aitareya III, 1, 13). A great deal has been written about these *mahāvākyas* in the context of the exposition of various schools of VEDĀNTA.

Mahā-vīra ('great hero')

Honorific title applied to many personalities in Hinduism, Buddhism and Jainism; epithet of the 24th Tīrthānkara, the founder/reformer of Jainism.

Mahā-yogi ('the great ascetic')

An epithet of ŚIVA.

Mahesh Yogi Maharishi

See INTERNATIONAL TRANSCENDENTAL MEDITATION SOCIETY.

Maheśvara ('the great Lord')

An epithet of ŚIVA.

Mahī-dāsa ('slave of the earth')

A celebrated Vedic ṛṣi (sage), son of the sage Viśāla and Itarā, a Sūdra girl. Neglected by his brahmin father, he was taught by earth (Mahī). He became known as Aitareya (Itarā's son) and is the author of the *Aitareya Brāhmaṇa*, *Āraṇyaka* and *Upaniṣad*.

Mahīpati (1715–90)

Biographer of the saints of Mahārāṣṭra from Dhyandeva onwards in the *Bhaktavijaya* and *Bhaktalīlāmṛta*.

Mahiṣāsura ('buffalo demon')

A mighty demon defeated by the goddess. (*See also* DEVĪ; DURGĀ; KALĪ.)

Mahmud of Ghazni (971–1030)

The first Muslim invader, who undertook major raids into India, defeated

Hindu princes and annexed large areas in north-western India. He is responsible for the destruction of the famous SOMANĀTHA temple in Gujarat and many other Hindu sancturies, which he plundered. His name is a symbol of fanaticism and hostility to Hindus.

Maitreya ('friendly')

A ṛṣi (sage), the son of Kuśarava, a disciple of PARĀŚARA, one of the main interlocutors in the *Viṣṇu* and *Bhāgavata Purāṇas*.

Maitreyī

One of the wives of YAJÑAVĀLKYA, famous for conducting philosophical conversations with her husband. (*See also* GĀRGĪ.)

Maitri

Ancient mystical philosopher, after whom the *Maitri Upaniṣad* was named.

Makara

A large aquatic animal (alligator, crocodile, dolphin?), the VAHANA (vehicle) of VARUṆA, often represented on Hindu temples.

Mākāra ('the five ms')

Requisites for tantric worship (taboos for Hindus generally): *madya* (wine); *māṁsa* (meat); *matsya* (fish); *mudrā* (a particular variety of parched grain); *maithuna* (extramarital sexual intercourse). (*See also* TANTRA (2).)

Māl ('great')

Tamil name for VIṢṆU and KṚṢṆA.

mala ('impurity')

Moral or physical pollution, especially bodily secretions, which makes one unfit for worship.

mālā

A garland, used to honour and decorate the image of a god, or a person; a string of beads, used to recite mantras or names of deities, such a *tulsīmālā*, made of beads from the wood of the TULASĪ plant, employed by many VAIṢṆAVAS to recite the MAHĀMANTRA. *Mālās* usually have a specific number of beads (often 108 or a fraction thereof).

Malaviya, Pandit Mohan (1861–1946)

Founder and first vice-chancellor of Benares Hindu University (1915). He was the co-founder of Hindu Mahāsabhā (1909), a right-wing political party with the aim of establishing a Hindu *rāṣṭra* (rule) in India. He was also editor of *Hindustan Times*.

manana ('reflecting')

The second step in the process of meditation (the first being *śravana* [listening] and the third *nididhyāsana* [contemplation, trance]).

manas ('mind')

Understanding, intelligence. In Indian philosophy *manas* is different from *citta*, *caitanya* (CONCIOUSNESS) and *ātman* (SELF) or *puruṣa* (spirit). *Manas* is the instrument through which sense impressions affect the *ātman*. It is comparable to the scholastic *sensus communis*, the faculty that mediates between the senses and the mind proper.

Manasā, also Manasā devī ('snake-goddess')

The sister of ŚEṢA, the serpent king, she is endowed with special powers to counteract the poison of serpents; also called Viṣaharā, 'destroyer of venom'. She is very popular in South India.

Mānasa, also **Mānasa-sarovara**

A lake in the Himālayas on Mount Kailāsa, believed to be native place of swans who return there every year to breed.

Mānasāra

An ancient treatise on architecture, providing much detail with regard to the building of houses and temples, the making of sculptures and the laying out of towns.

Mānava Dharmā-śāstra

See MANU-SMṚTI.

Mandākinī

The GAṄGĀ, especially the part that flows through KEDARNĀTH (2).

maṇḍala (1) ('circle', 'orb')

One of the ten sections of the *Ṛgveda*.

maṇḍala (2)

Complex geometric design, used in (tantric) rituals, to involve the entire cosmos. It is used in the ground plan of the Hindu temple, which is seen as a miniature cosmos.

maṇḍala (3)

Consecrated enclosed space, or any circular arrangements of religiously meaningful objects, e.g. *Braja-maṅḍala*, the area covered by places reminiscent of Kṛṣṇa around Mathurā–Vṛndāvana; *rasa-maṇḍala*, the circular platform on which the *rasa* dance is performed.

maṅḍala-nṛtya ('round dance')

The dance of the GOPĪS around Kṛṣṇa and Rādhā, as desribed in the *Bhāgavatam*.

Maṇḍana Miśra (eighth century CE)

Celebrated exponent of Purva MĪMĀṀSĀ, whom ŚAṄKARA (2) defeated in a long debate.

Mandara

The mountain that the gods and ASURAS used as stick during their CHURNING OF THE OCEAN. It has been identified with a mountain of that name in Bhāgalpur.

Māndhātṛ

An ancient king after whom the Māndhātṛ period (traditionally set at 2750–2550 BCE) has been named. Some peculiar myths surround him. His father, Yuvanāśva, having been childless for a long time, conceived him after drinking some consecrated water and gave birth to him from his right side. When Māndhātṛ grew up he had three sons as well as fifty daughters, all of whom were married to an old sage called Saubhari, who had assumed a youthful form.

maṇḍira

See TEMPLE.

Māṇḍukya Upaniṣad

One of the principal Upaniṣads, which teaches the four stages of CONSCIOUSNESS and being. Gauḍapada's *Kārikās* (glosses) on it were the seminal text for the development of Śaṅkara's ADVAITA VEDĀNTA.

Maṅgala

The planet Mars, identified with KĀRTTIKEYA, the god of war. Son of Śiva and the earth, he is also called Bhūmiputra (son of the earth) and Lohita (red). Maṅgalavāra (Tuesday) is named after him.

Maṅgalā ('the auspicious one')

An aspect of the Goddess (DEVĪ).

maṅgala ('auspicious', 'benedictory')

Maṅgala-stotra, an introductory verse to major literary works, invoking the blessings of gods and *gurus*, and often summarizing in a few words the intentions of the author.

Maṇidvīpa ('island of gems')

The paradise of the Goddess (DEVĪ). Situated above Brahmāloka, also called Sarvaloka ('all places'), it is described in glowing terms in the *Devī Bhāgavata Purāṇa* as of immense dimensions, consisting of eighteen concentric enclosures, each made of precious metals or gems, filled with precious objects and happy people. The innermost enclosure, made of *navaratna* (nine jewels), contains the seat of the Goddess: she is seated on a throne whose legs are Viṣṇu, Brahmā, Rudra and Maheśvara. She dispenses enlightenment and enjoyment and frees her devotees from the bondage of the world. Maṇidvīpa is described as being of immense dimensions, filled with lakes of nectar, gem-bearing trees, beautiful birds and surrounded by rivers of milk, honey and juices of all sorts. The mountains of the island are made of a variety of gems. All inhabitants enjoy the highest bliss for ever. To come to this place, a person only has to remember Devī seated in Maṇidvīpa at the time of death.

Māṇikkavācakar (*c.* 650–715 CE) ('the ruby-worded')

Born of brahmin parents near Madurai, he was for a time chief minister of the kingdom of Madurai. He became a SAMNYĀSI and one of the greatest of the 63 NĀYAṆMĀRS. He was author of the famous *Tiruvācakam* ('Sacred words'), a collection of Tamil hymns in praise of Śiva, widely used in Tamilnādū, and of the *Tirukovaiar*, describing the love between Śiva and Pārvatī. His IMAGE is worshipped in many South Indian Śiva temples.

Maṇimat

A demon, slain by BHĪMA (2). Followers of MADHVA spread the story that ŚAṄKARA was in fact Maṇimat, the illegitimate son of a widow, dedicated to misleading those destined to remain in SAṀSĀRA.

manomaya ('made of mind')

One of the sheaths of the self. According to Upaniṣadic teaching the self is 'layered', with a variable number of 'sheaths' surrounding the spiritual core, or *ātman* proper. The outermost layer consists of food (*annamaya kośa*), then comes the 'breath sheath' (*prānamaya kośa*), the 'mind sheath' (*manomaya kośa*), enveloping 'understanding' (*vijñānamaya kośa*), which surrounds the spirit–soul (*ātman*). All the 'sheaths' are perishable and subject to change; only the *ātman* (pure CONSCIOUSNESS) is eternal and unchanging. It is the aim of the process of LIBERATION to divest the *ātman* of these enveloping sheaths, through which it is connected with SAṀSARA.

mantra (1)

Vedic hymn, sacred text (if it is metrical and to be recited loudly it is called *ṛk*; if in prose and muttered in a low tone, it is called *yajus*; if intended for chanting it is called *sāman*).

mantra (2)

The Vedic SAṀHITĀS.

mantra (3)

Spell, charm, incantation, powerful formula or word. Part of the initiation ceremony into a *saṁpradāya* consists of transmission of a *mantra* from GURU to disciple, meant to be a personal inner guide, and not to be divulged to anyone else.

Manu (1)

A celebrated personality representing humankind, and ancestor of the human race (a human being is a *manuṣya*, a 'child of Manu').

Manu (2)

Name of each of the 14 progenitors and rulers of humankind presiding over one *manvantara*, a world age lasting 4,320,000 years. The first (who lived over 30 million years ago) was called Manu Svāyambhuva, 'the self-existent'. He is the father of the ten PRAJĀPATIS, progenitors of different races. He also is the reputed author of the *Manusmṛti* as well as a work on ritual. The present Manu is the seventh, called Vaivasvata, 'sun-born', also called Satyavrata. He was saved from the great flood by the intervention of Viṣṇu's fish AVATĀRA. (*See also* FLOOD.)

Manu-smṛti, also Mānava Dharma-śāstra ('Manu's Law')

The most influential of all Hindu codes, ascribed to the first MANU (2) Svāyambhuva. It gives an elevated position to brahmins. Its twelve books deal with creation (I), the sources of DHARMA and the duties of a BRAHMACĀRI (II), the duties of a householder (III and IV), the duties of women and dietary regulations (V), rules concerning vānaprastya (*see* VĀNAPRAṢṬHA) and SAMNYĀSA (VI), the duties of kings (VII), civil and criminal law (VIII), domestic laws (IX), the origin, development and rules of castes (X), general laws of morality, sins and expiation of sins (XI), consequences of good and bad actions, nature of the soul and transmigration, the way to release (XII).

mārga ('road', 'path')

This can be both an ordinary road and a spiritual path. Traditionally Hinduism is divided into the so-called *trimārga* (threefold path): *karmamārga* ('path of works', ritual activity); *jñānamārga* ('path of knowledge', meditation); and *bhaktimārga* ('path of devotion', worship of images).

Mārkaṇḍeya Purāna (eighth century CE?)

One of the Mahāpurāṇas, ascribed to Mārkaṇḍeya, son of Mṛkaṇḍa, who was remarkable for his austerities and his long life (he is also called Dīrghāyus, 'long-lived'). Most of the stories are told by birds knowledgeable in the Vedas. The *Devī-māhātmya* is part of it.

marriage (*vivaha*)

According to tradition, marriage did not exist in the early times. It was introduced by the sage ŚVETAKETU, after an incident involving his mother. Since then it has been of utmost importance to Hindus. Only a married couple was seen as a complete 'unit' for worship and participation in socially relevant acts. *Vivaha* was the most important SAṀSKĀRA (rite of passage), the only one for women. Hindu law recognized eight forms of marriage (including abduction and purchase of the bride), though the preferred mode was always the marriage arranged by the parents of bride and bridegroom. While traditional Hindu law allowed Hindu men to marry up to four wives, most Hindu marriages today are monogamous. The HINDU MARRIAGE ACT (1955 with many later amendments) provides a certain uniformity of procedures and regulations concerning marriage, divorce, children, property etc. Hindu marriage ceremonies are usually conducted by brahmin priests and involve a rich and ancient ritual. According to the *Ṛgveda*

A Hindu wedding taking place in the United Kingdom. The bride is placing a garland around the groom's neck.

the goal of marriage is to enable a man to offer to the gods and to beget a son who will ensure the continuity of the sacrifice. Woman was called 'half of man', and the domestic sacrifices could only be performed by husband and wife jointly. A son, *putra*, is so called because he pulls (*tra*) his parents out of hell (*pu*). He is important not only for the continuation of the family, but also for the spiritual welfare of his parents and ancestors in the world beyond. The last rites can normally only be performed by a male offspring (when no male relative was available, a girl had to be 'made a son' to qualify for this ritual).

In the Middle Ages the marriage of young children became a common custom (consummation being delayed, usually until puberty). Since child mortality was very high, many children were married and widowed several times before puberty. The custom is believed to have had its roots in a Hindu tradition that one should not have an unmarried girl who has reached puberty in the house. Nineteenth century reformers tried to abolish child marriage. Indian civil law prohibits it, and has set the legal age for marriage at 18 for girls and 21 for boys. (*See also* EQUALITY OF WOMEN.)

Maruts

The storm gods, sons of RUDRA, quite prominent in the *Ṛgveda*, friends and allies of Indra. Many legends surround their origin and their name (derived from Indra's injunction *ma rodih*, 'cry not').

mātā, also **mātājī** ('mother')

Honorific for religious women, especially the leaders of religious movements.

maṭha

A hermit's hut, a cell, a religious centre, 'monastery', often combined with a school.

Mathurā

One of the seven ancient holy cities of India, on the right bank of the Yamunā, about 150 km south of Delhi. It is the birthplace of Kṛṣṇa and an important centre of Kṛṣṇa worship for over 2,000 years, with many temples and *maṭhas*. Mathurā was famous for its school of sculptors (some of the most celebrated figures of Buddha came from it) that lasted from about 50 to 1200 CE and is also the site of an important archaeological museum.

matriarchy

There are several accounts in Sanskrit literature of realms ruled by women and matriarchal constitutions of tribes. At present the Nairs of South India provide the best example. Nair is a generic name covering the castes of Menons, Panikkars, Nambiars and others, mainly in today's Kerala. The women own the property, and inheritance is from mother to daughter. Relationship and descent are traced from women. Husbands often do not live with their wives but come only to visit. (*See also* EQUALITY OF WOMEN; WOMEN.)

Mātṛkas, also **Mātṛs** ('mothers')

The divine mothers; the spouses of Viṣṇu, Śiva, Brahmā and other deities. While often a large or an indefinite number of 'mothers' is mentioned, the 'seven mothers' (*saptamātṛkās*) Brahmī, Maheśvarī, Kaumārī, Vaiṣṇavī, Mahendrī, Varāhī and Cāmuṇḍā are often found represented together as a unit in temples.

Matsya ('fish')

The first of Viṣṇu's AVATĀRAS, associated with the salvation of MANU (2) from the Great FLOOD.

Matsya Purāṇa

One of the older Purāṇas, so called because it is said to have been revealed to MANU (2) by the MATSYA AVATĀRA of Viṣṇu, although it is mostly a ŚAIVA work.

Maurya

A royal dynasty founded by Candragupta (in 323 BCE) at Pataliputra (modern Patna) in MAGADHA. Traditionally there were ten Maurya kings whose rule lasted for 137 years. In the *Viṣṇu Purāṇa* the list reads: Candragupta, Bindusāra, Aśokavardhana, Suyaśas, Daśaratha, Sangata, Śāliśūka, Somaśarman, Śaśadharman and Bṛhadratha.

Maya

A DAITYA, considered the chief architect of the ASURAS, the counterpart of VIŚVAKARMAN (2) (architect of the DEVAS). The *Mahābhārata* mentions that he built a palace for the PĀṆḌAVAS. He is reputed to be the author of the *Maya-mata*, an extensive handbook on architecture.

māyā

('deceit', 'fraud', 'illusion', 'deception')

Personified as the bewitching power of VIṢṆU in the form of a beautiful woman at the time of the CHURNING OF THE OCEAN, which deprived the demons of AMṚTA. In Vedānta, especially in ADVAITA, *māyā* comes to mean the universal illusion that veils the minds of humans.

Māyon, also **Māyavan**

('the one who possesses *māyā*')

Tamil names for VIṢṆU.

meat eating

The *Ṛgveda* and later Vedic writings indicate that meat eating (even beef) was common in ancient India, especially in connection with animal SACRIFICES. When Jainism and Buddhism protested against the killing of animals both for ritual and commercial purposes, VEGETARIANISM also became popular in Hinduism, particularly among VAIṢṆAVAS, who ceased to perform animal sacrifices. Beef eating must have ceased long before MANU (2), because the MANU-SMṚTI provides for punishments for killing a COW almost as severe as those for killing a brahmin. Śaivas and Śāktas continue to eat meat, especially goat and chicken, but also buffalo and deer. (*See also* FOOD.)

Medātithi (*c.* 825-900)

Author of a celebrated commentary on the MANU-SMṚTI.

medha ('sacrifice')

This can be an element in words such as *aśvamedha* (horse SACRIFICE), as well as the quality that makes an animal fit for sacrifice (asses and camels, for instance, are unfit for sacrifice, because they lack *medha*).

medicine

Traditional Indian medicine was holistic, i.e. it aimed at restoring a balance between the various components of a person, believed to be disturbed in sickness. Thus the medical treatises by Caraka (*Caraka Saṁhitā*) and Suśruta (*Suśruta Saṁhitā*) contain, besides physiological diagnoses and remedies, instructions concerning the right lifestyle and the attainment of the ultimate goal. Ancient Indian medicine was quite advanced in its surgical procedures, its knowledge of the pharmaceutical properties of plants and its understanding of psychosomatic diseases. (*See also* AYURVEDA.)

meditation

A generic translation of a variety of Indian notions referring to interiorizaton (*manana*, reflecting on a text; *pratyahāra*, withdrawing the senses; *dhyāna*, a trance-like condition; *upāsana*, worshipful meditation on a deity, *samādhī*, contemplation); often Yoga is identified with meditation as such, although it consists of a variety of practices, whose ultimate aim, however, is in-depth meditation (*kaivalya*, understood as a return of the self to its own nature). Hinduism has been associated for ages with meditation, and contemporary GURUS usually establish themselves in the West as teachers of new meditation techniques.

megaliths

These are found in many places in India, and are associated with the MAGAS, who were famous for being able to move huge objects.

Megasthenes (fourth century BCE)

Greek ambassador to the Maurya emperor Candragupta at Pataliputra (Patna), whose book *Indika* remained for many centuries the main source of information in the West about ancient India. The work is known today only from quotes and references in other ancient writers.

melā ('gathering')

Generic designation of all popular festivals, usually with a religious background, such as the KUMBHA-MELĀ.

Melkote

Town in Karṇātaka, to which RĀMĀNUJA fled to avoid the persecutions of the Śaivite COLA king, and which under the HOYŚALA king, whom Rāmānuja converted from JAINISM, became an important centre of ŚRĪVAIṢṆAVISM.

Menā

An APSARA sent by Indra to seduce the sage Viśvāmitra to tempt him to desist from his austerities; she became the mother of ŚAKUNTALĀ.

merit (puṇya)

An important notion in Hinduism: the result of good *karma* and the condition for a good afterlife. Often the *aśva-medha*, the most prestigious of Vedic *yajñas* (SACRIFICES), was used as a measure of merit to be gained from a particular religious act, such as a dip in a sacred river at a particular time, or the giving of a gift to a brahmin.

Meru

The mountain in the centre of the world, on whose top lies SVARGA, Indra's heaven.

Meykaṇḍa(deva) (13th century)

Religious name of Śvetabana, a Śaiva philosopher, author of the *Śivajñana-bodha*, an important source for ŚAIVA SIDDHĀNTA, often commented upon by Tamil authors in later centuries.

milk

Hindus consider COW's milk the perfect FOOD and drink, the most *sattvik* (pure) of all. Milk from a *kapila* (brownish) cow was reserved for brahmins and for worship. Bathing an IMAGE in milk is a particularly solemn form of PŪJĀ. Advanced YOGIS subsist often on milk alone.

Mīmāṁsā ('disquisition')

This usually refers to the short form of Pūrva Mīmāṁsā ('earlier disquisition') over against Uttara Mīmāṁsā ('later disquisition', or Vedānta). It is one of the six orthodox (systems) (*darśanas*), devoted to the exegesis of the *karma-kānda* (the part dealing with ritual) of the Veda, focusing on the injunctions contained in them.

The earliest text is the *Mīmāṁsā Sūtra*, ascribed to JAIMINI. It is a collection of aphorisms analysing the elements of Vedic commands in connection with rituals. The *Mīmāṁsā Sūtras* were extensively commented on by ŚABARA in the so-called *Śābarabhāṣya*, which received many sub-commentaries by later writers such as KUMĀRILA BHAṬṬA and Pārthasārathi Miśra (14th century).

The Mīmāṁsakas held the Veda to be *apauruṣeya*, i.e. not composed by a person, either divine or human, but self-existent and eternal. That gave it supreme authority, and its WORD is the ultimate proof of the truth of a statement. They also insisted that only those portions of the Veda are *śruti* (revealed and therefore authoritative scripture) that contain an injunction; the rest (such as Upaniṣads) are mere eulogy, because they do not prescribe actions to be performed but only describe already existing entities.

In addition to explaining the meaning of certain Vedic injunctions, the Mīmāṁsakas analysed the nature and structure of LANGUAGE. They developed principles of interpretation which found application in the practice of Hindu law up to our own times. (*See also* ŚABDA.)

Mīnākṣī ('the fish-eyed one')

Title of the Goddess (DEVĪ) as worshipped in the main shrine of MADURAI in Tamilnāḍū. There is an ancient belief that fish feed their young by just looking at them; the Goddess is expected to give support to her devotees through her mere glance.

mind

The English word 'mind' is the translation of two Sanskrit terms with very different meanings and connotation in Hindu thought: (1) *manas* (which etymologically is close to Latin *mens* and English 'mind') is classified as the highest among the sense organs, the medieval *sensus communis*; (2) 'higher mind', i.e. spirit, consciousness, is rendered by terms such as *cit*, *caitanya*, *buddhi* etc.

Mīrābāī (1547–1614)

Rājasthani princess, an early and ardent devotee of Kṛṣṇa, she was married into a ŚAKTI-worshipping Rājput household at Chitor. She refused to worship the Goddess (DEVĪ), saying she was wedded to Kṛṣṇa. She was forced to leave Chitor, and fled to VṚNDĀVANA. Reconciled with her husband, she moved back to Chitor, but after his death she was mistreated by her in-laws and left again for Vṛndāvana. According to a local tradition she was absorbed into a Kṛṣṇa image while worshipping there. Her beautiful poems and songs are still recited by Kṛṣṇa BHAKTAS (devotees), and she is one of the favourite saints of northern India. (*See also* ANṬĀL.)

miracle

An essential ingredient especially of popular Hinduism. Apart from the *siddhis* (miraculous powers, e.g. making oneself small like an atom or big like a mountain) ascribed to famous YOGIS (and obtainable through methodic Siddha Yoga) every temple, big and small, boasts of miracles that happened to worshippers, from cures from incurable diseases to manifestations of life by the *mūrtis* (IMAGES), which are reported to have drunk the milk offered to them or to exude healing substances, or to show signs of menses etc. The epics and the Purāṇas, especially the Sthāla Purāṇas are full of stories of miracles and many Hindus also today claim to have witnessed miraculous events, which they report in religious magazines such as *Kalyān*. A contemporary GURU such as SATHYA SAI BABA is credited with miraculous powers: he has brought healing to many and is miraculously producing all kinds of objects, as reported in many books.

Mitākṣarā

A commentary by Vijñāneśvara (*fl.* second half of 11th century CE) on the *Yājñavalkyasmṛti* which enjoyed great authority all over India.

Mithilā

Capital city of Videha, in today's northern Bihār, the country over which King JANAKA ruled.

mithyā ('false', 'unreal')

Description of the visible world from the standpoint of ADVAITA VEDĀNTA: *brahma satyam, jagad mithyā* ('*brahman* is real, the world is false').

Mitra ('friend')

A name of the SUN. In the Vedas Mitra is usually associated with VARUṆA as guardian of morality: Mitra rules the day, and Varuṇa the night.

mleccha ('barbarian')

People who do not speak Sanskrit and do not observe the rules of life of the Āryans; a foreigner, an outcast.

moha ('delusion')

One of the 'three gates to hell', to be avoided by a religious person. (*See also* LOBHA, KRODHA.)

mokṣa

See LIBERATION.

Monier-Williams, Monier (1819–99)

Eminent lexicographer. Born in Bombay, he was the Boden Professor of Sanskrit at Oxford, founder of the Indian Institute at the University of Oxford (1883), compiler of a major Sanskrit dictionary, and the author of several scholarly works and translations.

month

Hindus use a lunar–solar CALENDAR, and their months do not coincide with those used in the Gregorian calendar. The year begins in spring with the month *Caitra* (March–April), followed by *Vaiṣakha* (April–May), *Jyaiṣṭha* (May–June), *Āṣāḍha* (June–July), *Śrāvana* (July–August), *Bhadra* (August–September), *Āśvina* (September– October), *Kārttika* (October–November), *Mārgaśīrṣa* (November–December), *Pauṣa* (December–January), *Māgha* (January–February), *Phālguna* (February–March). All the Hindu FESTIVALS are calculated according to this CALENDAR.

moon

The hundreds of synonyms and epithets for the moon in Hindu literature (e.g. *candra(mā)*, *soma*, *śaśī*, *śaśāṅka*, *rajanīkara*, *niśāketu*, *niśāpati*, *tārādhipati* etc.) indicate its great importance. In Vedic times the moon was believed to be the abode of the blessed forefathers. It was also believed to be the source of nectar, which was distilled from its rays. New moon (*āmavasya*) and full moon (*pūrnimā*) were the occasions of the archetype of all Vedic ritual sacrifices (*darśapūrnamāsa*), and the moon-days (*tithis*) are the basic time units for religious observances such as fasting. The moon is worshipped in the form of the god Soma in the Vedas, Candra in later times, and has many other names. (*See also* CALENDAR; SACRIFICE.)

mothers

See MĀTṚKĀS.

mṛtyu-saṃskāra

See ŚRADDHA.

Mudalvan

A Tamil god, later identified with ŚIVA.

mudrā ('seal')

This can also be a seal-ring, a mark, an impression, a gesture, a medal or stamped coin; mystery (in Tantricism); certain positions of fingers, e.g. *abhaya-mudrā*, gesture of reassurance.

muhūrta

In general, a short period of time, an instant; specifically, one-thirtieth of a day (48 minutes). (*See also* TIME, DIVISIONS OF.)

Muktananda, Swami

(1908–83)

Founder of Siddha Dham, a KUṆḌALINĪ Yoga meditation centre in Ganeshpuri, near Bombay. On a world tour in 1974 he also found many Western disciples. After his death Malti and Subhash Chetty (Swami Cidvilasananda and Swami Nityananda) continued the ashram activities.

mukti

See LIBERATION.

Müller, Friedrich Max

(1823–1900)

Son of the German poet Wilhelm Mūller, 'Max Müller', as he is usually called, spent most of his working life in Oxford. While active in many fields – he is called the founder of the discipline of comparative religion, did groundbreaking work in linguistics and in the study of fables, edited and translated Buddhist works – his contributions to the study of Hinduism were so impressive that Hindu pandits gave him the title *Mokṣa Mūlā* ('Root of Liberation'). He published the first critical text edition of the *Ṛgveda* with Sāyaṇa's commentary in six volumes (1849–73), initiated the 50- volume series *Sacred Books of the East*, to which he contributed several volumes of translations (Vedas, Upaniṣads, Gṛhya Sūtras), published a book on Ramakrishna (1898) after meeting Swami Vivekananda, and a course of lectures on *The Six Systems of Indian Philosophy* (1899). While some of his work has been superseded by more recent scholarship and some of his theories, such as the Āryan invasion of India and the chronology based on it, have become controversial, his name is held in high esteem in India as one of the pioneers of Indology in the West.

Muṇḍaka Upaniṣad

One of the principal Upaniṣads, famous for its distinction between *para* (higher) and *apara* (lower) knowledge.

muni

Someone who keeps silence, a sage, a saint; also a title of honour for religious persons.

muñja

A kind of grass or rush from which the girdle of a brahmin at initiation is made.

Munshi, Kanaiyalkal Maneklal

(1887–1971)

Prominent freedom fighter and Congress politician, instrumental in rebuilding and rededicating the ancient Śiva temple at Somnāth, founder of the Bharatiya Vidya Bhavan, an important cultural institution that promotes the study of Sanskrit and traditional Indian learning, and publishes a scholarly journal (*Bhāratīya Vidyā*) and a monograph series, Bhavan's Book University, with hundreds of volumes on Hindu shrines and saints, Hindu literature and art, translations and summaries of Hindu classics. It also has branches outside India, promoting the teaching of Sanskrit and Hindī.

Murāri

('the enemy of the demon Mura')

A favourite epithet of KṚṢṆA.

mūrti ('embodiment')

An IMAGE used in worship, the presence of the deity.

Murti, Tiruppatur Rameseshayyar Venkatachala

(1902–85)

Born into a South Indian brahmin family, educated both in the traditional and modern academic ways, for many years a professor of Philosophy at the Benares Hindu University, with guest professorships in many prestigious Western universities, although best known for his work *The Central Philosophy of Buddhism* (1955), one of the foremost Hindu philosophers and exponents of ADVAITA VEDĀNTA in our time. He published dozens of important papers on all aspects of Indian philosophy; some of these are found in H. C. Coward (ed.) *Studies in Indian Thought: Collected Papers of Prof. T. R. V. Murti* (1983).

Murugan

Tamil god of youth, beauty, divine freedom, the Lord of the World, war god; also known as Sey, Vel and Neduvel. The elephant and peacock are associated with him. Part of his cult is a frenzied kind of dance, the Veriyadal. He is

Music making from the Ho Tribe, Bihar.

worshipped with flowers, paddy, millet, and honey. Goats are sacrificed in his honour. He became āryanized as Subrahmaṇia. (*See also* KĀRTTIKEYA.)

music

The earliest form of Hindu music is the chanting of the Vedic HYMNS: Vedic recitation would have been fruitless if not done according to the tunes (*sāmans*) provided. The pitch is noted in modern editions of the *Ṛgveda* and has to be follwed by every reciter. Musical instruments are in evidence on ancient sculptures and were associated with particular deities: the vīna with Sarasvatī, the drum with Śiva, the flute with Kṛṣṇa, and so on. Music making was done not only for the entertainment of gods and humans but was also considered a religious exercise (*sādhana*). The professional study of music under a master followed a prescribed routine. It consisted mostly of mastering the RĀGAS and learning to develop these. There was no musical notation and all training was aural. Classical Indian music recitals have the atmosphere of worship, often made explicit by prayers at the beginning of the performance and the character of the music played.

Muyālahan ('the man of sin')

A dwarfish figure crushed by Śiva in his dance, symbolizing everything wicked and evil.

N

Naciketas

A son of the Vedic *ṛṣi* (sage) Uddālaka (also called Āruni) and a major figure in the *Taittirīya Brāhmaṇa* and the *Kaṭhta Upaniṣad.* The Naciketas SACRIFICE is named after him. The story goes that one day he saw his father offering cows of an inferior quality in a sacrifice intended to attain paradise, and he admonished his father and offered himself as a substitute victim. He asked his father to whom he should be sacrificed and his father, now very angry, replied, 'Death'. Naciketas subsequently went down to the underworld but Yama, the god of the dead, was absent and unable to receive him. Yama later apologized and offered Naciketas three boons. Naciketas asked for his father to recover from his anger, to be brought back to life, and for immortality. Yama at first tried to dissuade him from his last wish, suggesting that he ask for riches and sensual pleasures instead. Naciketas, pointing out the transience and futility of all terrestrial enjoyment, remained firm, and eventually Yama taught him the secret of the immortality of the ĀTMAN. Naciketas then returned to earth, and was reconciled with his father. Interpretations of the descent of Naciketas differ: some assume that Uddālaka actually killed his son in his anger, while others say it was a symbolic act.

nāda ('sound')

This is especially a mystical sound breaking forth at the time of ecstatic enlightenment.

nāḍi ('channel')

According to tantric physiology the (subtle) human body contains 35 million *nāḍis*, fine tubular vessels through which the psychic energy (*śakti*) moves. Fourteen of these are of primary importance, of which three, Īḍā, Piṅgalā and Suṣumnā constitute the central complex. Suṣumna runs through the hollow of the spinal cord, encircled by Īḍā and Piṅgalā.

naḍukal ('hero stones')

Large stones, often with carvings and inscriptions, erected by the ancient Tamils in memory of those fallen in battle.

Nāga

Mountain people, inhabitants of Nāgaland, in the northeast of India.

nāga (1)

Snake, more specifically the cobra. *Nāgas* are considered the guardians of subterranean treasures and receive extensive worship.

nāga (2)

Naked ascetics, quite often militant.

Naimiṣa

A forest near the Gomatī river, in which, according to tradition, the *Mahābhārata* was first recited to the assembled sages by the Sūta (a traditional narrator).

Naiṣkārmya-siddhi

Treatise by SUREŚVARA, a disciple of ŚAṄKARA (2), which expounds the final truth (*siddhi*) of ADVAITA VEDĀNTA.

naivedya

The offering of cooked food during the daily *mūrti-pūjā* (IMAGE worship).

nakṣatra

Constellation or lunar mansion, the position of the moon within one of the 27 or 28 parts into which astronomers divided the zodiac belt. The moon is seen in a different mansion each day. For ASTROLOGERS the position of the moon in a specific *nakṣatra* is the basis for all prognostications. They are personified as daughters of Dakṣa married to the moon.

Nakula

The fourth of the Pāṇḍava brothers, son of MĀDRĪ, famous for his skill with horses. (*See also* MAHĀBHĀRATA.)

Nām(a)dev(a) (1270–1350)

Mahārāṣṭrian poet-saint, born in Pandharpur, a centre of Viṣṇu worship, into a low-caste family of tailors. Converted from a dissolute life by JÑĀNEŚVARA to the worship of VIṬṬHOBĀ, together with twelve members of his family, he composed a very large number of *abhaṅgs* (HYMNS), which are still used in worship at Pandharpur.

nāma-rūpa ('name and form')

It is said that in the beginning 'reality' was one and undifferentiated: there were no specific things and no manifestation of anything. By obtaining 'name' and 'form', individual entities emerged and became manifest. Subsequently the expression *nāma–rūpa* was used by Indian philosophers as a shorthand for finiteness, individuality and particularity. *Nāma–rūpa* constitutes an entity as object, as opposed to consciousness as subject.

Nambūd(i)ris

The highest caste of BRĀHMAṆAS (2) (brahmins) in Kerala, often referred to as exemplars of CASTE consciousness; in former times a NAYAR had to precede a Nambūdri when he left his house, and announce his coming, to make sure that no OUTCASTE was in sight, because a mere glimpse would pollute him.

name

Names are considered the expression of the people bearing them. Names and name giving are consequently very important in Hindu traditions. Hindu parents are advised, when naming a child, to chose a name that is pleasant to hear, auspicious in meaning, and appropriate for their station. The revealed names of God are believed to be identical to the divine essence: 'taking the name' is the equivalent of entering religious life, and repeating the name (*nāma-japa*) is one of the most common religious exercises. There are litanies of a thousand names (*Sahasra nāma*) of the major deities that are recited by the devotees.

Nammāḷvār (ninth century?) ('our saint')

Also known as Śathakopa, he is considered the greatest among the ĀḶVĀRS. He

Statue of Nandi, Chamondi Hill, near Mysore.

is the author of *Tiruviruttam, Tiruvasariyam, Tiruvaymoli* and *Periya Tiruvandadi*. His icon is placed in many temples and his poems are part of the worship in ŚRĪVAIṢṆAVA temples.

Nanda (1)

A cowherd, who acted as Kṛṣṇa's foster father.

Nanda (2)

A dynasty of kings of MAGADHA, predecessors of the Mauryas.

Nandi

A bull, Śiva's VAHANA, son of KAŚYAPA and Surabhī (KĀMADHENU), the COW of plenty. His IMAGE can be seen in front of all Śiva temples, often in a separate chapel.

Nāra ('man')

Cosmic man; identified with ARJUNA.

Nārada (1)

One of the seven ṚṢIS to whom some Ṛgvedic *sūktas* (HYMNS) are ascribed.

Nārada (2)

One of the PRAJĀPATIS, inventor of the *vīna* and chief of the GANDHARVAS (2). He also descended to the netherworlds and praised their beauty.

Nārada (3)

Author of a *Bhaktisūtra*.

Nāradīya Purāṇa

One of the Vaiṣṇava MAHĀPURĀṆAS (ascribed to NĀRADA).

naraka ('hell')

A place of torture for sinners. The PURĀṆAS enumerate 28 *nārakas*, each designed to punish a specific sin. Although extremely painful, the sojourn of sinners in these hells is limited to the time it takes to atone for their crimes; they are not eternal. (*See also* AFTERLIFE.)

Nāra-Nārada

A pair of sages who according to the *Mahābhārata* visited the Śvetadvīpa ('White Island') where they encountered a race of perfect people and their worship of Viṣṇu.

Nāra-Nārāyaṇa

ARJUNA and KṚṢṆA.

Nārasimha, also Nṛsinha ('man–lion')

An AVATĀRA of Viṣṇu whose lower part is human, the upper part a lion. He appeared to save his devotee PRAHLĀDA from his father, the demon king HIRAṆYAKAŚIPU. He is widely worshipped in India.

Nārāyana ('the refuge of men')

One of the most exalted titles of VIṢṆU or KṚṢṆA.

Nārāyaṇīyam

A short rendition of the *Bhāgavatam*, composed in the 16th century by Meppattur Nārāyaṇa Bhattatiripad, regularly recited at the Kṛṣṇa temple in Guruvayur, Kerala.

Narbadā, also Narmadā

A holy river in central India, flowing to the Arabian Sea, on whose banks are such famous places of pilgrimage as Nasik. One particularly meritorious form of pilgrimage consists of going up the whole length of the river on one side and down on the other.

nāstika

A heretic, i.e. someone who denies the supreme authority of the Veda; follower of a non-orthodox system, such as Cārvāka, Buddhism or Jainism.

Naṭa-rāja ('king of dance')

An epithet of ŚIVA, often represented in art.

nātha ('lord')

Used in titles, e.g. Viśvanātha, 'Lord of the World', a title of ŚIVA.

Nātha Muni (ninth century)

Son of Īśvara Muni, first of the *ācāryas* (masters) of ŚRĪRAṄGAM who gave to the Tamil PRABANDHAM of the Āḷvārs the status of *śruti* in Śrīraṅgam and established himself as supreme teaching authority in ŚRĪVAIṢṆAVISM.

Nāthapanthis

See GORAKHNĀṬHA.

nationalism

Hindu nationalism had its first proponent in the Bengali novelist Bankim Chandra Chatterjee, who depicted the 1770 Samnyasi Rebellion as a Hindu uprising against foreign domination. He had his protagonists sing a hymn to Mother India, the BANDE MĀTĀRĀM, which subsequently became the national anthem of the Indian freedom movement. In it he identified the physical landscape of India and its people with the Great Goddess (DEVĪ), for whose liberation everything had to be done in the spirit of a struggle to attain salvation. This theme was continued by powerful personalities such as AUROBINDO GHOSE, Bal Gangadhar TILAK and others. Mahatma GANDHI too saw his efforts to free India from colonial rule as a religious mission, though not as a charge to establish a Hindu *rāṣṭra*. More radical Hindu nationalists, most of them affiliated with the RĀṢṬRĪYA SVAYAMSEVAK SANGH, and Hindu political parties have been pressing for a long time for the establishment of a Hindu *rāṣṭra*, claiming that HINDUTVA, Hindu-ness, is the very essence of India's identity. (*See also* HINDU JAGARAN.)

navarātrī ('nine nights')

The main feast in honour of ŚIVA, when a nightlong vigil is kept before the LIṄGA (3).

Nāyaṇ(m)ār(s) ('teachers')

A group of 63 ŚAIVITE poet-saints, who flourished between 700 and 1000 CE in South India, whose Tamil works, known as *Tirumurai*, are recited in Śiva temples. The Nāyaṇmārs disregarded distinctions of sex, caste or creed and among them were brahmins, oil sellers, toddy collectors, kings and princesses. (*See also* APPAR, MANIKKAVACAKAR, TIRUMULAR.)

Nāyar, also **Nāir, Nāyyar**

A group of *jātīs* in Kerala (for example Panikkar and Menon), who are considered ŚŪDRAS. They do not receive *upanayana* (initiation) and must stay seven feet away from a NAMBŪDRI brahmin. They held various service positions with Nambūdris.

Nayāyikas

Followers of the NYĀYA school of philosophy.

netherworlds

See PĀTĀLA.

neti-neti

A contracted form of *na iti, na iti,* 'not so, not so', an Upaniṣadic expression used to indicate the total otherness of the reality of *brahman* as compared to any object.

nidhi ('treasure')

Abode, receptacle, the ocean; an epithet of VIṢṆU.

nidi-dhyāsana ('contemplation')

Third stage of process of meditation, after *śravaṇa* and *manana*.

nidrā ('sleep')

Personified as the female form of BRAHMĀ; as Mahānidrā, 'great sleep', it marks the period between two creations, when everything is resting and hidden inside VIṢṆU.

nigama

The VEDA or a Vedic text; any authoritative scripture.

Nighaṇṭu

Part of the NIRUKTA, one of the Vedāṅgas; a glossary of obsolete and obscure Vedic words, attributed to Yāska.

Nīla ('blue')

A range of mountains north of Mount MERU.

Nīla-kaṇṭha, also **Nīla-grīva** ('blue-necked' or 'blue-throated')

An epithet of ŚIVA, whose throat darkened after drinking the poison HALĀHALĀ; symbol of Śiva's compassion for the world.

Nīmavat(s)

Followers of NIMBĀRKA, members of the Haṁsa *saṁpradāya*, with major centres in Braja, Bengal and Rajasthan.

Nimbārka, also **Nimāditya, Niyamānanda** (1125–62)

Telugu brahmin, founder of the (VAIṢṆAVA) Sanakādi (or Haṁsa) *saṁpradāya*, in which the role of the GURU becomes all important. His teaching is known as *Dvaitādvaitavāda*, a combination of ADVAITA and DVAITA. His commentary on the BRAHMASŪTRA is known as *Vedāntaparijātasaurabha*. For Nimbārka *brahman* is identical with Kṛṣṇa, who is omniscient, omnipotent and all-pervading.

nimeṣa ('twinkling of an eye')

A moment.

nir-guṇa ('without qualities')

This expression is used with reference to the 'higher *brahman*' by ŚAṄKARA (2), rejected by RĀMĀNUJA.

nirṛti ('death', 'decay', 'devolution')

Sometimes personified as a goddess (DEVĪ).

Nirukta

One of the VEDĀṄGAS; an etymological glossary to the Vedas, ascribed to Yāska. It consists of three parts: (1) *Naighaṇṭuka* (a list of synonyms); (2) *Naigama* (list of words used only in the Vedas); (3) *Daivata* (words relating to deities and rituals) with Yāska's commentary.

Niṣāda (1)

A forest tribe living in the Vindhya mountains, the Bhīls.

Niṣāda (2)

Outcastes, the children of a Brāhmana father and a Śūdra mother.

niṣ-kala ('without parts')

Undivided, whole; a characteristic of BRAHMAN.

niṣ-kāma ('without desire')

Niṣkāma karma: a desireless action does not result in *karma*, according to the *Bhagavadgīta*.

nīti

Polity, 'ethics', the art of living.

Nīti śāstra

Didactic works on the wisdom of life, usually in the form of animal fables and parables, interspersed with verses to remember, such as the famous PAÑCATANTRA and the *Hitopadeśa*.

nitya ('eternal', 'permanent')

Nitya karma: rituals that have to be performed daily until the end of one's life.

ni-vṛtti ('contraction')

The opposite of and counterpart to *pravṛtti* ('creation', 'expansion'). In a cosmological context it designates the phase in which the universe contracts and disappears. In a personal sense it signifies renunciation, abstinence and self-mortification.

niyama ('restraint')

A self-imposed or minor observance. In the YOGA SŪTRAS these are given as the complement to YAMA as a precondition for meditation, and are enumerated as purity (*śauca*), contentment (*saṁtoṣa*), self-mortification (*tapas*), scripture study (*svādhyāya*), self-surrender to the Lord (*īśvara praṇidhāna*).

non-violence

See AHIṀSĀ.

nyāsa ('placing', 'putting down')

Assigning different parts of the body to specific deities in worship by touching them and uttering appropriate MANTRAS (3).

Nyāya

One of the six orthodox systems of Hindu philosophy. While best known for its detailed treatment of logic and epistemology (*tarkaśāstra*) Nyāya also deals with metaphysical matters such as the nature of the self and means of final emancipation (*adhyātmavidyā*). The beginnings of Nyaya may be traced to the disputations of Vedic scholars and the debates of Upaniṣadic sages. The oldest text is the *Nyāya Sūtras*, ascribed to GAUTAMA (2), which were commented upon by later specialists. In the 12th century Nava Nyāya, the 'new school of logic', developed, focusing on the means of valid cognition (PRAMĀṆAS). The most important text is Gaṅgeśa's *Tattvacintāmani.*

The *Nyāya Sūtras* assert that a knowledge of the true character of the 16 categories it deals with leads the student to the attainment of the highest good. Nyāya uses a syllogism of five members: statement of the point to be proved (*pratijñā*), reason (*hetu*), illustrative example (*udahāraṇa*), corroborative instance (*upanaya*) and inference (*nigamana*).

Some later Nyāya works offer proofs for the existence of God, against the assertions of Buddhists and Cārvākas. The Lord is qualified by the absence (*abhāva*) of lawlessness (*adharma*), falsity (*mithyajnāna*), and error (*pramāda*), and by the positive presence of righteousness, knowledge and goodwill.

nyāya

Well-known maxims such as *andhaparaṁpara-nyāya*, the maxim of the blind following the blind.

Nyāya Sūtras (*c.* 300 BCE)

The basic text of the Nyāya *darśana* (system), ascribed to GAUTAMA (2), dealing with means of right cognition, objects of right cognition, doubt, disputation etc. commented upon by VĀTSYĀYAṆA (1).

O

Oldenberg, Hermann
(1854–1920)

One of the pioneers of Indology whose works proved to have wide appeal and lasting value. He initially focused on Buddhism, translating many texts for the Pali Text Society and the Sacred Books of the East, and was the author of the classic *Buddha: Sein Leben, seine Lehre, seine Gemeinde* (1881). His contributions to the study of Hinduism are equally substantial. His work on Vedic religion, originally published in 1894, was translated more than a century later into English: *The Religion of the Veda* (1988). His translations of Vedic hymns and of some Gṛhya Sūtras are part of the Sacred Books of the East series. His studies of the *Mahābhārata* were published posthumously (1922).

Om

See AUM.

Otto, Rudolf (1869–1937)

While best known for his *Das Heilige* (The Holy), an attempt to articulate a general theory of religion, he also has done considerable work on Hinduism, especially on VAIṢṆAVISM. He published an anthology of Vaiṣṇava texts (*Vischnu Narayana: Texte zur indischen Gottesmystik*), a comparative study of Śaṅkara and Meister Eckhart (in English: *Mysticism East and West*), and a broad-based comparison of Vaiṣṇavism and Christianity (*Die Gnadenreligion Indiens und das Christentum*). He also founded a museum for the history of religions at Marburg University and helped to draw the attention of European students to the theistic traditions of Hinduism.

outcaste

Pañcama, or 'fifth (*varṇa*)', is a designation of a large number of inhabitants of India who do not belong to one of the four VARṆAS. While many so-called outcastes never belonged to Hindu CASTE society, a large number were former caste members who as punishment for

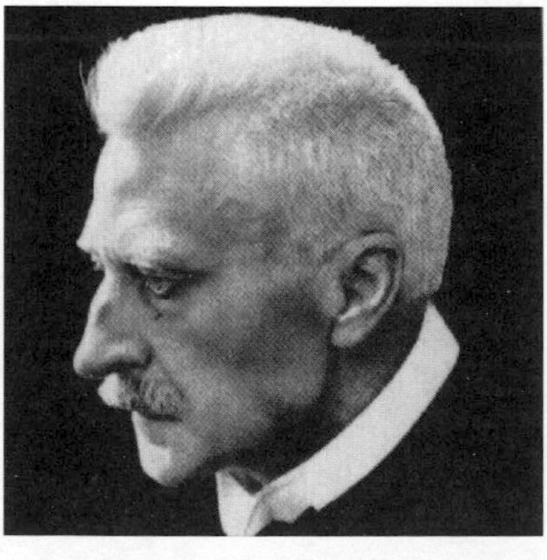

Rudolf Otto (1869–1937).

some serious infringement of caste regulations were excommunicated. Many outcastes originated from unlawful mixed marriages, others from neglect of rituals (former Buddhists or Jains). Certain professions, such as leather workers (*cāmārs*) and sweepers (*bhaṅgis*) and attendants at funerary sites (*dom*), were deemed hereditarily unclean, and could only be held by outcastes. Outcastes were not allowed to live in villages, to use the common wells or to share food with caste people, and they were often subjected to cruel punishment for minor offences. Mahatma GANDHI called them *Harijan*, 'God's people', and wanted to make them part of the Śūdra *varṇa*. The Indian constitution of 1950 outlaws untouchability and legally gives equal status to all Indians. In practice the former untouchables are still widely disadvantaged and attempts to improve their chances, such as those made by the Mandal Commission (1989) are met with violent resistance from the higher castes. Many former outcastes have organized themselves as DALITS ('oppressed') and are fighting for economic and social equality.

P

padapaṭha

The text of the Veda in which each word (*pāda*) stands distinct, not joined to preceding or following words.

padma

A lotus or lotus-like ornament; also a name of RĀMA. *Padma-āsana*: a lotus seat.

Padmanabha

One of Viṣṇu's VYŪHAS, bearing five shields as emblem.

Padma Purāṇa

One of the Vaiṣṇava MAHĀPURĀṆAS, deriving its name from the period when the world was a golden lotus.

pagala ('mad')

A type of saint, whose behaviour is abnormal, but still within certain recognized religious limits.

Pallavas

South Indian dynasty, *c.* 300–888 CE, whose capital was Kāñcīpuram; generous patrons of the arts and promoters of ŚAIVISM. Well-known Pallava monarchs are Mahendravarma I (600–30 CE), Narasimhavarma I (630–60 CE), under whose reign the seven *rathas* of MAHĀBALIPURA were constructed, Narasimhavarma II (695–722), under whom the famous Kailāsanāṭha temple in Kāñcīpura was built. Around 900 CE the Pallava kingdom was annexed by the COLAS.

pañca-lakṣana

See MĀHĀPURĀṆA.

Pañcāṅga ('five limbs')

Yearly almanac, which provides astronomical charts for every fortnight of a year, indispensable for astrologers, as well as for the determination of feast days. (*See also* ASTROLOGY; CALENDAR; FESTIVALS.)

Pāñcarātra ('five nights')

An ancient VAIṢṆAVA theological tradition, which accepts the separate reality of God, world and human being. It has become part of the theology of ŚRĪVAIṢṆAVISM. The name has also been explained as signifying the synthesis of five hitherto divided traditions, namely the Ekāntika, the Bhāgavata, the Nārāyaṇīya, the Vaikhānasa, and the Sātvata. The first promoter of the Pāñcarātra doctrine was Śāṇḍilya, the author of a *Bhaktisūtra*. The main sources for Pāñcarātra are the voluminous Pāñcarātra Āgamas, of which the best known are the *Ahirbudhnya*, the *Sanātkumāra* and the *Parameśvara*.

Pañcatantra (fifth century CE)

A collection of moral tales and fables in five (*pañca*) books (*tantra*), by Viṣṇuśarman, for the teaching of *nīti* (ethics) to young people. Its stories have been often retold and translated into many languages. Many of Aesop's fables are believed to be derived from it.

pañcāyata ('council of five')

A traditional committee of five members of the same CASTE, to oversee observance of caste rules. After independence *pañcāyats* were introduced all over India as village councils to decide on all issues concerning the interest of the local population.

pañcāyātana pūjā
('the [simultaneous] worship of five deities')

The worship of Gaṇeśa, Sūrya, Viṣṇu, Śiva and Devī was reputedly introduced by ŚAṄKARA (2) to reconcile the various Hindu SAṀPRADĀYAS. The practice suggests that all the various deities are but appearances of the one (invisible) BRAHMAN.

Pāṇḍavas

The five putative sons of Pāṇḍu, who was deterred by a curse from fathering his own children. While out hunting one day he shot an antelope that was in the process of mating. The dying animal, a transformed ṚṢI (sage), cursed him with death during sexual intercourse. He therefore refused to sleep with his two wives, and asked them to summon gods to father children for him. Kuntī, his first wife, had YUDHIṢṬHIRA from Dharma, BHĪMA from Vāyu and ARJUNA from Indra. Mādrī, his second and favourite wife, had NAKULA and SAHADEVA from the Aśvins. However, one day desire overcame him, and he died during intercourse with Mādrī, who ascended his funeral pyre at his wish, and became SATĪ. Since the five Pāṇḍava brothers were the sons of his two wives, they were treated as his sons. They were one of the major groups of protagonists in the *Mahābhārata*.

Pandharpur

Place of pilgrimage in Mahārāṣṭra, sacred to Viṭṭal or Viṭṭhobā (a form of Viṣṇu) made famous by TUKĀRĀM and his followers, the Vārkarīs.

paṇḍita ('learned')

An honorific applied to high personalities.

Pāṇḍu ('the pale')

Brother of Dhṛtarāṣṭra, king of Hastināpura. (*See* also MAHĀBHĀRATA; PĀṆḌAVAS.)

Pāṇḍya

A realm and a dynasty in South India, from *c.* 500 BCE to *c.* 1700 CE. The Pāṇḍyas derive their name and origin from the PĀṆḌAVAS. The early history and the extent of the kingdom is uncertain. Several Pāṇḍya rulers invaded Śrī Laṅkā, and they feuded with the PALLAVAS, the Ceras and the COLAS, whom they supplanted in the 13th century as the leading power of South India. One of their rulers, Neduvarman (*c.* 700 CE) became a ŚAIVA after marrying a Cola princess, and had 8,000 Jains killed in MADURAI. One branch of the Pāṇḍyas, the Nayyakas (1420–1736) became famous as builders of magnificent temples, including the Mīnākṣī temple at MADURAI (1600–50), the Raṅganātha temple in ŚRĪRAṄGAM (1620–89), and the huge temple at RAMEŚVARAM.

Pāṇini (sixth century BCE)

The most celebrated Indian grammarian, author of the AṢṬĀDHYĀYĪ ('eight chapter-work'), considered one of the greatest accomplishments of the human mind. From ancient times Pāṇinī was revered as a ṚṢI (sage) and his work was considered to be inspired by Śiva. The study of grammar was undertaken as a spiritual discipline and was considered indispensable for anyone aspiring to become a teacher of philosophy or religion.

panth(a) ('path', 'following')

This is used especially in contexts such as Kabīr Panth, followers of the path taught by KABĪR.

pāpa

See SIN.

pāpa-puruṣa ('man of sin')

The personification of all unpardonable sins: his head consists of brahmanicide, his arms of cow-killing, his nose of woman-murder, his belly of intoxication, his legs of theft of gold.

parama-haṁsa ('supreme swan')

An honorific title for a spiritual teacher.

paramārthika

('relating to the supreme reality')

Transcendent; the opposite to *vyavahārika*, relating to empirical reality. (*See also* VYAVAHĀRA.)

paramātman ('supreme soul')

The Absolute, BRAHMAN.

paraṁparā

The lineage of teacher and disciple, tradition. The Upaniṣads have long lines of teachers to whom their teachings are traced back. For members of Hindu religious orders it is important to memorize their *guruparaṁparā* to authenticate their tradition. A teaching not traced back to an acknowledged line of teachers is considered unsound and not conducive to LIBERATION.

Parāśara (14th century BCE?)

A *ṛṣi* (sage) to whom some of the Ṛgvedic *sūktas* (HYMNS) are attributed. He is also the narrator of the *Viṣṇu Purāṇa* and the author of a major work on DHARMAŚĀSTRA, commented upon by MĀDHAVA (2).

Paraśurāma

('Rama with the battle-axe')

The sixth AVATĀRA of Viṣṇu; the fifth son of Jamadagni and Reṇukā. He appeared in the TRETA YUGA to end the tyranny of the KṢATRIYAS, whom he is said to have annihilated 22 times. His story is told in the *Rāmāyaṇa*, the *Mahābhārata* and some PURĀṆAS.

Pargiter, Frederick Eden

(1852–1927)

Officer in the Indian Civil Service, High Judge in Calcutta, historian and student of classical India who rejected the Āryan invasion theory. He was the author of *Ancient Indian Historical Tradition* (1922) and *The Purāṇa Text of the Dynasties of the Kali Age* (1913).

Parijāta

The wonderful tree produced at the CHURNING OF THE OCEAN, whose blossoms perfumed the whole universe. It was placed in Indra's heaven, but when Kṛṣṇa visited it, his wife, Satyabhāmā, induced him to carry it away. In the ensuing fight Indra lost and Kṛṣṇa carried the tree to Dvāraka. After Kṛṣṇa's death the tree was returned to Indra's heaven.

parikrama

See CIRCUMAMBULATION.

Parikṣit

The grandson of Arjuna, father of

Janamejaya. When YUDHIṢṬHIRA retired from the throne, Parikṣit followed him as king of Hastināpura. He died from a snake-bite. In the interval between the bite of the snake and his death, the *Bhāgavata Purāṇa* was recited to him. (*See also* MAHĀBHĀRATA.)

Parliament of Religions

A gathering of representatives of all major religions, which took place in Chicago in 1893 in connection with the celebration of the 400th anniversary of Columbus' discovery of America. Swami VIVEKĀNANDA, the Hindu delegate, made a great impression through his speeches and became well known thereafter as an exponent of ADVAITA VEDĀNTA.

pariṣad

A gathering of brahmins for the purpose of studying and interpreting the Vedas. The term has also been appropriated by groups such as the VIŚVA HINDU PARIṢAD, giving it the more general meaning of 'association'.

Pārvatī ('daughter of the mountains')

An epithet of the consort of ŚIVA, mother of the six-headed KĀRTTIKEYA and the elephant-headed GAṆEŚA.

pāśa ('noose')

A designation (in certain schools of ŚAIVISM) of the bond that ties people to this finite existence and hinders them from reaching the Lord.

paśu ('bovine')

A designation (in certain schools of ŚAIVISM) of the unenlightened and unemancipated human condition.

Pāśu-patas

A Śaivite sect, said to have been founded by Śiva and later reorganized by Lakulin, the reputed author of the *Pāśupata Sūtra*. The teaching is classified as *bhedābheda* (difference–non-difference) and deals with five categories: *kāraṇa* (the cause, i.e. the creator, maintainer and destroyer of the universe); *kārya* (effect; created things); *yoga* (the way to achieve emancipation); *vidhi* (regulations and injunctions); and *dukhānta* (the final bliss).

Paśu-pati ('Lord of animals')

An epithet of ŚIVA, used to express his lordship over all living beings, collectively called *paśu*, 'bovines'.

Pātāla ('netherworlds')

Not to be confused with Western notions of netherworlds or hells (NĀRAKA). The seven netherworlds, called Atala (white), Vitala (black), Nitala (purple), Gabhastimat (yellow), Mahātala (sandy), Sutala (stony) and Pātāla are huge realms (each extending 10,000 *yojanas* – c. 130,000 km – beneath the surface of the earth), inhabited by DĀNAVAS, DAITYAS, YAKṢAS and great NĀGAS (1), filled with magnificent palaces and all kinds of treasures. NĀRADA (2), after visiting them, described them as more delightful than Indra's heaven.

Pātañjala Yoga

Also called Rāja Yoga, the 'royal' path, it is based on the YOGA SŪTRAS, ascribed to PATAÑJALI. Making use of the terms coined by SĀṂKHYA and taking over its worldview, the *Yoga Sūtras* describe the practice of the process of discriminative knowledge that leads to the liberation of the embodied spirit. Yoga is not mere theory, it also implies physical training, willpower and decisions. It deals with the human situation as a whole and aims at providing real freedom, not just a theory of liberation. Although much

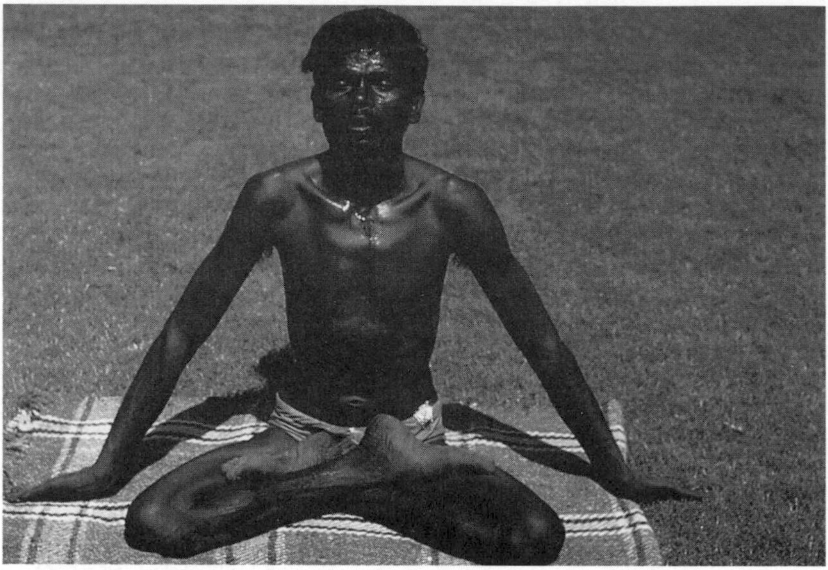

Pātañjala Yoga in practice.

of its concern is psychological, it differs radically from contemporary Western psychology: it assumes the reality of a spirit-soul, it has a strong ethical orientation, and it focuses on states of consciousness that presently are not recognized in modern Western thought.

The second *sūtra* defines Yoga as *citta-vṛttinirodha*, 'the quieting of all fluctuations of the mind'. *Citta*, mind, is the first evolved entity and its fluctuations, vibrations, irritations (*vṛttis*) cause the multiplicity of thoughts and material objects. If they cease, the mind is free. The impulse to seek that freedom is given by the experience of *kleśas*, 'afflictions' that beset life. They are identified as *avidyā* ('ignorance', illusion), *asmitā* ('mine-ness', egoism), *rāga* (passion, attraction), *dveśa* (aversion, hatred) and *abhiniveśa* (fear of death, attachment to life). While most of these terms may be self-explanatory, it is interesting to examine what the *Yoga Sūtras* mean by the term *avidy*ā. It is explained as 'mistaking the transient, impure and evil non-self for the eternal, pure and blissful self'. This *avidyā* is both the root of our unhappiness and also the cause for our search for liberation.

The practice of precepts and virtues is preliminary to Yoga but considered indispensable. Without ethical grounding, the powers acquired through Yoga practices proper could be used for evil purposes. The practice of virtues also produces many helpful side-effects. Thus the *Yoga Sūtras* assert that in the presence of a person grounded in *ahiṁsā*, non-violence, others will give up their enmity and that even wild animals become tame. The *Yoga Sūtras* offer practical advice on how to gain these virtues and how to counteract opposite trends. They analyse the root of all evil tendencies as contained in the triad of *lobha* (greed), *moha* (delusion), and *krodha* (anger) and offer advice on how to counteract these root vices in order to eradicate all sins.

While the Yoga that is taught in the West usually concentrates on the learning of a variety of postures supposed to be beneficial to health, Pantañjali says that any posture can be taken that is agreeable and allows a practitioner to sit in meditation for a length of time. The aim of Rāja Yoga is neither self-mortification nor physical exercise, but the achievement of inner freedom. Some YOGIS focus on the extraordinary faculties connected with Yoga, such as making oneself small like an atom or large like a mountain, understanding the languages of all peoples and even of animals, reading other people's minds, making onself invisible etc., but the *Yoga Sūtras* discourage the practitioner from cultivating them. They are more of a hindrance than a help on the path to freedom. There are certain dietetic rules to be observed as well: a yogi is to avoid spicy food, everything pungent, sour or salty. While the use of drugs, especially *bhaṅg* (hashish), is widespread among Yogis in India, Patañjali discourages this practice. *Kaivalya* is a state of mind that should be reached without any involvement of foreign substances.

Breath control, *prāṇayama*, is a central practice in Yoga. The Upaniṣads contain many speculations on *prāṇa*, life breath, and controlling one's breath is an ancient and widely practised method of purification. Some yogis succeed in controlling their breath to such an extent that they can reduce the metabolism to a point where it becomes possible for them to be buried for days or even weeks and emerge alive. The *Yoga Sūtras* do not encourage such extraordinary feats, but they consider breath control basic. Similarly, the ability to withdraw one's senses, *pratyahāra*, is essential. The senses, no longer occupied with transmitting impulses from the body, cease to hinder the mind from functioning according to its own 'mental' mode.

The central feature of Pātañjala Yoga is *samyama*, 'effort', consisting of the triad of *dhāraṇa–dhyāna–samādhi*, 'concentration–contemplation–trance'. They are not seen as flowing from a special 'psychic' capability but as resulting from strenuous effort. They completely interiorize consciousness and separate self-consciousness from everything that is not self, i.e. the body and sense-objects. By applying the technique to a number of dimensions of reality the yogi both identifies with and transcends each realm. The detail in which the *Yoga Sūtras* describe the process is highly technical and must be studied under the guidance of an experienced teacher. From a certain point onwards in the practice of Yoga the process becomes irreversible: *kaivalya*, complete introversion, becomes the 'natural' goal of the practitioner's mind. The state of mind shortly before reaching the final condition is defined as *dharmameghasamādhi*, '*dharma*-cloud trance' in which the finite, elementary nature of all things becomes experientially apparent to the yogi. A kind of zero-time experience precedes the entering into timelessness. *Kaivalya* is described as the spirit 'finding its own true state of nature', the coming home of the soul from the exile of involvement in the process of material evolution.

Patañjali (second century BCE)

A celebrated name, the reputed author of a treatise on Yoga (*Yoga Sūtras*), on medicine (*Carakasaṁhitā*) and on grammar (*Mahābhāṣya*), healer of body, mind and soul.

pāṭha ('reading')

This applies especially to the reading of a Vedic text. There are three *pāṭhas*: *saṁhitāpāṭha* (words read with *sandhi*, rules for combining vowels and consonants), *padapāṭha* (words read independently, without *sandhi*), and *kramapāṭha* (each word read twice, first combined with the preceding, and then with the succeeding word).

patita ('fallen')

Someone who is not qualified to partipate in (Vedic) rites.

Pauravas

Descendants of Puru of the lunar dynasty. *See* MAHĀ-BHĀRATA.

pavitra ('holy', 'sacred')

The sacred thread of upper CASTES.

peacock (*mayūra*)

The peacock is frequently employed in Indian art as a symbol both of vanity and wealth. The peacock is KUBERA's VAHANA (vehicle) and peacocks are often associated with Kṛṣṇa and his dalliance with the GOPĪS. The peacock is also associated with Śiva in the famous Śiva temple at Mylapur (Mayūrapura) in Madras.

penance

See PRAYAŚCITTA.

Pesh(a)was, also **Pesh(a)vas**

Originally a title (comparable to prime minister). The Peshvas of Mahārāṣṭra, towards the end of the rule of Aurangzeb, asserted themselves as independent rulers and founded a Hindu dynasty (with its capital in Pune) that seriously threatened first the Mogul and then the British rule of India. (*See also* ŚIVAJĪ.)

phala/phalaśloka
('fruit'/'verse of promise')

According to Hindu tradition each religious act, performed properly, carries its reward or 'fruit' (*phala*). Many religious texts end with verses (*śloka*) that promise specific benefits (*phala*) from reading all or part of the book, or keeping a copy or part of it in one's home.

pilgrimage (*yātrā*)

One of the most popular Hindu religious activities is visiting the countless holy places that dot India's landscape. For SAMNYĀSIS it is a duty to spend most of their time on pilgrimage. Pilgrimages are undertaken to have certain rites, such as *śraddha* (the last rites), performed, to redeem vows or to gain merit. Hindu ŚĀSTRAS regulate pilgrimage by defining the mode of travel, the resolve to be undertaken, the rituals to undergo. The more arduous the pilgrimage, the more meritorious it is deemed to be. Pilgrimage can also be undertaken by proxy in certain circumstances. At any given time millions of Hindus are on pilgrimage, and most of the sacred places are crowded by pilgrims from far and near all year long. Over the centuries pilgrimage has certainly helped to create a bond among Hindus, notwithstanding sectarian differences. (*See also* TĪRTHA.)

Pillai Lokācārya
(1205–1311)

A sixth-generation successor of RĀMĀNUJA as head of the Śrīvaiṣṇavas in ŚRĪRAṄGAM and author of *Tattvatraya*, a compendium of Śrīvaiṣṇava thought, arranged according to the three principles (*tattva*), *īśvara* (God), *jīvātma* (soul), and *acit* (nature). Several other works, such as *Mumukṣupatti*, *Tattvaśekhara* and *Śrīvācanabhūṣana*, are also attributed to him. Pillai Lokācārya recommends PRAPATTI (self-surrender) as the means to salvation. He became the main theologian of the Teṅgalai branch of ŚRĪVAIṢṆAVISM.

piṇḍa

A small ball of cooked rice, offered to

the ancestors in connection with the last rites by the nearest (male) relation. By connotation it then means (close) degree of relationship, such as in *sapiṇḍa*, forbidden to marry.

piśāca (fem. *piśācī*)

Fiend, evil spirit. It is the most malignant of ghosts, often mentioned in Vedas, Brāhmaṇas and epics. (*See also* BHŪTA; PRETA.)

pitāmaha

Paternal grandfather. A title of BRAHMĀ, especially in the *Mahābhārata*.

Pitāṁbara ('dressed in a yellow garment')

A name of VIṢṆU/KṚṢṆA.

Pīṭha, also **Pīṭha sthāna**

The 51 places where the limbs of Satī fell, when scattered by Śiva after his destruction of DAKṢA's sacrifice. Also called *śakti-pīṭhas*, they are important places of pilgrimage for Tantrikas. (*See also* KĀLIKĀ PĪṬHA.)

pitṛs

Fathers, forefathers, ancestors, to whom PIṆḌAS are offered.

planets

Hindus knew and observed the movements of the planets (Jupiter, Saturn, Mercury, Venus, Mars, together with the sun and the moon) from ancient times and used constellations to determine auspicious and inauspicious times. HOROSCOPES were based on planetary astronomy. (*See also* ASTROLOGY.)

Poddar, Hanuman Prasad (1892–1971)

Journalist, religious leader and founder of the Gītā Press in Gorakhpur, the largest publisher of Hindu religious literature in Sanskrit, Hindī and English. He was the founder-editor of *Kalyāṇ*, a Hindī religious monthly, and *Kalyāṇa Kalpātaru*, an English-language religious Hindu monthly, with large circulations.

Poṅgal

The greatest festival of Tamilnāḍū, and a public holiday. It is a combination of New Year and harvest/thanksgiving celebrations. One day is called *maṭṭu-poṅgal*, when COWS and oxen are decorated and worshipped as an expression of thanks for their work.

Pope, George Uglow (1820–1908)

Christian missionary, educator and scholar of Tamil. He taught at Tinnevelly, Tanjore and Ootacamund, and lectured in Tamil and Telugu at Oxford University; author and editor of many Tamil works, translator of the Tamil classic *Tirukkural* and the *Tiruvacakam* by MĀṆIKKAVĀCAKAR.

power

See ŚAKTI.

Prabandham

Also known as the 'Tamil *Prabandham*', the collection of hymns by the ĀḶVĀRS, undertaken by Nāṭha Muni, which is used in ŚRĪVAIṢṆAVA worship alongside Sanskrit hymns.

Prabhākara Miśra (*c.* 600–50 CE)

A famous MĪMĀṀSAKA scholar, founder of the Prabhākara school, author of *Bṛhati* and *Vivaraṇa*, and commentaries on the *Śābarabhāṣya*.

prācārya

A *guru*'s GURU.

pradakṣiṇa

See CIRCUMAMBULATION.

pradakṣiṇa pātha

A CIRCUMAMBULATORY pathway in a temple.

pradhāna ('the first')

Primary matter, inert matter, nature as opposed to spirit. According to SĀṀKHYA *pradhāna* is opposite of PURUṢA: it does not possess consciousness, but under the influence of *puruṣa* everything evolves out of *pradhāna* (*prakṛti*). The relationship between *pradhāna* and *puruṣa* is illustrated via the simile of a blind but strong person (*pradhāna*) carrying a lame but sighted person (*puruṣa*) on her shoulders. They do everything jointly, but the sighted person directs the blind one. ŚAṄKARA (2) argues against the possibility of an eternal material principle, and against *pradhāna* as the source of all things.

Pradyumna (1)

Kṛṣṇa's son by RUKMIṆĪ.

Pradyumna (2)

One of the names of KĀMA, the god of love.

Pradyumna (3)

Another name for SANAT-KUMĀRA, son of Brahmā.

Prahlāda

Son of the DAITYA king Hiraṇyakaśipu. As a boy he became an ardent devotee of Viṣṇu, proclaiming Viṣṇu sovereign, and thus enraging his father who had claimed world rulership. Hiraṇyakaśipu attempted to kill Prahlāda in many different ways but failed due to Viṣṇu's intervention. Finally Viṣṇu appeared as NĀRASIMHA (a man-lion) and killed Hiraṇyakaśipu.

Prajāpati ('Lord of creatures')

Progenitor, in a generic sense. In the Veda, Indra and other *devas* are called Prajāpati. Later the title is applied to Brahmā, the creator. Most commonly the title is given to the ten mind-born sons of Brahmā: Marīci, Atri, Aṅgiras, Pulastya, Pulaha, Kratu, Vasiṣṭha, Pracetas (Dakṣa), Bhṛgu and Nārada. Different sources give different numbers and different names for the Prajāpatis.

Prajñā-tīrtha

One of the names of MADHVA.

prakṛti ('nature')

In a general sense, matter, generative substance. *See also* PRADHĀNA.

pralaya

The dissolution of the world at the end of a KALPA.

pramāda ('error')

A mistake, the opposite of right knowledge (VIDYĀ).

pramāṇa

A means of establishing truth; traditionally six *pramāṇas* have been recognized: *pratyakṣa* (perception); *anumāna* (inference); *śabda* (verbal authority); *upamiti* (analogy); *arthāpatti* (presumption); *abhāva* (negation). Of these the CĀRVĀKAS accept one only, the VAIŚEṢIKAS two, the SĀṀKHYAS three, the NAYĀYIKAS four, the Prabhākara school of MĪMĀṀSA five, the Bhaṭṭa school of Mīmāṁsā and the VEDĀNTINS six. *Pramāṇas* are an important part of every Indian philosophical investigation.

prāṇa ('breath')

Breath is often identified with life. (*See also* PRĀṆAYAMA.)

prāṇava

See AUM.

prāṇayama ('breath-control')

An important part of ritual practice and of YOGA, a method of purification and a way to concentrate the mind.

prapatti ('self-surrender')

A central notion in BHAKTI, especially in VAIṢṆAVISM. It is the culmination of a long process of devotion and consists of five acts: the intention of submitting to the Lord; the giving up of resistance to the Lord; the belief in the protection of the Lord; the prayer that the Lord may save his devotee; the consciousness of utter helplessness. The oldest reference to *prapatti* may be *Bhagavadgītā* XVIII, 66.

prārābdha (karma)

Residual KARMA (2), karma left over from previous lives, which has to be lived through; fate, destiny.

Prārthana Samāj ('Prayer Association')

Founded in 1867 in Bombay by Dr Atmaram Pandurang (1823–98) as a Hindu reform movement. Its most prominent member was Justice Mahadev Govinda Ranade (1842–1901), who was responsible for many social reform initiatives and who exerted a major influence on the Indian National Congress, of which he was a founder member. The Prārthana Samāj established the Social Reform Movement and founded the journal *Indian Social Reformer*. It fought for the abolition of CASTE, the right of widows to remarry, the abolition of child MARRIAGE and the education of WOMEN. It was instrumental in the foundation of many associations dedicated to the upliftment of the depressed classes, tribal people and women.

prasāda ('grace')

FOOD that has been offered to the deity and that is shared among devotees as God's gift and blessing.

Praśastapāda (fourth century CE)

A famous scholar of the VAIŚEṢIKA school; author of the *Padārthadharmasaṅgraha*.

Praśna Upaniṣad

One of the principal Upaniṣads. It deals with six questions (*praśna*) which are asked of the sage Pippalāda.

prasthāna trayī ('the triad of proof-texts')

The major Upaniṣads, the *Bhagavadgītā*, and the *Brahmasūtras*, upon which a founder of a school of Vedānta has to comment.

prati-biṁba

See BIṀBA–PRATIBIṀBA; MADHVA.

pratijñā ('acknowledgement')

A vow, promise. In NYĀYA: the statement of the proposition to be proved, the first part of the five-membered Indian syllogism. The others are: *hetu* (reason); *udaharaṇa* (illustrative example); *upanaya* (corroborative instance); *nigamana* (inference: identical with the first statement).

Prātiśākhya

Treatises dealing with the phonetics of Vedic language, for example the *Taittirīyaprātiśākhya*, which belongs to the Black YAJURVEDA.

prati-sarga

Dissolution of the created universe; one of the *pañcālakṣana* (five topics of a Purāṇa).

prati-ṣṭhāpana

The solemn installation and consecration of an IMAGE (*mūrti*) through which the presence of a deity is called down and the image becomes an object of worship.

pratyāhāra

('withdrawal [of the senses]')

An important stage in PATAÑJALA YOGA.

pratyakṣa ('perception')

The first and most important means of proof. (*See also* PRAMĀṆA.)

pra-vṛtti ('progress', 'advance')

Active wordly life; projection. The opposite of NI-VṚTTI.

prayaścitta ('atonement')

Action prescribed as penance for violation of precepts, such as repetition of a formula or bathing. There are long lists of *prayaścittas* that match specific atonements for particular breaches of the law.

predestination

MADHVA teaches a kind of predestination, by insisting that certain persons (*nitya baddhas*) never reach release.

premā ('love')

In GAUḌĪYA VAIṢṆAVISM, a designation of the highest form of love for Kṛṣṇa, which transforms the devotee permanently.

preta ('ghost')

An evil spirit, the restless soul of a departed person who for some reason or other could not find a way to the beyond. There is a popular belief that people who commit suicide or people who have not atoned for a serious crime are condemned to haunt the world as *pretas*. Texts such as the *Pretakalpa* of the *Garuḍa Purāṇa* give instructions on how to meet *pretas* and what to do to give them release.

Pṛthivī ('the broad')

The earth, or the whole world. In the Vedas she is personified as mother of all beings. Her name is derived from PṚTHU, who gave her life and thus was considered her father.

Pṛthu

Son of VEṆA, the first rightful monarch on earth. He is credited with having introduced agriculture, and providing his subjects with peace and plenty.

pūjā

Worship, especially of an IMAGE, usually an offering of fruit, cooked food, water, incense, flowers etc. Each *saṁpradāya* (sect) has elaborate rules for the performance of *pūjā* which have to be strictly followed by the devotees. As an act of devotion *pūjā* is both service to the deity and a means to win his/her favour. *Pūjā* offered daily at the home shrine is a scaled-down version of the grand services performed at temples, especially at festive occasions. It has to include a minimum of sixteen acts: *avahana* (invitation of the deity); *āsana* (offering a seat); *svagata* (greeting); *padya* (washing the feet); *arghya* (rinsing the mouth and hands); *acamanīya* (water for sipping); *madhuparka* (offering water mixed with honey); *snāna* or *abhiṣeka* (bathing or sprinkling); *vastra* (clothing); *gandha* (perfumes); *puṣpa* (flowers); *dhūpa* (incense); *dīpa* (lamp); *naivedya* or *prasāda* (offering food); *nāmaskāra* or *praṇāma* (prostration); *visarjana* (send-off).

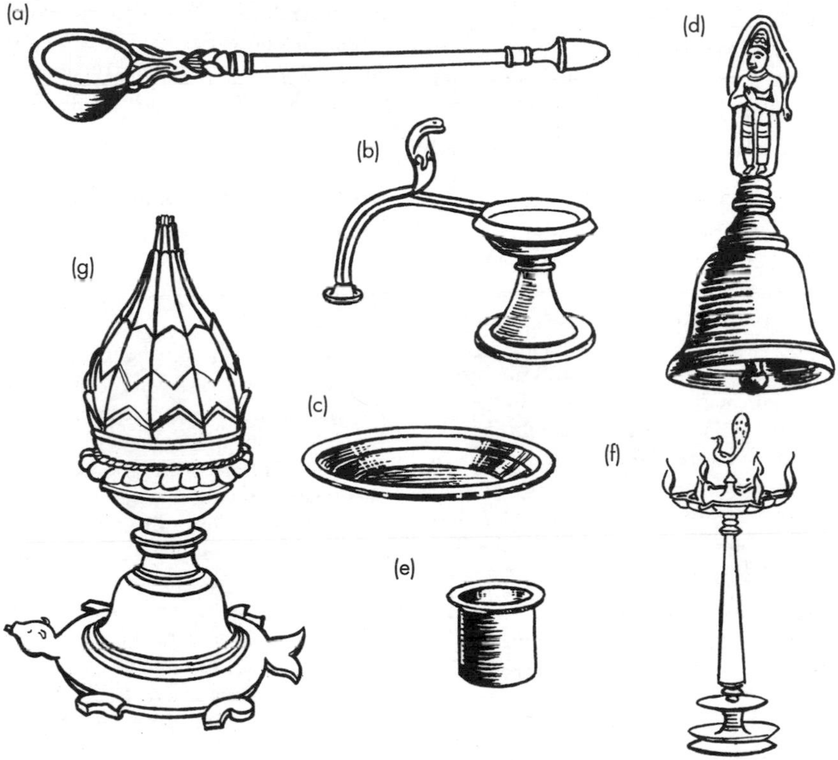

Pūjā implements: a) sruva *(spoon for offering* ghī *or water to deity); b)* ārati-dīpa *(used for waving burning camphor in front of deity); c)* pātra *(plate for* prasāda *– food offered to deity and then distributed to participants in worship); d)* ghaṇṭā *(bell, rung before deity); e)* pānapātra *(cup for offering water to deity); f)* dīpa *(oil lamp stand with multiple wicks); g)* padma *(lotus; can be opened up as flower during worship).*

punar-janma

See REBIRTH.

puṇya

See MERIT.

Purāṇa ('old (books)')

An important class of bible-like texts of varying length and age. Their origins may be traced back to the stories by which the people attending Vedic sacrifices were entertained. The Purāṇas themselves claim greater antiquity than the Vedas. The followers of various *saṁpradāyas* (sects) consider them to be revealed scriptures. They deal with the creation of the universe, genealogies of gods and patriarchs, myths associated with various deities, rules for living and descriptions of heavens and hells as well as of the end of the world. As a source for popular Hinduism they ares still of the utmost importance. Some, such as the *Viṣṇu Purāṇa*, the *Bhāgavata* or the *Devībhāgavata*, are often recited publicly through loudspeakers at places of prilgrimage. (*See also* MAHĀPURĀṆA.)

Purī

See JAGAN-NĀTHA PURĪ.

purity (*śuddhi, śauca*)

A central notion in Hinduism (as in all religions), with ritual, physical, psychological and spiritual dimensions. Ritual purity plays a great role in the Vedas; special rites are prescribed, particularly for brahmins to obtain ritual purity after being polluted. Pollution can be effected through contact with corpses, certain bodily fluids and association with OUTCASTES. The ĀRYA SAMĀJ introduced a special *śuddhi* ceremony to readmit to the fold of Hinduism the followers of other religions, whose ancestors had left Hinduism. Physical purity is part of the religio-hygienic routine which makes daily bathing also a religious obligation. Purity of the soul consists in the absence of greed, hatred and other negative attitudes. Purity of mind consists in disinterestedness, *niṣkāma karma*, activity without any selfish involvement, the eradication of all sense of egoity.

Pūrṇaprajñā ('full of wisdom')

One of the names of MADHVA.

purohita

A priest, who conducts the prescribed rituals for a particular family.

Puruṣa ('man', 'male')

The name of the cosmic man, whose sacrifice resulted in the creation of all things.

puruṣa

In SĀṀKHYA, spirit, the counterpart of matter (PRAKṚTI).

puruṣārtha

('the [four] aims of man')

These are *dharma* (righteousness), *artha* (wealth), *kāma* (sensual enjoyment), *mokṣa* (liberation).

puruṣottama ('supreme man')

A title of VIṢṆU/KṚṢṆA.

Puruṣottamācārya

(13th century)

A teacher of the NIMBĀRKA school, disciple of Śrīnivāsa and author of *Vedānta-ratna-mañjuṣa*. He enumerated the six constituent elements of BHAKTI: treating everyone with goodwill and friendliness, discarding what is contrary to it; refraining from all malice, backbiting, falsehood and violence; having strong faith in the protection of the Lord; praying to the Lord; discarding all false pride and egotism; entrusting oneself and all one's belongings completely to the Lord, being convinced that such complete resignation earns God's grace and mercy.

Pūrva Mīmāṁsā

('the earlier enquiry')

One of the six orthodox schools of Hinduism. *See* MĪMĀṀSĀ.

Pūṣan ('nourisher')

A vedic deity, identified with the SUN.

Puṣkara ('the blue lotus')

Name of a famous tank and place of pilgrimage near Ajmer, glorified in the *Puṣkara Purāṇa*.

puṣpa ('bud', 'blossom')

A flower; one of the essential ingredients of a PŪJĀ. Metaphorically used for virtues to be cultivated by a VAIṢṆAVA.

puṣṭimārga

('way of nourishment [grace]')

A school of VAIṢṆAVISM founded by Vallabha (1481–1533) which exalts the uncaused grace of God (*puṣṭi*) as the means of salvation. Vallabha considered it superior to all other forms of *bhakti-mārga*, entailing complete surrender of oneself and one's own to the GURU. The *puṣṭimārga* is open to all. The highest aim is *nitya līlā*, eternal enjoyment of the company of the Lord. The greatest models are the GOPĪS of Vṛndāvana.

Pūtanā

A demoness, who tried to kill the infant Kṛṣṇa by suckling him on her poisoned breasts. Kṛṣṇa killed her and thus saved her from her own wickedness.

putra ('son')

According to a popular etymology 'saviour' (*tra*) from hell (*put*, the place to which childless men were condemned), explaining the great importance of having a son. Only a son was qualified to perform the last rites for his parents, without which they would not be able to find rest. The son also continued the family line. In some cases a daughter could be 'declared a son', in order to perform the last rites. (*See also* ŚRADDHA.)

R

Rādhā, also Rādhikā

The favourite GOPĪ of Kṛṣṇa, wife of Ayana Ghoṣa, a cowherd of Vṛndāvana. Rādhā is seen as the earthly appearance of LAKṢMĪ. She is the focus of attention in GAUḌIYA VAIṢṆAVISM, at one and the same time mediatrix and role model for devotees. A large literature has developed around her and her worship even outshines that of Kṛṣṇa among the Rādhā-Vallabhis. She is the epitome of passionate devotion. (*See also* CAITANYA.)

Radhakrishnan, Sarvepalli

(1888–1975)

Born in Tirutani, Tamilnāḍū and educated in Christian schools and colleges, he rose not only to the highest office in the Republic of India (vice-president 1952–62; president 1962–67) but also became the most prominent and best-known exponent of Hinduism in the modern world. Beginning with an MA thesis on 'The Ethics of Vedānta', he systematially explored and explained Hinduism in a large number of English publications, such as *History of Indian Philosophy*, *The Hindu View of Life* and *Eastern Religions and Western Thought*. He had a distinguished academic career in India as professor of philosophy at the universities of Mysore and Calcutta, as vice-chancellor of Andhra University and Benares Hindu University, and was Spalding Professor of Eastern Religions at Oxford (1931–36). He also served as India's representative at UNESCO (1946–52), where he took a leading role in organizing important conferences. He was among the first to plead for dialogue among religions.

Radhasoami Satsang

Sect founded by Siv Dayal Singh in the mid-19th century, who declared Radhasoami, 'Lord of the Soul', to be the only appropriate name of God. Its teaching consists in guiding the aspirant through the lower reaches of the cosmos into higher realms of reality. Several branches split off from the original foundation, which adds the name 'Beas' to identify itself.

rāga

Musical mode, personified as male, with *rāgiṇī* as consort, often illustrated in miniatures (*Rāgamālā*).

rāgānuga bhakti

('passionate devotion')

A highly emotional form of BHAKTI developed by the CAITANYA school of GAUḌĪYA VAIṢṆAVISM, in which the passionate absorption in Kṛṣṇa of the GOPĪS of Vṛndāvana provides the model.

Rāghava

Rāma, a descendant of RAGHU.

Raghu

A king of the solar race and an ancestor of RĀMA. KĀLIDĀSA wrote the celebrated epic poem *Raghuvamśa*, the genealogy of Raghu and the life of Rāma.

Rahu

A mythical monster that consists of a disembodied head, and causes eclipses by swallowing the sun and the moon.

Rahu kāla ('Rahu-time')

An inauspicious time. It varies from day to day, and no new or risky untertaking should be commenced during this period.

Rāidās, also **Ravidās**
(15th century)

A BHAKTI poet from the *cāmār* (tanner) CASTE, who became the founder of a sect that perpetuates his memory. He took pride in showing the right way to brahmins, in spite of being an OUTCASTE. He has become a hero of the DALITS.

rāja-dharma

Rules of life for a king, prescribing a king's duties. There is a famous *Rāja-dharma* section in the Śāntiparvan of the *Mahābhārata,* and there are separate works on it as well.

Rājanya

another name for the KṢATRIYA caste.

rajas

See GUṆA.

rāja-sūya ('royal sacrifice')

A great sacrifice celebrated at the installation of a king, at which all vassals had to be present to acknowledge the sovereignty of the newly consecrated monarch.

Rāja Yoga

See PĀTAÑJALA YOGA.

rakṣaka ('saviour')

A designation of VIṢṆU, whose essence is salvation.

rākṣasa

A goblin, evil spirit, fiend, an enemy of the ĀRYAS. They play a major role in Hindu literature as disturbers of peace and as a constant threat to sages in their forest retreats.

Raktadantā ('red-toothed')

An epithet of DURGĀ.

Rāma, also **Rāmacandra**

The oldest son of king Daśaratha, ruler of Ayodhyā. According to traditional historians he lived *c.* 3800–3700 BCE He is considered to have been the seventh

Rāma with Sītā.

AVATĀRA of Viṣṇu. His story is told at great length in the RĀMAYAṆA. He is one of the most popular deities of India, considered the ideal ruler. Repeating his name, even wearing cloth on which his name has been printed, is a favourite religious exercise. In the countryside people use 'Rām, Rām' as a greeting.

Rāma Tīrtha, Swāmi

(1873–1906)

A professor of mathematics at Forman College, Lahore, he became a SAMNYĀSI in 1901 and went as a preacher of Vedānta to Japan and the United States (1902–04), where he gathered a large following. His *Collected Works,* consisting mainly of his lectures, have been published in 12 volumes by the Rama Tirtha Publishing League in Lucknow.

Ramakrishna 'Paramahamsa'

(1834–86)

Possibly the best-known modern Bengali Hindu saint, who became known worldwide through the Ramakrishna Mission. He spent most of his life as temple priest in Dakṣiṇeśvara, a new Kālī–Durgā temple outside Calcutta, where he experienced frequent trances in front of the image of the Goddess (DEVĪ). A circle of devotees gathered around him and one of them began noting down his utterances and conversations held over the years. The work became known in its English translation as *The Gospel of Ramakrishna* by M. One of his disciples, Swami VIVEKĀNANDA, began to form a religious order, the Ramakrishna Mission, after his death, which engaged in education, disaster relief, publication of religious books and preaching.

Shrine at the birthplace of Ramakrishna.

Ramana Maharṣi (1879–1950)

A widely recognized modern Hindu mystic, visited by seekers from both East and West. He experienced death as a boy of fourteen while fully conscious, and experientially understood the difference between the conscious, undying self and the body, the 'not-self'. Shortly after he left home and went to Tiruvanammalai to become a SAMNYĀSI. In spite of his vow of silence, people came to him, asking for his advice. He set up an ashram, and a group of permanent followers began to form. Soon he became a celebrity and was visited by many important personalities. His teaching remained the same: seek the true self. After his death his followers continued to operate his ashram and to publish journals and books reflecting his teachings.

Rāmānanda (1400–70)

Founder of the Śrī *saṁpradāya* (sect), in which Rāmā and Śita are prominently worshipped. Rāmānanda accepted people from all CASTES as well as WOMEN into his order. His twelve principal disciples formed twelve subsects, called *dvaras.* The headquarters of the Śrī *sampradāya*, called *bara sthāna*, is in Ayodhyā. As part of the initiation rites the Rāmānandis burn the name of Rāma into their skin and add the word *dāsa* (slave) to their names. Their greeting is 'Jay Sītā Rāma'.

Rāmānuja (1017–1137)

Founder of the school of VIŚIṢṬĀDVAITA Vedānta and the most important of the Śrīvaiṣṇava *ācāryas* (teachers). Called to YAMUNĀCĀRYA's deathbed, he promised to redeem his three unfulfilled wishes: to honour the memory of the sages Vyāsa and Parāśara, the authors of the *Viṣṇu Purāṇa*; to keep alive the hymns of NAMMĀḶVĀR, the greatest of the Tamil ĀḶVĀRS; and to write a commentary on the *Brahmasūtras* from a ŚRĪVAIṢṆAVA perspective. He consolidated the Śrīvaiṣṇava community, reformed worship at Śrīraṅgam and claimed the famous temple of TIRUPATI for his community. He experienced persecution from a Śaiva ruler and spent twelve years at MELKOTE, where he introduced a new code of worship. His teaching is known as Viśiṣṭadvaita, qualified monism. Rāmānuja held Viṣṇu to be both the material and the efficient cause of the universe; the material world is God's body. The relationship between God and the human being is that of whole and part (*amṣa-amṣi-bhāva*). Rāmānuja taught that by following God's will a person can earn God's grace and be saved. Salvation consists in being transferred to Viṣṇu's heaven (Vaikuṇṭha), being endowed with an incorruptible body and sharing God's bliss. The Śrīvaiṣṇava community later split into southern (TEṄGALAI) and northern (VADAGALAI) schools, but both recognize Rāmānuja as their greatest teacher.

Rāma-rājya ('the reign of Rāma')

An ideal condition believed to have prevailed under the rule of Rāma, the King of Righteousness, where people followed the law and the country was blessed by abundance and generally favourable natural conditions. Mahatma GANDHI translated it as 'Kingdom of God', which he wished to see realized in India. The term *Rāmarājya* has been taken up by Hindu nationalists and politicians as the goal of a Hindu state, replacing the present secular state of India.

Rāmarājya Pariṣad

('reign of Rāma assembly')

A political Hindu party, founded by Swami Karpatriji Maharaj in 1948 to promote a Hindu India.

Rāmāyaṇa ('Adventures of Rāma')

An ancient Sanskrit epic, ascribed to VĀLMĪKI, the first poet. It received its present shape perhaps as late as the second century CE, but contains much older materials (Indian scholars date Vālmīki to the third millennium BCE). It tells the life of Rāma from before birth until death. It is divided into seven sections (*kāṇḍas*), of which the first and the last are considered later additions, with greater variations among the various recensions than the rest: (1) *Bālakāṇḍa*: the birth and boyhood of Rāma; (2) *Ayodhyākāṇḍa*: description of the capital city Ayodhyā and the banishment of Rāma; (3) *Āraṇyakāṇḍa*: Rāma's wanderings in the forest during his fourteen-year exile and the abduction of Sītā by RĀVAṆA; (4) *Kiṣkindhyākāṇḍa*: Rāma's sojourn in the capital of the monkey-king Sugrīva; (5) *Sundarakāṇḍa*: Rāma's efforts to recover Sītā and his winning of allies to invade Laṅkā; (6) *Yuddhakāṇḍa*: the war with Rāvaṇa, his defeat and the recovery of Sītā, his return to Ayodhyā and coronation of Rāma; (7) *Uttarakāṇḍa*: Sītā's banishment, the birth of her two sons in the forest, her ordeal and reunion with Rāma, Sītā's death and Rāma's merging with Viṣṇu. The *Rāmāyaṇa*, both in its original as well as in vernacular recreations such as Tulsīdās's (Hindī) *Rāmcaritmanas* or Kambha's (Tamil) *Kambharāmāyaṇam*, has remained extremely popular in India and parts of it are performed in the yearly Rāmlīlās, theatrical recreations especially of the battle between Rāma and Rāvaṇa, and Rāma's entry into Ayodhyā. The *Rāmāyaṇa* has been edited in seven volumes in a critical edition by the Oriental Institute of the University of Baroda (1960–75).

Rām(a)dās(a), Swami

(1608–81)

Maharatta poet-saint, author of the *Daśabodha*, founder of the Rāmdāsi *saṁpradāya*, a very popular order which attracts mainly low-CASTE people. Its headquarters is in Sajjangad, near Satāra.

Rameśvaram ('Lord Rāma')

A famous place of PILGRIMAGE on an island between India and Śrī Laṅkā. Its 17th-century Ramanathaswamy temple, considered the most perfect example of Dravidian architecture, is set on the place where according to tradition Rāma established a Śivaliṅga (*see* LIṄGA (3)) to atone for the killing of Rāvaṇa, a brahmin by birth, who had abducted his wife Sītā. (*See also* RĀMĀYANA.)

Ranade, R. D. (1889–1957)

Eminent Indian scholar, professor of philosophy at Fergusson College, Pune, and at Allahabad University, vice-chancellor of Allahabad University and founder of Adhyatma Vidyapith at Nimbal. He was a lifelong student of mysticism and the author of *A Constructive Survey of Upanisadic Philosophy* (1926), *The Creative Period of Indian Philosophy* (1928), *Pathway to God in Hindi Literature* (1959), *Pathway to God in Marathi Literature* (1961), *Pathway to God in Kannada Literature* (1960) and of many books in Marathi, Hindī and Kannada.

rasa ('juice', 'taste', 'flavour')

In Indian aesthetics, a term for emotional experience in drama and poetry. Usually nine *rasas* are enumerated: *śṛṅgāra* (erotic love), *hāsya* (laughter), *karuṇa* (compassion), *krodha* (anger), *bibhatsa* (vexation), *vīrya* (heroism), *bhayānaka* (fearfulness), *adbhūta* (wonderment), *śānta* (tranquillity). The GAUḌĪYA VAIṢṆAVA school under the inspiration of CAITANYA used the *rasa* theory in the development of a religion based on emotion. Kṛṣṇa is called *akhila-rasa-amṛta-mūrti*, the perfect embodiment of all *rasas*, and devotees are instructed to develop all emotions in relation to Kṛṣṇa, culminating in *śṛṅgāra rasa*, which was most perfectly embodied in the GOPĪS, among whom RĀDHĀ stands out as Kṛṣṇa's favourite.

Rāṣṭrīya Svayamsevak Sangh

('National Volunteer Organization')

This was founded in 1926 by K. V. Hedgewar (1889–1940), a member of the HINDŪ MAHĀSABHĀ, to counteract the perceived rising Muslim influence in the Indian National Congress. It developed into a tightly organized paramilitary movement with many branches and front organizations attracting students, workers and businesspeople. It claims a membership of 5 million. Members of the RSS were instrumental in the development of the VIŚVA HINDŪ PARIṢAD. Its weekly, *The Organiser*, keeps pressing for the establishment of *Hindū rāṣṭra*.

ratha-mela ('chariot-festival')

A gathering at which the IMAGE of a deity is placed on an often multi-storeyed chariot and taken in procession through a town.

Ratī ('desire', 'lust')

Personified as wife of Kāma, the god of love, and a daughter of DAKṢA. She is also known by other names such as Kāmi, Revā, Prīti, Kāmapriyā and Māyāvatī.

ratna ('jewel')

This is used as title of distinction, and is the name of a medal given by the Indian government (*Bhāratаratna*).

Raurava ('dreadful', 'terrible')

One of the hells. (*See also* NĀRAKA.)

Rāvaṇa ('crying', 'screaming')

The demon king of Laṅkā, the chief of the RĀKṢASAS, half-brother of KUBERA, grandson of the *ṛṣi* Pulastya. Laṅkā was originally in the possession of Kubera, but Rāvaṇa ousted him. He had ten heads (he is also known as Daśagrīva or Daśavādana). He practised the most severe penances for 10,000 years to propitiate Brahmā, and offered one of his heads at the end of each millennium. Thus he gained invulnerability from *devas* and *asuras*, but it was foretold that he was doomed to die through a woman. He is a major figure in the RĀMĀYANA, where he is the main adversary of Rāma. He abducted Sītā, Rāma's wife, but did not do violence to her. He eventually succumbed to Rāma and his allies and lost his capital and his life.

Ṛddhi ('prosperity')

The wife of KUBERA, the god of wealth. Sometimes the name is also used for PĀRVATĪ, the wife of Śiva.

reality (*sat/satya*)

The quest for a 'reality' behind the deceptive appearance of things is as old as Hinduism. The Vedas contain the oft-quoted prayer 'from the unreal lead me to the real' (*asatya mā sat gamaya*), and the Upaniṣads' main interest is in finding the 'reality of the real' (*satyasa satyam*). All Hindu systems are ways of 'realization', i.e. methods of finding truth and reality. Reality is by definition imperishable, possesses consciousness and is blissful (*sat–cit–ānanda*).

rebirth (*punarjanma*)

From the time of the Upaniṣads onwards the universal belief in the endless round of rebirth (*saṁsāra*) became widely accepted in India together with the notion that it was the major task of a human being to break that cycle and attain a state of transcendent freedom. While rebirth, under the inexorable law of *karma*, took place in time, LIBERATION (*mokṣa*, *nirvāṅa*, *kaivalya*) meant reaching a timeless state. The major differences between the competing traditions arose from differences in understanding the nature of the ultimate condition and the means necessary to achieve it.

religious persecution

While Hinduism prides itself on tolerance towards followers of other religions, religious persecution is not unknown. There are historic instances of persecution (even execution) of Jains in South India under the instigation of the Śaivite saint SAMBANDHAR as well as persecution of Vaiṣṇavas by Śaivite kings. In more recent times radical Hindus locally instigated persecutions of Muslims and Christians. Many Hindu works contain not only polemics against other sects and followers of other religions, but also a great deal of invective and condemnation.

Renou, Louis (1896–1966)

Eminent French Indologist. He was professor of Sanskrit at the Sorbonne and author of the standard work *L'Inde classique* (three volumes).

renouncer/renunciation

See SAMNYĀSA/SAMNYĀSI; TYĀGA/TYĀGI.

revelation

See SĀKṢĀTKĀRA; ŚRUTI.

Ṛgveda

The oldest of the Vedic *saṁhitās* (collections), consisting of 1017 hymns (*sūktas*) divided into ten books (or into eight *aṣṭakas* or *khaṇḍas*) with an appendix of 11 so-called Vālakhīlyas, written in an archaic Sanskrit ('Vedic'). There are widely differing opinions regarding its age: since the time of Max MÜLLER (end of the 19th century) it has become customary to assign to it (fairly arbitrarily) the date of *c.* 1500–1200 BCE; many Indian scholars postulate a much earlier date (*c.* 4000–3000 BCE) based on astronomical markers in the texts. The hymns themselves are ascribed to various *ṛṣis* (sages) and addressed to a variety of *devatas* (deities). About a quarter are hymns to INDRA, next in frequency come AGNI hymns. While early Western Indologists considered them a kind of nature poetry, often clumsy and prosaic, modern scholars admit to not being able to understand most of what the *sūktas* are about. Some contemporary Indian scholars believe them to be an astronomical code, embedding the observations of the ancient Vedic Indians, which were used to construct fire ALTARS and to determine the times of SACRIFICES (*yajñas*). According to many Hindu schools of thought the *Ṛgveda* was not created by any human nor conceived by any deity but pre-existed from eternity and was arranged in its present shape by the mythical scholar VYĀSA. For many centuries it was orally transmitted from generation to generation by means of elaborate and complicated mnemonic devices. It was not to be divulged to strangers or to low-caste people. Only brahmins were authorized to teach and to recite it. Vedic hymns are still used in connection with SAṀSKĀRAS (rites of passage), especially at weddings and funerals. The beliefs expressed in the *Ṛgveda* have largely been superseded by more recent Purāṇic ones. But nominally adherence to the infallibility of the Veda is still the criterion of orthodoxy in Hinduism.

Ṛg-vidhāna

Texts that deal with magical effects of reciting the hymns of the *Ṛgveda*, attributed to ŚAUNAKA.

righteousness

See DHARMA.

rites of passage

See SAṀSKĀRAS.

ritual (*kriyā*)

Hinduism is strongly shaped by ritual: a brahmin's entire life is accompanied by ritual. Some of it is obligatory (*nitya*), i.e. non-performance for one year would lead to a loss of CASTE. Some is optional (*naimittika*) and performed for particular purposes (*kāmya*). Devotional Hinduism and tantric Hinduism have developed additional rituals that are deemed essential for their followers. Rituals are believed to be the means of joining the spiritual world and participating in the rhythms of the cosmos. Ritual initiation (UPANAYANA) is a prerequisite for membership in Hindu society; without it all works would be in vain. Similarly it is through ritual that a valid MARRIAGE is entered into, and through ritual alone a person can hope to find peace after death. (*See also* WORSHIP.)

Daily life by the river Ganges.

rivers

Rivers played a great role in early Vedic religion, where they were hymned as life giving. The SAPTASINDHU, the seven rivers, are a constant point of reference, among which the (now dried out) SARASVATĪ was praised as the greatest and the mother of all. When the Hindu heartland moved eastwards, the YAMUNĀ and the GAṄGĀ became the two most important and holy rivers. Many *tīrthas* (places of pilgrimage) are located along them, and the confluence of Yamunā and Gaṅgā (together with the invisible Sarasvatī) at Prāyāga is one of the holiest spots in India. In South India the KAUVERĪ is also called the 'Southern Ganges'. The NARBADĀ in Central India enjoys the unique distinction among the Indian rivers of purifying a person on sight. Most rivers are treated as female (although Indus, Brahmaputra, Sone, Gogra and Sutlej are male) and personified as goddesses. In many temples images of Gaṅgā (with the *makara*, alligator) and Yamunā (with the *kūrma*, tortoise) flank the entrance. Rivers were worshipped as nourishers as well as purifiers: ablutions in them cleansed a person from many sins.

ṛk

A hymn in general; a verse in the *Ṛgveda* as well as the entire *Ṛgveda*; worship, praise.

Roy, Ram Mohan (1772–1833)

Early Indian religious and social reformer, founder of the Brahmo Samāj, called 'father of Modern India'. Born into an orthodox Hindu family, he received a liberal education that included the study of Persian and Arabic, Sanskrit and later English. He was one of the first Indian employees of the British East India Company. Following a religious calling he left service and got in touch with the Christian missionaries at Serampore. He published many essays and tracts and worked towards establishing a Hindu monotheism. His best known accomplishment is his successful struggle for the abolition of SATĪ, the burning alive of a widow on her husband's funeral pyre, which was defended by many as part of the Hindu tradition. To respond to appeals from the pro-*satī* party he went to England, where he died. He is buried in Bristol.

Ṛṣabha

The son of Nābhi, the great-grandson of MANU (2) Svāyambhuva, and Meru, father of BHARATA (2). After leaving his kingdom to his son he became an ascetic of great austerity. He is also held to be the founder of Jainism.

ṛṣi

A sage or poet, especially one who composed Vedic hymns. The 'seven *ṛṣis*' (*saptarṣi*), the 'mind-born sons of Brahmā', are proverbial. Among them are Bhṛgu, Gautama, Bharadvāja, Viśvamitra, Vasiṣṭha, Atri and Aṅgiras (the lists given in various sources are not all the same). They are identified with the seven stars of the Big Dipper. There are many ancient and modern personalities to whom the title '*ṛṣi*' was given in recognition of their wisdom.

Ṛṣya-śṛṅga also Eka-śṛṅga ('deer-horned', 'unicorn')

He was a descendant of KAŚYAPA and an ascetic from childhood. He grew up in a forest without any other human being except his father. When the country of Aṅga was threatened by a severe drought King Lomapāda, advised by his brahmins, sent for Ṛṣyaśṛṅga to marry him to his daughter Śāntā, as rain was promised as a result of their union. Lured out from his hermitage by some beautiful young women, he married Śāntā and the desired rain fell. Śāntā was in reality the daughter of King DAŚARATHA, and Ṛṣyaṣṛṅga performed the SACRIFICE that resulted in the birth of Rāma. His story became very popular; it was used by SAMNYĀSIS to warn young ascetics against becoming familiar with women. It can be found in the *Bhāgavata Purāṇa*.

ṛta ('cosmic order')

The eternal moral law that governs the universe. It parallels *ṛtu*, the sequence of seasons, which in their regularity embody constancy and lawfulness. VARUṆA and MITRA are held to be the guardians of *ṛta*.

ṛtu

The seasons, of which the Indians count six: cool season (*śiṣira*); spring (*vasanta*); hot season (*grīṣma*); rainy season (*varṣa*); autumn (*śārada*); snowy season (*hīma*). Thus the word *ṛtu* sometimes stands for the number six, or any fixed period of time.

ṛtvik

A priest who officiates at a Vedic SACRIFICE. The four chief classes of priests are Hotṛ, Udgatṛ, Adhvaryu and Brāhmaṇa.

Rudra ('terrible', 'howler')

Mentioned in the Veda as a god of death and destruction, feared and kept away from sacrifices. Later identified with Śiva, he represents this god's fierce side. He is also known as Bhava, Śarva, Īśāna, Paśupati, Bhīma, Ugra and Mahādeva.

rudrākṣa-mālā

A rosary made of the fruit of the *rudrākṣa* shrub, worn by ŚAIVITES around the neck, used to count the repetitions of MANTRAS (3). There are some late Upaniṣads that glorify it and its effects.

Rukminī

Kṛṣṇa's principal queen in DVĀRAKA, mother of PRADYUMNA (1) as well as nine other sons and a daughter, called Carumatī.

Rūpa Gosvāmi (*c.* 1460–1540)

One of the six original disciples of CAITANYA. He was known as Dabir Khas, but renamed 'Rūpa Gosvāmi' by Caitanya. Through his efforts VṚNDĀVANA was rediscovered and rebuilt, and he is the author of important works on GAUDĪYA VAIṢṆAVISM, such as the *Bhaktirasāmṛtasindhu*, the *Ujjvala Nīlāmaṇī*, and many *stotras*.

S

Śābara (first century BCE) ('one who lives in the mountains', 'savage')

A celebrated MĪMĀṀSAKA and author of the *Śābarabhāsya*, a lengthy commentary on the *Mīmāṁsāsūtra*.

śabda ('word')

The object of lengthy treatises by grammarians and theologians, who attributed mysterious powers to it. As *śabdabrahman*, BRAHMAN in the form of a word or a sound, the word has absolute power. Basically there are two schools of thought as regards the nature of the word: one believes that words are mere conventional signs of communication; the other holds that there is an eternally pre-existing model (*akṛta*) of all words, which ensures that words are understood the same way everytime they are uttered.

Śacī

The wife of INDRA.

saccidānanda, also **sat-cit-ānanda** ('being/truth *(sat)* – consciousness *(cit)* – bliss (*ānanda*)')

The most popular designation/definition of the supreme being (BRAHMAN) in Hinduism.

Sacred Books of the East (SBE)

A series of 49 volumes of translations (into English) of sources of all Eastern religions (Buddhism, Jainism, Hinduism, Islam, Taoism, Confucianism, Zoroastrianism) planned and edited by Max MÜLLER, and originally published by Clarendon Press, Oxford, from 1879 to 1904 (reprinted 1965–6 by Motilal Banarsidass, Delhi). It was also intended to include the Bible, to make the series fully representative of all major book religions. However, church authorities did not allow this for fear it would make Christianity appear to be on the same level as all other religions. While many of the works selected have been translated again more recently, some of the translations have not been superseded as yet. SBE contains 21 volumes on Hinduism: selected hymns from *Ṛgveda* and *Atharvaveda*, some major Upaniṣads, the entire *Śatapatha Brāhmaṇa*, several *Dharmaśāstra* works, the *Manu-smṛti*, the *Bhagavadgītā* and Śaṅkara's and Rāmānuja's complete commentaries on the *Brahmasūtra*.

Sacred Books of the Hindus (SBH)

A series of 38 volumes of texts and translations of sources of Hinduism planned and edited by Major B. D. Basu, originally published from the Panini Office in Allahābad (1911–34; reprint AMS, New York, 1974).

sacrifice (*yajña*)

The central act of Vedic religion, considered indispensable for the continuation of the world and the well-being of society and individuals. The Vedas describe the creation of the world in terms of a sacrifice and derive the institution of the four VARṆAS from the sacrifice of a primeval *puruṣa* (human). In the course of time the ritual of sacrifice became very intricate and elaborate, and the performance of sacrifices became the prerogative of brahmins, who received an extensive schooling in everything pertaining to it. The roles of various classes of priests were precisely defined in the sacred books.

Besides the regular routine of sacrifices (such as new moon and full moon sacrifices, quarterly seasonal sacrifices, daily oblations) there were special sacrifices performed to obtain particular objectives: thus a person desirous of going to HEAVEN (after death) was enjoined to perform a special sacrifice; a king desirous of establishing his supremacy over his realm was to perform a horse sacrifice (*aśvamedha*), a complex ritual stretched out over a whole year. It is extensively described in the BRĀHMAṆAS, and has received a great deal of attention from Western Indologists. The last recorded *aśvamedha* was performed in the 18th century by a Rajput king.

Sacrifices were believed to provide strength to the gods, on whose activities depended the maintenance of the world. They were also used to expiate sins and to gain power. The sacrifice was supposed to have a great hidden power (*prabhāva*) which could become dangerous if not handled properly by brahmins.

Animals (especially goats), liquor (especially the fermented juice of the SOMA plant), plants and cooked FOOD (especially barley cakes) were the ingredients of Vedic sacrifices. Killing an animal in a sacrifice was not considered an act of violence (*hiṁsā*), since it was prescribed by the Veda and conferred on the victim the privilege of a higher REBIRTH. Some animals such as the camel or the donkey were not considered suitable for sacrifice: they were believed to be lacking *medha*, the sacrificial substance.

The *puruṣamedha* (human sacrifice) was ranked as the highest among the Vedic sacrifices, imitating the primordial sacrifice of the primeval *puruṣa*. Its protective power was considered so great that in ancient times no bridge was considered safe unless a human being had been sacrificed and built into its foundations.

Human sacrifice was a major feature of the Goddess religions of India. Several Purāṇas have lengthy descriptions of the ritual of human sacrifice, and there are historic records of regular human sacrifices in places such as Kāmākhyā (Assam), a centre of DEVĪ worship, and in Tanjore (Tamilnāḍū) far into the 19th century.

An important aspect of all sacrifices is the intention or purpose of the sacrifice (*yajñānta*) and the fee given to the officiating priest (*dakṣiṇa*). The gifts given to brahmins for their services were often considerable: cattle, houses, land, entire villages.

Under the influence of Buddhism and Jainism many Hindu communities abandoned animal sacrifices and substituted offerings of fruit, flowers and vegetables to honour the gods. (*See also* AGNICAYANA; PŪJĀ.)

sad-ācāra

('ethics', 'right behaviour')

Seen as an essential ingredient of all religion by Hindus. The specific *sadācāra* of various *saṁpradāyas* (sects) also contains dietary and liturgical precepts, which vary from one to the other.

Sadā-śiva

The form in which Śiva exercises his fivefold activities of attraction (*anugraha*), concealment (*tirobhava*), taking away (*adana*), preservation (*stithi*) and creation (*sṛṣṭi*), according to ŚAIVA SIDDHĀNTA.

ṣaḍ-darśana

('six philosophical systems')

The collective designation of the philosophies that are considered 'orthodox', namely SĀṀKHYA, YOGA, NYĀYA, VAIŚEṢIKA, Pūrva MĪMĀṀSĀ and Uttara Mīmāṁsā or VEDĀNTA. Nominally all accept the authority of the Veda as revealed.

sādhana ('means to realization')

A generic term for the complex of practices recommended by the various *saṁpradāyas* (sects) or individual GURUS.

sādhāraṇa dharma

('general law')

Moral obligations such as truthfulness, honesty, purity etc. valid for all people, irrespective of CASTE or sect.

sādhu (fem. *sādhvī*, 'good person')

Generic designation of those who have renounced and who dedicate themselves to the pursuit of religious aims, usually wearing garb that distinguishes them from ordinary people.

sage

See ṚṢI.

saguṇa ('with qualities')

One of the major theological controversies among Hindus is the question of whether the ultimate is *saguṇa* or *nirguṇa*. All theist systems ascribe qualities to the supreme, whereas ADVAITA VEDĀNTA denies them. The Upaniṣadic references to *brahman nirguṇa* (without qualities) are interpreted by VAIṢṆAVAS and other theists as meaning the absence of evil or limiting qualities; by Advaitins they are understood as signifying a total absence of all qualities, i.e. pure CONSCIOUSNESS. Those who ascribe qualities to the ultimate usually also conceive of God as having a body and living in a special abode.

sahā-mārga ('associate's way')

The third stage of *bhakti* (devotion) in ŚAIVA SIDDHĀNTA, consisting of yoga: withdrawal of senses from objects, breath control, suspsension of mind activity, recitation of MANTRAS (3) and directing the vital breaths through the six body centres.

Sahadeva

The youngest of the five PĀṆDAVAS, son of MĀDRĪ. He was an expert on astronomy. (*See also* MAHĀBHĀRATA.)

sahaja ('inborn', 'natural condition')

The designation for some tantric, antinomian forms of worship, which follow 'nature' or 'inborn instincts' rather than the Vedic law.

sahasra-nāma ('thousand names')

Litanies of a thousand names of major deities, which are recited by the devotees.

Śaiva Siddhānta

('the final truth of Śiva')

A major school of thought of South Indian ŚAIVISM, with a large following in Tamilnāḍū. Its most important text is the *Śivajñānabodha* by Meykaṇḍa (13th century), based on the recognized 28 Āgamas and the teachings of the 63 Nāyaṇmārs. It acknowledges a triad of principles: *pati* (the Lord, i.e. Śiva), *pāśu* (the unredeemed human person); and *pāśa* (the fetters, identified as *karma*, *māyā* and *aṇava*, 'atomicity', reduced consciousness). To gain freedom one must practise knowledge (*vidyā*), ritual (*kriyā*), austerities (*Yoga*), and a virtuous way of life (*cārya*). The supreme reality is Śiva, whose most fitting description is 'grace' or 'love'. Through his form of Sadāśiva he exercises his fivefold functions of attraction (*anugraha*), concealment (*tirobhava*), creation (*sṛṣṭi*), preservation (*stithi*), and destruction (*ādāna*). Only in a human form and through Śaiva Siddhānta can liberation be gained. All other systems lead to lower stages of reality. Liberation consists in the appearance of the hidden Śiva nature (*śivatva*) of the soul: humans then realize that their true and original Śiva nature was hidden and curtailed through sins. The enlightened person is conscious of Śiva's presence and whatever such a person does, whether the world thinks it good or bad, is Śiva's deed.

Śaivism

The worship of Śiva, probably the oldest of the Hindu traditions. Its beginnings go back to prehistoric times. LIṄGAS (3), the most typical expressions of Śiva worship, have been found in Indus civilization sites and some of the seals were interpreted as representing Śiva Mahāyogi and Śiva Paśupati, figures still prominent in Śiva worship. *Liṅgas* were also found in South India, which today is the centre of Śaivism.

In the *Ṛgveda* the word *śiva* (benevolent, gracious) is not used as a proper name but as an attribute of various deities. However the worship of RUDRA, which later became fused with Śaivism, is quite prominent. Rudra, 'the Howler', was feared rather than loved and his worship consisted in depositing offerings at crossroads imploring him not to come or do harm.

The earliest known Śiva community are the PĀŚUPATAS, worshippers of Śiva as Lord of Animals. Sophisticated Śaivite philosophies developed in South India (ŚAIVA SIDDHĀNTA) and in Kashmir (KASHMIR ŚAIVISM or Tṛka). Many important figures in the history of Hinduism, such as ŚAṄKARA (2), and many South Indian kings, were Śaivas. They built magnificent sanctuaries in honour of Śiva and established attractive festivals in places such as TANJORE, CIDAMBARAM and MADURAI. VĀRĀṆASĪ, the holiest city of Hinduism, is sacred to Śiva, who is worshipped in the Golden temple as Viśvanātha, Lord of the Universe.

Śaivite asceticism tended to run into extremes: groups such as the Kapālikas and Kālamukhas are said to eat human corpses and to besmear themselves with ashes taken from cremation grounds. They do this to demonstrate the identity of everything with the supreme Śiva and their indifference towards conventions of ordinary life.

Śaivism today is the second-largest segment of mainstream Hinduism, with several hundred million followers.

Śakadvīpa

The continent of the ŚAKAS. Śakadvīpa is also an alternative name for ŚVETADVĪPA, the 'white island continent', which is mentioned in the *Mahābhārata* as a place where perfect beings worship NĀRĀYAṆA, and which was visited by the sages NĀRA and NĀRADA (2). It is quite often mentioned in Hindu literature, but has not been satisfactorily identified.

Śakas

A people from the north, usually identified with the Yavanas. They are thought to be the Indo-Scythans described by Ptolemy. They invaded India between 200 BCE and 100 CE and founded a kingdom in north-western India. The Śaka era, beginning in 78 CE, still widely used in India, derives from them.

Śākaṭāyana

An ancient grammarian who lived before YĀSKA and PĀṆINĪ.

śākhā (1) ('branch')

With reference to the Vedas *śākhā* means a particular recension of a text as taught and transmitted by a particular family or school, showing some minor variations.

śākhā (2)

The smallest unit of the RĀṢṬRĪYA SVAYAMSEVAK SANGH.

sākṣāt-kāra

A bodily vision of the deity, the goal of many BHAKTI schools, believed to constitute the assurance of final salvation.

sākṣī ('inner witness')

Upaniṣadic notion of an immortal, unchanging 'witness' consciousness, which is the passive observer of everything else. The Upaniṣads use the simile of the two birds on one tree: one eats (ordinary consciousness) while the other only watches (witness consciousness). By focusing all attention on the 'witness consciousness' one can gain immortality. MADHVA calls the presence of Viṣṇu in the soul *śākṣī*.

śākta

A follower of ŚAKTI religion. (*See also* ŚĀKTISM.)

Śakti ('power')

Personified in the Goddess (DEVĪ). She is either conceived as consort of a male god, or as an independent supreme being, created from the united power of all the gods. In the first instance she is identified with the letter 'i' in *Śiva*: without it, he is *śava*, i.e. a lifeless corpse.

Śāktism

('the worship of power energy')

Personified in a female divinity, it is a common feature of all forms of Hinduism. Specifically it designates the traditon in which the Goddess (DEVĪ) is identified with the supreme principle and worshipped in an exclusive way. One of the major differences between Śāktism and other expressions of Hinduism is the identification of the Goddess not only with spirit (BRAHMAN), but also with nature or matter (*prakṛti*).

Śāktism may be a remnant of the prehistoric worldwide cult of the Great Mother. In India terracotta figurines of the Goddess, almost identical in shape, have been found in prehistoric sites, in the Indus civilization and in contemporary villages.

As a form of mainstream Hinduism Śāktism is especially prominent in modern Bengal and Assam. The main festivity is *Durgāpūjā*, celebrated during nine days in autumn, when the image of Devī *Mahiṣamārdiṇi* is displayed in homes and public places and processions take place in her honour.

The main literary sources of Śāktism are Devī Purāṇas and Tantras. True to the principle that Śakti embodies both mind and matter, Śāktism combines theoretical reflections on the identity of Śakti with *brahman* and the unity of everything with concrete forms of worship. The declared aim of Śāktism is *bhukti* and *mukti*, enjoyment and liberation in one. In Śāktism *vidyā* (knowledge) and *māyā* (delusion) are seen as one and the same.

There are two main branches of Śāktism: 'right hand' and 'left hand'. Right-hand Śāktism resembles other forms of BHAKTI: it consists of the worship of the image of the Goddess with fruits and flowers, the singing of hymns and the burning of camphor and incense. Left-hand Śāktism involves the use of the five 'ms', the transgression of ordinary morality in secret forms of worship. (*See also* DURGĀ; TANTRA (2).)

Śakuntalā

Daughter of the sage VIŚVAMITRA and the APSARA MENĀ, whom INDRA had sent down from heaven to seduce Viśvamitra. When Menā had to go back to heaven she left the child in the care of birds (*śakuntas*), and thus she was called Śakuntalā. She was brought up in a forest hermitage by a sage called Kanva. King Duṣyanta saw her, was charmed by her and asked her to marry him. She bore him a son, named BHARATA (4), who became a universl monarch. India was called Bhārata after him. The Śakuntalā story was very popular with Indian dramatists. One of the most famous plays by KĀLIDĀSA is *Śakuntalā* (translated into most Western languages).

śāla-grāma

A round ammonite, found in the Gandak river of Nepal, held sacred by VAIṢṆAVAS as an emblem of Viṣṇu. Most Vaiṣṇavas either carry a *śālagrāma* or keep one or more in their homes.

samādhi (1)

('concentration', 'mindfulness')

The title of one of the sections of the *Yoga Sūtras*.

samādhi (2)

A stage in the process of YOGA ('contemplation').

samādhi (3)

A memorial chapel erected over the tomb of a saint.

sāman ('tune')

As in *Sāmaveda*, the Veda containing the tunes according to which the hymns of the *Ṛgveda* are to be chanted.

Sāmaveda

The third of the four vedic *saṁhitās*, dealing with *sāmans* or melodies appropriate to the *ṛks* or verses of the *Ṛgveda*. The text as it is preserved exists in three recensions: Kauthuma, Rāṇāyanīya and Jaiminīya. The text was commented upon by Sāyaṇa in the 14th century. Most of the verses are identical with the verses in the *Ṛgveda*. The most ancient melodies have not been preserved; the notations which we possess are of a relatively late time. (*See also* VEDA.)

Sambandhar, also Jñanasambandhar

(seventh century)

A famous poet and preacher of ŚAIVISM in South India at a time when most had turned Jainas. While the King of Madurai had converted to JAINISM, his chief queen and his chief minister had remained Śaivites. With their help Sambandhar arranged a debate with a large number of Jain monks, whom he defeated. The king then re-converted to Śaivism. According to tradition Sambandhar persuaded the king to impale 8,000 Jains. In another part of the Tamil country he brought back a large number of Jains and Buddhists to Śaivism. His hymns are still widely sung in Śiva temples.

saṃdhyā (1), also sandhyā

('joining', 'twilight' [both of morning and of evening])

Personified as daughter of BRAHMĀ and wife of ŚIVA.

saṃdhyā (2)

Obligatory rituals to be performed by brahmins at dawn and dusk.

Saṃdhyābhāṣa
('twilight language')

Compositions with double meaning, used by Tantrikas; their 'surface' meaning is accessible to everybody, the second, 'secret', meaning is only understood by the initiates. (*See also* TANTRA (2).)

saṃhitā ('collection')

An expression used to designate the mantra portion of the Vedas (e.g. *Ṛgveda Saṃhitā*) or the later sectarian writings of VAIṢṆAVAS (e.g. *Ahirbudhnya Saṃhitā*), to which a great amount of authority was attributed due to their authors.

samīpa ('nearness [to God]')

One of the modalities of salvation in theistic Hinduism. Another would be SARŪPA (sameness of form).

saṁkalpa ('intention')

A declaration of intent at the beginning of a pilgrimage. Without it, the pilgrimage would not earn any merit.

Saṁkarṣaṇa

One of the four *vyūhas* (emanations) of Viṣṇu, characterized by lordship (*aiśvarya*) and heroism (*vīrya*).

Sāṁkhya ('number')

One of the six orthodox systems, founded by Kapila (sixth century BCE); it assumes that the whole universe consists of combinations of 24 elements (*tattvas*) in addition to *puruṣa* (spirit). Sāṁkhya is a dualistic system: spirit (*puruṣa*) and matter (*prakṛti*) have opposite but complementary characteristics. Everything originates from a combination of the two, and ultimate liberation is due to a separation of spirit from matter. Spirit is originally manifold, matter is one. Matter is characterized by three *guṇas* (elementary principles): *sattva* (lightness); *rajas* (passion); and *tamas* (darkness). These three are originally in equilibrium, but under the influence of spirit, evolution begins. The first product of the process is *mahat* (the great One), also called *buddhi* (the intellect). From *mahat* issues *ahaṁkāra*, the principle of egoity. When one suffers under the frustrations of life one begins a quest for freedom from misery. This quest leads to a reversal of the evolutionary process and a final separation of spirit from matter. The ultimate stage is called *kaivalya* (aloneness), when the spirit is all by himself and fully satisfied.

Sāṁkhya-kārikā

The oldest preserved text of the SĀṀKHYA system, ascribed to Īśvara Kṛṣṇa (third century CE). It explains in a brief and systematic manner the basic principles of Sāṁkhya.

Sāṁkhya-sūtra

Ascribed to Kapila (sixth century BCE), but probably later than the *Sāṁkhya-kārikā*. It consists of a brief exposition of Sāṁkhya in *sūtra* form.

sam-kīrtaṇa

Congregational singing of hymns, especially among GAUḌĪYA VAIṢṆAVAS, usually accompanied by cymbals and drums, often also by dancing. *Nāgara samkīrtaṇa*, popularized by CAITANYA, is public singing and dancing on the streets of towns.

samnyāsa ('renunciation')

The fourth and last ĀŚRAMA (2) (stage in life) of a brahmin, in which all attachment to home and possessions, including family, are to be given up. It has become popular to enter into *samnyāsa* without going through the āśramas of householder and forest dweller. Usually the formal entry into *samnyāsa* is preceded by a period of instruction in the particular customs of a *saṃpradāya* (sect) and solemnly confirmed through an initiation ceremony (*dīkṣā*) by the GURU. This includes stripping and symbolic self-cremation, the acceptance of a new name and the transmission of a MANTRA (3), through which the initiate becomes a member in the line of succession (*guru paraṁparā*). *Samnyāsa*, while freeing the initiate from all normal religious and social obligations, is strictly regulated by the rules of the *yatidharma* (*see* YATI).

samnyāsi
(fem. *samnyāsinī*, 'renouncer')

Someone who has taken up SAMNYĀSA. Normally acceptance by a GURU from an acknowledged order is a prerequisite for becoming a *samnyāsi*. However, there are cases of self-initiation, so-called *svatantra samnyāsis*. The number of *samnyāsis* and *samnyāsinīs* in India is fairly large: estimates range from 7 to 15 million. There are associations of *samnyāsis*, such as the Akhila Bhāratīya Sādhu Samāj, and some Hindu orders have also begun to accept non-Indians.

saṁpradāya ('tradition')

Usage, denomination, sect.

saṁsāra

The transient world, the cycle of birth and rebirth.

saṃskāra ('sacrament')

A rite of passage, through which a Hindu of the three higher VARṆAS becomes a full member of the community. While in former times a great number of *saṃskāras* were performed, today there are mainly four that are important in the life of a Hindu: birth (*jāta-karma*), initiation (*upanayana*, investiture with the sacred thread), marriage (*vivaha*), and last rites (*śraddha* or *antyeṣṭi*). A Hindu who wilfully neglects the *saṃskāras* is no longer a member of the community.

samudra manthana

See CHURNING OF THE OCEAN.

samvat

A Hindu era, beginning in 57 BCE, a widely used chronological system in modern India.

samyama

In PATAÑJALI YOGA, the triad of *dhāraṇa, dhyāna* and *samādhi.*

sanātana dharma ('eternal law')

A self-designation of 'Hinduism' by Hindus, implying either that the DHARMA is eternal or that it has been promulgated by an eternal lawgiver. Many Hindus derive from this explanation the universal validity of Hindu *dharma* for the whole of humankind and for all of history. 'Sanātanists' are those who rigidly adhere to traditional law.

Sanat-kumāra

The most prominent of the four mind-born sons of BRAHMĀ. (*See also* KUMĀRAS.)

Śāṇḍilya (*c.* 100 CE)

The author of the *Chāṇḍogya Upaniṣad*, of a law book, and of a *Bhakti-sūtra.*

Saṅgam ('confluence') (1)

The place near Prāyāga (Allāhabad) where the YAMUNĀ flows into the GAṄGĀ, merging with the (invisible) SARASVATĪ.

Saṅgam (2), also **Cankam**

An early period of Tamil literature (*c.* 1st century BCE).

Śaṅkara (1) ('auspicious')

Name of ŚIVA in his role of creator.

Śaṅkara, the founder of the school of Advaita Vedānta.

Śaṅkara (2), also **Śaṅkarācārya**

'Master Śaṅkara', a great reformer of Hinduism (eighth century CE). Born in Kālaḍi, Kerala, he entered SAMNYĀSA at a very early age. Defeating Buddhists and followers of other heterodox movements, he established ADVAITA VEDĀNTA through his commentaries on the major Upaniṣads, the *Bhagavadgītā* and the *Brahmasūtras*. He also wrote numerous hymns and many smaller treatises. He established *maṭhas* (religious centres) in four strategic places in the east (Purī), west (Dvāraka), north (Bādarīnātha), and south (Śṛṅgerī) and founded ten orders of *samnyāsis* (DAŚANĀMIS). By many he is considered the greatest among Indian religious thinkers. His followers consider him either an AVATĀRA of Śiva or a person inspired by him. One of his immediate disciples, Ānanda Giri, wrote a *Śaṅkara Digvijāya*, a report on the (spiritual) conquest of India by Śaṅkara, by defeating all his opponents in debate.

Śaṅkarācārya

The title given to the head monk of one of the *māṭhas* (religious centres) reputedly founded by ŚAṄKARA (2).

Śaṅkara Miśra (16th century)

A prolific writer, who produced major works on almost all of the orthodox systems of Hinduism.

Śaṅkara Deva (1449–1568)

A major teacher of VAIṢṆAVISM in Assam.

śaṅkha ('conch')

Used in many forms of Hindu WORSHIP; the blowing of the conch often opens or closes worship.

san-mārga

('the way of truth and reality')

The fourth and highest stage in ŚAIVA SIDDHĀNTA.

Sanskrit ('refined language')

The language in which much of classical Hindu literature has been written, considered a 'sacred' language, the language of the gods. For some time it was believed to be the root language of all Indo-European languages. (*See also* LANGUAGE.)

sant (1) 'saint'

Generic designation of all SAMNYĀSIS (renouncers).

sant (2)

Specific name for a group of late medieval religious poets and teachers, belonging to various denominations, Hindus (e.g. Tulsīdās), Sikhs (e.g. Gurū Nānak), and Muslims (e.g. Kabīr), usually from the lower strata of society, but widely influential on account of the appeal of their teachings.

sant sādhana

The teaching of the SANTS (2), focusing on the practice of the divine name (*nāma*), devotion to the divine *guru* (*satguru*) and the company of fellow devotees (*satsaṅg*).

Śāntā

The daughter of Daśaratha, she was adopted by Lomapāda, and married to ṚṢYAŚṚṄGA.

śānta ('tranquillity')

One of the eight RASAS of Hindu aesthetics.

śānti ('peace')

Often exclaimed (three times) at the end of recitiations of religious texts as a kind of blessing.

saṇtoṣa ('contentment')

One of the Hindu virtues, listed in the *Yogasūtras* as generating inner peace and happiness, a precondition for successful meditation.

saptarṣi

The seven great ṚṢIS (sages): the names are not the same in all the references.

Saptaśatī ('seven hundred [verses]')

A name of the *Devīmāhātmya*, which consists of seven hundred ŚLOKAS (couplets).

Saptasindhu, also **Saptasindhava**
('the seven rivers')

These are frequently mentioned in the Vedas. Their names are: Gaṅgā, Yamunā, Sarasvatī, Śutudri, Paruṣṇi, Marudvṛdhā, Ārjīkīyā. Not all are clearly identifiable today.

Sāradā Devī (1853–1920)

As RAMAKRISHNA PARAMAHAMSA's wife and, after his death, his successor as 'The Holy Mother' she had great influence on the formation of the Ramakrishna Mission. Ramakrishna never consummated the marriage with Sāradā Devī, worshipping her instead as Śakti incarnate. Her own vision of Kālī set off her personal spiritual development. As long as Ramakrishna was alive she took care of his material needs, especially cooking his food. After his death she grew into the role of the 'Holy Mother'. Her picture is found in all Ramakrishna Mission temples alongside that of Ramakrishna Paramahamsa and Swami Vivekānanda. In 1954 the Śāradā Maṭha was founded as independent monastic institution for women alongside the Ramakrishna Mission, which has only male monastics.

śaraṇa-gati
('taking refuge [in the Lord]')

The highest act of devotion in VAIṢṆAVISM, the last formal step in the process of becoming a *bhakta* (devotee). One of the last works of RĀMĀNUJA is the *Śaraṇagatigadya*, which extolls the salvific effects of this practice. Madhva wanted his followers to demonstrate this self-surrender outwardly by branding their bodies with the symbols of Viṣṇu. (*See also* PRAPATTI.)

Sarasvatī (1)

The wife of BRAHMĀ, goddess of speech and learning, inventor of the Sanskrit

Sarasvatī.

language and the Devanāgarī script, patroness of the arts and sciences, usually represented as seated on a lotus, with a *vīna* (lute) in one of her hands.

Sarasvatī (2)

Celebrated in the Vedas as a mighty river, flowing from the Himālayas to the sea, it later disappeared in the sands. Recent satellite photography has produced evidence of its course. It is believed to join underground the GAṄGĀ and the YAMUNĀ at the SAṄGAM (1) in Prāyāga. As the most sacred of the Vedic rivers, it formed the eastern boundary of the original Āryāvarta, the homeland of the Vedic people.

sarga ('creation')

One of the *pañcālakṣana* (five topics of a PURĀṆA). Most Purāṇic accounts of creation speak of several creations.

śarīra

See BODY.

Śarīraka-bhāṣya

The title of Śaṅkara's commentary on the *Brahmasūtras*.

sa-rūpa

('having the same form [as the Lord]')

One of the qualities of a released VAIṢṆAVA, who receives an incorruptible body like that of Viṣṇu.

Śarva

A name of ŚIVA, derived from *śaru* (arrow). Śarva symbolizes the power of Śiva to kill, and is often invoked together with YAMA, the custodian of the underworld. Śarva is the embodiment of cruelty.

Sarva-darśana-saṁgraha

('Synopsis of all philosophical systems')

A famous work by the Advaitin MĀDHAVA, in which he reviews and critiques 15 different systems (besides CĀRVĀKA and several schools of Buddhism and Jainism, he deals with all major Hindu systems).

Sarva-loka

See BRAHMA-LOKA.

śāstra ('teaching', 'rule')

An authoritative source for Hindu DHARMA, used either as a collective term or as designation of a single work, especially one dealing with law.

sat, also satya ('being', 'truth')

As in SACCIDĀNANDA, the designation of the supreme being as 'being/truth, consciousness, bliss; or in *sat-guru*, the 'true master', i.e. the supreme.

Śatākṣī ('hundred-eyed')

A name of the Goddess (DEVĪ).

Śata-rudriya

('[invocation of] Rudra with a hundred [names]')

A text in the White YAJURVEDA, through which RUDRA/Śiva is propitiated and asked to stay away from the sacrificer.

Śata-rūpā

('the one with the hundred forms')

The first woman; daughter of BRAHMĀ, mother or wife of MANU (2).

sat-guru ('the true teacher')

Usually identified with the supreme being.

Sathya Sai Baba (*b.* 1926)

('true father of truth')

A contemporary charismatic Hindu leader, who claims to be the reincarnation of the Sai Baba of Śirdi (Mahārāṣṭra) who died in 1918, as well as an AVATĀRA of Śiva and Śakti. He discovered, as a fourteen-year-old, his miraculous powers to cure illness by means of an ash-like substance that formed on the pictures of Sai Baba and that he himself is now creating freely. His followers number millions in India and abroad; hundreds of Sai Baba centres have come into existence, some large establishments with schools, hospitals and other facilities. He predicted that he will live to the age of 95, and that after his death a third and last incarnation of a Sai Baba will appear.

Satī ('faithful')

A daughter of DAKṢA and wife of ŚIVA, who killed herself out of anger at Dakṣa's contempt for Śiva.

satī

A wife who ascends the funeral pyre of her deceased husband. A *satī* was usually honoured by her community through a memorial. *Satī* was declared illegal in 1829, but still occurs occasionally. (*See also* WOMEN.)

Bhajan attended by the contemporary guru Sai Baba (left).

sat-putra-mārga
('the way of the true son')

The second stage of devotion according to ŚAIVA SIDDHĀNTA, consisting of preparing articles for Śiva PŪJĀ and meditating on Śiva as a form of light.

Śatru-ghna ('destroyer of enemies')

Twin brother of LAKṢMAṆA, half-brother of Rāma. He supported Rāma and killed Lavaṇa, a RĀKṢASA leader.

sat-sang
('community of true [devotees]')

Communal worship, usually consisting of singing hymns (*bhajan*) and listening to sermons. It is enjoined to devotees as a duty and as a means to sustain their faith.

sattva

See GUṆA.

satyāgraha ('truth-grasping')

A term coined by Mahatma GANDHI in South Africa, describing his insistence on claiming his rights, defined as the strength born of truth, love and non-violence.

Satya-loka

See BRAHMA-LOKA.

Satya-nāmi(s)

An order of SAMNYĀSIS claiming great antiquity. Persecuted and almost eradicated under Aurangzeb, they were revived in the late 18th century by Jagjivandās. They are found mainly in western India.

Satyārtha Prakāśa
('light of truth')

The title of the main work (in Hindī) by Swami Dāyānanda Sarasvatī, the founder of the ĀRYA SAMĀJ.

Satyavatī (1)

The daughter of Uparicara and the *apsara* (nymph) Adrikā. She was the mother of VYĀSA by the *ṛṣi* (sage) Parāśara, and later married King Śāntanu, and gave birth to VICITRA-VĪRYA and Citrāṅgada. She became the grandmother of the KAURAVAS and PĀṆḌAVAS. (*See also* MAHĀBHĀRATA.)

Satyavatī (2)

The mother of JAMADAGNI and grandmother of PARAŚURĀMA.

śauca ('purity')

One of the traditional Hindu virtues, whose practice is a prerequisite to PĀTAÑJALA YOGA.

saulabhya ('benevolence')

One of the (six) transcendental qualities of Viṣṇu according to RĀMĀNUJA.

Śaunaka

A famous sage, son of Śunaka, the reputed author of the *Bṛhaddevatā*, a major figure in the MAHĀBHĀRATA and the *Bhāgavata Purāṇa*, where he narrates large portions of VAIṢṆAVA lore.

Saura Purāṇas

A group of Upa-Purāṇas, dealing with Sūrya (the SUN).

sauśilya ('kindness')

One of the (six) transcendental qualities of Viṣṇu according to RĀMĀNUJA.

Savarkar, Vinayak Damodar
(1883–1966)

For many years chief ideologue of the HINDU MAHĀSABHĀ, and founder of the ABHINAV BHĀRAT SOCIETY, who attempted to 'Hinduize politics and to militarize Hinduism'. His essay

'Hindutva', in which he advocated a distinction between Hinduism as a religion (*Hindu dharma*), divided into many *saṁpradāyas* (sects), and Hinduism as a culture (HINDUTVA), which is supposed to be one, became seminal for the further development of political Hinduism.

Savitṛ ('generator')

A vedic name for the SUN, to whom many hymns are addressed. Also the title of an epic poem by AUROBINDO GHOSE.

Sāyaṇa (14th century)

Celebrated commentator of the entire *Ṛgveda* and author of other works. He was the brother of Mādhavācārya, and lived at the court of VIJĀYANĀGARA.

sayujya ('togetherness [with Viṣṇu]')

One of the forms of emancipation from SAṀSĀRA.

Schrader, Otto (1876–1961)

Renowned German Indologist, who pioneered the study of the VAIṢṆAVA *saṁhitās*. After studies in Indology in several European universities, he accepted an appointment as director of the library of the Theosophical Society at Adyar (Madras) where he learnt Tamil, Telugu, Kannada and Malayalam. He travelled widely to collect manuscripts for the library. He is best known for his pioneering work on PĀÑCARĀTRA. His *Introduction to the Pāñcarātra and the Ahirbudhnya Samhita* (1916), written while he was interned in Ahmednagar during the First World War, became seminal for the study of the Vaiṣṇava *saṁhitās*. After his return to Germany and as professor of Indology at Kiel University he concentrated on studies on the *Bhagavadgītā*. He was honoured with the title 'Vidyāsāgara' by the Bhārata Mahāmandal in Vārāṇasī in 1924.

second birth

Initiation (UPANAYANA) and investiture with the sacred thread given to the three upper VARṆAS (Brahmaṇas, Kṣatriyas, Vaiśyas) is called a 'second birth' and the initiated are called *dvijatis*, 'twice-born'.

secularism

The Indian constitution, written under prime minister Jawaharlal Nehru's government, declared India (Bhārat) 'a secular democracy'. Many traditional Hindus resisted 'secularism' and wanted India to be a Hindu *rāṣṭra* (state) and Hinduism declared the state religion (as Pakistan had declared Islam its state religion). 'Secularism' was interpreted by its defenders not as hostility towards religion or dismissal of religion, but as tolerance for all religions and impartiality towards all. One of the consequences of secularism was the injunction against teaching Hinduism in public schools. Secularism has become the main target of the Hindu political parties who accuse the Congress governments that ruled the country for over four decades of having legislated against Hindu DHARMA. They strive to overthrow secularism.

self

The nature of the self has been conceived in a great variety of ways in Hindu thought and is one of the main foci of all Hindu *darśanas* (philosophical systems). Many classical Hindu scholarly works begin with a review and critique of all major conceptions of the self before establishing their own positions. They all reject the materialist CĀRVĀKA notion that identifies the self with the physical body, and the Buddhist 'no-self' teaching. As far as Hindu systems are concerned, SĀṀKHYA and YOGA teach a plurality of individual selves (*puruṣa*) that are immaterial and eternal, uncreated and conscious.

According to VAIŚEṢIKA there are many different selves, distinguished by their *viśeṣas* (properties, specifics), which can be perceived by YOGIS. The ĀTMANS themselves are eternal and not bound by time and space, but their actions are limited by the physical organisms with which they are connected. NYĀYA assumes the existence of a spiritual self different from the body. MĪMĀṀSĀ postulates the existence of a soul/self distinct from the body, because without it Vedic statements such as 'the sacrificer goes to heaven' would not make sense. However, since Mīmāṁsakas only recognize the *karmakāṇḍha* of the Veda as 'revealed', they must refrain from making statements about the nature of the self. Vedāntins, for whom the *jñanakhāṇḍa* is revelation proper, focus on the nature of the self. They differ in their interpretation of Upaniṣadic statements such as 'this *ātman* [self] is the *brahman* [supreme being]'. The Advaitins understand it as an expression of complete identity, the liberated self merging without trace into the qualityless *brahman*. Dvaitins insist on a categorical distinction between Viṣṇu, the Supreme Being, and the individual souls (*jīvātmas*). Viśiṣṭādvaitins take a middle position. While for Advaitins the self is uncreated and indestructible, theistic schools of Vedānta usually consider the selves of individuals created by the Supreme God, and, together with matter, the body of God. Consequently the importance of self-knowledge differs. For Advaitins knowledge of the self is identical with emancipation; for the non-Advaitins, emancipation requires the knowledge of matter, selves and God.

Sen, Keshub Chandra

(1838–84)

One of the early members of the BRAHMO SAMĀJ, a non-brahmin who rose to leadership and brought about a split in the Samāj. Initially a great admirer of Christ and Christianity, he increasingly developed a notion that he was a superman initiating a new dispensation. Socially progressive and active in humanitarian work, he alienated many members of the Brahmo Samāj by his idiosyncracies and by violating the principles he had himself established.

service

See SEVA.

Śeṣa

A serpent with a thousand heads which serves Viṣṇu as couch during the intervals between creations. It is also called *ananta*, infinite, as a symbol of eternity. When Śeṣa yawns, the earth trembles. At the end of each KALPA Śeṣa vomits poisonous fire which destroys all creation. At the time of the CHURNING OF THE OCEAN the gods took Śeṣa as a rope, looping it around Mount Mandara. Śeṣa's hood is known as MAṆIDVĪPA, the island of jewels.

seva ('service')

In pre-modern Hinduism this is usually understood as temple service and care for the divine IMAGE. Traditional Hindu *saṁpradāyas* (sects) have very elaborate rituals which clearly define the range of (obligatory) *seva* and also list acts that are considered 'sins against *seva*'. With Hindu reform movements in the 19th century *seva* began to acquire the connotation of social service, support for the needy and material as well as spiritual comfort. To worship God in the poor and to serve God in the needy has become an accepted contemporary interpretation of *seva*.

Sey, also Seyon

Alternative names for the Tamil war god MURUGAN.

Śibi

An ancient tribe in north-western India, described as going about clad in the skins of wild animals and using clubs as weapons, believed to be the original Śiva worshippers.

siddha (1) ('accomplished')

Semi-divine beings, said to number 88,000, believed to be pure and holy.

siddha (2)

A person who has reached perfection within a specific SĀDHANA.

siddha-rūpa ('perfect form')

One's true and original being; in GAUḌĪYA VAIṢṆAVISM, one of the original characters of the Kṛṣṇa LĪLĀ in Braja, with which the devotees identify and through which they engage in *rāgānuga* (passionate) BHAKTI.

siddhi ('accomplishment')

Usually designates the exercise of occult faculties, such as making oneself invisible, understanding the languages of animals etc. They are mentioned in the *Yogasūtras* as potential obstacles on the way to KAIVALYA, but eagerly sought after by many lesser YOGIS. The Transcendental Meditation Society offered courses in *siddhis*.

śikha

The tuft of hair kept at the back of the head after tonsure. It is also called *choṭi*. It had to be worn by Hindu householders (supposed to cover the *Brahmārandhra*, the place at which the soul leaves the body at the time of death). It is shorn off during the initiation (*dīkṣā*) of a SAMNYĀSI.

śikhara

The 'spire' of a Hindu temple (of the Northern or *nāgara* type).

śikṣā

Phonetics, one of the six VEDĀṄGAS, which teaches proper pronunciation and recitation of the Veda.

Śikṣāṣṭaka

('eight couplets of instruction')

A short text said to be the only written work of CAITANYA, embodying the gist of his teachings.

śīla

See ETHICS.

silence

Keeping silent for extended periods of time (*maunasādhana*) is a common practice for Hindu ascetics.

śilpa ('skill', 'craft')

Artistic creation, production of something beautiful. It can be through architecture, painting, dance or music.

Śilpa-śāstra, also **Vāstu-śāstra**

The traditional teaching of temple building and IMAGE making, originally believed to have been imparted by semi-divine beings to human craftsmen. The two most important manuals are the *Mānasāra* and the *Mayamata*, supposed to be by the architects of the gods and the demons respectively. In addition to technical detail the *Śilpaśāstras* also contain mythological and religious materials.

śilpin

Traditional craftsman, architect, sculptor, artist.

sin (*pāpa, pātaka, doṣa*)

Offences against the moral and ritual law, which require penances (*prayaścittas*). Vedic religion used the distinction between *upapātaka* ('lesser sins'), such as teaching the Veda for money, adultery, killing a woman or a man from a low caste, and MAHĀPĀTAKA ('capital sins') which were difficult to atone for. The latter were *brahmaṇahatya* (killing a brahmin), *sūrapāna* (intoxication), *steya* (stealing gold from a brahmin), *guruvaṅganagama* (variously interpreted as incest or cohabitation with the *guru*'s wife), *mahāpātakasaṁsarga* (association with great sinners). The number of sins was greatly augmented by the various *saṁpradāyas* (sects), who declared infringements of their ritual as sins. Thus the GAUḌĪYA VAIṢṆAVAS enumerate 32 offences against worship (which can be atoned for) and 10 offences against the name, which are virtually unpardonable. Sins which are not atoned for lead to 'downfall', i.e. loss of CASTE in this life and punishment in the next.

Sītā ('furrow')

The daughter of King Janaka of Videha, wife of Rāma, a principal figure in the RĀMĀYAṆA. She was found in a furrow by her father while he was ploughing his field, and was also called Ayonijā, 'not born from a womb'. As Rāma's only wife she embodied all the virtues of a traditional Hindu woman and was held up as model for Hindu girls to follow throughout the ages. This notion has come under attack by Indian feminists.

Śītalā

The goddess of smallpox, widely worshipped in rural India.

Śiva ('graceful')

A deity, whose followers represent one of the ancient mainstream traditions of Hinduism. Early on identified with the Vedic RUDRA, Śiva appears in some late Upaniṣads and in the epics and Purāṇas as the focus of a vast mythology and

Śiva Nāṭarāja, King of the Dance.

philosophical reflection. Some seals found in Harappa–Mohenjo Daro were interpreted as Śiva Paśupati (Lord of the Animals) and Śiva Mahāyogi, motifs found in later Śaivism. LIṄGAS were also found in the Indus civilization; these have always been associated with ŚAIVISM. The oldest myth associated with Śaivism – the destruction of DAKṢA's sacrifice by Śiva at Kankhala, near Hardwar – suggests initial hostility towards Śaivism from the side of Vedic religion. Other myths, such as Śiva's drinking the poison HALĀHALĀ, which threatened to engulf the world, are seen by Śaivites as proof of Śiva's willingness to save the world at personal risk. The best-known iconic representation of Śiva is that of the Nāṭarāja (King of Dance), symbolizing the creative, salvific and destructive functions of Śiva. Śaivism has been a major component of Hinduism since at least the fifth century CE and has inspired its followers to magnificent temple buidings and rich poetry. VĀRĀṆASĪ, for millennia the most sacred city of Hinduism, is Śiva's abode: the 'Golden temple' is a Śiva sanctuary. ŚAṄKARA (2), the founder of Advaita Vedānta, was a Śaivite and so were many luminaries of India. Śiva is also known as Maheśvara ('Great God'), Gaṅgādhāra ('Bearer of the Gaṅgā'), Iśāna ('Ruler') and Viśvanātha ('Lord of the Universe'), among other names. Among the philosophical schools based on Śaivism are ŚAIVA SIDDHĀNTA and KASHMIR ŚAIVISM. Śaivism is a vigorous and active Hindu tradition today.

Śivajī (1627–80)

The son of Shahji Bonsle, a PESHWA, he rose up against the Mogul emperor Aurangzeb, and became the founder of the last great Hindu empire. From his capital city Pune he conquered large tracts of north-western India and the Deccan. He forced the Mogul emperor to conclude a treaty conceding his suzerainty over the conquered land. He was just and took care of the weaker sections of society, especially of women, and was much admired and loved by his people. He was very respectful towards brahmins, but as he came from a ŚŪDRA background they denied him coronation according to Vedic rites. In later centuries he acquired almost legendary status and a Mahratta nationalist political party established itself in 1962 under the name of 'Siv sena', Śivajī's army. It has become the ruling party in Mahārāṣṭra and is becoming an all-India party now.

Śivaliṅga

See LIṄGA (3).

Śivānanda, Swami (1887–1963)

Founder of Śivānanda Ashram and Yoga Vedānta Forest Academy in Hṛṣikeśa. Born into the illustrious family of Appaya Dikṣita in South India, he studied medicine and practised as a doctor for many years in Malaya before becoming a SAMNYĀSI in Hṛṣikeśa in 1924. As a medical doctor he selflessly attended to the poorest and most downtrodden, and continued to do so after founding the Śivānanda Ashram in 1932 and the Divine Life Society in 1936. In 1948 he established the Yoga Vedānta Forest Academy. He continued taking an interest in medicine, especially in AYURVEDA, and opened a dispensary and clinic. He also gave discourses on spiritual matters and began publishing pamphlets and books. The Śivānanda Ashram has an international following and both in letter and spirit promotes universalism in religion. It is one of the major establishments in Hṛṣikeśa and well known all over India. The activities of the ashram have been continued and broadened by Śivānanda's successor, Swami Cidānanda (born 1916).

śivatva ('Śiva-ness', Śiva nature)

ŚAIVA SIDDHĀNTA teaches that the true nature of all humans is *śivatva*, Śiva nature, which is hidden and curtailed through sin. When sin is removed, the Śiva nature reveals itself, bringing truth and happiness.

slavery

Slavery did exist in ancient India, and under the form of indentured labour it continued into the 20th century.

śloka ('couplet')

The smallest literary unit of the EPICS.

Śloka-vārtika

Celebrated work by Kumārila Bhaṭṭa of the MĪMĀṀSĀ school, a commentary to the first part of the *Mīmāṁsā Sūtras*, containing critiques especially of various Buddhist schools.

smaraṇa ('remembering')

The second stage in the process of MEDITATION.

smārta ('pertaining to *smṛti*')

A designation of ultra-orthodox traditional brahmins in South India.

smāsana

Burning place, crematorium.

smṛti ('what has been remembered')

Tradition, as opposed to ŚRUTI (revelation). In a generic sense, all authoritative writings pertaining to Hindu tradition that are not *śruti*, i.e. all works composed after the Veda, such as epics and Purāṇas. In a specific sense, works dealing mainly with law ascribed to inspired lawgivers, such as the *Manusmṛti*, *Yājñavalkyasmṛti*.

snake

See NĀGA.

social order

The Hindu social order is circumscribed by CATUR–VARṆA–ĀŚRAMA-DHARMA, i.e. the division into four 'classes' (VARṆA) and four 'stages of life' (ĀŚRAMA (2)). Theoretically all rights and duties are defined according to this schema. In practice each *varṇa* is subdivided into a very large number of *jātīs* ('sub-castes'), each with its own rules, and most people no longer follow the progression of the stages of life. CASTE is still a powerful factor in social life in India, and for many the ideal of SAMNYĀSA is still alive. Besides the caste society, which is largely identical with Hindu society, there are a large number of 'outcastes' or 'untouchables' (*nihṣpriya*), who began organizing under the name of DALIT ('oppressed') and are actively fighting for their rights. Modernization of society, the exigencies of industrialization, demands for equality by women, and abandonment of many old caste regulations have seriously challenged the Hindu social order. Hindu political parties are concerned with re-establishing a Hindu social order. (*See also* ĀRYA SAMĀJ; BHĀRATĪYA JĀNATĀ PARTY; HINDU MAHĀSABHĀ; RĀṢTRĪYA SVAYAMSEVAK SANGH; VIŚVA HINDŪ PARIṢAD.)

social reforms

Like Ram Mohan ROY, who succeeded in 1828 in having SATĪ banned, many Hindus have felt the need for reforming aspects of Hindu society, such as untouchability (Mahatma GANDHI), widow remarriage (RANADE, R. D.), FEMALE INFANTICIDE, education for women and others. There have been demands to abolish caste and to establish gender equality. (*See also* EQUALITY OF WOMEN.)

Soma

A name of the MOON.

soma

The fermented juice of a not yet satisfactorily identified plant, which was one of the main ingredients of Vedic SACRIFICE. A whole section of the *Ṛgveda* contains hymns that were used in *soma* libations. Indra is described as lover of *soma*, and the intoxication caused by *soma* consumption is frequently referred to.

Som(a)nāth(a),
also **Someśvara**
('Lord of the moon')

A celebrated Śiva sanctuary in Gujarat. It was destroyed and plundered by Mahmud of Ghazni in 1025, rebuilt by Kings Bhima and Bhoja, several times thereafter destroyed and rebuilt. Its final restoration took place through the initiative of K. M. Munshi, governor of Bombay Presidency, and the original *Śivaliṅga* (*see* LIṄGA (3)) was installed by Rajendra Prasad, president of India, in 1951.

son

A son was considered essential to the continuation a family line, and his birth was an occasion of joy. A married woman without a son was considered unlucky and only a son was entitled to light the funeral pyres of his parents, ensuring a good afterlife. In recent years it has often happened that pregnant women, after learning about the sex of the future child, would abort female foetuses. FEMALE INFANTICIDE – by drowning, poisoning, starvation, exposure – was quite frequent.

Sontheimer, Günther-Dietz (1934–92)

Scholar of Sanskrit, Hindi, Marathi and Hindu law. He was professor of the history of Indian religion and philosophy at the Süd-Asien Institut Heidelberg (Germany), author of *The Concept of Daya* and *The Joint Hindu Family*, studies of tribal deities (Khandobha) of Mahārāṣṭra, and producer of several films on tribal religions.

soul

See ĀTMAN; SELF.

Spaṇḍaśāstra

One of the two branches of KASHMIR ŚAIVISM.

sphoṭa ('boil')

A term used by grammarians and philosophers of language, such as BHARTṚHARI, to illustrate the sudden appearance of the meaning of a WORD after the individual letters have been enunciated. Also identified with the cause of the world, BRAHMAN. (*See also* ŚABDA.)

spirit

See SELF.

śraddhā

See FAITH.

śraddha, also antyeṣṭi, mṛtyu-saṃskāra

The last rites, the whole complex ritual (sometimes lasting a full year) required after the death especially of a brahmin.

śrauta (1)

Belonging to ŚRUTI.

śrauta (2)

One of the VEDĀṄGAS, dealing with ceremonial occasions: the *Kalpasūtras* or *Śrautasūtras* contain the ritual for (public) SACRIFICES.

śravaṇa ('listening')

The first of the three steps in MEDITATION.

Śrī ('good luck', 'fortune', 'prosperity')

A name for Viṣṇu's consort (LAKṢMĪ). The Sanskrit sign *śrī* is used as an auspicious emblem on the covers of books, the front of houses, and added as a honorific to names of eminent persons or books. In ordinary life today used as the equivalent to 'Mister'.

Śrī-bhāṣya

The title of RĀMĀNUJA's commentary on the BRAHMASŪTRA.

Śrīkaṇṭha (13th century)

An exponent of Śiva-viśiṣṭādvaita, author of the *Śrīkaṇṭhabhāṣya*, commented upon by Appaya Dīkṣita, a 16th-century Advaitin who belonged to the so-called Bhamati-school. (*See also* VIŚIṢṬĀDVAITA.)

Śrīraṅgam

Situated on an island in the Kauverī river, near Tirucirapalli, it houses the famous Raṅganātha (Viṣṇu) temple, surrounded by seven concentric walled-in enclaves, arguably the biggest temple complex in India. It became famous as the seat of the Śrīvaiṣṇava *ācāryas* (teachers), of whom RĀMĀNUJA is considered the greatest. He reordered temple worship and gave shape to the faith of the Śrīvaiṣṇava community. The history of the temple has been recorded in the *Śrīraṅga Māhātmya* and the *Koil Olugu*, which traces its origins back to the Saṅgam period (first century CE). Rāmānuja had to flee from Śrīraṅgam, and spent twelve years in a neighbouring country because of persecution of Vaiṣṇavas by the ruling Śaiva king. Later the temple was attacked several times and occupied by Muslim troops, but left largely untouched. Today it is a major place of pilgrimage and the centre of the southern branch of ŚRIVAIṢṆAVISM.

Śrīvaiṣṇavism

One of the four major Vaiṣṇava *saṁpradāyas* (sects), so called because of the role that Śrī (Viṣṇu's consort, LAKṢMĪ) plays in it. Śrīvaiṣṇavism, although representing an age-old tradition, received its doctrinal and ritual codification through the work of the *ācāryas* of ŚRĪRAṄGAM: NĀṬHA MUNI; YAMUNĀCĀRYA; and RĀMĀNUJA. Later Śrīvaiṣṇavism split into a northern school (VAḌAGALAI) with its centre in KĀÑCĪPURAM, and a southern school (TEṄGALAI) with its centre in ŚRĪRAṄGAM. The most renowned teacher of the former was Pillai Lokācārya (1205–1311), of the latter Vedānta Deśika (1269–1370).

The universally acknowledged greatest Śrīvaiṣṇava theologian was Rāmānuja, through whom Śrīvaiṣṇavism received its own *Brahmasūtra* commentary, the *Śrībhāṣya*. While emphasizing the lordship of Viṣṇu and the principle of salvation through Viṣṇu's grace alone, he ascribed to Śrī the important role of mediatrix. Śrī is the prototype of the GURU who leads forgetful souls back to Viṣṇu. She is also the embodiment of grace and mercy whose endeavours win the forgiveness of Viṣṇu for the devotee.

Śrī-vatsa

A mark on Viṣṇu's or Kṛṣṇa's chest, indicating the presence of ŚRĪ.

śṛṅgāra ('erotic love')

One of the RASAS of traditional Indian aesthetics.

Śṛṅgerī

A mountain retreat in Karṇātaka. It was named after Ṛṣyaśṛnga, who according to tradition had his abode there. It became famous as the main centre of Śaṅkara's DAŚANĀMI *saṁnyāsis*. Since the eighth century it has been occupied by an uninterrupted succession of Śaṅkarācāryas, called *jagad-gurus*, many of them of great fame, such as SUREŚVARA, a direct disciple of ŚAṄKARA (2), Vidyāśaṅkara (13th century) and MĀDHAVA (2). It contains, besides the ashram, a temple dedicated to Śāradā, the goddess of wisdom, and a residential school for instruction in Sanskrit and traditional Hindu studies, especially ADVAITA VEDĀNTA.

sṛṣṭhi

See CREATION.

śruti

('what has been heard', 'revelation')

The most sacred part of the scriptures of Hinduism. All Hindus consider the Veda (Saṃhitās, Brāhmaṇas, Āraṇyakas, Upaniṣads) as *śruti*. Depending on affiliation, Purāṇas, Śaiva Āgamas, Vaiṣṇava Saṃhitās and Tantras would be considered *śruti* by the followers of these *saṁpradāyas* (sects) as well. *Śruti* is the ultimate authority in matters of faith and practice: it can be interpreted, but not superseded or bypassed.

stotra ('[Sanskrit] hymn')

A large genre of religious composition, usually in verse form, that is used in public and private worship. Many *stotras* were composed by famous people such as Śaṅkara, Rāmānuja and Vivekānanda, or are part of Purāṇas and other scriptures. Collections of such hymns (*Stotramālās*) are quite popular.

strī-dharma ('women's law')

That part of the Hindu lawbooks that deals specifically with the duties of WOMEN.

study

Daily study of scriptures (*svādhyāya*) is a duty for all brahmins. Study is called the 'hightest austerity' in the Upaniṣads and has always been considered a religious necessity by Hindus. The support of students and teachers was one of the sacred duties of Hindu kings. Many temples maintain schools and the 'gift of knowledge' is considered the highest charity.

Subrahmaṇia

Āryan name for the Tamil god MURUGAN, introduced in the SAṄGAM (2) period.

Sudās

A Vedic king, famous for his SACRIFICES. The ṚṢIS (sages) VIŚVAMITRA and VASIṢṬHA lived at his court.

śuddha ('pure')

Especially in a ritual sense. (*See also* PURITY.)

śuddhi ('purification')

A ceremony introduced by the ĀRYA SAMĀJ to readmit (Indian) Muslims and Christians into the Hindu fold. (*See also* PURITY.)

Śūdra(s)

The fourth and lowest VARṆA (class), whose members do not receive UPANAYANA or wear the sacred thread, are not entitled to recite or listen to the Veda, and whose duty it is to serve the three higher *varṇas*, the 'twice-born'. (*See also* CASTE; SOCIAL ORDER.)

suffering

This is unavoidably associated with a bodily existence. Birth in SAṀSĀRA is indicative of a karmic necessity to atone (through suffering) for past misdeeds. Self-imposed suffering (TAPAS) is more effective than that imposed by others. All Hindu systems of thought have been devised to bring an end to suffering by providing LIBERATION from the cycle of rebirth.

suicide

While suicide is normally condemned by Hindus as a heinous crime, whose punishment consists in remaining a ghost (PRETA) and not finding rest after death, under certain circumstances and in certain places, for example at the SAṄGAM in Prāyāga, 'religious suicide' was permitted or even commended.

Śuka-deva (1760–1838)

The author of several works on YOGA and founder of the Cāraṇadāsis, a branch of YOGIS.

sukha-duḥkha
('enjoyment and pain')

A necessary conjunction of states for everyone living in SAṀSĀRA.

śukla-pakṣa ('bright part')

The fortnight of a lunar month beginning with the new moon (*āmavasya*). Its opposite is KṚṢṆA-PAKṢA.

Śukra (1)

The son of Bhṛgu and a priest of BALI and the DAITYAS, author of the *Śukranīti*, a law code. (*See also* BHĀRGAVAS.)

Śukra (2)

The planet Venus. *Śukravar*, Friday, is named after it.

sūkṣma śarīra ('subtle body')

The body formed of subtle matter that does not disintegrate at the time of death and that as the carrier of KARMA is responsible for rebirth. (*See also* BODY.)

sūkta

A Vedic HYMN.

Sumitrā

The wife of Daśaratha and mother of Śatrughna and LAKṢMAṆA.

sun

The sun plays a major part in Hindu mythology. It was worshipped in the form of Sūrya and glorified as one of three chief Vedic deities in the Saura Purāṇas (sun worship was supposed to bring relief from leprosy). Viṣṇu has also been connected with the sun, and his three strides have been associated with the journey of the sun from morning through midday to evening. One of the most celebrated temples of India is the sun temple at Konārak in Orissa, built in 1287.

Sundaramurti, Sundarar
(ninth century)

One of the 63 NĀYAṆMĀRS, author of *Tiruttondattogai* (part of the *Tirumulai*), famous for his many miracles and his practice of worshipping the deity as a friend (*sakhi*).

superimposition

See ADHYĀSA.

supreme reality

See BRAHMAN.

sura ('god')

The opposite of ASURA (demon).

Sūrdās (1479–1584)

Born blind, he achieved great fame as a singer and composer of songs glorifying Kṛṣṇa, collected in the *Sūrsāgar*, 'The Ocean of Sūrdās'. He was a follower of VALLABHĀCĀRYA and celebrated the Rādhā Kṛṣṇa LĪLĀ. Emperor Akbar is said to have visited him incognito to listen to his songs.

Sureśvara (ninth century)

A direct disciple of ŚAṄKARA (2) and author of such influential works of ADVAITA VEDĀNTA as *Naiṣkarmyasiddhi*, *Bṛhadāraṇyakabhāṣyavārttika* and *Taittirīyabhāṣyavārttika*. One of the points where he disagrees with other Advaitins is his positing of the locus of *avidyā* (ignorance) in *brahman* (the universal), not in the *jīvātmas* (individual consciousness).

Śurpa-nakhā
('one with nails like winnowing fans')

A sister of RĀVAṆA. She fell in love with Rāma and offered to marry him. He referred her to Lakṣmaṇa, who cut off her nose and ears, thus provoking the enmity of Rāvaṇa, who subsequently abducted Sītā. (*See also* RĀMĀYAṆA.)

Sūrsāgar

See SŪRDĀS.

Sūrya

See SUN.

Sūrya, the sun.

sustenance (*sthithi*)

One of the three divine cosmic functions ascribed to the Supreme Being. Within the *trimūrti* (Brahmā–Viṣṇu–Śiva) Viṣṇu is called the 'preserver'. He is immanent in everything, and under particular circumstances descends to earth as an AVATĀRA to save it from peril. (*See also* ANNIHILATION; CREATION.)

suṣupti ('deep [dreamless] sleep')

The third mode of CONSCIOUSNESS.

sūtra ('thread', 'string')

Short formulaic statements as well as collections of them, e.g. *Vedānta-sūtra(s)*, *Kalpasūtras* etc. There are *sūtras* on virtually every traditional subject of study. They had to be memorized by students and were commented upon by teachers.

sva-dharma ('one's own duty')

Specific obligations for a member of a particular VARṆA (social unit).

svādhyāya

See STUDY.

svapna sthāna ('dream state')

The second state of CONSCIOUSNESS.

Svarga ('heaven')

This refers especially to INDRA's heaven, the abode of blessed mortals, situated on Mount MERU. In later Hinduism it is usually considered a lower form of ultimate bliss, as compared to Viṣṇu's Vaikuṇṭha or the absorption in BRAHMAN. (*See also* INDRALOKA.)

Svarloka

See INDRALOKA.

svastika

From *svasti* (hail), an ancient solar symbol often found in Hindu temples as well as on the first pages of books. It is thought to be auspicious.

sva-tantra sādhus

Ascetics who do not belong to one of the recognized *sampradāyas* (sects) and have not received initiation through an acknowledged *guru*.

svayam-bhū liṅgas
('self-existent *liṅgas*')

A number of LIṄGAS (3) believed to have originated without human agency, and which are considered especially powerful, such as the *liṅga* formed of ice at Kedarnāṭh.

svayam-vyakta ('self-revealed')

IMAGES that appear in dreams and are believed not to be artificially made. They are considered more powerful than artificial ones.

Śveta-dvīpa ('white island')

Mentioned in the *Nārāyaṇīya* section of the *Mahābhārata* as lying to the north of Bhārata, inhabited by a race of white wise beings, worshippers of NĀRĀYAṆA, who communicated to NĀRA and Nārāyaṇa a doctrine of salvation.

Śvetaketu

A son of UDDĀLAKA, he received instruction in the *Chāṇḍogya Upaniṣad* regarding the identity of ĀTMAN and BRAHMAN. In the *Mahābhārata* he is mentioned as a *ṛṣi* (sage) who introduced the law of marital exclusivity.

Śvetāśvatara Upaniṣad

One of the principal Upaniṣads, belonging to the YAJURVEDA, containing a fairly systematic discussion of Śiva Advaita.

Śyāma ('black')

A name of KṚṢṆA.

T

Tagore, Debendranath
(1818–1905)

Religious and social reformer. Founder of Sādhāran Brahmo Samāj and of the forest retreat Śantiniketan, near Calcutta. Known as 'Maharṣi', he discarded the sacred thread and claimed to receive direct messages from the Almighty, which he communicated to his disciples. He compiled the *Brahmodharma*, an anthology from the Upaniṣads, the *Mahābhārata* and *Manusmṛti*.

Tagore, Rabindranath
(1861–1941)

Son of Debendranath Tagore, poet, painter, playwright, essayist, founder of the forest university Śantiniketan and the women's university Śrīniketan. He received the Nobel Prize for Literature in 1913 for his collection of poems *Gītāñjalī* and a knighthood in 1915. He was fond of the Baul songs of Bengal and wrote poetry and plays both in Bengali and English. Among his major prose works are *Sādhana* and *Creative Unity*. He lectured and travelled widely all over the world, and received many honours.

Taittirīya
('relating to Tittiri [the partridge])'

A Vedic sage, the pupil of YĀSKA, an authority referred to by PĀṆINĪ reputed to be the founder of a Vedic school of the Black YAJURVEDA. He is the author of the *Taittirīya Saṁhitā*, the *Taittirīya Brāhmaṇa* and the *Taittirīya Upaniṣad*.

tamas

See GUṆA.

tāmasa-śāstras
('scriptures of darkness')

The designation of all non-Vaiṣṇava scriptures by VAIṢṆAVAS.

taṇḍava

The dance of world destruction, performed by ŚIVA in Cidambaram. Its etymology is derived from Taṇḍu, one of Śiva's attendants, who invented the dance.

Tanjore

A city in Tamilnāḍū, famous for the Bṛhadīśvara (Śiva) temple, built by the COLA king Rajaraja I (985–1013), one of the largest in India. According to tradition the king built this temple in the hope of being cured from leprosy.

Tantra (1) ('ritual', 'rule')

The designation of a class of works connected to goddess worship.

Tantra (2)

A form of Hinduism in which śakti, the energy of Śiva, is worshipped. 'Right-hand' Tantra (*daksinācāra*) is a form of Goddess worship similar to that of Viṣṇu. 'Left-hand' Tantra (*vāmācāra*) involves the worshippers in secret rituals that are characterized as *pañca-makāras* (the '5 ms'), namely *madya* (intoxicating drinks), *māṁsa* (meat), *matsya* (fish), *mudrā* (parched grain and gestures), and *maithuna* (extramarital sexual intercourse).

Tantra-vārttika

A subcommentary by KUMĀRILA BHAṬṬA on part of the *Śābarabhāṣya*.

tapas ('heat')

Self-mortification. This is an important notion in Hinduism from the earliest times to the present. According to widespread belief, self-mortification leads to an accumulation of power which can be used to summon the gods to be of service. Many stories in the epics and Purāṇas tell of attempts by Indra and other gods to prevent ascetics from accumulating too much power through *tapas*, by either having them seduced or provoked to anger, through which all power was annihilated. Hindu scriptures enumerate a great variety of forms of *tapas*: besides fasting or not lying down to sleep, they recommend standing in water up to the neck, holding one arm up high, looking into the sun etc. One of the most celebrated forms is the 'five-fire' *tapas*: an ascetic is to build four blazing cow-dung fires, in each direction of the compass. With the midday sun overhead (as a fifth fire) he is to spend some time exposed to the heat of all these fires.

Tapo-loka

The second-highest of the worlds in the Hindu universe, below Satyaloka (*see* BRAHMĀ-LOKA).

Tārā ('star')

The wife of BṚHASPATI. She was abducted by Soma, the moon, and recovered by Brahmā. She was delivered of a child, fathered by Soma, whom she called Budha (Mercury).

tarka-śāstra

('the science of reasoning')

Formal logic, part of NYĀYA.

Tarka-bhāṣa

See KEŚAVA MIŚRA.

tarpaṇa

Libation, the sprinkling of water as part of certain rituals, especially connected with the commemoration of ancestors.

tat tvam asi ('that you are')

One of the MAHĀVĀKYAS (from the *Chāṇḍogya Upaniṣad*) teaching the unity of self (*tvam*) and absolute (*tat*).

tattva

('principle', 'element', 'that-ness')

True or essential nature.

Tattva-cintā-maṇi

A celebrated work by GAṄGEŚA, considered the basic text of Navya NYĀYA, dealing with the PRAMĀṆAS.

tattva-jñāna ('knowledge of principles, or of truth')

Metaphysics.

Telang, Kāśīnāth Trimbak

(1850–93)

Professor of law at Bombay University and notable Sanskrit scholar, as well as social reformer, editor of Bhartṛhari's *Nīti-śātaka* and *Vairāgya-śātaka* and Viśakhadatta's *Mudrā-rākṣasa*. He wrote important essays on the

Mahābhārata and the *Rāmāyaṇa* and entered into polemics with Western Indologists on several issues. He translated the *Bhagavadgītā* for the Sacred Books of the East (1880).

temples (*maṇḍira*)

While the Vedas do not mention temples (*yajñas* (sacrifices) were performed on temporarily established sites) these have been a hallmark of Hinduism since the fifth century CE. Hindu temples are not primarily places of meeting for a congregation to worship as community, but palaces for the god who is present in an IMAGE (*mūrti*) and who is worshipped individually by an appointed priest. In the course of centuries Hindus have developed a great variety of architectural styles for temples, the chief ones being the *nāgara* or North Indian, and the *drāviḍa*, or South Indian styles. All details of temple construction are laid down in the texts on *vāstuśāstra*. A village or a town was not deemed complete and habitable unless it had a temple. Some of the major temples are veritable temple cities and attract millions of worshippers every year. The major temples have Sthāla Purāṇas which record their histories and major events that took place at the site. To have a temple built has been a time-honoured activity among Hindus, still much in evidence in modern India and also among Hindus in the diaspora. (*See also* ARCHITECTURE.)

Teṅgalai

Southern school of ŚRĪ VAIṢṆAVISM, giving equal weight to Sanskrit and Tamil scriptures (Ubhāya Vedānta) with its seat in Śrīraṇgam. It is also known as the cat school, because it believes that God's grace saves without human effort, as a cat carries its kitten from fire without the kitten's active co-operation (*mārjaranyāya*). The Teṅgalais were also more tolerant with regard to CASTE affiliation of teachers. (*See also* PILLAI LOKĀCĀRYA.)

Thibaut, Georg (1848–1914)

Prominent German Indologist. After studying Indology in Heidelberg and Berlin, concentrating on Vedic studies, he became assistant to Max MÜLLER in Oxford in editing the *Ṛgveda*. In 1875 he moved to India, first as Anglo-Sanskrit professor and principal at the Benares Hindu College, then as professor and principal of Muir Central College. His work on Indian mathematics and astronomy was pathbreaking. He was co-editor of the Benares Sanskrit Series and translated a number of important works into English, e.g. ŚAṄKARA's (2) and RĀMĀNUJA's commentaries on the *Brahmasūtras*, which appeared in the Sacred Books of the East.

Tilak, Bal Gangadhar (1856–1920)

Poona-based lawyer, revolutionary, educator, founder of Fergusson College, editor of newspapers and author of several important, if controversial works: *Orion or Researches into the Antiquity of the Vedas* (1893), and *The Arctic Home in the Vedas* (1903), in which he postulated prehistoric origins of the Vedas. He wrote a Mahratti commentary on the *Bhagavadgītā*, *Gītā Rahasya* (1915), subtitled *The Gītā as a Gospel of Action*, which became very popular. Forbidden by the British authorities to organize political mass rallies, he used the local GAṆEŚA festival as an occasion for huge protest demonstrations. Since then GAṆEŚA CATŪRTHI has become a major religious festival in Mahārāṣṭra.

time

Most Hindu systems distinguish between divisible and indivisible time: the first is identified with empirical time and its divisions, the second is an uncreated principle of the universe. The *Ṛgveda* speaks of the rotating wheel of time as having 12 spokes, it connects the seasons with the ingredients of the all-important SACRIFICE. The *Maitri Upaniṣad* contains the famous passage: 'Time cooks all things in the great self. He who knows in what time is cooked is the knower of the Veda.' In the *Mahābhārata* time appears as fate (*daiva*) or even death. Time is seen both as giver of happiness and misery; its effects are considered inescapable. In the Purāṇas time (*kāla*) is often introduced as one of the uncreated principles on a par with *pradhāna* (matter) and *puruṣa* (spirit), emerging from the unmanifested being (*avyākta*). The *Yogavāsiṣṭha Rāmāyaṇa* has a large section devoted to *kāla*: time is said to be the cause for both the creation and the destruction of the universe. *Kāla* is compared to an actor, who appears on the stage, disappears and reappears again to perform his play. In the *Bhagavadgītā* Kṛṣṇa says about himself: 'Time am I, world-destroying, grown mature, engaged in subduing the world.' In one of the last sections of the *Mahābhārata*, the *Mauśalyaparvaṇ*, which is characterized by a deep sense of doom, the speaker tells us that his heroes 'met with destruction, impelled by time.' Time (in an embodied form) is described as wandering around the earth: 'He looked like a man of terrible and fierce aspect' and was 'none else but the Destroyer of all creatures'. The evil deeds the protagonists commit and which earn them their fate are ascribed to 'the perverseness of the hour that had come upon them'.

time, divisions of

Regardless of philosophical differences Hindus throughout the ages accepted certain divisions of empirical time which were used both in daily life and in astronomical/astrological calculations. Different systems were and are used, but these differences are not related to different ideological conceptions of time. The major divisions of time are effected by the revolutions of moon, sun and Jupiter (Bṛhaspati). The lunar month is divided into a dark half (KṚṢṆAPAKṢA) and a bright half (ŚUKLAPAKṢA); each half is divided into fifteen *tithis* (each with a specific name). The solar movement divides the year into six seasons (determined by entry into certain constellations) and twelve solar months. The seasons are *vasanta* (spring), *grīśma* (hot season), *varṣa* (rainy season), *śarād* (autumn), *hemānta* (winter), *śiśira* (cool season). The months (beginning with *Caitra* in spring) are neither identical with the months of the Western calendar nor with the lunar months. Every now and then an intercalary month is required to realign the beginning of spring with the beginning of the month *Caitra* (or *Meṣa*). Different schools of astronomers issue yearly calendars/almanacs (*pañcāṅga*) which are followed by different groups of people. Major feasts are sometimes celebrated on different days (even a month apart) because of disagreements between the calendars. For astronomical/astrological calculations the *nakṣatras* ('houses') are important: there are 28, each measuring 13°20′ of the ecliptic. Each *nakṣatra* is subdivided into 4 *pādas* of 3°20′ each. Over and above the lunar and solar cycles, the 12-year and 60-year cycles of Jupiter are important.

The 24-hour solar day is subdivided into 30 *muhūrtas* (48 minutes each). A *muhūrta* is subdivided into two *ghati* (of 24 minutes each). Each *ghati* is subdivided into 30 *kāla* (of 48 seconds each). Each *kāla* is divided into 2 pala (of 24 seconds each), and each *pala* into 6 *prāṇa* (of 4 seconds each). Each *prāna* is divided into 10 *vipala* (of 0.4 seconds each) and each *vipala* into 60 *prativipala* (0.000666 seconds each). One month in human terms is considered to be one day and night of the *pitṛ* (deceased forefathers); one human year is equal to one day and night of the *deva* (gods); one thousand years of the *deva* is equal to one day of Brahmā. History is reckoned in *manvantara*, 'ages of patriarchs' of which there are fourteen, each presided over by a specific MANU (2). The largest time-frame are the *kalpas* (eons) equal to 4,320,000 years, and subdivided into 4 *yugas*, each successively shorter and more wicked. (Kṛta Yuga, Treta Yuga, Dvāpara Yuga and Kali Yuga). We are at present living in a Kali Yuga (age of strife) which will end with a *pralaya* (total dissolution of the world) before a new age arises. As regards details of these calculations there is a certain amount of discrepancy among various authors. But the notion of a devolution of history, a gradual and irreversible worsening of the world situation is common to all, as is the idea of a cyclic destruction and creation of the universe, whether attributed to the action of a deity or to an impersonal process. (See also CALENDAR; FESTIVALS.)

time, philosophies of

Substantialist notions of time: In the VAIŚEṢIKA system, time is one of nine substances (*dravya*). It is described as 'of three kinds, being characterized by creation, sustention and destruction'. NYĀYA accepts the Vaiśeṣika notion of time as a substance and attempts to work out the epistemological implications. It holds that 'perception and the rest cannot be regarded as instruments of cognition on account of the impossibility of connecting them with any of the three points of time.' VIŚIṢṬĀDVAITA considers the physical universe to be 'the body of God' and thus invests nature with a degree of reality hardly parallelled anywhere else. Consequently time also acquires a substantiality of its own as the manifestation of God's eternity and omnipresence. It is eternal and all pervasive. Time is an instrument in the cosmic sport of God. In his 'sport manifestation' God functions as dependent on time.

Relativistic notions of time: for the Advaitin ŚAṄKARA (2) *brahman*, which is timeless, is the only reality. Time does not possess an independent reality of its own; it is only associated with events in time.

Momentariness vs. temporality: PATAÑJALI defines the end and purpose of YOGA to be 'the cessation of all modifications of consciousness' and endeavours to lead the practitioner to a transcendence of time and space. Since the ultimate condition is one of timelessness, time cannot be an aspect of reality. 'Temporality' is a figment of the imagination; however, the moments that cause the perception of time are real. The *Yogasūtra* says that one gains metaphysical knowledge by concentrating on the sequence of moments. As the commentator VYĀSA explains: 'Just as the atom (*paramāṇu*) is the smallest particle of matter (*dravya*) so a moment (*kṣaṇa*) is the smallest particle of time (*kāla*).' Physically a *kṣaṇa* is the amount of time an atom in motion takes to cross a space equalling the space it occupies. The sequence of such moments cannot be combined into a 'thing'. Notions such as 'hours' or 'days' are mental combinations. Time (*kāla*) is not a real thing, but is based on changes in the mind. The moment, however, is a real thing in itself and constitutive of the sequence. The sequence is constituted by an uninterrupted succession of moments. Past and future can be explained on the basis of change. The world that exists in this moment undergoes instant change. Patañjali accepts the notions of present, past and future. Unlike the present, however, past and future do not exist in manifest form. When the mental condition called *dharmamegha* is reached, the sequence of changes comes to an end and the sequence can no longer sustain even a *kṣaṇa*. In *dharmameghasamādhī* the YOGI reaches a zero-time experience before merging his consciousness in the timeless KAIVALYA.

tīrtha ('ford')

A place of PILGRIMAGE. There are thousands of places of pilgrimage in India, visited every year by millions of people. Each *tīrtha* offers something special, be it a particular blessing, the favour of a deity or a natural peculiarity. Usually pilgrims arriving at a *tīrtha* are being taken care of by local *paṇḍas* (guides) who for a fee show the pilgrims around and tell them what ceremonies to perform.

Tirukkural (first century CE?)

Ancient collection of aphorisms, in Tamil, often called the 'Tamil Bible' because of its popularity and wisdom.

Tirumal

Tamil name for VIṢṆU.

Tirumular

The legendary author of the 3,000 verse *Tirumaṇḍira*, an importance source for Śaiva Siddhānta. According to the *Periya Purāṇa* he was born in Kailāsa, entered the body of a dead cowherd, and spent 3,000 years composing the *Tirumaṇḍira*, one verse per year. The *Tirumaṇḍira*, one of the earliest works of Tamil Śaivism, is believed to have been written in the seventh or eighth century CE.

Tirupati ('Holy Lord')

Arguably the most popular and richest Hindu temple, in Andhra Pradesh, sacred to Veṅkaṭa, assumed to be HARI–HARA, i.e. a combination of Viṣṇu and Śiva. While it functioned as a Śaiva shrine for several centuries, RĀMĀNUJA declared the image to be Viṣṇu and introduced a mode of worship following the example of ŚRĪRAṄGAM. One peculiar custom at Tirupati is the offering of one's hair. Veṅkaṭa also has the reputation of fulfilling all the desires of his devotees, who deliver large donations of money and valuables into a huge *hundi* (chest). The temple complex is under the administration of the Tamilnāḍū Devasthānam Board and its enormous income is used, among other things, to support the Veṅkaṭeśvar University and a temple museum.

Tiru-vācakam ('sacred utterances')

The title of a celebrated collection of hymns in honour of Śiva, by MĀṆIKKAVĀCAKAR, one of the 63 Nāyaṇmārs.

tithi ('day')

The thirtieth part of a lunar month, the basic unit of the Hindu calendar, according to which sacred days and festivals are calculated. (*See also* TIME, DIVISIONS OF.)

Tolkappiam (second century CE)

An ancient Tamil grammar, considered the oldest Tamil text.

tradition

See SMṚTI.

transmigration

See REBIRTH.

trees

Trees are considered models of generosity and patience. Some trees are sacred to specific deities: the TULASĪ is sacred to Vaiṣṇavas, the bilva to Śaivites. Major trees in or near a village often become objects of worship, or shrines are built beneath them. There is also a ceremony

The wedding of trees.

called 'marriage of the trees', when two close-standing trees are united in a ritual not unlike that of *vivaha* (MARRIAGE).

Treta Yuga

The second of the four world ages. (*See also* TIME, DIVISIONS OF.)

trident (*triśula*)

Śiva's weapon. It is also carried by Śaivite NĀGAS (3) both as a symbol and a weapon.

triguṇa ('[possessing] three qualities')

The designation of matter (*prakṛti*) as composed of *sattva* (light), *rajas* (excitement) and *tamas* (darkness), affecting all material entities. (*See also* GUṆA.)

Trilocana ('three-eyed')

A designation of Śiva, who has a third eye in the middle of his forehead that is very destructive. He burned KĀMA to death with a glance from it.

triloka ('three worlds')

Variously understood as either comprising netherworlds (*nāraka*), earth (*bhūmi*) and heaven (*svarga*), or earth (*bhurloka*), sky (*bhuvarloka*) and planets (*svarloka*). The great gods are often called 'rulers of the three worlds'.

tri-mārga ('three ways')

The triad of *karmamārga* (path of action), *bhaktimārga* (path of devotion) and *jñānamārga* (path of knowledge).

tri-mūrti ('three forms')

The designation either of the triad of Brahmā (creator), Viṣṇu (sustainer) and Śiva (destroyer), or of the three aspects of either Viṣṇu, Śiva or Devī, each exercising these three functions.

A replica of the famous Tri-mūrti in the caves of Ganapuri (Elephants) near Mumbai (Bombay).

tripuṇḍra

A mark on the forehead consisting of three parallel lines, made with ashes from cowdung, which Śaivites have to apply before worship. Without wearing this sign all prayers would be fruitless. (*See also* ŚAIVISM.)

Tri-purā

A name of the Goddess (DEVĪ). A famous tantric text is called *Tripurārahasya*.

Tri-pura ('triple city')

An aerial tri-tiered phenomenon, which was destroyed by Śiva. The story according to the *Śiva Purāṇas*, is that three ASURAS (demons), desirous of immortality, asked MAYA, the divine artificer, to construct three aerial fortresses – one each of gold, silver and iron – of immense dimensions, and wonderfully equipped with all conceivable amenities. They terrorized the population of the earth from their triple city, and so humans and *devas* (gods) asked Brahmā for help. Brahmā told them that only Sthānu (an aspect of Śiva) could pierce all three cities with one shaft. Śiva accordingly had an armoured car made, with the help of all the gods, and shot a fiery arrow into Tripura, destroying it.

Triśaṅku ('three arrows')

A mythical king of the solar dynasty, he was first called Satyavrata but later called Triśaṅku because he had ruined his reputation through the three 'arrows' of adultery, cow killing and beef eating. He tried to persuade his family priest, VAŚIṢṬHA, to perform a SACRIFICE through which he would be able bodily to ascend to heaven. Triśaṅku was condemned by Vaśiṣṭha to become a *caṇḍāla* (OUTCASTE), but VIŚVAMITRA, who had been helped by Triśaṅku in times of famine, performed the ritual. Rejected by INDRA at the entrance to heaven, Triśaṅku remained suspended from the vault of heaven, head downwards, and can be seen as a star. Triśaṅku is often referred to in India as an example for a task only half accomplished.

tri-sthalī ('three places')

The most sacred places of PILGRIMAGE for Hindus: Vārāṇasī, Gayā and Prāyāga. There is a famous work by Narāyaṇabhaṭṭa, *Tristhalīsetu* ('Bridge of Three Places'), which describes them in detail.

tri-varga (1) ('three states')

The three aims of life: ARTHA (1) (wealth), KĀMA and DHARMA (law).

tri-varga (2)

Three conditions: loss, stability and increase.

tri-varga (3)

The three qualities of nature: *sattva*, *rajas*, *tamas*.

tri-varga (4)

The three higher VARṆAS: Brāhmaṇas, Kṣatriyas and Vaiśyas.

Tri-vikrama

A name of VIṢṆU, referring to the three strides he took at BALI's sacrifice.

truth

The Sanskrit word *satya* means both truth and reality; it is the central notion of Hindu ethics and philosophy/theology. Truthfulness is the highest and most inclusive virtue; the search for reality – *satyasya satya*, 'the reality of the real, the truth of truth' – is the ultimate aim of VEDĀNTA. The 'golden age' of humankind was called *satyayuga*, the age of truth when people were honest and did not need any laws. In Hindu philosophy much effort was spent on definining criteria for truth (PRAMĀṆAS). SAMNYĀSA is meant to be an uncompromising search for truth/reality not hindered by the necessities of conventions and the burden of everyday occupations. Mahatma GANDHI prided himself in reversing the adage 'God is Truth' into 'Truth is God' and he called his political method *satyāgraha*, 'truth- grasping'. His autobiography bears the title *My Experiments with Truth*. The Indian government adopted the Upaniṣadic formula *satyam eva jayate* (Truth will be victorious) as the crest on its official seal.

Tukārām(a) (1608–49)

Mahratta poet-saint. Born into a ŚŪDRA family in Dehu, near Pune, he grew up in a family that worshipped VIṬHOBA (Viṣṇu). Neglecting his family business, he spent his days composing *abhaṅgs* (songs) in the temple. His life is surrounded by many miraculous events. He is one of the most popular of all poet-saints, and his memory is kept alive by the Vārkarīs, a group of devotees of Viṭhoba at Dehu, who meet every fortnight to spend hours singing Tukārām's *abhaṅgs*.

tulasī

The sacred basil, a shrub identified with the presence of Viṣṇu, kept by each pious VAIṢṆAVA household in a pot, worshipped and used in rituals. Beads made from its wood (*tulsīmālā*) are worn by many Vaiṣṇavas around the arm and neck, and also carried along to count JAPA of the holy names.

Tul(a)sīdās(a) (1511–1637) ('servant of the *tulasī*')

Celebrated author of the *Rāmcaritmanas*, a Hindī (Avadhī) recreation of the *Rāmāyaṇa*, which has become the most popular religious book of North India, and of many hymns and poems celebrating the greatness of Rāma.

turīya ('the fourth [state]')

A designation of the highest stage of CONSCIOUSNESS, when subject–object duality disappears.

Tvastṛ

In the *Ṛgveda* he is the ideal artist and artisan, manufacturer of many wonderful contraptions, nourisher of all beings. His son Viśvarūpa, three-headed and six-eyed, became an enemy of Indra and was killed by him. In the Purāṇas Tvastṛ is identified with VIŚVAKARMA (2), the architect of the gods.

twice-born

See DVIJĀTI.

tyāga ('renunciation')

This applies especially to the formal act of becoming a SAMNYĀSI.

Tyāgarāja (1767–1847)

One of India's most famous musicians, a devotee of Rāma and composer of numerous songs (in Kaṇṇāḍa) with religious content, widely used in *bhajan* sessions.

tyāgi (fem. *tyāginī*) ('renouncer')

A renouncer, in a generic sense.

U

Udāyana (10th century)

Author of *Nyāyakusumañjāli*, a celebrated text.

ud-bhava ('appearance')

This applies especially to the appearance of Śiva from within the *Śivaliṅga* (*Śivaliṅgodbhava*, often represented in art) or other objects. (*See also* LIṆGA (3).)

Uddālaka

A teacher identified in the *Chāṇḍogya Upaniṣad* as the author of a new cosmology. His son ŚVETAKETU figures prominently in the Upaniṣads and the *Śathapatha Brāhmaṇa*. His other son, NACIKETAS, became famous for his dialogues with YAMA, as reported in the *Kaṭha Upaniṣad*. Among his students were YĀJÑA-VALKYA, ŚAUNAKA and Kahoda.

Uddhava

Kṛṣṇa's cousin, counsellor and friend, mentioned in the *Bhāgavatam*.

Uḍipī

A city in Karṇātaka state, headquarters of the Madhva *saṁpradāya* (sect), seat of its supreme pontiff. The change of pontiff which takes place every twelve years is a major occasion in Uḍipī. (*See also* VAIṢṆAVISM.)

Ugra-sena

King of Mathurā. He was deposed by KAṀŚA, and reinstated by Kṛṣṇa, who killed Kaṁśa.

Ujjainī ('victorious')

One of the seven ancient sacred cities, in Central India, a Śiva sanctuary, the site of the Amareśvara LIṄGA (3). It is one of the four places where the KUMBHAMELA is celebrated every 12 years. It was the capital of Vikramāditya, and famous for its astronomical observatory. Hindu astronomers use the longitude of Ujjainī as their first meridian.

Ujjvala Nīlāmaṇi
('burning sapphire')

The title of a celebrated work by RŪPA GOSVĀMI, dealing with *mādhuryabhakti*, the highest form of devotion according to the GAUḌĪYA VAIṢṆAVAS.

Ul, also **Ul vinai**
(Tamil, 'fate', 'destiny')

A major factor in Tamil folk religion, addressed in the TIRUKKURAL as the greatest power.

Umā ('light')

Another name for SATĪ, Śiva's consort.

Umāpati
('lord of Umā', 'Uma's husband')

A frequent designation of Śiva.

unborn (*aja*)

An epithet of the ultimate, ĀTMAN and BRAHMAN.

universe (*jagat*; *viśva*)

The Hindu universe, as described in the Purāṇas, is geocentric: the earth is the centre, but not the best part of it; it is suitable only for 'work', for gaining liberation from *saṁsāra*. The universe as a whole is encompassed by the shell of the WORLD EGG, 500 million *yojanas* in diameter. Inside this egg there are concentric layers of firm continents surrounded by oceans containing different liquids. It contains the heavens of the various deities as well as the netherworlds and the hells. Most Hindu schools of thought accept a periodic creation and destruction of the universe in a succession of world ages (*kalpas*) and they also assume the simultaneous existence of a multitude of parallel universes. (*See also* COSMOLOGY; DVĪPA; TIME, DIVISIONS OF.)

unreality (1)

In logic, *abhāva* (non-existence), accepted by some schools as a separate entity.

unreality (2)

In Vedānta, *asat(ya)*, the whole of finite beings, in contrast to *sat(ya)* (reality) which by definition must be unchanging, eternal and conscious.

unrighteousness

See ADHARMA.

untouchability

See OUTCASTE.

untruth (*anṛta*)

The opposite of ṚTA, the right order of things; it is seen as destructive and a negative power.

upadeśa ('instruction')

The teaching of a GURU.

Upa-deśa-sahasrī
('thousand instructions')

The title of a popular ADVAITA work, attributed to ŚAṄKARA (2).

upadhyāya ('teacher')

Used today as the Indian equivalent of the academic title 'doctor'.

upamāna, also **upamiti**

Analogy. One of the acknowledged PRAMĀṆAS.

upa-nayana

Initiation. *Upanayana* is given only to members of the three upper CASTES (usually only to boys). Its outward sign is the JANĒU (sacred thread). (*See also* SAṀSKĀRA.)

Upaniṣads

Derived from *upa* (near), *ni* (down), *sad* (sit), this is the designation of the fourth and last part of the VEDAS (also called VEDĀNTA) containing mystical teachings. It is the basis of the *jñānamārga* and Vedānta *darśana*. The so-called 'principal Upaniṣads' are *Bṛhadāraṇyaka*, *Chāṅḍogya*, *Īśa*, *Kena*, *Aitareya*, *Taittirīyā*, *Kauśītaki*, *Kaṭha*, *Muṇḍaka*, *Śvetaśvatara*, *Praśna*, *Maitri*, and *Māṇḍukya*. The traditional number of Upaniṣads is 108. Several hundred Upaniṣads are known, some of very recent origin such as an *Allah Upaniṣad* and a *Khrist Upaniṣad*. The Upaniṣads belong to the *prasthāna-trayī*, and every Vedānta *ācārya* (master) had to write a commentary on the principal Upaniṣads, the first and longest being that by ŚAṆKARA (2).

upa-pātakas ('lesser sins')

In contrast to MAHĀ-PĀTAKAS (great sins), breaches of DHARMA that can be atoned for relatively easily. (*See also* SIN.)

Upa-purāṇas ('lesser Purāṇas')

In contrast to the MAHĀ-PURĀṆAS (great Purāṇas). The classification is not always unambiguous. Thus ŚĀKTAS classify the *Devībhāgavatam* as a *Mahāpurāṇa*, while VAIṢṆAVAS consider it an *Upapurāṇa*.

upāsana

See WORSHIP.

upavāsa ('fasting')

A very popular form of penance. There are a number of fast days in the Hindu CALENDAR, varying from *saṁpradāya* (sect) to *saṁpradāya*. In its strict sense it entails total abstinence from food and drink. Often it is understood as a restriction of one's diet, either quantitatively or qualitatively. Many Hindus untertake fasting in fulfilment of vows. GANDHI undertook 'fasts unto death' several times in an attempt to move rioting Muslims and Hindus to reconciliation.

Upa-vedas

('lesser' or 'complementary' Vedas)

The four traditional arts and sciences: (1) *Ayurveda* (medicine); (2) *Gandharvaveda* (music and dancing); (3) *Dhanurveda* (archery, martial arts); (4) *Sthāpatyaveda* (architecture).

Uṣas

The dawn, daughter of heaven and sister of the ĀDITYAS, praised in the Vedas for her charms and her immortality.

utsava ('feast')

Especially a temple feast. The *utsavabera* is the processional IMAGE of a temple which is taken out on feast days.

Uttara Mīmāṁsā

('later Mīmāṁsā')

VEDĀNTA. (*See also* MĪMĀṀSĀ.)

V

vac ('speech', 'word')

In the *Ṛgveda* (*Vāksūkta*) personified as a goddess, through whom everything is created, and through whom the ṚṢIS receive their inspiration.

Vācaknavī

Upaniṣadic female philosopher, who challenged YAJÑAVĀLKYA.

Vācaspati Miśra (ninth century)

A versatile Advaitin writer, known as a *sarvatantrasvatantra* (independent commentator on all systems of philosophy). He wrote commentaries on Śaṅkara's *Brahmasūtrabhāṣya* (the *Bhāmatī*), on the *Sāṁkhyakārikās* (the *Vaiśāradī*), on the *Yoga Sutras* (the *Yogabhāsya*), and on the *Nyāya Sūtras* (the *Nyāyavārttika*). He held that the individual human beings were the seat of ignorance.

vācika japa

The repetition of a MANTRA (1) with words, i.e. audibly (in contrast with *mānasa japa*, which entails mental repetition only).

Vaḍagalai

The northern school of ŚRĪVAIṢṆAVISM, preferring the Sanskritic tradition over the Tamilian. Its headquarters are in KĀÑCĪPURAM. It is also known as the 'monkey school', from its insistence that a person, in order to be saved by God, has to co-operate actively, like the young of a monkey, which must cling to its mother if it wants to reach safety in a fire (*mārkatanyāya*). (*See also* VEDĀNTA-DEŚIKA.)

vāda-vāda ('disputation', 'dialogue')

One of the traditional methods of engaging scholars from other schools of thought.

vahana ('vehicle')

Usually an animal carrying a god, e.g. Viṣṇu has the bird GARUḌA as his *vahana*,

Garuda, the vahana *(vehicle) of Viṣṇu.*

Śiva the bull NANDI, Indra an elephant, Durgā a tiger etc. In temples the *vahanas* are represented before the main entrance, and often in a separate temple.

vaidhi-bhakti

('devotion consisting of following commands [*vidhi*]')

This is considered the first stage in the development of BHAKTI.

vaidik(a) dharma ('vedic religion')

A self-designation of 'Hinduism'.

Vaikuṇṭha

The paradise of Viṣṇu, the destination of those who have been saved through Viṣṇu's grace.

vairāgi (fem. *vairāginī*) ('renouncer')

Specifically VAIṢṆAVA ascetics, who usually wear white (in contrast to Śaivite *samnyāsis*, who wear ochre).

vairāgya ('renunciation')

A generic expression, synonymous with TYĀGA and SAMNYĀSA.

Vairāgya śatakam

('century of renunciation')

A celebrated poetic treatise by BHARTṚHARI, which urges mortals to practise renunciation before it is too late.

Vairocana

A name of BALI.

Vaiśampāyana

A celebrated sage, the original teacher of the Black YAJURVEDA. He was a disciple of the sage VYĀSA, from whom he heard the *Mahābhārata*, which he later recited before King JANAMEJAYA.

Vaiśeṣika

One of the six orthodox systems of Hinduism. The oldest text, the *Vaiśeṣika Sūtras*, are ascribed to Kaṇāḍa. Its name derives from its assumption of the existence of *viśeṣas*, ultimate qualifiers of primary substances such as atoms, time, space etc. It emphasizes DHARMA as the means to prosperity and salvation. It is often grouped with the NYĀYA system as 'Nyāya–Vaiśeṣika'. It assumes a plurality of independent selves and the eternity of atoms, the smallest units of matter.

Vaiṣṇava Saṁhitās

A large number of voluminous texts belonging to the PĀÑCARĀTRA tradition, which acquired high authority among VAIṢṆAVAS as the source for regulations of life and ritual. Most are associated with specific centres of Vaiṣṇavism in South India. Examples are the *Parameśvara Saṁhitā* (Śrīraṅgam), *Ahirbudhnya Samhitā*, and *Sanatkumāra Saṁhitā*.

Vaiṣṇavas

Devotees of Viṣṇu, numerically the largest segment of mainstream Hinduism (500 million plus), divided into a number of *saṁpradāyas* (sects).

Vaiṣṇavism

A conference in the 14th century established the division of Vaiṣṇavas into four major constituencies (*catuḥsampradāya*) with which all others have to affiliate in order to receive recognition. They are: (1) Śrīvaiṣṇava *saṁpradāya* (sect), established by the *ācāryas* (masters) of Śrīraṅgam, among whom RĀMĀNUJA is the greatest. Their centres are in Śrīraṅgam and Tirupati; (2) Brahmā *saṁpradaya*, also called the Madhva *saṁpradāya*, founded by MADHVA. Its centre is in Uḍipī; (3) Kumāra *saṁpradāya*, founded by NĀRADA (3), also called the Hamsa *saṁpradāya*, or Nimbārka *saṁpradāya*, after its best-known representative, NIMBĀRKA, with its headquarters in Govardhana; (4) Rudra *saṁpradāya*, founded by Viṣṇusvami, also called Vallabha *saṁpradāya*, after Vallabha (1479–1531), its best-known reformer, with its headquarters in Gokula.

While all later *saṁpradāyas* are supposed to be affiliated with one of the four, there are two major *saṁpradāyas* that are often mentioned separately: the GAUḌĪYA VAIṢṆAVA *saṁpradāya* (affiliated with the Madhva *saṁpradāya*), founded by CAITANYA, with its centre in Navadvīp, and the Śrī *saṁpradāya*, founded by RĀMĀNANDA, with its headquarters in Ayodhyā.

Vaiṣṇavism is characterized by *upāsana* (ritual worship) and *sāraṇāgati* (taking refuge in Viṣṇu). Vaiṣṇavas subscribe to *ahiṁsā* (non-violence), vegetarianism, selflessness and active altruism. Vaiṣṇavism has brought forth an extremely rich literature both in Sanskrit and Indian vernaculars as well as artistic productions (music, dance, sculpture, architecture). Major revival movements within Vaiṣṇavism have been founded by the ĀḺVARS of South India, the North Indian BHAKTI movements and the Neo-Caitanyite Mission (19th–20th centuries), which has reached the West in the form of the INTERNATIONAL SOCIETY FOR KRISHNA CONSCIOUSNESS.

Vaiśya

The third of the VARṆAS (classes), the lowest of the twice-born, composed of traders, farmers and artisans.

Vāla-khīlyas (1)

Eleven hymns in the *Ṛgveda* that are added as an appendix, due to their spurious nature.

Vāla-khīlyas (2)

Mythical pygmy sages, the size of a thumb, able to fly swifter than birds, the guardians of the sun chariot.

Valiyon

The Tamil name for BALADEVA, the elder brother of Viṣṇu. He is described as having a light complexion, one earring and a ploughshare as a weapon. His emblem is the palmyra tree.

Vallabhācārya, also Vallabha (1481–1533)

A Telugu brahmin, founder of a school of theistic Vedānta called Śuddhādvaita (pure non-dualism). He emphasized most strongly the role of grace in the process of salvation. He elevated the *Bhāgavata Purāṇa* to the position of the most authoritative scripture. He also considered revelation the only way to acquire knowledge of God. (*See also* PUṢṬIMĀRGA.)

Vālmīki

The author of the RĀMĀYANA, the first poet (*Ādikāvi*). His name is derived from *vālmīka*, an anthill. According to legend he led the life of a brigand before being converted to Rāma worship. Doing penance he meditated so long and so intensely that ants built their hill around him, leaving only his eyes visible. He received the banished SĪTĀ into his hermitage and educated her two sons.

vāmācāra ('left-hand way')

See TANTRA.

Vāma-deva (1)

A name of ŚIVA.

Vāma-deva (2)

A Vedic *ṛṣi* (sage), author of many hymns.

Vāma-deva (3)

An Upaniṣadic sage.

Vāma-deva (4)

The name of a *daśanāmi saṃnyāsi*, founder and president of the Akhil Bhāratīya Sant Samiti (1986).

Vāmana

The dwarf AVATĀRA of Viṣṇu. (*See also* BALI.)

Vāmana Purāṇa

One of the Upapurāṇas, dealing with the dwarf AVĀTARA of Viṣṇu.

vaṃśa

Genealogy, lists of succession of *ṛṣis* (sages) as found attached to some BRĀHMAṆAS (1); also one of the *pañcālakṣana* (five subjects of a Purāṇa).

vaṃśānucarita

The third of the *pancālakṣana* (subjects of a Purāṇa). It consists of the genealogies of various gods and patriarchs.

Van Buitenen, Johannes Adrianus Bernardus
(1925–89)

Dutch–American Indologist, professor of Sanskrit at Chicago University, translator of Rāmānuja's *Gītābhāṣya*, Yamunācārya's *Āgamaprāmuanya*, and the *Mahābhārata* (incomplete).

vāna-praṣṭha ('forest dweller')

The third stage in a brahmin's life. (*See also* SAMNYĀSA.)

Varāha ('boar')

One of the AVATĀRAS of Viṣṇu, who in this form saved the earth from being submerged in the ocean.

Varāha Purāṇa

One of the UPA-PURĀṆAS, in which the exploits of Viṣṇu's Varaha AVATĀRA are described.

Vārāṇasī

Vārāṇasī and the Ganges.

One of the seven ancient holy cities of India, and probably one of the oldest cities on earth, it is situated on the Gaṅgā, in today's Uttar Pradesh. Its name comes from the names of two rivers (Vārāṇa and Asī) that formed the borders of the ancient town; it is also known as Kāśī (the shiny one), Avimuktaka (place of highest liberation). From time immemorial it was a holy city (it was an ancient place by the time of Buddha) and a centre of Hindu learning. Its major temples, especially the Viśvanāṭha ('Golden') temple, were destroyed and rebuilt several times under Muslim rule. The present shrine, built on part of the original temple (the other part is occupied by a mosque), was constructed in 1783 by Rānī Ahalyabāī. Many Hindus come to Vārāṇasī to die in the hope of finding instant liberation from rebirth. Besides its many traditional places of Hindu learning, Vārāṇasī is the seat of the Kāshī Sanskrit Vidyāpīth and the Benares Hindu University.

Vārāṇasī has been the object of much literature, ancient and modern. One of the most extensive descriptions of ancient Vārāṇasī is found in the *Kāśīkhaṇḍa* of the *Skandha Purāṇa*. Vārāṇasī has been praised in countless hymns and poems throughout the ages.

Vārkarīs

See TUKĀRĀM(A).

Varma

A name, designating affiliation with the Kṣatriya VARṆA.

varṇa ('colour')

The largest social unit, based on birth. The four *varṇas* are Brāhmaṇas (priests, scholars, counsellors), Kṣatriyas (soldiers, administrators, nobles), Vaiśyas (landowners, businesspeople, artisans) and Śūdras (servants, landless labourers, menials).

varṇāśrama dharma

The (Hindu) law regulating the rights and duties of the four VARṆAS according to their station in life (ĀŚRAMA (2)), considered binding for all members of Hindu society. (*See also* SOCIAL ORDER.)

varta ('economy')

One of the focal points of Hindu statecraft (the other being *daṇḍa*, justice, the power of punishment).

Varuṇa

A major Vedic deity, associated with creation and the upholding of law. Varuṇa is the ruler of the universe, controller of the destiny of humankind. His consort is Vāruṇī, the goddess of wine.

vasanta

Spring, also personified as a deity.

Vasiṣṭha ('wealthiest')

A Vedic ṚṢI (sage), composer of many hymns. He is one of the seven great *ṛṣis* and one of the ten PRAJĀPATIS. As owner of Kāmadhenu, the 'cow of plenty', he could obtain all wishes. A law book is also attributed to him. In the Veda Vasiṣṭha appears as family priest of king Sudās and as the enemy of his rival Viśvamitra. The name Vasiṣṭha occurs frequently in the epics and Purāṇas, and not all the stories connected with this name agree with the Vedic tradition. There is also a *Vāsiṣṭha Rāmāyaṇa* (also known as *Yogāvasiṣṭha*) which offers a philosophical, advaitic rewriting of the epic.

vāstu-puruṣa

A figure in the shape of a person enclosed by a quadrangle, subdivided into a number of smaller squares, used as the basic ground plan for the construction of a TEMPLE.

vāstu-śāstra

See ŚILPA-ŚĀSTRA.

Vasu

The eight Vasus are described in the *Ṛgveda* as attendants of INDRA: Āpa (water), Dhruva (the pole star), Soma (the moon), Dhara (earth), Anila (wind), Anala (fire), Prabhāsa (dawn), Pratyūṣa (light). They are also called Aditi's children.

Vasu-deva

The son of Śura of the YĀDAVA clan of the lunar dynasty, father of Kṛṣṇa. He married the seven daughters of Āhuka. Devakī, the youngest, became the mother of Kṛṣṇa. After Kṛṣṇa's death he also died and four of his wives became SATĪS (2) with him.

Vāsudeva

The patronymic of Kṛṣṇa.

Vātsyāyaṇa (1)

The author of a commentary on the *Nyāyasūtra*.

Vātsyāyaṇa (2)

The author of the *Kāmasūtra*.

Vāyu, also Pavana ('air, wind')

Personified in the Vedas, often associated with INDRA. In the Purāṇas he is the king of the GANDHARVAS (2), the father of BHĪMA (2) and HANUMANT.

Vāyu Purāṇa

A Purāṇa in which Vāyu announces *dharma* in connection with the Śvetakaḷpa, the age preceding the present one. It is considered to be the oldest among the MAHĀPURĀṆAS and to conform most closely to the definition of a Purāṇa as *pañcalakṣana* (five topics).

Veda

From the root '*vid*', to know; 'knowledge', with the connotation of revelation. The Vedas are the foundation of Hinduism and their acceptance as ultimate authority is the criterion of orthodoxy. Veda in the narrower sense comprises the four *saṁhitās*, collections of hymns written in Vedic, an archaic form of Sanskrit. The date of their composition, as well as the place, have been the object of major scholarly disputes. Indian tradition dates the Vedas to about 4000 BCE and assumes a northwest Indian origin. Western scholars, since Max MÜLLER, assume a date of 1500–1200 BCE and consider them the products of nomadic invaders of India from the area of southern Russia. Veda in the wider sense includes, besides the *saṁhitās*, the Brāhmaṇas, voluminous treatises dealing with the technicalities of sacrifice, the Āraṇyakas, 'forest treatises', and Upaniṣads, texts for persons who have renounced and no longer participate in the routine of ritual.

The *saṁhitās* consist of the *Ṛgveda* (Veda of mantras), the *Sāmaveda (Veda* of melodies), the *Yajurveda* (Veda of rituals), and the *Atharvaveda* (Veda of incantations). The most important is the *Ṛgveda*, a collection of 1,017 hymns (with an additional 11 VĀLAKHILYAS (1)) divided into ten books or eight *maṇḍalas*. Every hymn is addressed to one or more Vedic deities, is attributed to a Vedic ṚṢI (some of them women), and has to be recited at a certain pitch to accompany a ritual. While much of Vedic ritualism has become obsolete, many Vedic hymns are still recited at occasions such as birth-ceremonies, initiation, marriage and cremation.

The text of the *Ṛgveda* has been meticulously preserved over thousands of years through oral transmission. Various mnemotechnic devices were employed to ensure faultless memorization and recitation. The various texts of the Veda were transmitted by particular *śākhās* (branches) of brahmin families. For example, the White Yajurveda was passed on by the Vajasaneyi *śākhā*. Certain Hindu schools of thought, such as Pūrva MĪMĀṀSA, consider the Veda *apauruṣeya* (not the work of a person, either divine or human) and pre-existent. Others consider it the utterance of the Supreme Being revealed to *ṛṣis*. Learning and recitation of the Veda was the prerogative of brahmins. Persons not belonging to the twice-born castes were not allowed to either recite or listen to it and severe punishment was meted out for transgressions. (*See also* appendix 2, HINDU SCRIPTURES.)

Vedāṇgas ('limbs of the Veda')

Six auxiliary sciences to be studied in order to understand and use the Veda correctly: *śikṣā* (phonetics and pronunciation); *chandas* (verse metres), *vyākāraṇa* (grammar), *nirukta* (etymology, explanation of obsolete words), *jyotiṣa* (astronomy), *kalpa* or *śrauta* (ritual).

Vedānta ('end of Veda')

This can mean both the Upaniṣads and systems of Upaniṣadic philosophy and theology. The Upaniṣads were the last portion of the Veda (in the wider sense) and, according to Vedāntins, constitute the core purpose of the Veda, because they teach final emancipation from the cycle of birth and death. An attempt was made to systematize their teaching in the BRAHMA-SŪTRAS (also called the *Vedāntasūtras*). The lengthy commentaries upon these composed by various authors from different backgrounds gave rise to many schools of Vedānta. Vedānta in one form or other has been the major Hindu philosophy of religion for the past 1,200 years and has many contemporary academic and religious exponents. (See appendix 3, The Ten Principal Schools of Vedānta.)

Vedānta Deśika (1269–1370)

The most prolific exponent of ŚRĪVAIṢṆAVISM after RĀMĀNUJA, and believed to be the AVATĀRA of the bell of the temple at TIRUPATI. He wrote works in Sanskrit and Tamil as well as in Manipravāla, a mixture of the two. Many of his writings are subcommentaries on Rāmānuja's commentaries and are widely used by students of VIŚIṢṬĀDVAITA. He became the main authority for the northern school (VAḌAGALAI) of Śrīvaiṣṇavism. His works include *Rahasyatrayasāra*, *Nyāsa Viṁśati* and *Saṅkalpa Suryodaya*.

Vedānta-karikāvalī

A short manual of VIŚIṢṬĀDVAITA Vedānta by the 18th-century scholar Bucci Venkaṭācārya.

Vedānta-paribhāṣa

A short manual of ADVAITA Vedānta written by the 17th-century scholar Dharmarāja Adhvarin.

Vedānta-sāra

A short ADVAITA VEDĀNTA manual written by Sadānanda, a celebrated Advaitin who lived in the first half of the 15th century. He is the author of *Vedāntasāra*, a concise compendium of Advaita, much in use even today.

Vedānta-sūtra

See BRAHMA-SŪTRA.

Vedārtha-saṅgraha

('the gist of the meaning of the Veda')

A small work by RĀMĀNUJA, in which he critiques Advaita understandings of the Upaniṣads and advances his own from the standpoint of VIŚIṢṬĀDVAITA.

vedi

A Vedic sacrificial altar. The *Śulvasūtras* contain exact rules for the construction of altars for specific purposes. The most elaborate was the altar in the form of a falcon used for the solemn AGNICAYANA. It consisted of 10,800 bricks (the number of hours in a Vedic year) in five layers (the five seasons) representing the year, and with it the universe. Contemporary scholars believe they have found correlations between the dimensions of the altars and the distances of sun, moon and planets as well as their orbits.

Vedic civilization

A major dispute has developed about

the age and origin of Vedic civilization. While the majority of Western scholars, following the lead of Max MÜLLER, assume that Vedic civilization in India was the result of an invasion by semi-nomadic, cattle-breeding Āryan people from outside India around 1500–1200 BCE, following the decline of the Mohenjo Daro/Harappan city culture, most Indian scholars contend that Vedic civilization developed in India itself around 4000 BCE and that the so-called Indus civilization (renamed Indus–Sarasvati civilization) was a late phase of Vedic civilization, which spread eastwards to the Gangetic plains after the desiccation of the original homeland in what is today Sindh. While there is neither literary nor archeological evidence for an invasion from outside India, satellite photography and archaeogeography seem to have established that the river-bed of the Sarasvatī, described in the *Ṛgveda* as the mightiest of rivers, beside which the Vedic people had settled, had completely dried out by 1900 BCE. It is to be expected that both groups of scholars would engage in debate to validate their assumptions.

Vedic religion

The religion based on the Veda was strongly focused on SACRIFICE (*yajña*), which was believed to be the source of everything. Vedic religion was also characterized by the division of VARṆAS, believed to have originated at the *puruṣayajña* with which humankind began. Vedic religion was polytheistic: Indra, Agni, Varuṇa and Mitra were the main deities; however, as one Vedic verse has it, 'Indra is known by many names; all the different names design but One.' Vedic religion was the basis of later Hinduism, which received influences from other sources. Many Hindus would call their religion 'vedic', emphasizing the continuity of practice and belief from Vedic times to today.

vegetarianism

Vedic Indians were meat eaters; they even consumed cattle after they had been sacrificed. Vegetarianism apparently developed under the influence of Buddhism and Jainism, religions that insisted on *ahiṁsā*, 'non-killing', repudiating animal sacrifice and meat eating. Among Hindus VAIṢṆAVAS are the strictest vegetarians (Bengali brahmins eat fish, which they do not consider against their religion); ŚAIVAS and ŚĀKTAS continue animal sacrifices and also eat meat. Neo-Hindu movements are proponents of strict vegetarianism for ethical as well as health reasons. Accepting the doctrine of rebirth and the possibility that a human might be reborn in an animal, they view animal slaughter and meat eating as tantamount to cannibalism. (*See also* FOOD.)

Vel

A name of MURUGAN, the Tamil god of war, also known as Sey and Neduvel. His priests were known as Velan.

Veṇa

A mythical king, son of Anga, who angered the brahmins of his realm by forbidding SACRIFICES to anyone but himself. When their remonstrations did not help they killed him with blades of *kuśa* grass. When lawlessness overtook the kingless country they drilled the left arm of the dead king and produced Niṣāda, who proved to be wicked and useless. They drilled the right arm and obtained Pṛthu, who cultivated the earth (*pṛthivī*) and was a just ruler, restoring the privileges of the brahmins. His story is told in the *Mahābhārata* and in several Purāṇas.

Vendan

A Tamil form of INDRA, worshipped in Maridan.

Veṅkaṭeśvara ('Lord of Veṅkaṭa')

A title of Viṣṇu as worshipped in TIRUPATI, situated on the Veṅkaṭa hill.

vetāla

A ghost or goblin, which especially haunts cemeteries, animating dead bodies. (*See also* BHŪTA; PRETA.)

vibhava

The appearance (of Viṣṇu) in a visible, bodily form (like an *avatāra*).

Vibhīṣaṇa ('terrible')

The younger brother of RĀVAṆA, a virtuous man opposed to the activities of the RĀKŚASAS. He became an ally of Rāma and was made king of Laṅkā after Rāvaṇa's death.

vibhuti

Miraculous powers, dealt with in a section of the YOGA-SŪTRAS. It is also used to designate the ash-like substance forming on pictures of SATHYA SĀI BĀBĀ, which is said to have miraculous properties.

Vicitra-vīrya

A king who plays a major role in the *Mahābhārata*.

vidhi ('injunction', 'command')

According to MĪMĀṀSA only that part of the Veda is authoritative that gives injunctions with regard to things to be done, the rest being mere 'eulogy' (*arthavāda*).

Vidura

The son of VYĀSA by a slave girl, called 'the wisest of the wise', adviser to both PĀṆḌAVAS and KAURAVAS, and ally of Pāṇḍavas in the Great War. (*See also* MAHĀBHĀRATA.)

vidyā ('knowledge', 'wisdom')

According to the Upaniṣads the highest aim of life and the only means to find full emancipation from SAṀSĀRA. It arises from discrimination (*viveka*) between the eternal self and the transient world of the senses. Indian philosophers have developed diverse interpretations of its meaning and its acquisition.

Vidyābhūṣana Baladeva (18th century)

A follower of the CAITANYA school, author of a commentary on the *Brahmasūtras* from a Caitanyite perspective, the *Govinda Bhāṣya*.

Vidyāpati (1400–1507)

Poet, author of the celebrated *Gītagovinda* extolling the love between RĀDHĀ and KṚṢṆA.

Vidyāraṇya

See MĀDHAVA.

Vijaya-nagara ('city of victory')

The last Hindu state in India, founded in 1336 by Harihara and Bukka, MĀDHAVA becoming the first prime minister. It covered a large area on the Deccan, up to modern Cennai (Madras). Its capital was beautified through many temples, the largest and most famous being the Virupakṣa, sacred to Śiva. Sixteenth-century European travellers described it as the richest kingdom in Asia and its capital comparable in size to Rome. The *rāyas* of Vijayanagara were patrons of Tamil, Telugu and Kanarese poetry and encouraged Sanskrit studies. They fully supported orthodox Brahminism and the revival of Vedic animal (and human) SACRIFICES. Muslim forces conquered and destroyed the city in 1565. The remnants of the rulers of Vijayanagara moved to Chandragiri and the empire disintegrated.

Vijñāna-bhikṣu (15th century)

The founder of a school of VEDĀNTA called Sāmānya-vāda. He attempted to show the compatibility of SĀṀHKYA and Vedānta in his commentary to the *Brahmasūtras* called *Vijñānāmṛta Bhāsya*. He also wrote a commentary on the *Śavaragītā* of the *Kūrma Purāṇa*.

Vikramāditya (95 BCE–78 CE)

A legendary king, whose identity has been variously established, from whose reign the beginning of the Vikram era dates (57 BCE). His capital was Ujjainī, and he was renowned as a soldier and politician, as well as a patron of the arts. He was said to have assembled at his court the 'nine jewels', men highly accomplished in their fields of endeavour: Dhanvantari, a physician; Kṣapaṇaka, Śaṅku, and Vetāla Bhaṭṭa, poets; Amarasinha, a lexicographer; Ghatakharpara, Kālidāsa and Vararuci, poets and dramatists; and Varāhamihira, an astronomer. The title Vikramāditya was also used by other kings.

village religion

The discrepancy between the sophisticated Hindu systems such as VEDĀNTA and the down-to-earth religious practice of Indian villages was noticed early. Village religion in India is characterized by locality: the most important objects of worship are usually local heroes and goddesses, often former members of the village community. Worship is offered not only in formal temples but at improvised shrines, under trees, at peculiarly shaped stones, at places where apparitions were sighted, etc. A number of studies of village religion in different parts of India have been undertaken recently.

Vindhya

A range of mountains that stretch across Central India, dividing the Madhyadeśa, homeland of the Āryas, from the south, the Deccan. Many events described in epics and Purāṇas relate to the Vindhyas.

violence (*hiṃṣa*)

This is normally considered a vice by Hindus. It is justified, however, if sanctioned by the ŚĀSTRAS: the killing of animals in SACRIFICE is not considered sinful, because it is done on the strength of a Vedic injunction, and by being sacrificed an animal obtains a higher existence. The killing of enemies by Kṣatriyas (warrior class) is also permitted, or even required, if involved in a just (dharmic) war. As Kṛṣṇa explains to Arjuna in the *Bhagavadgītā*, a warrior must fight in order to fulfil his duties and to contribute to the wellbeing of the world (*lokasangraha*). Unconditional *ahiṁsā* (non-violence), as GANDHI taught it, is not part of mainstream Hindu tradition.

Virāj, also **Virāṭ**

('splendid', 'excellent')

A primordial being, variously described as the male half of BRAHMĀ or as an issue of PURUṢA, the prototype of all male creatures. In VEDĀNTA it is the name of the intellect that rules over the aggregate of bodies.

virāja

The mythical river that divides Vaikuṇṭha from Śivaloka.

Vīra-śāivas

See LIṄGĀYATS.

virtues

The most common list of traditional (universal) Hindu virtues is provided in the five YAMA (non-violence, truthfulness, honesty, continence and non-covetousness) and five NIYAMA (purity, contentment, ritual actions, study, making the Lord the motive of one's actions) as listed in Patañjali's *Yogasūtra*, as preparation for higher meditation. Specific virtues are enjoined on members of particular *saṁpradāyas* (sects), such as fasting on specific days, observing feasts, contributing to temple worship etc.

vīrya ('strength')

One of the attributes of Viṣṇu, according to RĀMĀNUJA.

Viśiṣṭādvaita

The interpretation of VEDĀNTA developed by RĀMĀNUJA and his followers, in opposition to ŚAṄKARA's Advaita. While maintaining the ultimate oneness of all reality, Rāmānuja postulates a multiplicity of real beings: the world of material things as well as that of living beings, in addition to BRAHMAN, identical with Viṣṇu. The universe is seen as God's body. As a consequence both the way to salvation and the ultimate end are conceived differently from Śaṅkara's Advaita: for Rāmānuja human effort aided by divine grace is required, and the final state is not one of complete dissolution of individual existence but one of eternal companionship with Viṣṇu together with all the released.

Viṣṇu ('the all-pervader')

He appears in the *Ṛgveda* as INDRA's younger brother, but emerges in epics and Purāṇas as the Supreme Being, with the largest numerical following. He is usually shown together with his consort *Śrī* or LAKṢMĪ. He is essentially a saviour god, called *muktidātā*. His worship is joyous and often emotional.

Pictorially he is represented as having a dark blue body, with four arms, holding *cakra* (a discus, sign of world-power, called Sudarśana), *gada* (a mace, called Kaumodakī), *padma* (a lotus), and *śaṅka* (a conch, called Pañca-janya). On his breast is the curl called Śrīvatsa and the jewel Kaustubha, on his wrist he wears the jewel Syamantaka. Usually he is represented standing or seated on a lotus, with Lakṣmī beside him. In some temples he is also pictured lying on the coils of ŚEṢA, the world snake, who represents eternity. His VAHANA (vehicle) is GARUḌA.

Viṣṇu.

He is worshipped in a litany of thousand names (*sahasranāma*). His most popular names are Acyuta ('unfallen'), Ananta ('infinite'), Caturbhuja ('four-armed'), Hari, Hṛṣīkeśa ('Lord of the sense organs'), Janārdana ('worshipped by men'), Keśava ('the radiant'), Lakṣmīpati ('husband of Lakṣmī), Madhusūdana ('destroyer of the demon Madhu'), Nāra, Nārāyana, Pitāṁbara ('clothed in yellow'), Puruṣottama ('the supreme person'), Vaikuntanāṭha ('lord of heaven'), Yajñeśvara ('lord of sacrifice). Since KṚṢṆA is considered by his followers not just as an *avatāra* of Viṣṇu but Viṣṇu appearing as such (*svayam bhagavān*), the titles of Viṣṇu and Kṛṣṇa are often used interchangeably.

His community is divided into a great many different *saṁpradāyas* (sects). The most characteristic feature of Viṣṇu is his appearance in the form of AVATĀRAS (incarnations), whose most prominent are RĀMA and Kṛṣṇa. A rich mythology has been created around Viṣṇu as well as a sophisticated theology. (*See also* RĀMĀNUJA, VAIṢṆAVAS, VIŚIṢṬĀDVAITA.)

Viṣṇu Purāṇa

The Purāṇa dealing with Viṣṇu, his AVATĀRAS, his legends, his worship etc. It is one of the oldest (fifth century CE?) and best corresponds to the definition of a Purāṇa as dealing with five subjects (*pañcalakṣana*): primary creation, secondary creation, genealogies of gods and patriarchs, reigns of MANU (2), history. It is very popular among Hindus and considered *śruti* (revelation) by many VAIṢṆAVAS.

Viṣṇu-gupta

Minister of Candragupta Maurya (322–298 BCE), usually identified with CĀNAKYA (or Kauṭilya), the celebrated author of the *Kauṭiliya Arthaśāstra*.

Viṣṇu-sahasra-nāma

('thousand names of Viṣṇu')

A litany of a thousand names or titles of Viṣṇu, found in the *Mahābhārata* and several Purāṇas. It has been commented upon by ŚAṄKARA (2) and by PARĀŚARA Bhaṭṭa, and is often recited in VAIṢṆAVA worship. The *Cāraka Saṁhitā*, a work on medicine, recommends recitation of the *Viṣṇusahasranāma* in cases where medical remedies no longer help and in former times it was recited during childbirth.

Viṣṇu-smṛti

One of the older, authoritative codes of law.

Viṣṇu-svāmi (1200–50)

Founder of the Rudra (VAIṢṆAVA) *saṁpradāya* (sect).

Viśva Hindū Pariṣad

('Universal Hindu Assembly')

A movement founded in 1964 by about 150 Hindu religious leaders in Bombay to reawaken Hindu consciousness (Hindu *jagaran*) and to bring about worldwide co-operation among Hindus. It also attempts to articulate a common platform for Hinduism, to modernize the Hindu tradition and to give political power in India back to Hindus. It supports Hindu political parties and has held several major public events to draw attention to Hindu concerns. It is very active in the Hindu diaspora and has attracted the support of leading figures in economy and culture.

Viśva-karma (1) ('all-maker')

A Vedic *deva*, who is addressed in two hymns as 'all-seeing, mighty in mind and power, the father who made us, the one above the seven *ṛṣis* (sages).'

Viśva-karma (2)

The architect, engineer and master craftsman of the gods, the author of *Viśvakarmavāstuśāstra*.

Viśva-mitra

A celebrated figure who, though born as a KṢATRIYA, rose to brahminhood through intense *tapas* (self-mortification) and became one of the SAPTARṢIS (Seven Sages). He was the arch rival of VASIṢṬHA, another Maharṣi (Great Sage). Viśvamitra is the sage of the third *maṇḍala* of the *Ṛgveda,* which contains the famous *gāyatrī*, Vasiṣṭha that of the seventh. Both were at some time *purohitas* (family priests) of the famous King SUDĀS. The epics and Purāṇas contain many stories about the enmity between Viśvamitra and Vasiṣṭha.

Viśva-nāṭha ('universal Lord')

A title of Śiva and name of the most famous of the temples in VĀRĀṆASĪ, of which Śiva is patron deity.

Viśva-nātha Cakra-varttin (1664–1754)

One of the most prolific scholarly exponents of GAUḌĪYA VAIṢṆAVISM and author of numerous commentaries on major works by Rūpa and Jīva Gosvāmi, as well as of dramas and plays with Caitanyite plots. Among his best-known works are *Sarārtha Darśinī*, a commentary on the *Bhāgavatam*, a *Gītābhāṣya*, *Bhaktirasamṛtasindhubindu* and *Ujjvalanīlāmanikiraṇa*, short summaries of the two main works of RŪPA GOSVĀMI.

viśva-rūpa ('all forms')

A title of Viṣṇu, the form in which ARJUNA beheld KṚṢṆA in the eleventh chapter of the *Bhagavadgītā*.

Viṭṭhobā, also **Viṭṭal**

A Mahārāṣṭrian form of the name of Viṣṇu. His sanctuary is in PAṆḌHARPUR.

vivaha

See MARRIAGE.

viveka ('discrimination')

Discrimination between what is self, eternal, and what is non-self, transient. It is one of the preconditions as well as the means for liberation from SAṀSĀRA.

Viveka-cūḍā-maṇi ('crest jewel of discrimination')

A famous short work, ascribed to ŚANKARA (2), teaching how to gain LIBERATION through VIVEKA.

Vivekānanda, Swami (1863–1902)

The monastic name of Narendra Nath Dutt, a disciple of RAMAKRISHNA 'PARAMAHAMSA' and founder of the Ramakrishna Mission. He was sent by the rāja of Rāmnād as Hindu delegate to the World Parliament of Religions in Chicago in 1893 and impressed the West by his forceful reinterpretation of Vedānta and his practical plans for the upliftment of India. He founded ashrams in India, which became centres for spiritual and material support, and established Vedānta societies in America and England, to propagate Indian spirituality in the West. He also became one of the proponents of Hindu nationalism and is one of the most celebrated figures of the Hindu renaissance.

vrata ('vow')

A voluntary religious practice, taken up by individuals in fulfilment of certain promises made. They usually consist of particular fasts, pilgrimages or repetitions of prayer formulas to gain healing for a sick family member or friend, obtain help in difficult situations, or to give thanks for divine support received. They are an important aspect of popular Hinduism.

Vrātyas

A heretical group. There is much controversy about the identity of the Vrātyas. Some claim they were non-Āryan immigrants from the Middle East, others think they were lapsed high-caste Āryans, while some (associating the name with the term *vrata*, 'vow') consider them to be a 'people who took a vow', religious mendicants who adopted a particular lifestyle.

Vṛndāvana, also **Vṛndāban, Vrindaban, Brindaban** ('Vṛnda forest')

One of the most popular Hindu pilgrimage centres, in western Uttar Pradesh, near Mathurā, associated with

Kṛṣṇa's youthful exploits, especially his dalliance with the GOPĪS, the milkmaids of Braja, as described in the *Harivaṃśa* and the *Bhāgavatam*. It owes its present status and popularity to its rediscovery and revival by CAITANYA and his associates, who settled there in the late 16th century and began building major temples, identifying the locations mentioned in the BHĀGAVATAM and starting a prolific literary activity. Its closeness to Delhi (120 km to the north) and its accessibility from the Agra–Delhi trunk road has created an enormous influx of visitors in recent years. Many retired people spend their lives in Vṛndāvana, participating in the rich fare of temple worship, *raslīlā* performances (re-enactments of the life of Kṛṣṇa) and presentations by famous religious leaders.

Vṛṣṇi

A descendant of Yadu, of the lunar dynasty, an ancestor of Kṛṣṇa, also called Varṣṇeya. (*See also* YĀDAVAS.)

Vṛtra

The antagonist of INDRA in the *Ṛgveda*, sometimes identified with drought or darkness, the embodiment of everything oppressive, whom Indra slays, thereby relieving his followers.

vyākaraṇa

Grammar, one of the six VEDĀṆGAS, a major preoccupation in Hindu scholarship. Study of grammar was an indispensable prerequisite for any higher studies, and in itself was considered a religious discipline. The major grammarians, such as PĀṆINĪ, enjoy a high status.

Vyāsa ('arranger')

A celebrated sage, the arranger of the Vedas, and the compiler of the *Mahābhārata* and all the Purāṇas. According to tradition he was the illegitimate child of PARĀŚARA and SATYAVATĪ (1) (before her marriage to King Śāntanu) and retired to the forest to practise austerities immediately after birth. He was called upon by his mother to beget sons on the widows of her son Vicitravīrya, and became the father of Pāṇḍu and Dhṛtarāṣṭra as well as of Vidura and Śuka. He was called Kṛṣṇa because of his dark complexion, and Dvaipāyana because of his birth on an island (*dvīpa*) in the Yamunā. He is one of the seven *cira-jīvins*, or deathless persons. (The others are Aśvathāmā, Bali, Hanumān, Vibhīṣana, Kṛpa and Paraśurāma).

vyavahāra ('conduct', 'action', 'transaction', 'procedure')

In general it denotes all manner of dealings, especially legal procedure. In Vedānta, especially in ADVAITA VEDĀNTA, it is used to desribe the mundane, innerwordly, imperfect standpoint (*vyavahārika*) over against the perfect, eternal (*paramārthika*) perspective on reality.

vyūhas ('arrangement')

In VIŚIṢṬĀDVAITA, the fourfold form of BRAHMAN, manifesting himself as Vāsudeva (possessing all six divine attributes), Saṅkarṣaṇa (possessing knowledge and strength), Pradyumna (endowed with lordship and virility) and Aniruddha (possessed of potency and splendour) for purposes of meditation by the devotees and creation of the universe. Each of the four descends into three sub-vyūhas who are the presiding deities of the twelve months of the year. Their names are Keśava, Nārāyaṇa, Mādhava, Govinda, Viṣṇu, Madhusūdana, Trivikrama, Vāmana, Śrīdhara, Hṛṣīkeśa, Padmanābha and Dāmodara.

W

war (*vigraha*)

Hindu history, from the Vedas onwards, is replete with stories of wars, climaxing in the Great Bhārata War, with which the KALI YUGA, the age of strife, began. Wars of defence and of conquest were considered the legitimate occupation of Kṣatriyas (the warrior class). Conventions of fair warfare included the rule that only Kṣatriyas were to engage in warfare, that non-combatants should be spared, that no one was to attack another from behind, at night, or in a position in which he could not defend himself. Wars according to chivalric conventions were called *dharmayuddha* and seen as a means to win fame and a good afterlife; wars in which these conventions were violated, or which were caused by greed and lust, were called *kuṭayuddha* or *asurayuddha*. Warfare was developed as one of the traditional sciences, and received the attention of many writers on statecraft (*ārtha śāstra*). Battles were usually initiated with long rituals and prayers, and wars were regarded as 'sacrifice'.

water

Besides its practical uses, water was always important in Hindu RITUAL: daily ritual ablutions are prescribed, additional ablutions were done to atone for sins, the sprinkling of water (*tarpaṇa*) for the benefit of deceased ancestors is part of daily ceremonies, the rivers are considered sacred and must not be polluted. Gaṅgā (Ganges) water, especially, said not to putrefy, is taken away by pilgrims and used as medicine and for libations, especially in connection with the last rites.

wheel (*cakra*)

An ancient solar symbol, used also to denote universality of domination or teaching. A universal monarch is a *cakravartin*, and the *cakra* is a popular symbol for the DHARMA as well. CIRCUMAMBULATION is the customary form of worship of an object.

Whitney, William Dwight (1827–94)

The first professor of Sanskrit at Yale University, long-time president of the American Oriental Society, he published a Sanskrit grammar which is still used, and wrote many essays on language. His translation of the *Atharvaveda* was published posthumously (1905).

Wilkins, Sir Charles (1750–1836)

A member of the Indian Civil Service, he was the first Englishman with a substantial knowledge of Sanskrit. His *Sanskrit Grammar* (1779) was path-breaking, and his translation of the

Bhagavadgītā (1785) inspired many Europeans. He became co-founder of the Asiatick Society of Bengal (1784). He also translated the *Hitopadeśa* and Kālidāsa's *Śakuntalā*, which prompted Goethe's admiration for Indian drama.

Wilson, Horace Hayman
(1786–1860)

Sanskrit scholar. He was the first Boden Professor of Sanskrit at Oxford University, the translator of Kālidāsa's *Meghadūta*, the *Viṣṇu Purāṇa*, and author of *Lectures on the Religion and Philosophy of the Hindus* and *Sanskrit Grammar*.

Winternitz, Moriz (1863–1937)

A diverse and creative Indologist, who promoted the study of Hinduism in many fields. While studying Indology at Vienna, he wrote a thesis on the Hindu marriage ritual, comparing it with other traditions. He published a critical edition of the *Āpastambīya Gṛhyasūtra* (1887) and worked as an assistant to Max MÜLLER in Oxford. As professor of Indology in Prague from 1899 on, he prepared the general index to the 49 volumes of the Sacred Books of the East series and became instrumental in initiating the critical edition of the *Mahābhārata*. His three-volume *History of Indian Literature* (1905–22) has remained a standard reference work.

wisdom

See VIDYĀ.

women

In Vedic times women were the equals of men in almost every respect: they shared rituals and sacrifices, learning and honours. Some sacrifices, such as the harvest sacrifice (*sītā*) and the sacrifice to secure good husbands for their daughters (*rudrayāga*), could only be performed by women. Women chanted the SĀMANS and composed many of the hymns of the *Ṛgveda*. There was a provision for change in gender (*uha*) in many ritual formulae to alternately have a woman or a man perform the ritual. Women were also teachers of Vedic lore, and girls were given the same education as boys.

By the time of MANU (2) the role of women in society was drastically curtailed, and women were considered unfit for Veda study. Women were treated like ŚŪDRAS: they could not eat or walk with their husbands, or converse with them on anything of consequence. The epics and Purāṇas, while extolling some women such as Sītā and Draupadī, generally exhibit a negative attitude towards women: they describe them as vicious, sensual, fickle, untrustworthy and impure. Women's only sacrament was marriage and only through service to their husbands, regardless of their behaviour, could they hope to find salvation. A faithful woman (*satī*) was supposed to accompany her husband (if she was childness) on the funeral pyre. Childless widows could expect a grim fate: they could not remarry, and were almost without any rights.

After centuries of subordination and repression Hindu women found advocates in the reformers of the 19th and 20th centuries: they agitated for the abolition of *satī*, fought for the right of women to get an education, to remarry, to earn an income. The Hindu Marriage Act of 1955 (with later amendments) gives women the right to divorce their husbands and to remarry, to own property independently, and establishes legal parity of women with men. (*See also* EQUALITY OF WOMEN.)

Woodroff, John (1865–1936)

Writing under the pen name Arthur Avalon, he translated and wrote many books on Tantric Hinduism, until then all but unknown in the West. Among his best-known works are *Introduction to Tantra Śāstra*, *Principles of Tantra*, *Maha-nirvāṇa-tantra*, *Wave of Bliss*, *Śakti and Śakta* and *The World as Power*.

word

From early on Hindus were conscious of the importance of the word and its power; the entire Veda is testimony to this in a general way and some of its *sūktas* (hymns), especially the *Vāksūkta*, explicitly affirm the creative power of the word through which everything has been made and everything is sustained. The power of the brahmins rested entirely on the power of the word, whose custodians they were. The continued interest of Hindus in language and grammar is evidenced by a long tradition in these disciplines and works of lasting value such as PĀṆINĪ's *Astādhyayī* and BHARTṚHARI's *Vākyapadīya*. (*See also* LANGUAGE; ŚABDA.)

world egg (*bramāṇḍa*)

The tradition that the universe evolved out of a primordial egg is found in many different versions. The Vedas speak of a world egg floating on the primordial ocean and giving birth to various creatures. The first being to come forth from the world egg was Viśvakarma, the Vedic creator god. In Manu's account of creation the desire of Svayambhū Bhagavān appeared as a golden egg shining with the brilliance of a thousand suns. From it issued BRAHMĀ, the creator god. Remaining in the shape of an egg for a full year, he divided himself through the power of meditation into two halves out of which were fashioned heaven and earth. Purāṇic cosmography describes the universe as being contained within the shell of the world egg (*aṇḍakaṭaha*), whose diameter is calculated at 500 million *yojanas*.

worship

The various Sanskrit terms translated by 'worship', such as *yajña*, *pūjā*, *upāsana*, and others, indicate varieties of worship that evolved throughout the ages. In Vedic times SACRIFICE (*yajña*) was the most comprehensive term, encompassing public and domestic rituals, from the offering of hundreds of cattle to the burning of a stick of firewood. When theistic religions developed, PŪJĀ, the offering of flowers, fruit and incense in a formal or informal setting, became the predominant form of worship. *Upāsana* is the most generic expression, encompassing both outwardly visible ritual worship as well as interior acts of devotion, meditation and self-surrender. Usually Hindus distinguish between acts of worship that are mandatory (*nitya*) and those that are optional (*naimittika*). Overall, worship in some form or other is typical for Hinduism and the great variety of forms as well as the lavishness of execution especially in connection with temple festivals is quite unique.

Y

Yādavas

The descendants of King Yadu, the son of King YAYĀTI of the lunar dynasty. Kṛṣṇa was born among the Yādavas, who were known as pastoralists but also established a kingdom in Dvārakā, in Gujarat. When Dvārakā was submerged by the ocean, all its inhabitants perished. The founders of the Vijayanāgara empire claimed to be descendants of those Yādavas who were not present at Dvārakā when it was destroyed.

Yādava-prakāśa (11th century)

Advaitin *guru*, the first teacher of RĀMĀNUJA, who rejected his interpretation of the Upaniṣads, which he criticized in his *Vedārthasaṁgraha*.

Yadu

See YĀDAVA.

yajña

See SACRIFICE.

Yajña-vālkya

A celebrated sage, reputedly the author of the White YAJURVEDA, the *Śatapatha Brāhmaṇa* and the *Bṛhadāraṇyaka Upaniṣad*, as well as the *Yājñavalkyasmṛti*, a code of law second in importance only to the MANUSMṚTI. He figures prominently in the epics, especially in the *Rāmāyaṇa*, where he is represented as a dissenter from traditional religion.

yajñopavīta

See JANĒU.

Yajur-veda

The second of the VEDA *saṁhitās* (collections), a book for priests, containing ritual formulas for full and new moon *yajñas* (SACRIFICES), the *rājasūya*, the *aśvamedha*, and the SOMA sacrifices. It insists on strict observance of the prescribed ritual and considers the *yajña* so important that even the gods have to follow the commands of the brahmins. It is divided into many *śākhās* (schools) and is available in two recensions, the White (*Vājasaneyī*) and the Black (*Taittirīya*) Yajurveda.

yakṣas

Semi-divine beings, the attendants of KUBERA, the god of wealth.

Yama ('restrainer')

The Vedic god of the realm of the dead, son of Vivasvat (the Sun); his twin sister is Yamī or Yamunā. They are described as the first human pair, the first to die, and the first to depart to the netherworlds, and Yama is the judge of all who have died. In the epics and Purāṇas he becomes the overseer of a vast complex of hells (NĀRAKA), each specializing in particular punishments for specific sins committed. He sends his servants to fetch the dying soul and becomes a symbol of terror, from which devotion to Viṣṇu saves. He is also called *Dharmarāja*, *Daṇḍadhāra*, *Pretarāja*, death, time, and ender.

yama

('rule', 'universal moral duty', 'major observance')

Their number is usually given as ten, although the lists differ between various writers. One such list enumerates the following: continence (*brahmacarya*); compassion (*dāya*); forbearance (*kṣānti*); charity (*dāna*); truthfulness (*satya*); integrity (*akalkatā*); non-violence (*ahiṁsā*); non-stealing (*asteya*); kindness (*mādhurya*); and self-restraint (*dama*).

In the YOGA SŪTRAS their number is given as five (complemented by five NIYAMA). (See appendix 4, The Eightfold Practice of Yoga: Aṣṭāṅga Yoga.)

Yamunā, also Kālindī, Sūryajā, Triyāmā

A major river in northern India, which joins the GAṄGĀ at Prāyāga (Allahābad). She is sacred especially to VAIṢṆAVAS, whose holy cities of Mathurā and Vṛndāvana are situated on her. In the Purāṇas she is said to be the daughter of the Sun by his wife Sanjñā. Yamunā is often represented in art as a female goddess figure, often paired with Gaṅgā.

Yamunācārya (10th century)

The second of the *ācāryas* (masters) of ŚRĪRAṄGAM, and a grandson of NĀTHA MUNI, the immediate predecessor of RĀMĀNUJA. He was the author of the *Āgamaprāmānya* in which he established the validity of the Vaiṣṇava ĀGAMAS as sources of orthodox religion.

yantra ('loom')

A symbol of the Goddess (DEVĪ), used as a meditation device in ŚĀKTISM. It usually consists of a combination of triangles and other geometric figures. On it are inscribed the monosyllabic mantras that constitute the body of the Goddess. The design is intended to focus on the centre, usually formed by the sign ŚRĪ and a dot, the mantra-body of the Goddess. There are many different *yantras*, the most celebrated being the Śrī Yantra, whose construction is provided in several tantric texts.

The Śrī-Yantra (the Yantra of the illustrious one) consists of nine superimposed triangles, converging on the central spot (bindu)*; the latter symbolizes the unmanifested potentiality of all things; the triangles symbolize the successive stages of creation, emanating from the* bindu.

Yāska

The author of the NIRUKTA, the oldest explanation of obsolete and uncommon words in the Veda.

Yaśodā

The wife of the cowherd Nanda and foster mother of Kṛṣṇa.

yati ('pilgrim')

A generic designation for *samnyāsis* ('renouncers'). The rules by which they are to abide are known as *yatidharma*. A major collection of such has been made by Viśveśvarasarasvatī in his *Yatidharmasaṅgraha*. (*See also* TYĀGA.)

Yatīndra-mata-dīpikā

('the lamp of the teaching of the king of the renouncers')

A popular work by Śrīnivāsa (18th century) explaining systematically the philosophy of VIŚIṢṬĀDVAITA, the teachings of RĀMĀNUJA.

Yayāti

A mythical figure about whom a great variety of stories circulate in the epics and Purāṇas, and who became the subject of many plays. The *Mahābhārata* introduces him as the fifth king in the lunar dynasty, the son of Nahuṣa, the father of Yadu and Puru, who became the founders of the lines of the Yādavas and Pauravas. His infidelity brought upon him the curse of old age and infirmity from Śukra, the father of his wife Devayānī. Śukra agreed to transfer the curse to one of his sons, if one was willing to bear it. Puru did so, and Yayāti enjoyed a thousand years of sensual pleasures. He then restored youth to Puru.

Yoga

One of the six orthodox systems. Derived from the word *yuj* (to join, to yoke, to combine), Yoga is often used in India as an equivalent of religious practice, or as a generic term for a system of philosophy or religion. In a more specific sense, Yoga may either mean a set of physical exercises (*Haṭhayoga*) or a system of meditation and concentration (*Rāja Yoga*). The latter is also often called PĀTAÑJALA YOGA, with reference to Patañjali's YOGA SŪTRAS, which are its principal text, or Sāṁkhya Yoga, because of the close proximity of the SĀṀKHYA system to the philosophy underlying Yoga. It places little emphasis on physical exercises (*āsanas*) but insists on ethical preparation (*yama-niyama*) and a process of interiorization (*saṁyama*) in order to lead the spirit (*puruṣa*) to the realization of its original nature (*kaivalya*), free from admixture with matter (*prakṛti*). The practice of Yoga is fairly universal among SAMNYĀSIS and also quite popular among Hindus generally.

Yogānanda, Swami

(1893–1952)

Founder of the Yogoda Sat Sangha (1917). Born Mukunda Lal Ghosh, he came to the USA in 1920, and began teaching a simplified form of KUṆḌALINĪ Yoga. He was the founder of Self-Realization Fellowship (1937): its headquarters are near Los Angeles, and the author of *Autobiography of a Yogi*.

Yoga-nidrā ('Yoga sleep')

The trance-like condition of Viṣṇu between the destruction of a universe and the creation of a new one; personified in Devī Mahāmāyā, the Great Illusion.

Yoga Sūtras

Ascribed to PATAÑJALI, these consist of 196 brief aphorisms, arranged in four parts entitled *samādhi* (concentration), *sādhana* (practice), *vibhuti* (extraordinary faculties) and *kaivalya* (emancipation). The teaching of the *Yoga Sūtras* has also been called *aṣṭāṅga Yoga* (eight-limbed Yoga) because of its structure in eight stages. (See appendix

4, The Eightfold Practice of Yoga: Aṣṭāṅga Yoga.) The most important exercise is *samyama* (effort), consisting of a repeated application of the triad concentration– contemplation–trance to the various dimensions of reality until *kaivalya* is reached, a point of no return.

Yogavāsiṣṭha Rāmāyaṇa

See VĀŚIṢṬHA.

yogi

In a general sense every serious practitioner of a spiritual path; more specifically the practitioners of Yoga in one of its forms.

yoni ('womb')

This is both physiological and metaphorical. Stylized images of the *yoni*, representing ŚAKTI, are found in conjunction with the LIṄGA (3) in Śiva temples; without the *liṅga* they serve in DEVĪ temples as objects of worship. Metaphorically BRAHMAN is called 'the *yoni* of the universe' in the *Brahmasūtras*.

Yudhi-ṣṭhira ('firm in battle')

The oldest of the five PĀṆḌAVAS, the son of YAMA, a model of calmness, prudence and justice. He was brought up at the court of the KAURAVAS, and the blind king Dhṛtarāṣṭra chose him rather than his own son Duryodhana as his successor, thereby causing the mortal feud between the Kauravas and Pāṇḍavas. Yudhiṣṭhira with his four brothers had to go into exile to Vāraṇāvata (Vārāṇasī?). After the MAHĀBHĀRATA war he was formally crowned emperor of Hastināpura and reigned righteously for many years. At the end he departed together with his remaining family for the Himālayas, and finally was enthroned in INDRALOKA (Indra's heaven).

Z

Zimmer, Heinrich (1890–1943)

One of the best-known interpreters of Hindu thought and mythology. After studying Hebrew literature, German philology and history of art at Berlin, he discovered his interest in ancient India. Dismissed from his position in Heidelberg by the Nazi government (because of his Jewish wife), he first moved to Oxford and then to the USA where he became visiting professor at Columbia University. His writings cover a wide range, from mythology to medicine, from Buddhism to Jainism to Hinduism. His early writings were in German: *Kunstform und Yoga* (1926), *Ewiges Indien* (1930), *Indische Sphaeren* (1935). His English works were posthumously edited by his former student Joseph Campbell: *The Art of Indian Asia* (1955), *Philosophies of India* (1951), *Myths and Symbols in Indian Art and Civilization* (1946), *The King and the Corpse* (1947). Zimmer had a gift for presenting Indian ideas in an intellectually and aesthetically accessible and appealing way, and created a great amount of interest in Hinduism among the general public.

Chronology

The chronology of Ancient India up to the time of Buddha is at present the focus of fierce scholarly debates. The majority of Indian scholars assume a date of 4000 BCE for the *Ṛgveda*, rejecting also the so-called 'Aryan invasion theory', whereas the majority of Western scholars maintain the invasion theory and date the *Ṛgveda* to 1500–1200 BCE. The chronology offered here represents largely the traditional Indian position.

Indians who do not use the Western (Gregorian) calendar have several other systems of dating. The most common eras used in today's India are *samvat* (beginning 57 BCE) and *saka* (beginning 78 CE).

On the basis of the more recent research, based on archaeology and astronomy, the following chronology can be tentatively established:

c. 4000 BCE	Earliest Vedic hymns
c. 3500 BCE	Early Harappan civilization
c. 3100 BCE	Traditional dates for the 'Great Flood' and Manu Vaivasvata
c. 3000–2750 BCE	Traditional date for Yayāti Period
c. 2750–2550 BCE	Traditional date for Māndhātri Period
c. 2700–1500 BCE	Mature Indus civilization
c. 2350–1950 BCE	Traditional date for Rāmacandra period
c. 1900 BCE	Age of *Rāmāyaṇa*
c. 1500–500 BCE	Major *Upaniṣads*, development of early *Sāṁkhya*, early *Pūrva Mīmāṁsā*
c. 1400 BCE	Great Bhārata War – Age of Kṛṣṇa. Early version of *Mahābhārata*
c. 1200 BCE	Early *Sūtra* literature. Consolidation of Vedic civilization: *Manusmṛti*
624–544 BCE	Life of Gautama Buddha according to traditional reckoning
527 BCE	End of Mahāvīra's earthly life according to Jain tradition
518 BCE	Persian invasion under Skylax and conquest of the Indian satrapy for Darius I
c. 500 BCE–500 CE	Composition of *Śrauta Sūtras*, *Gṛhya Sūtras*,

	Dharma Sūtras, *Vedāṅgas*; the basis of the orthodox systems; composition of the epics and the original *Purāṇas*
c. 500–200 BCE	Composition of the *Bhagavadgītā*
c. 500–200 BCE	Bādarāyaṇa's *Vedānta Sūtra*
c. 490–458 BCE	Reign of Ajataśatru, king of Magadha
c. 400 BCE	Pāniṇi's Aṣṭādhyayī (Grammar)
c. 400–200 BCE	Jaimini's *Pūrvamīmāṁsā Sūtra*
327–325 BCE	Alexander of Macedonia's invasion of India
c. 322–298 BCE	Reign of Candragupta of Magadha
c. 300 BCE	Megasthenes, Greek Ambassador to Magadha
c. 300 BCE	Kautilīya's *Ārthaśāstra* (according to some scholars: 100 CE) Gautama's *Nyāya Sūtra* and Kaṇaḍa's *Vaiśeṣika Sūtra*
c. 273–237 BCE	Reign of Aśoka
c. 200 BCE–100 CE	Invasions of Śuṅgas, Iranians, Śakas and Kuśānas, who founded kingdoms in India
c. 200 BCE–200 CE	Peak period of Buddhist and Jain influence
c. 150 BCE–100 CE	Patañjali's *Mahābhāṣya*
c. 115 BCE	Besnagar inscription of Heliodorus with a mention of Kṛṣṇa worship
c. 100 BCE–500 CE	Patañjali's *Yoga Sūtra*
c. 100 BCE–100 CE	Upavarśa's commentary on *Pūrvamīmāṁsā Sūtra* and *Vedānta Sūtra*
c. 100 BCE–400 CE	*Śabara-bhāśya* on Jaimini Sūtras
c. 100 BCE–800 CE	Composition of *Tirukkural*
c. 100 BCE	Early Mathurā sculpture; images of gods in temples
c. 25 BCE	Indian embassy to Emperor Augustus of Rome
c. 50 CE	First documentation of images of gods with several pairs of arms
c. 10	Indian embassy to Emperor Trajan of Rome
c. 100–500	Expansion of Hinduism in South–East Asia
c. 100–200	*Yājñavalkyasmṛti*
c. 100–300	*Viṣṇudharma Sūtra*
c. 100–400	*Nāradasmṛti*
c. 200–500	Composition of *Viṣṇu Purāṇa*
c. 250–325	*Sāṁkhya Kārikā* of Īśvarakṛṣṇa
c. 300–600	Composition of some of the older *Purāṇas* in their present form
c. 300–888	Pallava rulers in South India (Kāñcīpuram)
c. 319–415	Gupta empire of Mathurā
c. 400–500	Vatsyayana's *Kāma Sūtra*
c. 400	Composition of *Harivamṣa Purāṇa*, *Ahirbudhnya Saṁhitā*. Age of Kalidāsa, the greatest Indian dramatist. Spread of Vaiṣṇavism, especially Kṛṣṇa cult. Beginning of Tantricism
c. 400–500	Vyāsa's *Yoga-bhāṣya*

c. 450–500	Huna invasions
c. 500	*Devī-māhātmya* (in *Markaṇḍeya Purāṇa*). Spread of Śāktism into larger areas
c. 500–800	Composition of *Kūrma Purāṇa*
547	Kosmas Indikopleustes travels to India
c. 600–650	Poet Bana, author of *Kadāmbarī* and *Harsacarita*
c. 600–800	Peak of Pāñcarātra Vaiṣṇavism
c. 600–900	Late (metrical) *smṛtis;* composition of *Agni Purāṇa* and *Garuḍa Purāṇa*
after 600	Strong development of Vedānta
c. 600–800	Brahmanical renaissance; successful fight against strongly tantric Buddhism
c. 640	King Harṣa of Kanauj sends embassy to China
c. 650–1200	Several independent kingdoms in western, central, eastern and southern India
c. 650–700	Life of Kumārilabhaṭṭa and Māṇikkavācakar
since c. 700	Prevalence of *bhakti* religions Flourishing of Kaśmīr Śaivism
c. 700–750	Gauḍapada, author of a *kārikā* on the *Māṇḍukya Upaniṣad* and Paramaguru of *Śānkarācārya*
c. 788–820	Life of Śaṅkarācārya [according to some: c. 700]
c. 800–900	Composition of the *Bhāgavata Purāṇa* in its present form; *Śukra-nīti-sāra*
c. 800–1250	Cola dynasty in Tamiḷnādu
c. 825–900	Medathiti, writer of a commentary on *Manu-smṛti*
c. 900	Udāyana's *Nyāyakusumañjalī*
c. 900–1100	*Śiva Purāṇa*; Saivite Tantricism in Indonesia Composition of *Yogavasiṣṭharāmāyaṇa* and *Bhaktisūtra*
999–1026	Mahmud of Ghazni repeatedly raids India
1025–1137	Life of Rāmānuja
1026	Muslims loot temple of Somnāth
c. 1100	Buddhism virtually extinct in India. Life of Abhinavagupta. Composition of Hindu Tantra
c. 1100–1400	Composition of *Śākta Upaniṣads*; rise of Vīraśaivism in South India
c. 1150–1160	Composition of Kalhana's *Rājatarāṅginī*, recording the history of Kaśmīr
c. 1150	*Śrīkaṇṭha-bhāṣya*. Building of Jagannāth Temple at Puri
c. 1197–1276	Life of Madhvācārya
1211–1236	Reign of Iltutmish, first sultan of Delhi; beginning of Muslim rule over large parts of India
c. 1216–1327	Rule of Pāndyas at Madurai; foundation of the famous Mīnākṣi and Śiva Temple of Madurai
c. 1250	Beginning of *Śaiva-siddhānta*. Building of Sun Temple in Konāraka

c. 1275–1675	Jñāneśvara of Mahārāṣṭra and other *bhakti* mystics
1288	Marco Polo at Kalyan
c. 1300–1386	Life of Sāyaṇa, famous commentator on the Vedic *Saṁhitās* and *Brāhmaṇas*
1327	Muslims loot temple at Śrīraṅgam
c. 1333	Ibn Battuta's travels in India
1336–1565	Kingdom of Vijayanāgara, last Hindu empire in India, extending as far as Malaysia, Indonesia and the Philippines
c. 1340	Life of Mādhava, author of *Sarvadarśanasaṅgraha* and *Pañcadaśī*
c. 1350–1610	Vīraśaivism as the state religion of Mysore
c. 1350–1650	Composition of many works of the Pūrvamīmāṁsakas
c. 1360	Life of Vedāntadeśika
c. 1400–1470	Life of Rāmānanda
c. 1420	Life of Mīrābāī
1440–1518	Life of Kabīr
c. 1449–1568	Life of Śaṅkaradeva, great Vaiṣṇava preacher in Assam
c. 1469	Birth of Gurū Nanak, founder of Sikhism
c. 1475–1531	Life of Vallabha
c. 1485–1533	Life of Caitanya
1498	Vasco da Gama, after having rounded the Cape of Good Hope, lands on the Malabar coast
c. 1500	Composition of *Adhyātma Rāmāyaṇa* and of Sādānanda's *Vedānta-sāra*
c. 1500–1800	Peak of Durgā worship in Bengal
c. 1500–1600	Life of Sūrdās of Agra
c. 1550	Life of Brahmānanda Giri, author of a famous commentary on Śaṅkara's *Śarīraka-bhāṣya*
1510	Portuguese occupy Goa
c. 1526–1757	Moghul rule in India, destruction of most Hindu temples in North and Central India
c. 1532–1623	Life of Tulāsidāsa
c. 1542	The Jesuit missionary Francis Xavier lands in Goa
c. 1548–1598	Life of Ekanātha
1580	Akbar the Great invites some Jesuit missionaries from Goa to his court for religious discussions
c. 1585	Life of Harivaṃṣa, founder of the Rādhā-Vallabhis
1608–1649	Life of Tukarāma
1608–1681	Life of Rāmdās
1610–1640	Composition of Mitramiśra's *Vīramitrodaya*, famous digests of the *dharma-śāstras*
c. 1630	Composition of Śrīnivāsadāsa's *Yatīndramatadīpikā*
1631	Death of Mumtaz, in whose honour Shah Jahan built the famous Taj Mahal or Agra

1651	The (British) East India Company opens first factory on the Hugli (Bengal)
1657	Dara Shikoh translates the Upaniṣads into Persian
1661	Bombay becomes a British possession
1664	Śivajī declares himself king of Mahārāṣṭra
c. 1670–1750	Life of Nagojibhaṭṭa, author of numerous works on grammar, *dharma-śāstra*, yoga etc.
1675	Foundation of the French colony of Pondichéry
1690	Foundation of Calcutta through East India Company (Fort St. George)
c. 1700–1800	Life of Baladeva, author of *Govinda-bhāṣya*
c. 1750	Composition of the (reformist) *Mahānirvāṇa-tantra*
1757	Battle of Plassey; Clive is master of India
1784	Asiatick Society founded in Calcutta by Sir William Jones
1818	Defeat of the last Maratha Peshwa
1828	Rām Mohan Roy founds Brahma Samāj
1829	Law against *satī*
1829–1837	Suppression of the *thags*
1834–1886	Life of Ramakrishna Paramahamsa
1835	Introduction of English school system in India
1842–1901	Life of M.D. Ranade, great social reformer
1857	The so-called 'Mutiny' ('First Indian War of Independence' in more recent history books)
1858	The British Crown takes over the administration of India from the East India Company
1875	Foundation of *Ārya Samāj* by Swami Dāyānanda Sarasvatī
1885	Foundation of *Indian National Congress* in Bombay
1909	Foundation of Hindū Mahāsabhā by Pandit Mohan Malaviya
1913	Nobel prize in literature for Rabindranath Tagore
1920	Mahatma Gandhi begins first All-India Civil Disobedience Movement
1925	Foundation of *Rāṣṭrīya Svayamsevak Sangh*
1947	Partition of India and creation of the Indian Union and Pakistan as independent nations
1948	Assassination of Mahatma Gandhi
	Foundation of *Rām Rājya Pariṣad*
	Pandit Nehru elected prime minister of the Indian Union; Sri Cakravarti Rajagopalacari appointed governor general
1950	India declared a republic within the Commonwealth; acceptance of the constitution. Death of Sri Aurobindo Ghose and Ramana Maharṣi
1951	Inauguration of the *Bhūdān* movement by Vinoba Bhave. Foundation of the *Bhāratīya Jana Sangh*

1955	The Hindu Marriage Act passed in parliament
1956	Reorganization of states (provinces) according to linguistic principles
1961	Portuguese colonies in India (Goa, Damao and Diu) liberated in a military action
1962	Dr Rajendra Prasad, the first president of the Republic of India (since 1950), dies; Dr Sarvepalli Radhakrishnan, vice-president, succeeds him
1964	Death of Jawaharlal Nehru; Lal Bahadur Sastri succeeds him as prime minister. Foundation of Viśva Hindū Pariṣad (VHP)
1965	Conflict with Pakistan (West). Indira Gandhi succeeds Sastri as Prime Minister
1984	Sikh agitation for an independent Khalistan; Central government forcefully evicts Sikh extremists from Golden Temple in Amritsar/Punjab; Indira Gandhi assassinated by two of her Sikh guards
1985	Rajiv Gandhi, Indira's eldest son, elected prime minister
1991	Rajiv Gandhi assassinated by Tamil extremist.
1992	Hindu agitation on behalf of temple on Rāma's presumed birthplace in Ayodhyā culminates in destruction of Babri-Masjid and major rioting in many Indian cities
1998	Electoral victory of Hindu parties: establishment of a Bharatiya Janata Party minority government Celebration of Kumbhamela at Hardwar with millions of pilgrims attending

Appendices

Appendix One: The Philosophical Schools of Hinduism

Āstika ('orthodox', i.e. those that accept the Veda)
- Sāṁkhya
- Yoga
- Nyāya
- Vaiśeṣika
- Pūrva Mīmāṁsā
- Uttara Mīmāṁsā (Vedānta)

Nāstika ('unorthodox', 'heretical')
- Cārvākas
- Buddhists
- Jainais

Appendix Two: Hindu Scriptures

I. *Śruti* ('Revealed' writings) = Veda (in wider sense)
- Veda (in narrower sense): *Four Saṁhitās*:
    - *Ṛg-veda*
    - *Sāma-veda*
    - *Yajur-veda*
    - *Atharva-veda*
- *Brāhmaṇas*
    - *Ṛgveda*: 1) *Aitareya (Aśvalāyana)*
      2) *Kauśītakī (Samkhāyana)*
    - *Yajurveda*: 1) *Taittirīya*
      2) *Sātapatha*
    - *Samaveda*: eight, of which the most important are:
      1) *Prauḍha (Pañcaviṁśa)*
      2) *Tāṇḍya*
      3) *Sadviṁśa*
    - *Atharvaveda*: *Gopatha*
- *Āraṇyakas*: 1) *Bṛhad*
  2) *Taittirīya*
  3) *Aitareya*
  4) *Kauśītakī*

- *Upaniṣads* (108) = 'Vedānta'

II. *Smṛti* ('Tradition')

- *Itihāsa*
  - *Rāmāyaṇa*
  - *Mahābhārata* (Including *Bhagavadgītā*)
- *Purāṇas*
  - 18 *Mahāpurānas:*
    - 6 Vaiṣṇava (*sāttva*) Purāṇas:
      Viṣṇu-Purāna
      Nāradīya-Purāṇa
      Bhāgavata-Purāṇa
      Garuḍa-Purāṇa
      Padma-Purāṇa
      Vāraha-Purāṇa
    - 6 Śaiva (*rājasa*) Purāṇas:
      Matsya-Purāṇa
      Kūrma-Purāṇa
      Liṅga-Purāṇa
      Śiva-Purāṇa
      Skanda-Purāṇa
      Agni-Purāṇa
    - 6 Brahmā (*tāmasa*) Purāṇas:
      Brahmā-Purāṇa
      Brahmāṇḍa-Purāṇa
      Brahmavaivarta-Purāṇa
      Mārkaṇḍeya-Purāṇa
      Bhaviṣya-Purāṇa
      Vāmana-Purāṇa
  - 18 *Upapurāṇas*
  - Numerous *Sthālapurāṇas*
- *Smṛtis* (= Codes of Law)
  - *Manū-smṛti*
  - *Yajñavālkya-smṛti*
  - *Viṣṇū-smṛti* etc.

III. *Sūtras*:

- *Śrautasūtras*
- *Gṛhyasūtras*
- *Kalpasūtras*
- *Dharmasūtras*
- *Śulvasūtras*

IV. *Vedāṅgas* (Auxiliary sciences connected with Veda-study):

1) *Śīkṣa* (Phonetics)
2) *Chandas* (Metre)
3) *Vyakāraṇa* (Grammar)
4) *Nirukta* (Etymology)
5) *Jyotiṣa* (Astronomy)
6) *Kalpa* (Ritual)

V. *Upavedas* (Sciences not connected with Veda-study)

1) *Ayur-veda* (Medicine)
2) *Gandharva-veda* (Music and dancing)

3) *Dhanur-veda* (Archery)
4) *Sthāpatya-veda* (Architecture)

VI. Sectarian scriptures

- *Saṁhitās* (Vaiṣṇava)
- *Āgamas* (Śaiva)
- *Tantras* (Śākta)

Appendix Three: The Ten Principal Schools of Vedānta

Each is listed with its founder and his main work, a commentary on the *Brahmasūtra*.

Advaita Vedānta: Śaṅkara (788–820) *Śarīrakabhāṣya*
Viśiṣṭādvaita Vedānta: Rāmānuja (1017–1136) *Śrībhāṣya*
Dvaita Vedānta: Madhva (1238–1317) *Aṇuvakhyāyana*
Bhedābheda: Bhāskara (9th century) *Brahmasūtrabhāṣya*
Dvaitādvaita: Nimbārka (11th century) *Vedāntaparijātasaurabha*
Śuddhādvaita: Vallabhācārya (1473–1531) *Aṇubhāṣya*
Acintya Bhedābheda: Baladeva (18th century) *Govindabhāṣya*
Dvaitādvaita: Śrīpati (1350–1410) *Śrīkarabhāṣya*
Śivādvaita: Śrīkaṇṭha (13th century) *Śrīkaṇṭhabhāṣya*
Samānyavāda: Vijñānabhīkṣu (16th century) *Vijñānāmṛta*

Appendix Four: The Eightfold Practice of Yoga: Aṣṭāṅga Yoga

Remote Preparation:

- *yama* (practice of precepts)
    - *ahiṁsā* (non-violence)
    - *satya* (truthfulness)
    - *asteya* (non-stealing)
    - *brahmacarya* (continence)
    - *aparigraha* (absence of greed)
- *niyama* (practice of virtues)
    - *śauca* (purity)
    - *samtoṣa* (contentment)
    - *tapas* (discipline)
    - *svādhyāya* (study, especially of sacred lore)
    - *īśvara pranidhāna* (surrender to God)
- *āsana* (postures)
- *prāṇayama* (breath control)
- *pratyāhāra* (withdrawal of senses)

Direct Preparation:
These are collectively called *samyama* (effort) and successively applied to various categories of objects

- *dhāraṇa* (concentration)
- *dhyāna* (contemplation)
- *samādhi* (trance)

Beginning of Real Yoga:
This comprises the exercise of extraordinary powers and the practice of advanced forms of meditation, leading to *kaivalya*, complete isolation and freedom.

Thematic Bibliography

General

Aiyangar, S.K. *Some Contributions of South India to Indian Culture*. Calcutta, Calcutta University, 1942

Aiyar, C.P. Ramaswamy *Fundamentals of Hindu Faith and Culture*. Trivandrum, Government Press, 1944

Altekar, A.D. *The Position of Women in Hindu Civilization from Prehistoric Times to the Present Day*. Benares, Motilal Banarsidass, 1956

Altekar, A.D. *State and Government in Ancient India*. Delhi, Motilal Banarsidass, 1962 (4th edn)

Auboyer, J. *Daily Life in Ancient India from Approximately 200 BC to AD 700*. New York, Macmillan, 1965.

Basham, A.L. *The Wonder that was India*. New York, Grove Press, 1959

Bhattacharya, H. (gen. ed.) *The Cultural Heritage of India*, 6 vols. Calcutta, Ramakrishna Mission Institute of Culture, 1957–62 (2nd edn)

Brockington, J.L. *The Sacred Thread. Hinduism in its Continuity and Diversity*. Edinburgh, Edinburgh University Press, 1981

Carpenter, J.E. *Theism in Mediaeval India*. London, Constable & Co., 1921

Carstairs, G.M. *The Twice-Born*. London, Hogarth Press, 1957

Diksitar, V.R. *Studies in Tamil Literature and History*. London, Luzac, 1930

Dowson, J. *A Classical Dictionary of Hindu Mythology and Religion, Geography, History and Literature*. London, Routledge & Kegan Paul, 1961

Farqhar, J.N. *An Outline of the Religious Literature of India*. Benares, Motilal Banarsidass, 1967 (repr.)

Filliozat, J. *The Classical Doctrine of Indian Medicine: Its Origins and its Greek Parallels*, trans. D. R. Chanama, Delhi, Munshiram Manoharlal, 1964

Fuller, C.J. *The Camphor Flame: Popular Hinduism and Society in India*. Princeton, Princeton University Press, 1992

Ghoshal, U.N. *A History of Indian Political Ideas: The Ancient Period and the Period of Transition to the Middle Ages*. Oxford, Oxford University Press, 1959 (3rd edn)

Heimann, B. *Facets of Indian Thought*. London, Allen & Unwin, 1964

Hutton, J.H. *Caste in India: Its Nature, Function and Origins*. Oxford, Oxford University Press, 1961 (3rd edn)

Kane, P.V. *History of Dharmasastra*, 5 vols. (7 parts). Poona, Bhandarkar Oriental Research Institute, 1930–62
Kapadia, K.M. *Marriage and Family in India*. Oxford, Oxford University Press, 1959 (2nd edn)
Karve, I. *Hindu Society: An Interpretation*. Poona, Deshmukh Prakashan, 1961
Klostermaier, K. *A Survey of Hinduism*. 2nd ed., Albany, State University of New York Press, 1994
Lannoy, R. *The Speaking Tree*. Oxford, Oxford University Press, 1971
Majumdar, D.N. *Caste and Communication in an Indian Village*. Bombay, Asia Publishing House, 1962 (3rd edn)
Meenaksisundaram, T.P. *A History of Tamil Literature*. Annamalainagar, Annamalai University, 1965
Prabhu, P.H. *Hindu Social Organisation: A Study in Socio-Psychological and Ideological Foundations*. Bombay, Popular Prakashan, 1963 (4th edn)
Raghavan, V. *The Indian Heritage*. Bangalore, Indian Institute of Culture, 1956
Rajagopalachari, R.C. *Hinduism: Doctrine and Way of Life*. Bombay, Bharatiya Vidya Bhavan, 1959
Rice, E.P. *Kanarese Literature*. Calcutta, Association Press, 1921
Sarkar, S. *The Aboriginal Races of India*. Calcutta, Bookland, 1954
Schwartzberg, J.E. (ed.) *Historical Atlas of India*. Chicago, University of Chicago Press, 1978. 2nd rev. ed. 1990
Seal, B.N. *The Positive Sciences of the Hindus*. Delhi, Motilal Banarsidass, 1958 (repr.)
Sharma, R.S. *Sudras in Ancient India*. Delhi, Motilal Banarsidass, 1958
Srinivas, M.N. *Caste and Other Essays*. Bombay, Asia Publishing House, 1965 (2nd edn)
Thomas, P. *Hindu Religion, Custom and Manners*. Bombay, D.B. Tareporevala Sons & Co., 1961
Thurston, E. and Rangachari, K. *Tribes and Castes of South India*, 4 vols. Madras, Government Press, 1929
Upadhyaya, K.D. *Studies in Indian Folk Culture*. Calcutta, Indian Publications, 1964
Volwahsen, A. *Living Architecture: Indian*. New York, Grosset & Dunlap, 1969
Walker, B. *The Hindu World: An Encyclopedic Survey of Hinduism*, 2 vols. New York, Praeger, 1968
Winternitz, M. *A History of Indian Literature*, trans. S. Ketkar and H. Kohn, 3 vols. Calcutta, University of Calcutta, 1927–67 (repr.)
Wiser, W.H. *Behind Mud Walls 1930–60*. Berkeley, University of California Press, 1963
Zaehner, H. *Hinduism*. Oxford, Oxford University Press, 1962
Zimmer, H. *Myths and Symbols in Indian Art and Civilization*. New York, Harper & Row, 1963 (4th edn)

Geography

Ali, S.M. *The Geography of the Puranas*. New Delhi, People's Publishing House, 1966

Bhardwaj, S.M. *Hindu Places of Pilgrimage in India: A Study in Cultural Geography*. Berkeley, University of California Press, 1973

Choudhuri, D.C. Roy. *Temples and Legends of Bihar*. Bombay, Bharatiya Vidya Bhavan, 1965

Cunningham, A. *Ancient Geography of India*. Calcutta, Archaeological Survey of India, 1924

Dave, J.H. *Immortal India*, 4 parts. Bombay, Bharatiya Vidya Bhavan, 1959–62 (2nd edn)

Eck, D.L. *Banaras: City of Light*. Princeton, Princeton University Press, 1983

Havell, E.B. *Benares, The Sacred City: Sketches of Hindu Life and Religion*. London, W. Thacker & Co., 1905

Jha, M., (ed.) *Dimensions of Pilgrimage*. New Delhi, Inter-Indian Publications, 1985

Mate, M.S. *Temples and Legends of Maharastra*. Bombay, Bharatiya Vidya Bhavan, 1962

Morinis, E.A. *Pilgrimage in the Hindu Tradition: A Case Study of West Bengal*, South Asian Studies Series. New York and New Delhi, Oxford University Press, 1984

Panikkar, K.M. *Geographical Factors in Indian History*. Bombay, Bharatiya Vidya Bhavan, 1955

Ramesan, R. *Temples and Legends of Andhra Pradesh*. Bombay, Bharatiya Vidya Bhavan, 1962

Spate, O.H.K. *India and Pakistan: A General and Regional Geography*. New York, Dutton, 1963 (rev. ed.)

Srinivasan, D.M. (ed.) *Mathura: The Cultural Heritage*. New Delhi, American Institute of Indian Studies, 1989

Vaidyanathan, K.R. *Sri Krishna, the Lord of Guruvayur*. Bombay, Bharatiya Vidya Bhavan, 1974

History

Derret, J.D.M. *History of Indian Law (Dharmasastra)*. Leiden, Brill, 1973

Drekmeier, C. *Kingship and Community in Early India*. Stanford, Stanford University Press, 1962

Gibb, H.A.R. (ed.) *Ibn Battuta: Travels in Asia and Africa*. London, Routledge & Kegan Paul, 1957 (2nd edn)

Majumdar, R.C. *The Classical Accounts of India*. Calcutta, Firma K. L. Mukhopadhyay, 1960

Majumdar, R.C. (gen. ed.) *The History and Culture of the Indian People*, 11 vols. Bombay, Bharatiya Vidya Bhavan, 1945–78

Majumdar, R.C. *Hindu Colonies in the Far East*. Calcutta, Firma K.L. Mukhopadhyay, 1963 (2nd edn)

Majumdar, R.C., Raychaudhuri, H.C. and Datta, K. *An Advanced History of India*. London, Macmillan, 1965 (3rd edn)

Marshall, J. *Mohenjo Daro and the Indus Civilization*, 3 vols. London, Oxford University Press, 1931

Marshall, P.J. (ed.) *The British Discovery of Hinduism in the Eighteenth Century,* European Understanding of India Series. Cambridge, Cambridge University Press, 1971
Panikkar, K.M. *Asia and Western Dominance.* London, Allen & Unwin, 1955 (3rd edn)
Panikkar, K.M. *A Survey of Indian History.* Bombay, Asia Publishing House, 1947
Pargiter, F.E. *Ancient Indian Historical Tradition.* Delhi, Motilal Banarsidass, 1962 (repr.)
Pargiter, F.E. *The Purana Text of the Dynasties of the Kaliage.* Oxford, Oxford University Press, 1913
Parpola, A. *The Sky Garment: A Study of the Harappan Religion and the Relation to the Mesopotamian and later Indian Religions.* Helsinki, Finnish Oriental Society, 1985
Piggott, S. *Prehistoric India.* Baltimore, Penguin Books, 1961
Possehl, G.C. (ed.) *Harappan Civilisation: A Contemporary Perspective.* Warminster, Aris & Philips, 1982
Renou, L. *Vedic India.* Calcutta, Sunil Gupta, 1957
Saletore, B.A. *Ancient Indian Political Thought and Institutions.* Bombay, Asia Publishing House, 1963
Sankalia, H.D. *Indian Archeology Today.* New York, Asia Publishing House, 1962
Sastri, K.A. Nilakantha. *The Colas,* 3 vols. Madras, University of Madras, 1935
Sastri, K.A. *The Culture and History of the Tamils.* Calcutta, Firma K.L. Mukhopadhyay, 1964
Sengupta, N.C. *Evolution of Ancient Indian Law.* London, Probsthain, 1953
Sengupta, P.C. *Ancient Indian Chronology.* Calcutta, University of Calcutta, 1941
Sharma, R.K. (ed.) *Indian Archeology. New Perspectives.* Delhi, Agam Kala Prakashan, 1982
Shendge, M. J. *The Civilized Demons: The Harappans in Rgveda.* New Delhi, Abhinav, 1977
Smith, V. *History of India.* Oxford, Oxford University Press, 1955
Spellman, J.W. *Political Theory of Ancient India.* New York, Oxford University Press, 1964
Thapar, R. *A History of India,* 2 vols. Baltimore, Penguin Books, 1966
Tod, J. *Annals and Antiquities of Rajasthan,* ed. William Crooke, 3 vols. Delhi, Motilal Banarsidass, n.d
Vyas, S.N. *India in the Ramayana Age.* Delhi, Atura Ram & Sons, 1967
Wheeler, M. *The Indus Civilization.* Cambridge, Cambridge University Press, 1953

Sacred Books

Balasundaram, T.S. *The Golden Anthology of Ancient Tamil Literature,* 3 vols. Madras, South India Saiva Siddhanta Book Publishing Society, 1959–60
Coburn, T.B. *Devi Mahatmya: The Crystallization of the Goddess Tradition.* Delhi, Motilal Banarsidass, 1984

Pusalker, A.D. *Studies in Epics and Puranas of India*. Bombay, Bharatiya Vidya Bhavan, 1955
Rocher, L. *The Puranas*. In J. Gonda, *A History of Indian Literature*, Wiesbaden, Otto Harrassowitz, Vol. 2, fasc. 3
Santucci, J.A. *An Outline of Vedic Literature*, American Academy of Religion Aids to the Study of Religion Series. Missoula, Scholars Press, 1977
Sukthankar, V.S. *On the Meaning of the Mahabharata*. Bombay, Asiatic Society, 1957
Thomas, P. *Epics, Myths and Legends of India*. Bombay, Taraporevala, 1961
Tilak, B.G. *The Arctic Home in the Vedas*. Poona, Tilak Bros., 1956 (repr.)
Tilak, B.G. *Vedic Chronology*. Poona, Tilak Bros, 1909
Tilak, B.G. *Orion or Researches into the Antiquity of the Veda*. Bombay, Sagoon, 1893; repr. Poona, Tilak Bros., 1955

Religions

Aiyer, V.G. Ramakrishna *The Economy of a South Indian Temple*. Annamalai, Annamalai University, 1946
Ayyar, C.V. Narayana *Origin and Early History of Saivism in South India*. Madras, University of Madras, 1936
Ayyar, P.V. Jagadissa *South Indian Festivities*. Madras, Higginbothams, 1921
Banerjea, J.N. *The Development of Hindu Iconography*. Calcutta, University of Calcutta, 1956 (2nd edn)
Barz, R. *The Bhakti Sect of Vallabhacarya*. Faridabad, Thompson Press, 1976
Beane, W.C. *Myth, Cult and Symbols in Sakta Hinduism: A Study of the Indian Mother Goddess*. Leiden, Brill, 1977
Bhandarkar, R.G. *Vaisnavism, Saivism and Minor Religious Systems*. Benares, Indological Book House, 1965 (repr.)
Bharati, A. (L. Fischer) *The Tantric Tradition*. London, Rider & Co., 1965
Bloomfield, M. *The Religion of the Veda*. New York, G.B. Putnam's, 1908
Bloomfield, M. *Gorakhanatha and Kanphata Yogis*. Calcutta, Association Press, 1938
Brown, C.M. *God as Mother: A Feminine Theology in India, An Historical and Theological Study of the Brahmavaivarta Purana*. Hartford, Claude Stark, 1974
Carman, J.B. *The Theology of Ramanuja. An Essay in Inter-religious Understanding*. New Haven and London, Yale University Press, 1974
Carman, J.B. and Marglin, A. (eds.) *Purity and Auspiciousness in Indian Society*. Leiden, Brill, 1985
Chattopadyaya, S. *The Evolution of Theistic Sects in Ancient India*. Calcutta, Progressive Publishers, 1963
Chaudhuri, R. *Doctrine of Srikantha*, 2 vols. Calcutta, Pracyavani, 1959–60
Courtright, P.B. *Ganesa: Lord of Obstacles, Lord of Beginnings*. New York, Oxford University Press, 1985
Crooke, W. *Popular Religion and Folklore in Northern India*, 2 vols. 1896; repr. Delhi, Munshiram Manoharlal, 1968
De, S.K. *Early History of the Vaisnava Faith and Movement in Bengal*. Calcutta, Firma K.L. Mukhopadhyay, 1961 (2nd edn)

Diehl, C.G. *Instrument and Purpose: Studies on Rites and Rituals in South India*. Lund, Gleerup, 1956

Farqhar, J.N. *Modern Religious Movements in India*. Oxford, Oxford University Press, 1914; repr. Delhi, Munshiram Manoharlal, 1967

Fergusson, J. *Tree and Serpent Worship*. London, W.H. Allen, 1868

Fuller, C.J. *Servants of the Goddess: The Priests of a South Indian Temple*. Cambridge, Cambridge University Press, 1984

Gatwood, L.E. *Devi and the Spouse Goddess: Women, Sexuality and Marriage in India*. Delhi, Manohar, 1985

Getty, A. *Ganesa*. Oxford, Oxford University Press, 1936

Ghurye, G.S. *Indian Sadhus*. Bombay, Popular Prakashan, 1964 (2nd edn)

Gonda, J. *Aspects of Early Visnuism*. Utrecht, 1954; repr. Delhi, Motilal Banarsidass, 1965

Hardy, E.T. *Viraha Bhakti* Delhi, Oxford University Press, 1983

Hawley, J.S. and Wulff, D.M. (eds.) *The Divine Consort: Radha and the Goddesses of India*. Berkeley, University of California Press, 1982

Ions, V. *Indian Mythology*. London, Paul Haymlyn, 1967

Kakati, B.K. *The Mother Goddess Kamakhya*. Gauhati, Lawyers' Book Stall, 1948

Keith, A.B. *The Religion and Philosophy of the Veda and Upanisads*. Cambridge, MA, Harvard University Press, 1925

Kennedy, M.T. *The Chaitanya Movement*. Calcutta, Association Press, 1925

Kinsley, D. *Hindu Goddesses*. Berkeley, University of California Press, 1986

Kinsley, D. *The Sword and the Flute: Kali and Krsna, Dark Visions of the Terrible and the Sublime in Hindu Mythology*. Berkeley, University of California Press, 1975

Klostermaier, K. *Mythologies and Philosophies of Salvation in the Theistic Traditions of India*. Waterloo, Ont., Wilfred Laurier University Press, 1984

Kramrisch, S. *The Presence of Siva*. Princeton, Princeton University Press, 1981

Lorenzen, D.N. *The Kapalikas and Kalamukhas: Two Lost Saivite Sects*. Berkeley, University of California Press, 1972

Macdonell, A.A. *Vedic Mythology*. Benares, Indological Bookhouse, 1963 (repr.)

Macnicol, N. *Indian Theism*. London, Oxford University Press, 1915

Mahadevan, T.M.P. *Outline of Hinduism*. Bombay, Cetana, 1960 (2nd edn)

Mookerjee, A. and Khanna, M. *The Tantric Way: Art – Science – Ritual*. London, Thames & Hudson, 1977

Nandimath, S.C. *Handbook of Virasivism*. Dharwar, L.E. Association, 1941

Pandey, R.B. *Hindu Samskaras: Socio-religious Study of the Hindu Sacraments*. Benares, Vikrama Publications, 1949

Pandeya, L.P. *Sun Worship in Ancient India*. Delhi, Motilal Banarsidass, 1972

Paranjoti, *Saiva Siddhanta*. London, Luzac, 1954 (2nd edn)

Pareckh, M.C. *The Brahmo Samaj*. Calcutta, Brahmo Samaj, 1922

Payne, A.A. *The Saktas*. Calcutta, YMCA Publishing House, 1933

Pillai, G.S. *Introduction and History of Saiva Siddhanta*. Annamalai, Annamalai University, 1948

Rai, L. *The Arya Samaj*. London, Longman, 1915

Roy, D.K., and Devi, J. *Kumbha: India's Ageless Festival.* Bombay, Bharatiya Vidya Bhavan, 1955

Sakare, M.R. *History and Philosophy of the Lingayata Religion.* Belgaum, publ. by the author, 1942

Schour, K. and McLeod, W.H. (eds.) *The Saints: Studies in a Devotional Tradition of India.* Delhi–Benaresi–Patna–Madras, Motilal Banarsidass, 1987.

Sharma, H.D. *Brahmanical Asceticism.* Poona, Oriental Book Agency, 1939

Sheth, Noel, *The Divinity of Krishna.* Delhi, Munshiram Manoharlal, 1984

Shinn, L.D. *The Dark Lord: Cult Images and the Hare Krishnas in America.* Philadelphia, Westminster, 1987

Shulman, D.D. *Tamil Temple Myths: Sacrifice and Divine Marriage in the South Indian Saiva Tradition.* Princeton, Princeton University Press, 1980

Siegel, L. *Fires of Love – Waters of Peace: Passion and Renunciation in Indian Culture.* Honolulu, University of Hawaii Press, 1983

Siegel, L. *Sacred and Profane Dimensions of Love in Indian Traditions as exemplified in the Gitagovinda of Jayadeva.* Oxford, Oxford University Press, 1978

Singer, M. (ed.) *Krishna: Myths, Rites and Attitudes.* Chicago, University of Chicago Press, 1969

Sirkar, D.C. *The Sakta Pithas*, Delhi, Motilal Banarsidass, 1948 (rev. ed.)

Staal, J.F. *AGNI: The Vedic Ritual of the Fire Altar,* 2 vols. Berkeley, University of California Press, 1983

Staal, J.F. *The Science of Ritual.* Poona, Deccan Institute, 1982

Stevenson, M. *The Rites of the Twice Born.* Oxford, Oxford University Press, 1920

Strickman, M. (ed.) *Classical Asian Rituals and the Theory of Ritual.* Berlin, Springer, 1986

Underhill, M.M. *The Hindu Religious Year.* Calcutta, Association Press, 1921

Vidyarthi, L.P. *Aspects of Religion in Indian Society.* Meerut, Vednat Nath Rammath, 1962

Vogel, J.P. *Indian Serpent Lore.* London, Probsthain, 1926

Waghorne, J.P. and Cutler, N. (eds.) *Gods of Flesh/Gods of Stone: The Embodiment of Divinity in India.* Chambersburg, Anima Publications, 1985

Welborn, G. and Yocum, G.E. (eds.) *Religious Festivals in South India and Sri Lanka.* Delhi, Manohar, 1985

Whaling, F. *The Rise of the Religious Significance of Rama.* Delhi, Motilal Banarsidass, 1980

Whitehead, H. *The Village Gods of South India*, Religious Life of India Series. Calcutta, Association Press, 1921 (2nd edn)

Wilson, H.H. *Religious Sects of the Hindus.* London, Trübner & Co., 1861; repr. Calcutta, Punthi Pustak, 1958

Woodroffe, J. (Arthur Avalon) *Introduction to Tantra Sastra.* Madras, Ganesh & Co., 1963 (4th edn)

Yamunacarya, M. *Ramanuja's Teachings in his Own Words.* Bombay, Bharatiya Vidya Bhavan, 1963

Zvelebil, K. *Tiru Murugan.* Madras, International Institute of Tamil Studies, 1982

Philosophies

Balasubramanian, R. *Advaita Vedanta*. Madras, University of Madras, 1976
Cenkner, W. *A Tradition of Teachers: Sankara and the Jagadgurus Today*. Delhi, Motilal Banarsidass, 1983
Chandavarkar, B.D. *A Manual of Hindu Ethics*. Poona, Oriental Book Agency, 1965 (3rd edn)
Chatterji, S. and Datta, D.M. *An Introduction to Indian Philosophy*. Calcutta, University of Calcutta, 1968 (7th edn)
Coward, H.G. *Bhartrhari*. Boston, Twayne Publishers, 1976
Creel, A.B. *Dharma in Hindu Ethics*. Columbia, MO, South Asia Books, 1977
Dasgupta, S.N. *History of Indian Philosophy*, 5 vols. Cambridge, Cambridge University Press, 1961–2 (3rd edn)
Eliade, M. *Yoga: Immortality and Freedom*. Bollingen Series 41. Princeton, Princeton University Press, 1969 (2nd edn)
Feuerstein, G. *The Philosophy of Classical Yoga*. Manchester, University of Manchester Press, 1982
Gächter, O. *Hermeneutics and Language in Purvamimamsa, A Study in Sabara Bhasya*. Delhi, Motilal Banarsidass, 1983
Ghate, V.S. *The Vedanta*. Poona, BORI, 1926; repr. 1960
Heimann, B. *Indian and Western Philosophy: A Study in Contrasts*. London, Allen & Unwin, 1937
Hiriyanna, M. *Outlines of Indian Philosophy*. London, George Allen & Unwin, 1958 (4th edn)
Larson, G.J. *Classical Samkhya*. Delhi, Motilal Banarsidass, 1969 (2nd edn)
Lott, E.J. *God and the Universe in the Vedantic Theology of Ramanuja: A Study in his Use of the Self–Body Analogy*. Madras, Ramanuja Research Society, 1976
Maitra, S.K. *The Ethics of the Hindus*. Calcutta, University of Calcutta, 1963 (3rd edn)
Marfatia, M.I. *The Philosophy of Vallabhacarya*. Delhi, Munsiram Manoharlal, 1967
Matilal, B.K. *Logic, Language and Reality*. Delhi, Motilal Banarsidass, 1985
McKenzie, J. *Hindu Ethics*. Oxford, Oxford University Press, 1922
Neufeldt, R. (ed.) *Karma and Rebirth: Post-classical Developments*. Albany, State University of New York Press, 1986
O'Flaherty, W.D. *Siva: The Erotic Ascetic*. New York, Oxford University Press, 1981
O'Flaherty, W.D. (ed.) *Karma and Rebirth in Classical Indian Traditions*. Berkeley, University of California Press, 1980
O'Flaherty, W.D. and Derret, J.D.M. (eds.) *The Concept of Duty in Southeast Asia*. New Delhi, Vikas, 1978
Radhakrishnan, S. *Indian Philosophy*, 2 vols. London, Allen & Unwin, 1948 (2nd edn)
Raja, K. Kunjunni. *Indian Theories of Meaning*. Adyar, Adyar Library and Research Centre, 1963
Raju, P.T. *The Philosophical Traditions of India*. London, Allen & Unwin, 1971

Riepe, D. *The Philosophy of India and its Impact on American Thought.* Springfield, Charles C. Thomas, 1970
Sastri, G. *A Study in the Dialectics of Sphota.* Delhi, Motilal Banarsidass, 1981
Sharma, A. *The Purusarthas: A Study in Hindu Axiology.* East Lansing, Asian Studies Center, Michigan State University, 1982
Sharma, B.N.K. *A History of Dvaita School of Vedanta and its Literature*, 2 vols. Bombay, Booksellers Publishing Co., 1960–1
Sharma, B.N.K. *Madhva's Teaching in His Own Words.* Bombay, Bhavan's Book University, 1961
Sharma, B.N.K. *Philosophy of Sri Madhvacarya.* Bombay, Bharatiya Vidya Bhavan, 1962
Singh, S. *Vedantadesika.* Benares, Chowkhamba, 1958
Sinha, J. *History of Indian Philosophy,* 2 vols. Calcutta, Sinha Publishing House, 1956–61
Sinha, J. *Indian Psychology*, 2 vols. Calcutta, Sinha Publishing House, 1958–60
Sinha, J. *Indian Realism.* London, K. Paul, French, Trübner & Co., 1938
Sivaraman, K. *Saivism in Philosophical Perspective.* Delhi, Motilal Banarsidass, 1973
Srinivasacari, P. *The Philosophy of Visistadvaita.* Adyar, Theosophical Society, 1946
Sundaram, P.K. *Advaita Epistemology.* Madras, University of Madras, 1968
Tagore, R. *Sadhana.* Calcutta, Macmillan, 1950
Taimni, I.K. *The Science of Yoga.* Wheaton, Theosophical Publishing House, 1972 (3rd edn)
Vidyabhusana, S.C. *A History of Indian Logic.* Calcutta, University of Calcutta, 1921
Zimmer, H. *Philosophies of India*, ed. J. Campbell. Princeton, Bollingen Foundation, 1951

Political Hinduism

Golwalkar, M.S. *Bunch of Thoughts.* Bangalore, Vikrama Prakashan 1966 (2nd edn)
Heimsath, C.H. *Indian Nationalism and Hindu Social Reform.* Princeton, Princeton University Press, 1968
Jhangiani, M.A. *Jana Sangh and Swatantra: A Profile of the Rightist Parties in India.* Bombay, Manaktalas, 1969
Panikkar, K.M. *Hindu Society at Cross Roads.* Bombay, Asia Publishing House, 1956
Panikkar, K.M. *Hinduism and the Modern World.* Bombay, Bharatiya Vidya Bhavan, 1956
Rudolph, L.I., and Rudolph, S.H. *The Modernity of Tradition.* Chicago, Chicago University Press, 1967
Sarma, N.S. *Hindu Renaissance.* Benares, Benares Hindu University, 1944
Sen, S.P. *Social Contents of Indian Religious Reform Movements.* Calcutta, Institute of Historical Studies, 1978
Smith, D.E. *India as a Secular State.* Princeton, Princeton University Press, 1967
Thapar, R. *India in Transition.* Bombay, Asia Publishing House, 1956

Varma, V.P. *Modern Indian Political Thought*. Agra, Laksmi Narain Agarwala, 1968 (4th edn)

Vyas, K.C. *The Social Renaissance in India*. Bombay, Asia Publishing House, 1957

Art and Architecture

Bhattacharya, T. *The Canons of Indian Art: A Study of Vastuvidya*. Calcutta, Firma K.L. Mukhopadhyay, 1963 (2nd edn)

Bussabarger, R.F. and Robins, B.D. *The Everyday Art of India*. New York, Dover, 1968

Goetz, *The Art of India*. New York, Crown, 1964

Harle, J.C. *The Art and Architecture of the Indian Subcontinent*. Harmondsworth, Penguin, 1987

Kramrisch, S. *The Art of India: Traditions of Indian Sculpture, Painting and Architecture*. London, Phaidon, 1954

Kramrisch, S. *The Hindu Temple,* 2 vols. Calcutta, University of Calcutta 1946; repr. Delhi, Motilal Banarsidass, 1977

Liebert, G. *Iconographic Dictionary of the Indian Religions: Hinduism, Buddhism, Jainism*. Leiden, Brill, 1976

Rowland, B. *The Art and Architecture of India: Buddhist, Hindu, Jain*. Baltimore, Penguin Books, 1967 (2nd edn)

Popley, H.A. *The Music of India*. Calcutta, YMCA Publishing House, 1950

Swarup, B. *Theory of Indian Music*. Allahabad, Swamy Brothers, 1958 (2nd edn)

Zimmer, H. *The Art of Indian Asia,* 2 vols. New York, Bollingen Foundation, 1955

Individual personalities

Abbot, J.E. (ed. and trans.) *The Poet Saints of Maharastra*, 12 vols. Poona, Scottish Mission Industries, 1926–41

Bihari, B. *Minstrels of God*, 2 vols. Bombay, Bharatiya Vidya Bhavan, 1956

Brunton, P. *Maharsi and his Message*. London, Rider & Co., 1952

Deheja, V. *Antal and her Path of Love*. Albany, State University of New York Press, 1990

Deming, W.S. *Ramdas and Ramdasis*, Religious Life of India Series. Oxford, Oxford University Press, 1928

Godman, D. (ed.) *Be as you Are: The Teachings of Ramana Maharsi*. Boston, Arkana, 1985

Gold, D. *The Lord as Guru: Hindi Saints in the Northern Indian Tradition*. New York, Oxford University Press, 1987

Harper, M.H. *Gurus, Swamis, and Avataras: Spiritual Masters and their American Disciples*. Philadelphia, Westminster Press, 1972

Keay, F.E. *Kabir and his Followers*. Calcutta, Association Press, 1931

Madhavananda, Swami, and Majumdar, R.C. (eds.) *Great Women of India*. Calcutta, Advaita Ashrama, 1954

Majumdar, A.K. *Caitanya: His Life and Doctrine*. Bombay, Bharatiya Vidya Bhavan, 1969

Oman, I.C. *The Mystics, Ascetics and Saints of India*. Delhi, Oriental Publishers, 1973 (repr.)
Osborne, A. *Ramana Maharshi and the Path of Self-Knowledge*. Bombay, Jaico, 1962 (2nd edn)
Pareckh, M.C. *Brahmarshi Keshub Chander Sen*. Rajkot, Bhagavat Dharma Mission, 1926
Pareckh, M.C. *Sri Swami Narayana*. Rajkot, Bhagavat Dharma Mission, 1936
Pareckh, M.C. *Vallabhacarya*. Rajkot, Bhagavat Dharma Mission, 1936
Raghavan, V. *The Great Integrators: The Saint Singers of India*. Delhi, Ministry of Information and Broadcasting, 1966
Ruhela, S.P. and Robinson, D. (eds.) *Sai Baba and his Message*. Delhi, Vikas, 1976
Sastri, K.S. Ramaswami *Sivananda: The Modern World Prophet*. Rishikesh, Divine Light Society, 1953
Sharma, S.R. *Swami Rama Tirtha*. Bombay, Vidya Bhavan, 1961
Tendulkar, D.G. *Mahatma: Life and Work of M.K. Gandhi*, 8 vols. Bombay, V.K. Jhaveri, 1951–8
Westcott, G.H. *Kabir and the Kabir Panth*. Calcutta, Susil Gupta, 1953 (2nd edn; repr.)
Williams, R.B. *A New Face of Hinduism: The Swaminarayan Religion*. Cambridge, Cambridge University Press, 1984
Yogananda, Paramahamsa. *Autobiography of a Yogi*. Bombay, Jaico, 1960

Thematic Index

A. Mythology

History, historic personalities and scholars

Bādarāyaṇa
Bahiṇabāī
Basava
Besant
Bhave
Blavatsky
Buddha
Caitanya
Chinmoy
Cinmayananda
Cokamela
Dāyānanda Sarasvatī
Ekanāṭha
Gandhi
Golwalkar
Hedgewar
Janābāī
Jñānasambandhar
Jñāneśvara
Kabīr
Krishna Prem
Krishnamurti
Lalla
Madhva
Malaviya
Manikkavacakar
Mīrābāī
Muktananda
Nāmadeva
Nammāḷvār
Nāṭha Muni
Nimbārka
Rāīdās
Rāma Tīrtha
Rāmadāsa
Ramana Maharṣi
Rāmānanda
Rāmānuja
Roy
Sambandhar
Śaṅkara
Śaṅkaradeva
Sathya Sāī Bābā
Savarkar
Sen
Śivānanda
Śukadeva
Sundaramūrti
Tagore, R.
Tagore, D.
Tilak
Tūkarām
Tulsīdās
Tyagārāja
Vijñānabhīkṣu
Vivekānanda
Yamunācārya
Yogānanda

Rulers and dynasties:
Akbar
Colas
Dara Shukoh
Gupta
Hoyśalas
Mahmud of Ghazni
Maurya
Pallavas
Paṇḍya
Peshawas
Śakas
Śivajī
Vikramāditya
Viṣṇugupta

Traditional scholars:
Abhinavagupta
Āpastamba
Āryabhaṭṭa
Bhartṛhari
Bhāsa
Bhāskara
Dandin
Gaṅgeśa
Gauḍapāda
Gopāla Bhaṭṭa
Gorakhnāṭha
Īśvara Muni
Jaimini
Jayadeva
Keśava Miśra
Kumārila Bhaṭṭa
Kureśa
Mādhava
Mahīpati
Mandana Miśra
Meykaṇḍa
Pāṇinī

Concepts, doctrines, rituals, symbols

macrocosm–microcosm
matriarchy
matter
medicine
meditation
miracle
mokṣa
music
name
nationalism
outcaste
pramāṇa
preta
purity
Rāmarājya
real, reality
rebirth
religious persecution
revelation
sacrifice
sanātana dharma
sarga
secularism
self
seva
sin
social reform
social order
study
temples
time
truth
universe
unreality
varnāśrama dharma
vedic religion
vedic civilization
vegetarianism
village religion
war
women
word

Doctrines:
ahaṁkāra
akṛti
akṣara
ānanda
antaryāmi
apauruṣeya
aspṛśya
āśrama
aṣṭāvaraṇa
ātman
avatāra
avidyā
avyakta
bhakti-mārga
brahmacarya
brahman
brahma-vidyā
cat school
caturvarṇāśramadharma
daṇḍa
guṇa
guru
karma-mārga
loka
Mahāpralaya
māyā
meat eating
nāḍi
pañcayata
paraṁparā
phala, phalaśloka
prapatti
puṣṭimārga
rāgānuga bhakti
rasa
ṛṣi
ṛta
saccidānanda
ṣaḍdarśana
sādhana
sahāmārga
sākṣātkāra
sākṣī
śakti
sphoṭa
vidyā

Rituals:
Agnicayana
ashes
aṣṭamūrti
aśvamedha
circumambulation
confession

Buddhism
Cārvākas
Dānavas
daśanāmis
Divine Light Mission
Divine Life Mission
Gaudīya Vaiṣṇavism
Harījan
International Society for Kṛṣṇa Consciousness (ISKCON)
International Transcendental Meditation Society (TM)
Jainism
Jana Sangh
Jānatā Party
Kāṇphata
Kashmir Śaivism
Kaula
Liṅgāyats
Mīmāṁsā
Nambūdiris
Nīmavats
Nyāya
Pāñcarātra
Rāṣṭrīya Svayamsevak Sangh (RSS)
Śaivism
Śaiva Siddhānta
Śāktism
Sāṁkhya
Śrīvaiṣṇavism
Vaiṣṇavas
Viśiṣṭādvaita
Viśva Hindū Pariṣad (VHP)
Yoga
Yādavas

Scriptures, commentaries, other writings:
Adhyātma Rāmāyaṇa
Āgama
Agni Purāṇa
Ahirbudhnya Saṁhitā
Aitareya Brāhmaṇa
Aitareya Upaniṣad
Aṣṭādhyāyī
Atharvaveda
Ātmabodha
Bhāgavata Purāṇa
Bhagavadgītā
Bhāmatī
Bhaviṣya Purāṇa
Brahmāṇḍa Purāṇa
Brahmā Purāṇa
Brahmasūtra
Brahmavaivarta Purāṇa
Bṛhadāraṇyaka Upaniṣad
Bṛhaddevatā
Bṛhadsaṁhitā
Devī Bhāgavata Purāṇa
Devī Māhātmya
Dharmaśāstra
Drāviḍa Prabandham
Gītagovinda
Gītārahasysa
Gṛhya Sūtra
Harivaṃśa (Purāṇa)
hymns
Īśa(vasya) Upaniṣad
Kālikā Purāṇa
Kaṭha Upaniṣad
Kathāsaritsāgara
Kauśītakī
Kena Upaniṣad
kramapāṭha
Kūrma Purāṇa
Liṅga Purāṇa
Mahābhārata
Mahābhāṣya
Mahāpurāṇa
Mahānārāyaṇa Upaniṣad
mahāvākyas
Māṇḍukya Upaniṣad
Manusmṛti
Mārkaṇḍeya Purāṇa
Matsya Purāṇa
Muṇḍaka Upaniṣad
Nāradīya Purāṇa
Nārāyanīyam
Nirukta
Nīti śāstra
Nyāya Sūtras
Padma Purāṇa
Pañcatantra
Praśna Upaniṣad
Rāmāyaṇa
Ṛgveda
Ṛgvidhāna
Sacred Books of the East (SBE)